Improving science education

Improving science education

The contribution of research

Edited by
**Robin Millar, John Leach and
Jonathan Osborne**

Open University Press
Buckingham · Philadelphia

Open University Press
Celtic Court
22 Ballmoor
Buckingham
MK 18 1XW

email: enquiries@openup.co.uk
world wide web: www.openup.co.uk

and
325 Chestnut Street
Philadelphia, PA 19106, USA

First Published 2000

A catalogue record of this book is available from the British Library

ISBN 0 335 20645 X (pb)   0 335 20646 8 (hb)

Library of Congress Cataloging-in-Publication Data
Improving science education: the contribution of research/Robin Millar,
John Leach, and Jonathan Osborne (eds).
     p. cm.
   Includes bibliographical references and index.
   ISBN 0-335-20646-8 – ISBN 0-335-20645-X (pbk.)
   1. Science – Study and teaching – Research. I. Millar, Robin.
II. Leach, John, (John T.) III. Osborne, Jonathan.
Q181.I62 2000
507'.1–dc21   00–033989

Typeset by Graphicraft Limited, Hong Kong

Printed and bound in Great Britain by
Marston Book Services Limited, Oxford

This book is dedicated to the memory of Rosalind Driver
(1941–1997)

Contents

Acknowledgements

The editors acknowledge financial support from the Schools of Education at the University of Leeds and King's College London, and the Department of Educational Studies at the University of York, without which this project could not have been undertaken. We are also grateful to the contributors to the book and their institutions, who funded their own travel to the writing meeting held in York in 1999. Open University Press also granted us an advance on royalties to help fund this meeting, for which we are grateful.

We also acknowledge the thoughtful and helpful comments of John Gilbert, Derek Hodson and David Treagust, who refereed the book proposal.

All contributors have agreed to donate their share of the royalties from sales of this book to Macmillan Cancer Relief.

Introduction

Robin Millar, John Leach and Jonathan Osborne

The growth of science education research

In the past 20 years or so, there has been an enormous increase in the amount of science education research carried out and reported. This is immediately apparent in the science education sections of libraries. New journals have been established, and in the older journals there has been a steady increase in both the number of editions per year and the number of papers per edition. Several publishers now carry extensive science education research lists, with many new titles being published each year. Associations have been formed within countries and across national boundaries to promote research in science education.

However, this in itself has begun to raise some questions and concerns. Two of the major ones are:

- Why is the impact of research on practice apparently so slight?
- Is there any sense that the field of science education research is making 'progress'? (Do newer studies build on earlier ones? Is the effort *cumulative*? Are there any areas of agreement about theoretical frameworks and terminology, or about research approaches, procedures or tools, or even about areas of work that are more or less worthwhile? And are there findings that command general assent?)

These are the questions which this book is about. As we enter a new millennium it seems timely to take stock of what we have achieved in science education research, and to reflect on where we now ought to be going.

The book also has another function: it has been planned and written as a tribute to Rosalind Driver, to acknowledge and mark her contribution to the development of science education research as a field. Ros was one of the key figures in the science education research effort of the past 20 years. She died in October 1997. As the Notes on contributors at the end of the book indicate, all of the main contributors worked with Ros in some capacity in the past, and counted her as a friend.

A number of tributes, lectures and articles dedicated to Ros have already appeared (Osborne *et al.* 1997; Leach and Scott 1998; Millar and Osborne 1998; Scott 1998; Solomon 1998; Leach 1999; Monk and Osborne 2000; Fensham in press). In initiating the process that led to this book, we were concerned that it should be a fitting tribute to Ros. The last thing Ros would have wanted was an uncritical eulogy. A fitting tribute to her work would, itself, have to be a valuable addition to the literature. So we asked ourselves: is another edited collection on science education research really needed? We decided that a book which looked critically at the achievements of science education research, written by some of the major contributors to the field, would be timely and valuable – both in what it might itself have to say, and as a means of putting some important issues more firmly on the agenda.

A number of interrelated strands can be seen in Ros' work. She first made her mark with her PhD work on what she termed children's 'alternative frameworks' for explaining phenomena – a term which quickly passed into general use. She pursued this interest through her involvement in the work of the Assessment of Performance Unit (APU) and later in the Children's Learning in Science Project (CLISP). From very early in this work, she was aware of the serious weakness of an inductive (or empiricist) view of the process of learning science (Driver 1975, 1983). This concern about epistemological issues led to a critique of the so-called 'process approach', and also to a determined effort to tease out the relationship, in the context of learning science, between personal construction of meaning on the one hand, and induction into a corpus of public knowledge on the other. This led to several important papers in which she (often with colleagues in her group) articulated and defended a social constructivist perspective on science learning. By the early 1990s, Ros was becoming increasingly aware that the ideas learners develop in science classrooms about events and phenomena are shaped not only by their experiences of seeing and discussing those events and phenomena, but also by their ideas about science and scientific knowledge itself. She explored these issues in a major research project whose main results were published in *Young People's Images of Science* (Driver *et al.* 1996). This led in turn to an interest in how students construct arguments about natural phenomena and events and how they use evidence to support their views, which Ros began to develop in her time at King's College London. This interest is now being followed up in a research project based closely on the one she had planned shortly before her death.

Ros' other major interest was in curriculum issues. She was a member of the working party which drafted the first National Curriculum (NC) in England and Wales in 1989. This made her very aware of how little precise advice science education researchers could offer to curriculum policymakers. Ros co-directed a research project which was drawn upon in the first revision of the NC in 1991. When a further revision was carried out hurriedly in 1995, she was instrumental in convening a large group of science education researchers to synthesize research findings in a form that might be useful to those charged with the task of drawing up the revised curriculum orders. Although the contribution of research was greater than in 1989, its impact was still limited. However, the more fundamental issues which researchers and others were raising about the shape and direction of a science curriculum for all pupils were simply not on the agenda. Ros became convinced that the science education community needed to 'get its act together' well ahead of the next revision (in 2000), and think through its position clearly. Her vehicle for doing this was a seminar series. With Jonathan Osborne, she put this idea to the Nuffield Foundation, who funded a series of four seminars and two open meetings for the discussion of fundamental curriculum issues in science, which led to the report *Beyond 2000: Science Education for the Future* (Millar and Osborne 1998). Sadly Ros did not live to see this exercise completed.

Ros' abiding interest was always in 'the work', and in the issues it raised. So this book does not set out to privilege her own work in any way, exactly as she would have wanted. Many chapters do make reference to Ros and to her work, and acknowledge its influence. But some also raise critical points. We wanted the book to be a serious reflection on the state of the field of science education research, recognizing its real achievements, but also frank and honest about its deficiencies and weaknesses. For science education research is still a very young field. Like other areas of the social sciences and humanities (and unlike the mature natural sciences), it is certainly pre-paradigmatic, in the Kuhnian sense. We and others like us still have much work to do to establish it securely as a respected and valued research discipline.

The structure of this book

Chapters in this book are organized in three sections, each one addressing an important area of scholarship in science education, and each corresponding with an area in which Ros Driver made a significant contribution. The first section considers research on teaching and learning in science. In each chapter, the authors outline a piece of recent or current research in which they are involved, and use this to explain why they think research on this topic (or using this approach or method) is important and valuable; what contribution they believe such studies can make to our knowledge of science education; and how insights from the work might usefully inform practice. Section 2, in contrast, considers the role and purpose of science in the school curriculum. It explores questions about what we ought to be attempting to teach in science programmes. These are questions about underlying commitments and values, which cannot be answered by empirical enquiry – though of course finding out what is and is not possible, and investigating empirically the outcomes of practices, may draw to our attention factors which convince us that change is needed. Indeed, this is one major reason why many science education researchers find themselves drawn into value questions about the content of curriculum. The four chapters in the final section turn their attention to the achievements and future goals of research in science education. Each section begins with a brief overview of the constituent chapters.

The Notes on contributors at the end of the book provide short accounts of each contributor's work and their relationship with Ros Driver.

How the book was produced

At the time of Ros Driver's death, several people within the science education research community suggested that something should be done to mark her contribution to the field. The idea for this book and its three sections emerged from discussions between us over a period of several months. As editors, we wanted to invite people to contribute to the book who had something valuable to say on one or other of its themes, and who had known and worked with Ros.

We were conscious that we were asking authors to contribute a piece of writing which was rather different from a normal journal article or book chapter. In agreeing to contribute to the book, authors were accepting the challenging brief of reflecting critically on research in science education. At an early stage, we decided to hold a meeting of all chapter authors at which drafts would be reviewed. This took place in September 1999, at the University of York. We worked intensively and in a spirit of great collegiality over the three days of the meeting. Drafts of all the chapters were circulated in advance, and several detailed critiques of each chapter were written. Each chapter was then discussed by the group of contributors and editors. This process certainly led to significant improvements in the content of several chapters, and in the coherence of the book as a whole. In a sense, every author has contributed to every chapter in the book. All the contributors found it a productive experience in both personal and professional terms.

References

Driver, R. (1975) The name of the game. *School Science Review*, 56(197): 800–4.
Driver, R. (1983) *The Pupil as Scientist?* Milton Keynes: Open University Press.

Driver, R., Leach, J., Millar, R. and Scott, P. (1996) *Young People's Images of Science*. Buckingham: Open University Press.

Fensham, P. (in press) Science content as problematic – issues for research, in H. Behrendt, H. Dahncke, R. Duit, *et al.* (eds) *Research in Science Education: Past, Present, and Future*. Dordrecht, the Netherlands: Kluwer.

Leach, J. (1999) Rosalind Driver (1941–1997): a tribute to her work in science education, in M. Méheut and G. Rebmann (eds) *Proceedings of the 4ᵗʰ European Summerschool in Science Education*, pp. 12–30. Paris: Université Paris 7 Denis Diderot.

Leach, J. and Scott, P. (1998) Rosalind Driver (1941–1997). *Science Teacher Education*, Spring: 47–51.

Millar, R. and Osborne, J. (eds) (1998) *Beyond 2000: Science Education for the Future*. London: School of Education, King's College.

Monk, M. and Osborne, J. (eds) (2000) *Good Practice in Science Teaching: What Research Has to Say*. Buckingham: Open University Press.

Osborne, J., Leach, J. and Scott, P. (1997) Professor Rosalind Driver (1941–1997). *Studies in Science Education*, 30: 1–4.

Scott, P. (1998) Ros Driver, 1941–1997. *Physics World*, 11(1): 59.

Solomon, J. (1998) About argument and discussion. *School Science Review*, 80(291): 57–62.

Section 1   RESEARCHING TEACHING AND LEARNING IN SCIENCE

The volume of research on teaching and learning science has mushroomed in the past 20 or so years. However, some of the most stringent criticisms of science education research have been directed at work on teaching and learning. Three of the more significant of these criticisms are:

- There is little evidence that recent studies build upon established knowledge claims from earlier work.
- The theories of learning, and of science, that underpin much of the work are empiricist and therefore fatally flawed.
- There is little evidence that students understand science better as a result of changes in practice that are based on research.

The last of these points raises perhaps the most serious challenge to research on teaching and learning science: what possible future can such research have, if it cannot be shown to lead to measurable improvements in students' learning?

We therefore asked the authors of the chapters in this first section to address some of these points of criticism, through an account of a recent piece of their own empirical work on teaching and/or learning science. Specifically, we asked them to explain why the work is important and worth doing; to show how it builds upon previous theoretical and empirical work; to identify the contribution that the work makes to the knowledge of the science education community; and to specify the messages that the work has for the practice of teaching science. The chapters in Section 3 by Gaalen Erickson (Chapter 15), Richard Gunstone and Richard White (Chapter 16), and Piet Lijnse (Chapter 17) also explore general issues about the achievements of research on teaching and learning science.

Research has been carried out to illuminate our understanding of different aspects of the teaching and learning process in science. The chapters of this section are examples of research addressing four different aspects of teaching and learning science, namely evaluation of the effectiveness of specific *teaching situations*, studies of *assessing and evaluating* of student learning in science, studies of *developing science teachers*, and how *theorizing learning* can inform our understanding of science classrooms.

The first two chapters in this section are examples of research which investigates the effectiveness of specific teaching situations. The research described in Chapter 1 addresses teaching and learning about the nature of science. It is almost taken for granted nowadays in policy statements on science education, and in the science education research literature, that students should learn about 'the nature of science' through their science education. Many of these arguments are presented in chapters in Section 2 of this book. Less is known, however, about *how* students learn about the nature of science, and what might be involved in teaching it. Nancy Brickhouse, Zoubeida Dagher, Harry Shipman and William J. Letts, IV begin their chapter by questioning some assumptions about students' learning in this area. They ask if students do indeed hold unique views of 'the nature of science', or if key features of the context influence the opinions expressed, and whether students' ability to articulate sophisticated positions about the nature of science is constrained by features of the context in which questions are asked. They go on to describe the design and evaluation of a college astronomy course which has the dual aims of promoting understanding of key scientific concepts, and promoting students' understanding of the relationship between evidence and explanation in astronomy. They conclude that their study provides evidence that students do not hold unique views of 'the nature of science', and that this makes good sense, given the differences between disciplines such as ecology and biochemistry. Drawing upon findings from the study, they offer suggestions for teaching about the nature of science on college-level courses.

The focus of Chapter 2 is on teaching and learning about one concept area: energy. The contents of science curricula around the world are very similar, with topics such as energy being taught to millions of students of a given age at any time. Numerous research studies have been conducted with the aim of understanding students' learning of these topics, and improving teaching. Andrée Tiberghien's chapter presents findings from a programme of research conducted over a number of years on teaching and learning about energy as part of the French secondary school physics curriculum. The chapter begins by presenting perspectives on modelling in physics, and learning physics. These perspectives are then drawn upon to explain how teaching situations were designed. Examples of students' responses to these teaching situations are presented to illustrate the kinds of improvement in learning that can be obtained from such an approach.

Chapters 3 and 4 describe studies of assessment and evaluation in science education. (Readers interested in assessment might also refer to Chapter

10 by Svein Sjøberg in Section 2, and Chapter 18 by Paul Black in Section 3.) Chapters 3 and 4 make the case for assessment as an instrument through which science teachers can be empowered to change their practice and improve students' learning. In Chapter 3, Beverley Bell presents a study of formative assessment in the science classroom. Discussing her work alongside debates about cognition, learning and language in the classroom, she theorizes formative assessment as a sociocultural activity. This theorizing leads to an account of meaning-making and social relationships in the classroom, which have broad implications for the practice of science education.

In Chapter 4, Björn Andersson presents a study of national evaluations of science education in Sweden. By describing the process of generating assessment instruments that are valid measures of students' attainment against curriculum goals, Andersson problematizes the whole notion of national evaluation. He then introduces the notion of *developmental validity*: the idea that the validity of an assessment instrument can be judged in terms of the extent to which it facilitates educational practices that promote the desired learning outcomes, as well as its capacity to provide generalizable, objective knowledge of the attainment of students in a system. The chapter then presents examples from the Swedish national evaluation and discusses them in terms of developmental validity.

Chapters 5 and 6 both focus on developing science teachers. In Chapter 5, Hilary Asoko presents a case study of one student teacher's early attempts to teach science in the primary classroom. The chapter begins by setting out some of the potential problems when beginning primary teachers, who have usually studied little science, begin to teach science. A case study is used to illustrate the difficulties likely to be faced by many student teachers in trying to draw out appropriate conceptual teaching points from the teaching activities typically used in primary science classrooms. The chapter concludes with a discussion of the implications for the practice of training primary teachers to teach science.

In contrast to Asoko, Justin Dillon in Chapter 6 addresses the development of secondary science teachers during their careers. The chapter begins by recognizing the difficulties involved in implementing recommendations about practice that arise from research, and our lack of knowledge about how individual teachers develop through their careers. A study of middle managers in English school science departments is then presented. The study is used to illustrate why models of teacher development that neglect the relationships between individuals and institutions are likely to fail. The chapter concludes by making a case for further research into the development of individual teachers in institutions, in order to produce knowledge which will usefully inform the implementation of recommendations from research on teaching and learning.

In Chapters 7 and 8, attention is turned to how theories of learning can inform our understanding of science classrooms, leading to implications for practice. In Chapter 7, Peter Hewson and John Lemberger take the seminal work of Hewson and others on conceptual change as their starting point. They show how student–student discussions of problems in genetics can be interpreted in terms of the notion of *status*. The chapter concludes with a discussion of how perspectives on the process of conceptual change have progressed over the last 20 years, and of the implications of notions of status for the practice of science teaching.

In contrast to Hewson and Lemberger, Eduardo Mortimer and Phil Scott in Chapter 8 take the work of Vygotsky and his followers as their theoretical base. Within this perspective, the teacher is viewed as centrally important in introducing scientific knowledge into classroom discourse, and in controlling classroom discourse with a view to promoting learning aims that are scientifically consistent. The chapter presents a framework for analysing classroom discourse which evaluates utterances in terms of whether they are consistent with, or in contrast to, the teacher's aims. The chapter ends with an evaluation of the significance of the work to perspectives on science learning, and the practice of science teaching.

1 Why things fall: evidence and warrants for belief in a college astronomy course

Nancy W. Brickhouse, Zoubeida R. Dagher, Harry L. Shipman and William J. Letts, IV

Introduction

Science educators have argued for decades that the science curriculum must address not only learning science, but also learning about the *nature* of science (Matthews 1994). In other words, it is insufficient to know specific theories of science and not know how knowledge claims are justified, what counts as evidence, or how theory and evidence interact.

Driver *et al.* (1996) identify five rationales for teaching about the nature of science. These are:

- A utilitarian argument: 'an understanding of science is necessary if people are to make sense of the science and manage the technological objects and processes they encounter in everyday life' (p. 16).
- A democratic argument: 'An understanding of the nature of science is necessary if people are to make sense of socioscientific issues and participate in the decision-making process' (p. 18).
- A cultural argument: 'an understanding of the nature of science is necessary in order to appreciate science as a major element of contemporary culture' (p. 19).
- A moral argument: 'an understanding of the nature of science can help develop awareness of the nature of science, and in particular the norms of the scientific community, embodying moral commitments that are of general value' (p. 19).
- A science learning argument: 'an understanding of the nature of science supports successful learning of science content' (p. 20).

Arguments like these have made the nature of science part of curriculum debates across the globe. In England and Wales, the nature of science is incorporated into the National Curriculum (NC) (Driver *et al.* 1996). The nature of science is a significant part of the US National Science Education Standards (NRC 1995) and appears as part of many state standards documents (e.g. in Delaware).

We wonder, however, if it is possible to talk meaningfully about a 'universal nature' of science. Some researchers have argued that learning about the nature of science is invariant to content understanding. For example, Kuhn *et al.* (1988) investigated the ability of young children to make distinctions between theory and evidence. They conclude that the ability to coordinate theory and evidence is a general ability rather than a domain-specific one. However, the contexts for the questions the researchers asked were not embedded in the conceptual content of science. Instead, the 'theories' they used are more like people's everyday theories – for example, what kind of food makes people more likely to catch a cold? Since these kinds of theory are familiar and require little understanding of scientific theories, it is not surprising that understanding content had little influence on the responses to the reasoning questions.

Some research makes generalizations about what students understand about the nature of science without considering the possibility of how this might vary from one scientific domain to the next. In some cases, the research is large-scale in nature and utilizes surveys to assess general principles about the nature of science. Whereas Driver *et al.* (1996) designed problems that are embedded in school science content, the conclusions that are drawn are generalized to all science content. In other cases, the research is an assessment of a particular classroom intervention, yet neither the intervention nor the assessment takes into account the role of science content (Abd-El-Khalick *et al.* 1998). Finally, some researchers implement interventions that are based in specific subject matter, yet assess student learning without regard for student understanding of subject matter, and generalize to all science content (Carey *et al.* 1989; Roth and Lucas 1997).

Over a decade ago Millar and Driver (1987) argued that how students actually used science process skills was dependent on their understanding of science content. A similar rationale may well be appropriately applied to teaching about the nature of science. Samarapungavan (1992) has argued that changes in children's reasoning on theory–choice tasks can be accounted for by changes in their understanding of the underlying scientific concepts. While the recent work of Driver *et al.* (1996) does not directly address this possibility, their data are consistent with the idea that students' warrants for belief in scientific ideas and their abilities to coordinate theory and evidence vary somewhat with content. For example, they found that students talked differently about evidence and explanation when given a story about rusting than they did when given a story about balloons filled with air.

Finally, recent scholarship questions the validity of constructing meta-narratives of science (Gallison and Stump 1996; Stanley and Brickhouse in press). General descriptions of science, intended to apply to all the practices of the sciences, may be for the most part false or misleading. Science studies increasingly emphasize the local character of the sciences and the diversity of practices that are carried out under the name of science. For example, Hacking (1996) describes different styles of reasoning and how they are a manifest part of the different sciences. Similarly, factors that drive research in one area may not be significant in another. For example, while theoretical development may be the motivation for scientific inquiry in some areas, in other areas technological advancement or the solution of practical difficulties may be more important.

Here we wish to explore how student views of the nature of science vary with science content. In particular, we consider the following areas: distinction between explanation and evidence; warrants for belief or for scepticism; and nature of observation.

Context of the study and data collection

This chapter draws on data collected in a university astronomy course taught by a member of the research team (HS) who wants his students to learn about how astronomers acquire new knowledge. This is a non-major course that fulfils general education requirements of the university. Due to the large number of students on the course (340), much of the content is taught through traditional lectures. However, the instructor also uses some small group work during class and gives assignments and test questions that require extended writing. The instructor is well-known on campus as being committed and effective. He has been a leader for reforming undergraduate science education so that instruction is more responsive of the needs of our students and more demanding in terms of requiring understanding.

The research began when the instructor for the course expressed an interest in knowing whether his instruction was effective in teaching about the nature of science. The research team examined the syllabus, met with the instructor, and decided that, based on the content of the course, we would investigate student learning in three areas: students' learning about the nature of evidence, students' learning about the relationship between science and religion, and students' learning about the nature of theories (Brickhouse et al. 2000a).

On the first day of class, the instructor asked for volunteers to be interviewed for this study. From the 70 volunteers, we sampled all six of the education majors and randomly selected 14 other names. Most of the interview students came from a variety of majors in the College of Arts and Sciences. These students were interviewed three times by a research team member other than the instructor, using a semi-structured protocol. In addition to interview transcripts, data sources included student responses to assignments and exams.

In addition, we also utilized responses to assignments and exams from all 340 students. Research team members also took field notes for each class and collected artefacts such as handouts and overhead transparencies. This provided the team with an understanding of the context of the course to better make sense of the assessment data.

Data analysis

Our data provided us with access to how students talk and write about science. We do not attempt to infer underlying universal beliefs about science based on our data. Instead we approach our data with a more realistic view of what it is: data on how students talk and write about science. As such, we expect that how students talk and write will depend not only on what they have learned, but also on the social context in which they are talking and writing (Goffman 1958; Brickhouse *et al.* 2000b).

The data were analysed by reading through all the interviews and artefacts to find data that addressed how students talked about evidence. From this, three categories were formed: student talk and writing about the relationship and distinction between evidence and explanation; student justification for belief or scepticism; and student talk about the nature of observation in astronomy.

Data on student views of the relationship between evidence and explanation were separated into categories based on whether the subject was gravity, evolution, or Big Bang Theory (BBT). Data were then coded with a scheme developed by Driver *et al.* (1996). An ability to distinguish clearly between evidence and explanation is characterized as model-based reasoning: theories are evaluated in the light of evidence, but this relationship is often complex; theories are conjectural; there is a possibility of multiple models to explain evidence; descriptions and explanations are clearly distinguishable; theories are not logically deduced from data and we can never be certain they are correct. Driver *et al.* (1996) also describe relation-based reasoning – reasoning that makes some distinction between description and explanation, but both are explained in terms of observables. However, we will not elaborate on this since we saw no evidence of this reasoning with our students.

Driver *et al.* (1996) also describe phenomenon-based reasoning, which is thinking that makes no distinction between evidence and explanation and views inquiry as a purely empirical endeavour that is driven by a simple desire to learn about the behaviour of phenomena. A few students were not placed in any of these categories because their statements were too ambiguous to make a reasonable judgement regarding which category would be most appropriate.

In analysing students' warrants for belief or scepticism, the data were separated into topic categories. We then listed the warrants and whether these warrants were used to justify belief or scepticism.

Data were coded for the nature of observation into categories for evolution by natural selection, stellar evolution, BBT, and black-hole explanations of quasars, based on whether the students said that theory served as a motivator for observation or whether they said they believed scientists observed because they simply wanted to know what was there. We focused on these topics because we have the largest amount of data about them. Comments about the credibility of astronomy arose spontaneously and were recorded.

Do students make a distinction between an explanation and the evidence it explains?

How theoretical constructions and evidence relate to one another is central to understanding about the nature of science. These theoretical constructions include any kind of idea that is used to explain evidence. Theories and laws are both explanatory, although they provide somewhat different kinds of explanation. The research literature tends to refer to all theoretical constructions as 'theories', regardless of whether the ideas to which they are referring have the explanatory power of those ideas that are called scientific theories. Here we use the more general term 'explanations' since we are interested in a broad range of ideas that can be used to explain evidence.

In the initial interview we gave the students a list of topics that either had been or would be part of the course and asked them whether they believed each to be a theory, and why. The topics were: stellar evolution, creationism, general relativity, gravity, BBT, Darwin's ideas on evolution, black hole explanations of quasars, speciation and degeneracy pressure in white dwarf stars. We then asked which they strongly believed in and why. Finally, we asked if they had trouble believing in some of the topics and why. We repeated the question on the final interview with minor changes in the topics: we deleted speciation and degeneracy pressure in white stars and added expansion of the universe and Steady State Theory (SST). All of the data on gravity and evolution by natural selection were generated in interviews, primarily from these questions. Data about BBT were generated both from these interview questions as well as from a mid-term essay exam question that asked: 'Why do scientists believe that the Big Bang Theory, rather than some other idea, describes the evolution of the universe? Be as specific as you can in your reference to the evidence'.

In interviews, students talked mostly about evolution, BBT, and gravity because they were most familiar. Student talk varied significantly depending on which of these ideas was being discussed. In the case of gravity, students talked only about the phenomenon of gravitational force. They did not talk about gravity as a theoretical construction. Two typical examples follow:

> *Dionne:* Gravity I don't think is a theory.
> *Interviewer:* Why don't you think it's a theory?
> *Dionne:* Because how else would we be planted here? You know? Otherwise we'd be floating around and stuff. I think it's been proven. Why else would stuff fall towards the earth and like with the planets?

> *Sandy:* Well gravity I guess really isn't a theory. It's a measurement more. Gravity in itself is . . . they have a definite measurement for it as 9.8 whatever the measurement is, so I'm not sure I would classify that as a theory. It exists.

We found only one student who distinguished between gravity as a phenomenon and gravity as a theory. Although his understanding of gravity may not be exactly correct, there is a clear distinction between an explanation and a phenomena.

> *Brian:* Like Newton with gravity. The apple bonked him on the head and so he said hey, why did that happen? So he started thinking about it and doing tests. Dropping stuff off of tables and stuff and developed this theory of a force inside the earth that keeps us from floating away.

In the case of evolution, the students convincingly separated talk about explanation and about evidence. Everyone said that natural selection was a theory. In the final interview, they nearly all referred to data introduced to them in a required book for the course, *The Beak of the Finch* (Weiner 1994). For example:

> *Stacy:* Originally Darwin talked about the theory of natural selection and that it was a process that took a long time and when a couple of scientists tracked the life cycle of finches they were able to follow Darwin's theory almost to a tee. The only difference is that in their experiment the time-span was much shorter than Darwin had predicted or anticipated.

In the case of BBT, only one or two students perhaps conflated explanation and evidence. The rest convincingly separated them, as is shown in this excerpt from exam two:

Tyrone: The Big Bang Theory said that the universe had a hot beginning, while the Steady State believed that the universe was cold. Both these theories were argued, each had a reason to think there [*sic*] theory was right because there was evidence to prove the basis and none to disprove it. All of this changed with the discovery of primeval helium and microwave radiation. Their experiments showed that the universe began from a hot beginning, thus eliminating Steady State Theory.

Whereas the separation between explanation and evidence is consistently clear in student talk and writing about BBT or evolution by natural selection, the separation is virtually non-existent in the case of gravity. There are several explanations for what appear to be substantially different ways of talking and writing about these theories.

One explanation is that gravity *is* a fact, a law and a theory. For an epistemological realist, there is the fact and phenomenon of gravitational force. The word 'gravity' is commonly used to refer to the force that attracts objects to the earth. In everyday talk, as well as in science classes, it is common for the phenomena and the explanation for the phenomena to be called 'gravity' and to be talked about in indistinct ways. In science textbooks, the phenomena of gravitational force acting on objects is introduced very early. For example, this is from a first-grade textbook:

The ball is falling.
A force pulls it to earth.
The force is called gravity.
Gravity pulls everything to the earth.

(Mallinson *et al.* 1991: 146)

This sort of treatment in which there is a description of an observation, followed by an explanation or interpretation of a definition, and then finally a generalization is typical throughout the elementary years, whenever gravity is taught.

There is also the law of gravitation, which is the mathematical relationship between sizes of objects, distances between objects, and the force of attraction between them. This is commonly seen in high-school and college textbooks, but can also be found in middle-grade textbooks, in which gravity is still presented with the section on forces. The law of gravitation is explained as follows: 'Gravitational force is an attraction between any two objects that have mass. As mass increases, the attraction increases. The sun and planets have large masses, thus the attraction between them is very great ... Gravitational force depends also on the distance between masses. As distance increases, gravitational force decreases' (Mallinson *et al.* 1991: 282).

In high-school physics texts the law of gravitation first appears in a more formal, usually mathematical way. This progression in teaching about gravity is consistent with the recommendations of benchmarks (AAAS 1993).

It seems appropriate for students to talk about gravity as a force and as a law. However, they fail to recognize gravity as a theory or explanation for *why* things fall. They do not recognize that 'gravity' is also a theoretical construct that explains why things fall.

In spite of our estimation that student talk about gravity is not much beyond the first-grade textbook, students tended to express very high levels of confidence in their understanding. Thus, they did not re-evaluate their discourse during the course. No one gave a thorough explanation for why objects fall to the earth beyond 'things fall because of gravity'. Although students express little need for evaluating their understanding of gravity, scientists have questioned the adequacy of the theory of gravitational force. In particular, the lack of a mechanism to explain this strange attraction was a concern to Isaac Newton (Matthews 1994) that he noted in the General Scholium to the *Principia*. George Berkeley attempted to solve the problem of gravitational force by arguing that gravity was not real. It was simply a useful fiction to make the mathematics work out (Matthews 1994). While we realize that simply understanding that there is a force between any two objects in the universe does not mean that students (or scientists for that matter) can explain why this force exists, we maintain that an understanding of Newton's theory of universal gravitation goes beyond a simple statement that 'things fall because of gravity'.

Furthermore, students are likely have had no exposure to other explanations for why things fall. In other words, they cannot conceive of what another explanation might be for why things fall. Several students stated this explicitly by responding to our question regarding belief by asking 'How else would we be planted here?' (if there were no such thing as gravity).

In the case of BBT, the instructor for the class spent time talking about BBT and SST – two theories of the origin of the universe – and how we came to believe one of these theories was better than the other. In a sense, the instructor was teaching the sorts of consideration that were used to justify a scientific knowledge claim or what Norris (1997) refers to as the 'justificatory shape of science'. Students were able to articulate evidence that could be better explained by BBT than SST. In other words, students understood not only the possibility of multiple explanations, but could describe at least one of these other explanations in some detail.

Finally, evolution, like gravity, can be thought of as both a phenomenon and an explanation. There is the phenomenon of organisms evolving. There is also an explanation for why they evolve. However, students did not conflate the explanation and the phenomena in this case. They seemed to understand the theory of natural selection. Many of them also understood this to be a different explanation for the origin of species than many religious accounts. Evolution and gravity are different in that we experience the phenomenon of gravity from birth, whereas evolution is likely to be learned as both a phenomenon and a theory in school and is not experienced as a phenomenon at the everyday level of consciousness.

How do students justify scientific beliefs?

One of the goals of science education is the acquisition of justified belief, or knowledge, about the natural world (Driver *et al.* 1996; Norris 1997). Thus, we sought to understand whether students had merely acquired beliefs about astronomy, or whether they had acquired beliefs they could justify. Furthermore, if they were sceptical of the ideas presented in class, we wanted to know how they justified their scepticism.

The instructor wanted students to develop a disposition to use evidence as a warrant for belief. He wanted students to distinguish between ideas that were adequately supported by evidence and those that were not. However, citing one piece of evidence is not adequate for justifying belief. Justification for belief in a particular idea is strongest when the warrants are multiple. For example, belief based on evidence, on logical criteria, on consistency with other supportable beliefs, on reliable authorities, on absence of competing ideas, and on good outcomes from acting on the belief are examples of reasonable criteria for justifying belief. None of these alone are particularly good warrants. To understand student warrants for belief or scepticism we analysed students' responses to the same questions as mentioned before: 'Given a list of topics covered in the course, which of these do you believe strongly in? Which of these do you have more difficulty believing in?'

Student responses justifying belief or scepticism were highly variable from one topic to the next. At the beginning of the semester, students commonly stated that they did not know enough about the topics listed to give an opinion on belief. They gave thorough commentary only on those topics that they believed they understood. The only topic students frequently expressed strong belief in was gravity. They typically also had an opinion about evolution, which most found credible. A few students also had an opinion on BBT, but were much more sceptical of it.

Students said they believed strongly in gravity. Many referred to it as a fact or law. All students said they found the fact that we are not floating in the air to be undeniable, absolute, and good reason to believe unquestioningly in gravity. Students rarely gave any justification for this belief other than 'because things fall'.

Students also said they believed strongly in evolution, with most of the students citing evidence as justification for their belief. Particularly at the end of the semester, students were likely to cite the evidence presented in the course text, *The Beak of the Finch* (Weiner 1994), as convincing evidence. Several students also talked about extinction and its causes as a good reason to believe in evolution. Another reason students gave for believing in evolution was that it was sensible to them:

> *Marge:* Darwin's ideas on evolution. I think and believe in that, about the survival of the fittest and cross-breeding kind of helped variation and everything. So yeah, I pretty much believe in that.

Although most students believed in evolution, half of the students gave some reasons for scepticism. The reasons included: lack of evidence (for two students what was meant by this was the lack of direct evidence; one student simply said it was not totally proven); lack of universal acceptance by the general public; conflicts with religious views; and lack of understanding adequate for acceptance.

Maggie's talk about evolution was somewhat typical of those who accepted evolution for themselves, but who were also aware that it was a controversial idea among the public:

> *Maggie:* Darwin's ideas would be a theory because they are his ideas and they are not . . . there are so many different ideas about evolution. There really isn't one fact about evolution. Lots of people have different ideas about what happened.

Justification for BBT was expressed differently than justification for evolution. Although at the end of the course most of the students justified belief in terms of evidence (for example, microwave background radiation, helium concentrations), about half justified belief in terms of BBT being a better explanation of the data than SST. Nearly half the students said that learning more about BBT helped to make it more plausible to them. Two said that they accepted BBT because it was accepted by scientists. Students were generally better able to justify their belief in BBT with a larger number of different reasons than were given for evolution or gravity. Whereas for gravity only one student gave more than one warrant for belief and for evolution only three students gave more than one warrant for belief, in the case of BBT only three students justified their belief with only one warrant. Tyrone was particularly strong in giving a variety of warrants for belief in BBT, including a couple of different citations of evidence and its sensibility. He even seemed to recognize his dependence on scientists to report data truthfully (Norris 1997):

> *Interviewer:* Can you tell me specifically what makes [BBT] so compelling?
> *Tyrone:* I guess it was just a lot of the evidence that Dr Shipman told us about and then we read about. Like the Big Bang Theory how it

disproved the Steady State Theory by the microwave radiation background, rays that were found and the helium that was in space . . . the actual data, but that's confusing but you know, if you followed the line you sort of understood it. So taking that scientists correctly put down their data then I believe it.

Students were more sceptical of BBT than they were of either gravity or evolution. Their warrants for scepticism, however, changed somewhat during the course. Whereas the most common justification for scepticism at the beginning of the course was the implausibility of BBT, at the end of the course the most common justification for scepticism was the lack of direct evidence. The following quote was typical of this particular view:

Brenda: Big Bang is a scientific theory.
Interviewer: And again, why do you say it's a theory?
Brenda: Because it has to do with time and planets and stuff like that. But you know, it's not proven. No one was there when it happened.

Relativity was treated very differently from evolution or BBT because it was not viewed by students as having philosophical dimensions. It was also somewhat unusual because both the theory itself and the data that support it were not as well understood by the students. (Although about one fifth of the course was devoted to issues of relativity, student evaluations of the course indicate that students believed the topic of relativity to be the most difficult on the course.) Less than half of the students used evidence to justify belief in relativity. Most of these did not name any specific evidence as significant. For example, Roland justified belief in relativity as follows:

Roland: We proved it. The rules worked. He [the instructor] showed us so much concrete evidence of how the rules of general relativity work. And I think he told us it has been experimentally tested too. I didn't really understand that but . . . I talked about it with my parents and they were saying that it was experimentally tested.

An equal number of students justified belief in relativity by saying that they accepted it because scientists do. A few students said they believed in it because it was what they were taught, while others said they believed in it because it made sense to them. For example:

Lana: We haven't experienced it or anything, but I guess going by what other people say because I don't know for myself, the scientific community believes it to be true and I'll go along with that.

There was very little scepticism of relativity expressed. However, a few students said they were sceptical of it because they did not understand it well:

Brian: Well, I have difficulty believing in relativity because it's kind of an abstract idea. I mean I just don't understand the point of even stating it because it has to do with moving at the speed of light and everything and I mean it's just not concrete to me. I just have trouble visualizing because I can't move at the speed of light and nothing that I know can besides light so it's tough to visualize it.

Students gave about as many reasons to believe in stellar evolution as to not believe. They believed in it because of the evidence and because they knew that it is generally accepted by scientists. However, they were very sceptical of the quality of the data. In particular, the fact that the data are indirect was a significant problem for many of the students. For example, Sandy explained why stellar evolution is 'still a theory' in terms of uncertainty about the evidence:

Sandy: That's the way they think it is but they can't be absolutely sure with the technical problems they have. They don't have all the technical, the technical knowledge to get the measurements and everything. The distance and everything of not being there to actually see close up. I mean other than the Hubble telescope. But you still can't see all the mechanics that are happening. So some of it is just their conclusion but it may not be accurate.

This is particularly surprising because it is the instructor's area of research and the first month of class sessions was devoted to stellar evolution, as was most of the first exam. Students also read and made suggestions for a recent research proposal written by the instructor to the National Aeronautics and Space Administration (NASA). In spite of this relatively thorough treatment of the topic, students did not find the evidence to be compelling.

Students expressed even more scepticism regarding the black hole explanation of quasars. At the end of the course only two students gave a reason for believing in it. There was no justification given for belief that was mentioned more than once. At the end of the course nearly all the students expressing scepticism based their justification on the indirect nature of the evidence:

Jessica: They were thinking the final stage of some stars is black holes but they don't really . . . they're not 100 per cent sure that there are black holes because they can't see them and so it's kind of hard to find them.

Although we do not believe that the scepticism expressed here is much reason for concern (after all, we may well have produced this scepticism in the interviews by asking the students which of the ideas they had more trouble believing), we find it somewhat surprising that ideas such as BBT and evolution, that might conflict with religious views, were not treated any more sceptically than ideas like the black hole explanation of quasars or stellar evolution. The main reason given for scepticism was not conflict with religious belief, but had to do with the nature of the evidence being indirect.

Nature of observation

The nature of observation can vary considerably from one scientific domain to another. Whereas some scientists rely heavily on recorded electronic signals from instruments, others observe phenomena directly. Regardless, however, all scientists must make decisions about what is relevant data and what is. mere noise. These decisions are made on the basis of the scientists' knowledge of both the phenomena and the instrumentation. But perhaps most importantly, scientists decide what observations to make based on a desire to test a particular idea.

Data in the previous section are consistent with student responses to a question in interviews one and three that asked them how observations in biology and astronomy were different. The most commonly cited difference was that observations in biology dealt with tangible objects whereas in astronomy the size and scale of the universe as well as the limitations of technology did not permit direct observation. Unprompted, five students said in interviews that because of this they found the knowledge claims in biology to be more credible than the knowledge claims in astronomy! Karen, for example, talked at great length about the difficulties and her scepticism of astronomical knowledge:

> *Karen:* I would think that biology is a more precise science. Astronomy has a lot of guessing in it . . . I mean [biology] is more concrete because it's right there. We're studying people. We're studying plants. We're studying animals. We are not studying, like in astronomy you're studying stars and space. But we are not that close to space and it's hard to study something we don't know much about. Something that is not here.

When students gave examples of observations in biology, they nearly always gave examples of macroscopic, direct observations of plants and animals, rather than the microscopic ones. Karen continued to discuss how astronomers 'stumbled upon things and found like pulsars' and how this made astronomers change their theory. Karen viewed this changing of theory as a sign of weakness in astronomical knowledge. The instructor attempted to avoid the dogmatism that often accompanies science classes by teaching students about changes in theory and the resolution of competing theories.

However, we suspect if the students have only *one* of their science courses taught in this manner, they may conclude, as Karen did, that this domain of science is simply not as certain as other domains.

Students also viewed biology and astronomy differently in terms of whether theories motivated scientists to observe certain kinds of data. Most students recognized observations such as the size of finches' beaks, to be motivated by trying to test the theory of evolution by natural selection. In the case of astronomical theories such as stellar evolution, BBT, or the black hole explanation of quasars, most students said that astronomers just like to look around at the universe to learn about it.

We were not entirely surprised by these results since we asked 18 members of the class to answer the question 'Why do astronomers make observations?' at the beginning of the semester and found that only 33 per cent of these students wrote that observations are made to test theories or hypotheses. Their ideas may have inadvertently been reinforced by the fact that in class the instructor described two serendipitous astronomical observations related to BBT and the pulsar discovery. Although serendipitous discoveries are atypical and the recognition of them as significant requires theoretical knowledge, it is conceivable that this led some students to be somewhat more likely to say that astronomers observe just because they like to learn new things. In the case of evolution, on the other hand, observations were understood to be made for the purpose of testing the theory.

Conclusions and implications

This study provides further evidence of how students' talk about the nature of science differs, depending on the particular scientific topic under discussion. The relationship between theory and evidence, warrants for belief, and nature of observation are described in different ways in the different disciplines discussed in the course. These differences have several implications for science education researchers and for teachers.

We believe that researchers should be cautious in making claims about students having any particular view of 'the nature of science' which is, implicitly, independent of the subject under discussion. For example, students in our study population had relatively complete pictures of BBT while simultaneously viewing the theory of gravity as simply a one-word explanation for falling. It would seem problematic to ascribe a single view of the nature of theory, for instance, to such a student. Our findings affirm those of Ryder *et al.* (1999) that student understanding varies with contexts. We suggest that future research about the nature of science be more fine-grained and concentrate on student analyses of particular theories, warrants, observations and so on.

It follows, then, that attempts to teach the nature of science should be thoroughly embedded in particular science content. The standard textbook practice of including an introductory chapter which attempts to frame the nature of science for an entire scientific discipline like biology may well be problematic. Can students understand the nature of observation and experiment with a single description when a field includes subdisciplines as varied as ecology and biochemistry?

Our findings also have implications for teaching practice. We have found that introducing multiple theoretical explanations for a single phenomenon can be quite powerful. The instructor of this course has, for example, extended this treatment to introduce and test multiple explanations for why things fall: one based on Newton's picture and the other based on Aristotle's ideas of a world consisting of earth, water, air and fire. Topics for this treatment need to be selected with care. Areas where the connection between evidence and explanation is rather remote or abstract seem less promising.

This research has been supported by the National Science Foundation, but opinions and findings are those of its authors, not those of the Foundation.

References

AAAS (American Association for the Advancement of Science) (1993) *Benchmarks for Scientific Literacy*. New York: Oxford University Press.

Abd-El-Khalick, F., Bell, R.L. and Lederman, N.G. (1998) The nature of science and instructional practice: making the unnatural natural. *Science Education*, 82: 417–36.

Brickhouse, N.W., Dagher, Z.R., Letts, W.L. and Shipman, H.L. (2000a) The diversity of students' views about evidence, theory and the interface between science and religion in an astronomy course. *Journal of Research in Science Teaching*, 37(4): 340–62.

Brickhouse, N.W., Lowery, P.A. and Schultz, K. (2000b) What kind of a girl does science? The construction of school science identities. *Journal of Research in Science Teaching*, 37(5): 441–58.

Carey, S., Evans, R., Honda, M., Jay, E. and Ungar, C. (1989) 'An experiment is when you try it and see if it works': a study of grade 7 students' understanding of the construction of scientific knowledge. *International Journal of Science Education*, 11(5): 514–29.

Driver, R., Leach, J., Millar, R. and Scott, P. (1996) *Young People's Images of Science*. Buckingham: Open University Press.

Gallison, P. and Stump, D.J. (eds) (1996) *The Disunity of Science: Boundaries, Contexts, and Power*. Palo Alto, CA: Stanford University Press.

Goffman, E. (1958) *Presentation of Self in Everyday Life* (monograph 2). Edinburgh: University of Edinburgh Social Sciences Research Centre.

Hacking, I. (1996) The disunities of the sciences, in P. Gallison and D.J. Stump (eds) *The Disunity of Science: Boundaries, Contexts, and Power*, pp. 37–74. Palo Alto, CA: Stanford University Press.

Kuhn, D., Amsel, E. and O'Loughlin, M. (1988) *The Development of Scientific Thinking Skills*. London: Academic Press.

Mallinson, G.G., Mallinson, J.B., Froschauer, L., Harris, J.A., Lewis, M.C. and Valentino, C. (1991) *Science Horizons*. Morristown, NJ: Silver, Burdett & Ginn.

Matthews, M.R. (1994) *Science Teaching: The Role of History and Philosophy of Science*. New York: Routledge.

Millar, R. and Driver, R. (1987) Beyond processes. *Studies in Science Education*, 14: 33–62.

Norris, S.P. (1997) Intellectual independence for nonscientists and other content-transcendent goals of science education. *Science Education*, 81: 239–58.

NRC (National Research Council) (1995) *National Science Education Standards*. Washington, DC: National Academy Press.

Roth, W-M. and Lucas, K.B. (1997) From 'truth' to 'invented reality': a discourse analysis of high school physics students talk about scientific knowledge. *Journal of Research in Science Teaching*, 34, 145–79.

Ryder, J., Leach, J. and Driver, R. (1999) Undergraduate science students' images of science. *Journal of Research in Science Teaching*, 36(2): 201–20.

Samarapungavan, A. (1992) Children's judgments in theory choice tasks: scientific rationality in childhood. *Cognition*, 45(1): 1–32.

Stanley, W.B. and Brickhouse, N.W. (in press) Teaching sciences: the multicultural question revisited. *Science Education*.

Weiner, J. (1994) *The Beak of the Finch*. New York: Vintage.

2 Designing teaching situations in the secondary school

Andrée Tiberghien

Introduction

The relationship between research in science education and effective teaching in the framework of any educational system raises the question of the role of research in designing teaching situations. Such design for each domain of physics can be an endless task. In this chapter I present an approach to designing situations based on teaching and learning where the knowledge to be taught, students' understandings of that knowledge and teaching resources are each viewed as important, and with the potential to influence each other. The theoretical bases of such designs are first presented and then three types of situation are analysed.

Theoretical bases

The theoretical elaboration presented here has been developed following a series of empirical studies carried out in the COAST research group (France), with data mainly collected in classrooms during practical work at the upper secondary school level (Bécu-Robinault 1997a, 1997b; Buty 1998; Le Maréchal 1999); it is also rooted in a collaboration with teachers (Gaidioz *et al.* 1998). The results obtained, together with theoretical approaches to modelling (Tiberghien 1994), to didactical situations (Brousseau 1988), and to didactical transposition (Chevallard 1991) constitute the main bases of this research-based design of physics teaching situations.

Knowledge

First of all, it is necessary to note that in English, the single word 'knowledge' is the only one available, whereas in French there are two words:

savoir(s) and *connaissance(s)*, with the associated verbs. This makes it difficult to present in English the theoretical framework constructed in the French language.

The theoretical position on knowledge is based on Chevallard's (1991) work – a French researcher in didactics of mathematics – who, to deal with knowledge, uses the metaphor of life and ecology. Knowledge 'lives' within a group of people called an institution and the relation between an individual and a piece of knowledge is termed 'understanding of knowledge'.

From this perspective, the official curriculum corresponds to the knowledge to be taught and the distinction between *scientific knowledge* and this *knowledge to be taught* is recognized. The process of developing this knowledge to be taught is termed *didactical transposition*. This transposition is made under several kinds of constraints, imposed by the educational system.

The design of teaching situations corresponds to another step of the didactical transposition – that is, from the knowledge to be taught to the knowledge that is effectively taught. This transposition is the main aspect of this chapter; it involves a *manipulation* of knowledge. The whole knowledge to be taught cannot be presented as such to the students, it has to be manipulated in order to decompose it into smaller pieces and integrate it into activities. Consequently, in a research-based teaching situation, this manipulation should be theoretically based and *made explicit* (rather than being treated, implicitly, as being as close as possible to the 'true' knowledge). In the work presented here, two complementary ways of analysing knowledge are presented: modelling and semiotic registers.

Modelling

The modelling approach is a common base from which to analyse the knowledge to be taught, the knowledge that is *actually* taught and students' understanding of that knowledge. This approach deals with the knowledge communicated by word, gesture or writing – in other words, knowledge which 'lives'.

Since we are only addressing physics teaching, the treatment of the modelling approach is restricted to understanding the inanimate material world. The following hypothesis is made: when a person or a group of people explain, interpret or predict situation(s) in the material world, most of the time their productions entail observable objects or events, and/or physical parameters, and/or relations between them, and this involves a modelling activity. This activity involves both the world of objects and events and the world of explanatory or theoretical frameworks, as well as models derived from these explanatory or theoretical frameworks (Tiberghien 1994). The world

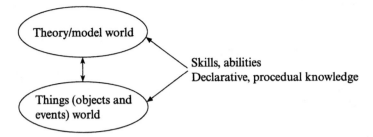

Figure 2.1   Categorization of knowledge based on a modelling activity

of objects and events refers to all observable aspects of the material world, whereas the world of theories and models refers to theoretical aspects and elements of the material situations, in terms of various principles, parameters or quantities (see Figure 2.1).

The nature of modelling activity in physics is not developed here, as this kind of analysis has been made by several epistemologists (for example Bunge 1973; Bachelard 1979; Giere 1988). In the case of students' knowledge, it is stated that explanations or predictions can be based on people's explanatory systems (which will be called a 'theoretical framework') (Carey 1985; Vosniadou and Brewer 1994). This theoretical framework is not unique – individuals draw upon frameworks according to the objects and events in question, and the social situation.

Compared to other categorizations of knowledge, such as the classification into procedural and declarative knowledge that is very often used in problem-solving research, our categorization is transversal. That is, both worlds can include declarative and procedural knowledge. Consider, for example, the statement 'The red pen is on this table'. This statement, in itself, involves declarative knowledge in the world of objects and events. By contrast, the statement 'The force of the system "pen" on the system "table" is equal to that of the system "table" on the system "pen"' is also declarative, but is sited in the world of the theory or model.

This method of decomposing knowledge allows for the interpretation of a major characteristic of students' difficulties when they learn physics, as shown in all the studies on students' conceptions of which Ros Driver was a pioneer (Driver 1973; Driver *et al.* 1985). After receiving tuition the students are able to solve physics problems with formulae, but they are not able to use formulae and the associated theory to predict and interpret experiments. The modelling perspective allows for the interpretation of these difficulties in terms of difficulties in establishing links between the worlds of objects/ events and theories/models.

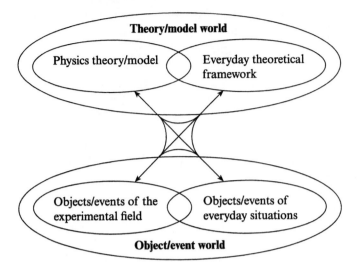

Figure 2.2 The two worlds of modelling

Different types of knowledge are involved in modelling (see Figure 2.2): the students can use their everyday knowledge, which may or may not overlap with the taught physics theory/model.

Semiotic registers

Another way of decomposing knowledge is to take into account its representation. Duval (1995) uses the concept of *semiotic registers*. Graphs, algebra, geometrical mathematics, linguistic forms and drawings are all different semiotic registers. These registers constitute the degrees of freedom at the disposal of a person to transform an idea, as yet unclear, into an object of thinking for him or herself (see p. 21). From this perspective, a hypothesis on learning is that an individual's understanding of a concept (or, more generally, an idea) develops when relations are established between different semiotic registers associated with that idea.

Learning and activities

The position on learning and activities that underpins the work described in this chapter is related to the position on modelling and semiotic registers described in the last section:

- The learners' existing theoretical framework is fundamental to their understanding of the whole situation. The situation includes all physical, mental, affective aspects.
- Acquisition of science understanding (conceptual, methodological and/or practical) requires the learner to construct links between the worlds of object/event and theory/model.
- When students change registers to make explicit their ideas (for example, when they transfer ideas from an algebraic register to a graphical register or linguistic register in written or oral form), this process in itself plays a role in helping them to construct meaning from the underlying idea (Duval 1995).

A specific hypothesis, on which the design of situations is based, deals with the relationships between learning and students' activities. It is considered that the learners' activities, during which they construct meaning and establish links between the two worlds and/or between semiotic registers, allow them to acquire physics knowledge. This implies that the learner interacts with their environment, which includes all the human and material resources in the situation.

The concept of *devolution* helps to specify the relationship between the teacher and the students: 'Devolution is the act by which the teacher makes the student take responsibility for a learning situation or problem, and accepts the consequences of this transfer him/herself' (Brousseau 1998: 303). The *didactical contract* (Balacheff *et al.* 1997) consists of the 'rules of the game' and the management of the teaching situation:

> The teacher must therefore arrange not the communication of knowledge, but the devolution of a good problem. If the devolution takes place, the students enter into the game and if they win learning occurs. But what if a student refuses or avoids the problem, or doesn't solve it? The teacher then has the social obligation to help her [*sic*]. Then a relationship is formed which determines – explicitly to some extent, but mainly implicitly – what each partner, the teacher and the student, will have the responsibility for managing and, in some way or other, be responsible to the other person for. This system of reciprocal obligation resembles a contract.
>
> (Brousseau 1998: 31)

The consequence is often that, rather than addressing learning situations or problems in terms of the underlying concepts, students address them in terms of what they think the teacher will expect them to do.

The design of three types of teaching situation

To design relevant teaching situations, the knowledge to be taught, and the sequence in which this knowledge is introduced, has to be made explicit.

When working from the perspective of modelling, involving the two worlds, curriculum designers are faced with the task of selecting a set of material situations coherent with the theory/model, which itself has to be specified. Given this coherence, the theory/model should lead the students or the teachers to interpret and/or predict events that are relevant to the learning goals, and, furthermore, this relevance should be taught explicitly. This design is also guided by the students' prior knowledge; both the material situations and the theory/model should be 'learnable' for the duration of the sequence.[1] Finally, the learning hypotheses about the role of activities leads to the choice of resources, which causes the students to take responsibility for constructing an understanding of the knowledge.

In France, such situations were rested at the upper secondary school level (age 15–17) in physics. They were designed within a group which included teachers and researchers. The organization of this type of work is rather similar to that done in the Children's Learning in Science Project (CLISP) (Scott and Driver 1998). Over a period of three years, a group of 15 teachers and three researchers worked together designing teaching sequences, the teachers using these sequences, the researchers observing in the classroom and on videotape in the case of one or two groups of students.

The situations that were studied are research products, and as such they need to be validated (Artigue 1990). This chapter only deals with a type of validation consisting of a comparison between students' actual activities during the session, and what was intended in the design. For this purpose, data needed to be collected throughout the teaching situations. Accordingly, at least two pairs of students were videotaped throughout a teaching situation. A case study methodology was used. The students' verbalizations were transcribed in their entirety, and notes were made of the students' gestures as relevant to the experiment.

The three cases presented below correspond to teaching situations included in two different parts of the curriculum.[2] The first is part of a sequence for students in the first year of higher secondary school (age 15–16),[3] addressing the topic 'sound'. The two other teaching situations are part of a sequence of the official curriculum of the second year addressing energy, though this is only studied by students who chose the scientific orientation.[4] For these situations, the sequences themselves are presented before an account of the design of the situations.[5]

Choosing the knowledge to be taught in the teaching sequences

The first teaching sequence deals with sound. In physics, sound is associated with waves and their propagation. The students at this level do not have any knowledge about waves. Their prior knowledge of sound comes almost exclusively from everyday experience where sound is strongly related to sense perception (Vince 1999). Consequently, it was decided to start from this type of knowledge and to design settings to help students to acquire several levels of modelling. The first is a model which can be directly related to events perceived by hearing: the sound chain. This chain gives three categories to interpret the material situations: source; medium of propagation; and receptor of sound. The second model includes the vibration, its frequency and its amplitude, its displacement and its velocity. Vibration is directly related to movement (back and forth motion of a vibration, and displacement of a vibration in a medium). This last model is then developed with the concepts associated with waves, including a particular model of matter.

This analysis leads to a teaching sequence in three parts: emission, propagation and reception of sound; sound waves and their propagation; musical acoustics. The first part aims to help students to develop and relate the two phenomenologies, corresponding respectively to classes of sound events perceived by hearing and to classes of mechanics events which can be perceived by touching or seeing. The students should be able to differentiate high- and low-pitched sounds and sounds of different volumes (loud, soft), and relate these to the frequency and amplitude of vibrations.

This first part of the teaching sequence might appear pointless for students at this relatively high level of teaching, since they might already be expected to know and relate these two types of phenomena. However, research studies show that this is not the case for sound (and may not be so for other aspects of physics). As a matter of fact, even if students are familiar with a domain, they may still remain unaware that the studied phenomena are a class of events explained by given theory/model. The familiarity of a situation can prevent students from selecting the right events. The modelling approach guides the designer in making explicit some aspects of knowledge necessary to understand physics; these aspects may be obvious and implicit to the expert and unknown to the students. This is why the design of the first situation of this part is presented in this chapter. It illustrates what we term 'constructing a phenomenology'.

The two other teaching situations are included in a sequence on energy. The part of the material world chosen as the object of study for students may draw upon either everyday social life (energy is what we pay for, what makes technical systems from toys to satellites work), or upon physics teaching traditions (i.e. mechanics and thermodynamics). Neither the selected part of the material world nor the corresponding theory/model are inevitable choices.

The first step of the teaching sequence took energy in everyday life as its reference, in accordance with the official curriculum. In several other curricula where this choice is made, the place of physics theory within teaching is not very well specified; the word 'energy' has multiple meanings before the introduction of physical quantities and measurements. In the framework of the modelling approach, it was decided to propose a seed of theory/ model as a part of the knowledge to be taught, this theory/model being understandable by the students and useful to interpret a variety of material situations with the support of a symbolic representation (the energy chain). The design of the corresponding teaching situations illustrates the second case, which we term 'constructing meaning for a qualitative theory'. In the second step of the sequence, the aim is to differentiate energy from power by introducing a quantitative aspect of energy: its relation with power as a flow of energy per unit time. This corresponds to the third case, which we term 'constructing a new concept by differentiation and by relationships within a theoretical network'. The following steps develop quantitative relations between energy and mechanical, electrical and calorimetric physics quantities.

Case 1: constructing a phenomenology

In the situation illustrating this case, the students are already aware of the concept of a sound chain. In a prior session they had to interpret a variety of situations in terms of an emitter, a medium of propagation or a receptor. Such a categorization is a basic theoretical aspect, since it implies a way of dividing up the world (Levy-Strauss 1962). The first situation of the introductory practical session of the sequence on sound is presented here.

Knowledge involved in the situation

The aim is to help learners to go from 'sense perception observation to theory-driven observation' (see Chapter 11). That is, to transform their sense perception into 'thinking' objects and making them explicit by means of debate, writing texts and possibly making drawings.

The students' activities should lead them to construct the idea that vibration is a common behaviour of all emitters. As shown in Figure 2.3, the knowledge involved is physics knowledge, everyday knowledge, the overlap between them, and several links inside and between the two worlds.

Characteristics of the design

The knowledge to be constructed, together with the learning hypotheses, suggest that students should be given the opportunity to develop their sense

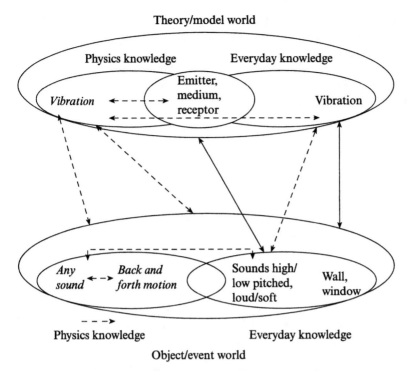

Theory/model world

Object/event world

Figure 2.3 Knowledge to be constructed, and students' prior knowledge. In italics and broken lines: what students have to construct. In solid and continuous lines: prior knowledge.

perception corresponding both to sound and to back and forth motion. The students therefore have to hear, to see and to *touch* objects producing sound.

The specification of the teaching situation is not detailed here (see Barde 1998; SOC 1999), only the main characteristics are presented. The main resource of the situation consists of a variety of objects (tuning fork, tambourine, low frequency generator with loudspeaker, cigarette paper to create a whistling sound and a pendulum which can move when the light pendulum bob touches the tambourine) with which the students can create events such as sound and observable movements of vibration. These objects are available for each group of students (they are handed from one group to another if necessary). The students are allowed and *advised* to touch the membrane of the loudspeaker and of course the other objects. The associated resources are:

- The same written question for each object: 'Name the source of sound, and explain the behaviour of the source, possibly with a schema sketch for each experiment'.
- A written question aiming to elicit the common characteristics of the perceived events: 'Is there any common behaviour among all these sources of sound?'

The organization of the situation is very common. The students work in groups of two, and have to write a report (answers to the questions). The teacher manages the groups, gives help when a group asks for it and regularly invites the students to make explicit *what is for them* the behaviour of the source. This invitation can modify the type of didactical contract if necessary: the students give themselves permission to write what they think, and they know that there is no single right answer.

Students' activities

Two main features of these activities in relation to the design are presented (for an extensive analysis, see Barde 1998).

- The videotapes and direct observations in the classroom show that verbalization takes place, but it is not straightforward, as the dialogue (turns No. 194, 198) in Table 2.1 shows. This is because students need to ask themselves how the membrane moves, and what is the distinction between the air, the membrane movement and the sound.
- The frequent touching of objects which emit sound, and in particular the membrane of the loudspeaker at different frequencies of the LFG, in spite of the fact that the designers did not plan this high number of touching and hearing actions. Let us note that even in the next two practical sessions, the students still touch sound sources when they are not specifically requested to do so. This result supports the hypothesis that the actions on objects involving sense perception, and the associated mental activities, are intrinsically linked. Table 2.1 illustrates this simultaneity.

The analysis of the whole session shows that there are more relations between sound and movement made by students than any other type of relation (Barde 1998). Thus, for this group of students the design of the situation is validated, in that the students made the intended links between sound production and movement of the source. However, it appeared that some other students 'do not play the game completely' – that is, they do not take time to debate and write full sentences from their sense perceptions.

Table 2.1 Extract of transcription of a group of two students, where Min. = the time following the end of the teacher's introduction, No. = the number of dialogue turn.

Min.	No.	Student	Gestures	Dialogue
23	194	Nicholas	Touching the loudspeaker membrane	it moves, it makes/how can we say that/that the air doesn't move (laugh) it doesn't move
24	198	Nicholas	Touching the loudspeaker membrane	this/you know you have the air, it passes/therefore it's according to the sound which passes the/ there it's regular but you put the sound with low pitched sound and the high pitched sound and all the sound doesn't move the same it propagates differently the air/the sound it's a propagation of the air
24	199	Christian		yes but what makes the noise, it's when the membrane moves
28	257		Hitting the tambourine	it's always the membrane
32	319	Nicholas	Hitting the tuning fork	the source of sound is the vibration of the tuning fork because when we hit it, it vibrates but we don't see it
32	328	Nicholas	Holding the pendulum bob against the tuning fork	huh, yes because it vibrates, it's logical
33	331	Christian		yes so in fact it's always the vibration roughly

One reason might be that the students are not interested, another that they do not consider themselves to be allowed to make explicit their own thinking with their own words, and all the more so because of the problems they experience in verbalizing their ideas.

In conclusion, when students 'play the game' the designed resources result in them mobilizing the relevant prior knowledge and elaborating different kinds of relevant links (see Figure 2.3). This leads to the hypothesis that when the knowledge to be taught involves constructing phenomena, a major role of the teaching resources is to allow students frequently to use sensory perception, with the possibility of simultaneous verbalization.

Case 2: constructing a meaning for a qualitative theory

This case involves a type of situation in which a part of the knowledge to be taught is reconstructed for didactical reasons (termed 'the seed of a theory/ model'). Such an elaboration of the knowledge to be taught seems to be fruitful both as a tool which is 'learnable' for the majority of students, and as a tool which can be used by them to understand the material world in a wide variety of situations. Furthermore, the tool offers common support for all the students in a classroom.

The situation presented here is the first practical session on energy following a teaching session aimed at creating a need for an energy theory/model (Tiberghien 1996).

Knowledge involved in the situation

The aim of this situation is to develop an understanding of a 'seed' of a physics theory/model – that is, something from which further understanding can grow – introduced through a text (see Table 2.2). This text categorizes the world into three parts: reservoirs, transformers and transfers, and proposes a symbolic representation for this categorization.

Three experiments were designed. The choice of the first one, a battery and a bulb, is based on the results of studies of students' conceptions showing that the idea of a battery as a reservoir of energy is close to the students' prior knowledge. The second experiment (an object hanging by a string attached to the axle of a generator connected to a bulb: when the object falls the bulb lights), and the third (a battery connected to a motor, the same object as the generator; an object hanging by a string attached to the axle of the motor rises up), involve events in mechanics, electricity and light.

The students' activities, when they elaborate the energy chain, should let them construct relations between elements of the theory/model and elements of the experiments (see Figure 3.4, an example of an energy chain). The overlap between everyday knowledge and physics knowledge should play a large part in this session.

Characteristics of the design

The main resources available in the situation are the text and the experiments. The students have to construct a symbolic representation which constrains

Table 2.2 A simplified version of the 'seed' of the theory/model. The left column presents the conceptual definitions for the target domain. The right column presents the symbols used to draw the energy chain.

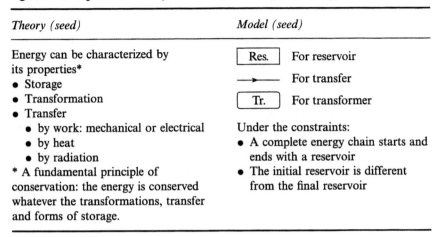

Theory (seed)	Model (seed)

Energy can be characterized by its properties*
 • Storage
 • Transformation
 • Transfer
     • by work: mechanical or electrical
     • by heat
     • by radiation
 * A fundamental principle of conservation: the energy is conserved whatever the transformations, transfer and forms of storage.
	☐ Res. For reservoir
	 ⟶ For transfer
	 ☐ Tr. For transformer
	
	 Under the constraints:
	 • A complete energy chain starts and ends with a reservoir
	 • The initial reservoir is different from the final reservoir

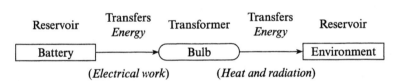

Reservoir   Transfers *Energy*   Transformer   Transfers *Energy*   Reservoir

Battery ⟶ Bulb ⟶ Environment

(*Electrical work*)   (*Heat and radiation*)

Figure 2.4 The energy chain for a battery–bulb experiment

the specification of the elements involved in the experiments and which corresponds to a different semiotic register from those of the resources (linguistic forms for the text and material objects for the experiments) (see Tiberghien 1996 for detailed presentation).

The students carry out three successive tasks to construct the chains (each experiment is given after the drawing of the previous chain). After the first chain ('battery–bulb'), the teacher hands out a sheet showing the correct chain, without comment. During this session, the teacher only *manages* the different groups. This is because the students need time to think by themselves without having to understand further information from the teacher. During the next teaching session the teacher takes the initiative to *discuss* and to state the relevant interpretations of these experiments.

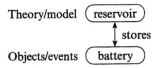

Theory/model   (reservoir)

stores

Objects/events   (battery)

Figure 2.5   Example of a simple relationship between the two worlds

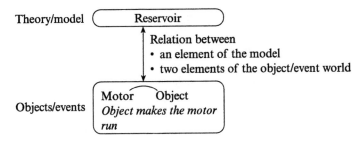

Theory/model   (Reservoir)

Relation between
• an element of the model
• two elements of the object/event world

Objects/events   Motor   Object
Object makes the motor run

Figure 2.6   Example of a complex relationship between the two worlds

Students' activities

A series of research studies were conducted (reported in Tiberghien and Megalakaki 1995). They show that students establish three types of relation between the worlds and that the number of complex relations and of intermediary interpretations (presented below) increases between the first and the second tasks, whereas the number of simple ones decreases.

In a simple relation, an element of one world is directly associated with an element of the other world. For example battery–bulb 'the reservoir stores the energy/thus it is the battery/in the battery there is energy/OK?' (see Figure 2.5).

There is a complex relation when several elements or relations between elements of one world are associated with one element or several elements or a relation between elements of the other world (see Figure 2.6). For example (object falling 124–6):

> *Peggy:* I would have thought that the reservoir/that would be the motor plus object together and . . .
> *Fabien:* Why the motor plus object?
> *Peggy:* The motor plus object that makes the motor run, and after we would put the bulb/and after we would put the environment.

The intermediary is more an interpretation than a relationship, because the elements of the two worlds are considered at the same level. For example (object falling 168–9):

> *Lionel:* Which [energy] goes through the motor/which goes through the bulb?
> *Fulvia:* The object produces the energy/OK? The object/it falls and that produces the energy which goes through the motor which arrives at the bulb/and the bulb shines/do you get it?

The use of both everyday knowledge and physics knowledge can get in the way of devolution. If the didactical contract is such that the students consider that only the taught knowledge (that given in the text and that already taught on electricity) has to be used, they cannot construct meaningful relationships between the two worlds. The teacher's role is to establish such a contract.

These results emphasize three significant characteristics of the design. First, students collect data in the form of experience of the material world. This is recorded in linguistic forms (in the world of object/event). Second, the same experience is recorded in terms of the taught model in symbolic language (in the world of theory/model). Third, presenting students with an explicit theory/model, even if in the form of a 'seed', introduces an aspect of the status of scientific knowledge. The sequence of the three tasks seems necessary to make the students construct complex links between the world of object/event, and the world of theory/model.

Case 3: constructing a new concept by differentiation and relations

This case is typical of much practical work in physics teaching in the upper secondary school (Millar *et al.* submitted; Tiberghien *et al.* submitted). This situation follows the session presented in Case 2. A detailed analysis of this has been made by K. Bécu-Robinault (1997a, 1997b).

Knowledge involved in the situation

This situation aims to help students to construct a quantitative aspect of energy, integrating it in a relational network involving energy, power and time, with power in relation to voltage and current. This requires a differentiation between energy and power, power being the 'flow' of energy. This relational network is associated with several semiotic registers: series of numbers; functional relations with the rules of algebra; symbolic representation of the energy chain; and linguistic forms. This 'density' of theory, which is a characteristic of physics, is introduced through this situation. The students are expected to know the properties of energy and the energy chain. They are also expected to know, from everyday life, of the existence of apparatus for measuring energy consumption, which has to be paid for.

This situation involves constructing an understanding of power, which is complex in the sense that this physical quantity is not associated with a direct observable in the experiment. Only the relation between power, energy and time allows for the prediction of events. Thus, several steps are necessary to 'stage' this knowledge.

Characteristics of the design

This situation is broken down into five parts: handling and measurement; data processing of two series of measurements (E, t) to find a mathematical relation; assigning a name to the constant coefficient between E and t; inserting power into a symbolic representation; and modifying the value of power by modifying the experiment.

This design differs in one sense from the previous cases, and from much practical work at this teaching level and at the university level. The resources initially provided (an experiment, with associated instructions and questions) lead the students to construct other resources such as the measurements and the data table. In this case, the students' responsibility for elaborating these resources should be carefully taken into account. If the teacher wants all students to work on correct data, the guidance that is provided may be in the form of 'recipes' to avoid errors. Then, in order that the students have the opportunity to be responsible for constructing their knowledge, the questions should fit with students' capabilities. Another reason to design carefully the questions associated with the resources, as has been shown (Bécu-Robinault 1997b; Hucke and Fischer 1998; Sander *et al.* 1998), is that the students' activities involve only the aspects of the world which are specified in the question, and no more.

Students' activities

Only one important aspect is mentioned. A new type of relationship between the two worlds has to be constructed by the students: the condition of validity of a model or, more specifically in this case, of a relation between

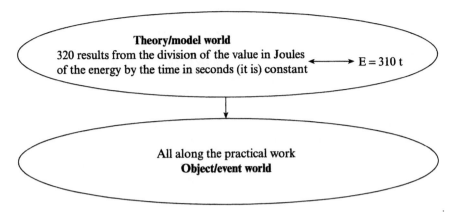

Figure 2.7   Extract of dialogue and its analysis in terms of the two worlds

physical quantities. The example presented in Figure 2.7 takes place during part three when the students have to assign a name to the constant
coefficient between energy and time (from a series of measurements) (P–M,
dialogue turns 497–505):

> *P:* It is an average value . . . which results from the division . . . of the
> value in Joules of the energy by the time in seconds . . . it is constant.
> *M:* It is a constant it is a constant value.
> *P:* . . . it is a constant value all along the practical work.

Discussion of the three cases

At a large granularity of analysis, the three cases are similar. All three take
place during practical work in physics teaching, the organization of the class
is in small groups (mainly pairs of students), and the teacher goes from one
group to another. In each case, students have a sheet and they have to
manipulate an experiment and to write in an exercise book.

However, at a fine granularity of analysis of knowledge (Minstrell 1992),
major differences appear as is shown in Table 2.3.

In conclusion, the analysis of knowledge in terms of modelling and of
semiotic registers is a guide to designing teaching situations which actually
allow the students to deal with and construct the target knowledge. This
kind of research should lead to the design of teaching tools for teachers in
order to help them carry out teaching situations which are more fruitful for
their students' learning.

Table 2.3   Specific characteristics of the three cases

	Case 1: *constructing a* *phenomenology*	*Case 2:* *constructing a* *meaning for a* *qualitative theory*	*Case 3:* *constructing a new* *concept by* *differentiation and* *relations*
Main resources	*Material objects* which make sound, and which it is possible to touch. Two short questions.	A *text* giving a theory/model. Three experiments to see and touch.	An *experimental device with measurement apparatus*. Technical information on setting-up the apparatus and reading and writing measurements. A series of questions which suppose students' elaboration of resources.
Students' productions	Transforming sense perception into concepts.	Establishing links between conceptual information and the experiments.	Building the relations between concepts and constructing a conceptual network. Establishing relations between the conceptual network and the experiment.
Intended learning	New concept of vibration which allows relations to be established between different types of objects/events (back and forth motion and sound).	Specification of the concept of energy. Elaboration of links between theory/model and object/event.	Elaboration of the relationship: energy = power × time. Relations are made between the conceptual networks themselves, rather than individual elements in each network.
Worlds and their links involved in the designed situations			

Notes

1 We do not discuss the aspect of teaching duration in this chapter, though we acknowledge its crucial role.
2 At this level of education, the current underlying goal of the official French curriculum is to improve students' understanding of the material world in terms of physics knowledge. In 2000/1 the official curriculum will be different and it seems that the underlying goal will be the understanding of how physics functions.
3 This year is called *indifférenciée*, which means that all students have the same programme.
4 The French educational system is very different from most of the Anglo-Saxon ones in the sense that students have to choose *a set* of disciplines rather than individual disciplines. For example, physics programmes for students in the human sciences orientation are different from those in the experimental sciences and mathematics orientations.
5 The design is also highly constrained by the organization and the resources of schools; in the cases presented the design is supposed to respect these constraints. This aspect will not be discussed here, even though it has a crucial influence.

References

Artigue, M. (1990) Ingénierie didactique. *Recherches en Didactique des Mathématiques*, 9(3): 281–307.
Bachelard, S. (1979) Quelques aspects historiques des notions de modèle et de justification des modèles, in P. Delattre and M. Thellier (eds) *Elaboration et Justification des Modèles*, vol. 1, pp. 3–18. Paris: Maloine.
Balacheff, N., Cooper, M., Sutherland, R. and Warfield, V. (eds) (1997) *Theory of Didactical Situations in Mathematics: Didactique des Mathématiques, 1970–1990 by Guy Brousseau*. Dordrecht: Kluwer Academic Publishers.
Barde, J. (1998) *Activité de Modélisation en Situation de Travaux Pratiques sur le son en Classe de Seconde*, mémoire du DEA de didactique des disciplines scientifiques. Lyon: Université de Lyon 1.
Bécu-Robinault, K. (1997a) 'Rôle de l'expérience en classe de physique dans l'acquisition des connaissances sur les phénomènes énergétiques' ['Role of experiment in physics classroom in the knowledge acquisition of energetic phenomena'], unpublished doctoral thesis. Université Lyon 1.
Bécu-Robinault, K. (1997b) Activité de modélisation des élèves en situation de travaux pratiques traditionnels: introduction expérimentale du concept de puissance. *Didaskalia*, 11: 7–37.
Brousseau, G. (1998) *Théorie des Situations Didactiques*. Grenoble: La Pensée Sauvage Éditions.
Bunge, M. (1973) *Method and Matter*. Dordrecht: D. Deidel publishing company.
Buty, C. (1998) Modelling in geometrical optics using a microcomputer, in D. Psillos and H. Niedderer (eds) *Working Paper 7: Case Studies of Labwork in Five European*

Countries. Lyon: European Project, Labwork in Science Education (Contract NOERB-SOE2-CT-95-2001).

Carey, S. (1985) *Conceptual Change in Childhood.* Cambridge, MA: MIT Press (Bradford Books).

Chevallard, Y. (1991) *La Transposition Didactique,* 2nd edn. Grenoble: La Pensée Sauvage.

Driver, R. (1973) 'Representation of conceptual frameworks in young adolescent science students', unpublished PhD thesis. University of Illinois at Urbana-Champaign.

Driver, R., Guesne, E. and Tiberghien, A. (1985) *Children's Ideas in Science.* Milton Keynes: Open University Press.

Duval, R. (1995) *Sémiosis et Pensée Humaine, Registres Sémiotiques et Apprentissages Intellectuels.* Berne: Peter Lang.

Gaidioz, P., Monneret, A., Tiberghien, A. *et al.* (1998) *Introduction à L'énergie. Collection: Appliquer le Programme.* Lyon: Centre Régional de Documentation Pédagogique de Lyon.

Giere, R.N. (1988) *Explaining Science. A Cognitive Approach.* Chicago: University of Chicago Press.

Hucke, L. and Fischer, H.E. (1998) The link of theory and practice in traditional and in computer-based university laboratory experiments in Germany, in D. Psillos and H. Niedderer (eds) *Working Paper 7: Case Studies of Labwork in Five European Countries.* Dortmund: European Project, Labwork in Science Education (Contract NOERB-SOE2-CT-95-2001).

Le Maréchal, J.F. (1999) Modelling students' cognitive activity during resolution of problems based on experimental facts in chemical education, in J. Leach and A.C. Paulsen (eds) *Practical Work in Science Education,* pp.195–209. Lyon: Université Lynon 2.

Levy-Strauss, C. (1962) *La Pensée Sauvage.* Paris: Plon.

Millar, R., Le Maréchal, J.F., Buty, C. and Tiberghien A. (submitted) A 'map' of labwork: developing a tool for exploring the nature and effectiveness of labwork in science education.

Minstrell, J. (1992) Facets of students' knowledge and relevant instruction, in R. Duit, F. Goldberg and H. Niedderer (eds) *Research in Physics Learning: Theoretical Issues and Empirical Studies.* Keil: IPN.

Sander, F., Niedderer, H. and Schecker, H. (1998) Learning processes in computer-based physics labwork in a course on Newtonian mechanics, in D. Psillos and H. Niedderer (eds) *Working paper 7: Case Studies of Labwork in Five European Countries.* European Project: Labwork in Science Education (Contract NOERB-SOE2-CT-95-2001). Bremen: University of Bremen.

Scott, P.H. and Driver, R.H. (1998) Learning about science teaching: perspectives from an action research project, in B.J. Fraser and K.G. Tobin (eds) *International Handbook of Science Education,* pp. 67–80. Dordrecht: Kluwer Academic Publishers.

SOC (Groupe de Recherche – Developpement sur San, Optique, Chimie) (1999) http://www2.ac-lyon.fr/enseigne/physique/docs/soc/index01.html

Tiberghien, A. (1994) Modelling as a basis for analysing teaching-learning situations. *Learning and Instruction,* 4(1): 71–87.

Tiberghien, A. (1996) Construction of prototypical situations in teaching the concept of energy, in G. Welford, J. Osborne and P. Scott (eds) *Research in Science Education in Europe*, pp. 100–14. London: Falmer Press.

Tiberghien, A. and Megalakaki, O. (1995) Characterisation of a modelling activity case of a first qualitative approach of energy concept. *European Journal of Psychology of Education*, X(4): 369–83.

Tiberghien, A., Veillard, L., Le Maréchal, J.F., Buty, C. and Millar, R. (submitted) An analysis of labwork tasks used in science teaching at upper secondary school and university levels in several European countries.

Vince, J. (1999) Teaching and learning about sounds: study of explanatory systems and analysis of knowledge to be taught in order to develop a multi-representational modelling software, in M. Méheut and G. Rebmann (eds) *Theory, Methodology and Results of Research in Science Education* (Fourth European Science Education Summer School) pp. 238–42. Paris: Laboratoire de Didactique des Sciences Physiques, Université D. Diderot.

Vosniadou, S. and Brewer, W.F. (1994) Mental models of the day-night cycle. *Cognitive Science*, 18(1): 123–83.

Formative assessment and science education: a model and theorizing

3

Beverley Bell

Introduction

In this chapter I discuss the findings of a research project exploring formative assessment in some science lessons, for the dual purposes of improving the classroom practice of teaching and learning science, and developing theoretical underpinnings for research. First, the findings are discussed in a descriptive model of formative assessment to inform the professional practice of teachers. Second, the findings are discussed in a way to link the activity of formative assessment to the literature and theoretical debates on learning, cognition and language. In this chapter, I theorize formative assessment as a sociocultural and discursive activity (Bell and Cowie in press).

Formative assessment

One of the purposes of assessment within education is that of informing and improving students' ongoing learning. Assessment which is intended to enhance teaching and learning is called formative assessment. Formative assessment is defined here as: 'the process used by teachers and students to recognise and respond to student learning in order to enhance that learning, during the learning' (Cowie and Bell 1996: 2). This definition parallels that of Sadler (1989), Gipps (1994) and Black and Wiliam (1998), having the common components of the teacher giving feedback to the student, the teachers and/or students taking an action to improve learning during the learning, and self-assessment. Self-assessment is always a part of formative assessment as students must be able to understand and use the criteria with which they are assessed, in order to bridge the gap between what they know or can do and the desired goal. And it is the consequences of formative assessment that are all important (Cowie in press).

Formative assessment is important as other research findings have linked it with improved learning. In a review of studies of formative assessment, Black and Wiliam (1998: 61) state that: 'the research reported here shows conclusively that formative assessment does improve learning. The gains in achievement appear to be quite considerable, and as noted earlier, amongst the largest ever reported for an educational intervention'.

Formative assessment is also an important aspect of teaching for conceptual development as discussed, for example, in Driver (1989). Giving feedback to students about how their existing concepts relate to the scientifically accepted ones, and helping them to modify their thinking accordingly, is both a part of formative assessment and of teaching for conceptual development.

In this chapter, formative assessment is that which is exemplified by such practices as getting students to brainstorm their ideas about 'energy' before the start of a lesson on energy; responding to the student comment that 'there is no gravity on the moon as there is no atmosphere'; and stopping the class in the middle of the practical work to address a safety concern that has arisen. Formative assessment, here, is not equated with continuous summative assessment, in which marks or grades are collected over a period of time and collated into an overall grade at the end of the teaching segment.

While there has been much written on the importance of formative assessment to improve learning and standards of achievement (Harlen and James 1996), there has been little research on the process of formative assessment itself. And, as Black and Wiliam (1998) suggest, there is a need to explore views of learning and their interrelationships with assessment. This chapter addresses these two gaps in the literature while reporting on the research funded by the New Zealand Ministry of Education in 1995–6 to investigate classroom-based assessment and which is more fully reported in Bell and Cowie (1997, 1999, in press). The main aim of the research was to investigate assessment in Year 7–10 classrooms where the teacher of science was taking into account students' thinking, and in particular formative assessment.

One of the key findings was a model to describe and explain the formative assessment processes as carried out by the ten teachers and their students (Bell and Cowie 1997; Cowie and Bell 1999). The current literature on formative assessment (Cowie 1997) initially acted as a framework to make sense of the qualitative data collected. However, the model evolved from the initial data analysis as more qualitative data was collected and as the teachers reflected on and took action in their classroom as a result of the ongoing debates in 11 teacher development days (Bell and Cowie 1999). The model, then, is one that the teachers and researchers (Bronwen Cowie and myself) co-constructed, for communication to other teachers who may be wishing to improve their professional practice.

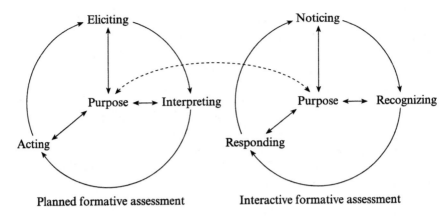

Figure 3.1   A model of formative assessment

A model of formative assessment

The teachers within the project undertook two types of formative assessment: planned formative assessment and interactive formative assessment (Cowie and Bell 1999). These two types of formative assessment are illustrated in Figure 3.1. The process of planned formative assessment was characterized by the teachers eliciting, interpreting and acting on assessment information. For example, one of the teachers started a lesson with a test of ten short questions. He did this to elicit what the students had understood and remembered from the previous lesson; to interpret the students' prior learning; and to use that information to make the final decisions about his lesson for that day. It also gave feedback to the students as to their learning.

The purpose for the planned formative assessment determined how the information was collected, interpreted and acted upon. Hence, these four aspects (eliciting, interpreting, acting, purpose) are interrelated and mutually determining. The main purpose for which the teachers said they used planned formative assessment was to obtain information from the whole class about progress in learning the science as specified in the curriculum. This assessment was planned in that the teacher had planned to undertake a specific activity (for example, a survey or brainstorming) to obtain assessment information on which some action would be taken. The teachers considered that the information collected as part of the planned formative assessment was 'general', 'blunt' and concerned their 'big' purposes. It gave them information which was valuable in informing their interactions with the class as a whole with respect to 'getting through the curriculum'. This type of formative assessment was planned by the teacher mainly to obtain feedback to inform her or his teaching. The purpose for doing the assessment strongly influenced the other three aspects of the planned formative assessment process.

The second type of formative assessment was interactive formative assessment. Interactive formative assessment was that which took place during student–teacher interactions. It involved the teachers noticing, recognizing and responding to student thinking during these interactions.

For example, one teacher noticed that some of the students in the class thought that matter expanded upon cooling. She recognized that this was not the scientifically accepted idea, and she responded by calling the class together and initiating a discussion on the heating and cooling of substances. The teacher mediated the learning of the students.

Interactive formative assessment differed from the first form (planned formative assessment) in that a specific assessment activity was not planned. The interactive assessment arose out of a learning activity. While the details of this kind of formative assessment were not planned, and could not be anticipated, the teachers were prepared to do interactive formative assessment, and they used teaching approaches that allowed it to occur. Hence, the teachers were prepared to do interactive formative assessment, but they could not plan for or predict what exactly they and the students would be doing, or when it would occur. As interactive formative assessment occurred during student–teacher interaction, it had the potential to occur any time students and teachers interacted. The teachers and students within the project interacted in whole class, small group and one-to-one situations.

An overview of the model of formative assessment

Six key features of the model were identified (Cowie and Bell 1999) as were other characteristics of formative assessment (Bell and Cowie 1997). One key feature of the model is that the detailed data generated by the research and underlying the model is a valuable contribution to the existing literature on formative assessment. Knowing about the details of the formative assessment processes raised the awareness of the ten teachers in the research project about what they do by way of formative assessment in their classrooms (Bell and Cowie 1997, 1999). That is, the teachers were doing formative assessment but they were not always aware of exactly what they were doing that could be called 'formative assessment'. The increased awareness enabled the teachers to reflect in new ways on their practice. It was perceived by the teachers to be the main aspect of their teacher development during the two years of the research project (Bell and Cowie 1997). Feedback obtained to date suggests that other teachers and researchers are also interested in this clarification of the formative assessment process. The research findings lend themselves to the development of workshop materials for use in teacher education programmes to develop teachers' skills of formative assessment, both with respect to knowing about formative assessment and to being able to carry it out in the classroom.

The other five key features of the model discussed here are ones that indicated a fruitful way of theorizing about formative assessment as a part of teaching and learning. First, formative assessment was seen as a purposeful, intentional activity. A central role was given to purpose in both types of formative assessment by the teachers – that is, the teachers felt their purposes for doing formative assessment determined what they actually did. Purpose influenced each of the aspects of planned formative assessment (eliciting, interpreting and acting) and interactive formative assessment (noticing, recognizing and responding).

The second significant feature of the model is the action taken as part of both planned and interactive formative assessment. The action means that formative assessment can be described as an integral part of teaching and learning and that it is responsive to students. The teachers in the research made the claim that they did not think they could promote learning in science unless they were doing formative assessment (Bell and Cowie 1997).

Third, formative assessment could be viewed as a situated and contextualized activity. The formative assessment was shaped by the setting or context in which it was done (Cowie in press). That is, the formative assessment was shaped by the setting of the community, school, classroom, curriculum, teaching and learning activities, the intentions of the teachers and students, and the existing thinking of both the teachers and the students. For example, the feedback given and the action taken as part of a formative assessment was influenced by the students' age and level of educational achievement.

The fourth key feature was the partnership that teachers and students entered into during the process of formative assessment, with the sharing of constructed meanings by the teacher and students during the process. The teacher and students had to share their constructed meanings in order for the students to undertake self-assessment. That is, the students had to share the constructed meanings of the teacher, if they were to understand the gap between what they knew and what the intended learning goal was.

The central role of language in formative assessment was the fifth feature. The teachers and students used language in both planned and interactive formative assessment to communicate their constructed meanings, to give feedback and to suggest possible actions to improve learning. Formative assessment depended entirely on the ways in which teachers and students used language.

In summary, the research findings suggested that formative assessment can be viewed as a purposeful, intentional activity; an integral part of teaching and learning; a situated and contextualized activity; a partnership between teacher and students; and involving the use of language to communicate meaning. These key findings are used as the basis in the second half of this chapter to link the research findings on formative assessment to current theorizing on learning as a sociocultural and discursive activity.

Theorizing about formative assessment

My purpose for theorizing about formative assessment is to account for formative assessment within the current debates on cognition, learning and language in the classroom, rather than within the current debates on account-ability in education. Within science education, education and other literature, current debates cluster around sociocultural views of cognition and learning which are variously described as 'social cognition' (Resnick 1991; Augoustinos and Walker 1995; Salomon and Perkins 1998); a 'social constructivist' view of learning (Driver *et al.* 1994; Bell and Gilbert 1996); 'situated learning' (Lave and Wenger 1991; Hennessy 1993); 'apprenticeship', 'guided participa-tion' and 'participatory appropriation' (Rogoff 1995); 'distributed cognition' (Salomon 1993; Carr 1998); 'mediated action' (Vygotsky 1978; Wertsch 1991; Wertsch *et al.* 1995) and 'discursive activities' (Harré and Gillett 1994). These categories and associated descriptions are not mutually exclusive, as there is much overlap and lack of clarity. This is due to various categories having been developed from within different disciplines – for example, anthropology, sociology, psychology and education. Different and similar words are used, different meanings are constructed and different emphases highlighted. Elsewhere (Bell and Cowie in press), I have discussed in more detail how these sociocultural views of learning can be used to theorize about formative assessment. Both social and cultural perspectives automatically give priority to languages, which are central to formative assessment.

In the second half of this chapter, I will theorize formative assessment as a sociocultural activity, using one of the views listed above: that of learning and mind as discursive activities. I have selected this sociocultural view as it does not have much visibility in science education debates to date and it enables the notions of language-in-use, meaning, the non-mentalistic posi-tion, units of analysis, and power to be highlighted. These notions open up possibilities for future research.

Learning and formative assessment as a discursive practice

If we view learning and formative assessment as discursive activities, we are predominantly giving attention to *language-in-use*. In the classroom set-ting, we are focusing on the ways language is used to promote thinking and learning. And like other sociocultural views, the goal of discursive psychology is to account for the way social practices, including language, determine how and what children think and learn in a classroom. The role of language (and other symbol) use is central to discursive psychology, in which we are examining human functioning in actual social and cultural settings. A discursive activity or practice is:

> the repeated and orderly use of some sign system, where these uses are intentional, that is, directed at or to something ... Discursive activities are always subject to standards of correctness and incorrectness. These standards can be expressed in terms of rules. Therefore, a discursive practice is the use of a sign system, for which there are norms of right and wrong use, and the signs concern or are directed at various things.
>
> (Harré and Gillett 1994: 28–9)

In short, a discursive activity is an intentional, normative action, using sign systems. The focus of discursive psychology is what talk and writing is being used to *do* – that is, what language is being used to achieve, rather than language being seen as an abstract tool to state or describe things. Language is seen as functional and is intentionally, purposefully used by people, for example to justify, explain, blame, excuse, persuade and present an argument. Hence, the notion of language-in-use relates to that of communication. Likewise, in formative assessment, teachers and students are using language for a particular purpose, that of learning of science. As noted previously, the teachers involved in the research used language to communicate their constructed meanings, to give feedback and to suggest possible actions to improve learning.

Meaning is central to a discursive view, as it is in other sociocultural views of learning and cognition. Meaning is also central to formative assessment. For formative assessment to occur, students and teachers have to disclose to each other, on an ongoing basis, the meanings that they are making in the lesson. Knowing what a situation means to a person enables us to understand what that person is doing (Harré and Gillett 1994). We understand the behaviour of an individual when we grasp the meanings that are informing a person's activity:

> [Wittgenstein] came to realise that understanding and the phenomena of meaning or intentionality in general could only be approached by looking at what people actually do with word patterns and other word signs. He formulated the doctrine that meaning is the use to which we put our signs. He studied the use of language in 'language games', by which he meant complex activities involving both the use of language and the use of physical tools and actions, where they are ordinarily encountered ... [he] came to see that mental activity is not essentially a Cartesian or inner set of processes but a range of moves or techniques

defined against a background of human activity and governed by informal rules. These rules, unlike the rules-laws at work in supposed inner, cognitive processes, were the rules that people actually followed. They are most evident when we consider the correct and incorrect ways of using words . . .

(Harré and Gillett 1994: 19–20)

Language and other semiotic (sign) systems play an important part in producing meaning, especially meaning as it shapes human action (Wertsch 1991). Meaning here is viewed as being produced only in a social setting, and as a process, not a fixed entity inherent in a linguistic package. As a social practice, language is seen as having no fixed meaning outside the context in which it is used. Our perception of the world is seen as being shaped by the language we use to describe it: objects, activities and categories derive their epistemological status from the definitions we create for them. Within this view, thought and language are no longer separated (Augoustinos and Walker 1995).

It is usual to think of concepts as the basis of meaning, understanding and thinking. But concepts are expressed by words and words are located in languages. Thus, the discourses constructed jointly by persons and within sociocultural groups become an important part of the framework of interpretation and meaning. The communicability of thoughts is secured by the mutual intelligibility of a shared symbolic system, such as a common language (Harré and Gillett 1994). The grasp of the use of a word/concept is seen as an active discursive skill, rather than an inner cognitive skill, and learning is seen as the increasingly skilled use of social practices. In formative assessment, the teacher can access only the language used by the student, and not a so-called 'conceptual understanding'. Therefore, in a discursive view of learning and mind, the theorizing is on only the social aspects of learning and no functional value is given to a consideration of the individual aspects. Like other sociocultural views of learning, a discursive view informs us that it is the whole of what goes on in classrooms that determines the formative assessment, not just what is happening inside an individual's head.

Therefore, another feature of a discursive view is the *non-mentalistic* view of 'cognition' and 'mind'. If priority is given to languages in defining what are psychological phenomena, then to present and understand cognition, it must be done in terms of the ordinary languages through which we think, rather than looking for abstract representations of them (Lemke 1990; Harré and Gillett 1994). Discursive psychology considers thinking not as a mental activity, but as the activity of operating signs (for example, language). Hence, discursive approaches to thinking and learning differ from other sociocultural views in that they see no distinction between thoughts and language. Discursive approaches see problems in the assumptions that cognitive phenomena (such as 'attitudes', 'emotions' and 'categories') can be identified and located in an internal cognitive world – inside the head. Rather, attention is given to the discourse itself and not the assumed underlying internal, static, mental states. Instead, discursive psychology is more interested in how people discursively constitute psychological phenomena to do certain things. The social processes *are* the cognitive processes. For example, categorization, as a psychological phenomena, is 'something we do, in talk' in order to accomplish social actions (persuasions, blamings, denial, refutations, accusations) (Edwards 1991: 94), and because 'some constructions are so familiar, pervasive and common-sensical . . . they give an effect of realism or fact. People therefore come to regard some constructions not as versions of reality, but as direct representations of reality itself' (Augoustinos and Walker 1995: 269).

Any internal cognitive realm is conceptualized as a form of situated practice. There is no notion of internal representation or model to assume cognitive mediation. (Augoustinos and Walker 1995). Discursive (as poststructuralist) psychology is critical of social cognitive concepts such as representations, schemas, attitudes and categories which are hypothesized to be stable mental categories located within the head. The position taken by Lemke (1990) and O'Loughlin (1992) is to deny the functional significance of individual mental processes (Nuthall 1997). Their position is a relativist one, rather than realist, and as such may be unacceptable to many in the science education community. However, their denial is not a denial of the 'reality' of cognition so much as a denial of the value of talk about cognition (Nuthall 1997). Hence, a discursive approach questions the notion of a knowable reality by emphasizing the sociohistorical and political nature of all knowledge claims. Such a poststructuralist view of psychology stresses that words do not have independent, objective meaning outside the social and relational context in which they are used (Augoustinos and Walker 1995). The whole point of discursive psychology is to get away from 'mythical' mental activities (Harré and Gillett 1994), the mind being considered as a non-mentalistic entity. Discursive psychology is not interested in mental representations but in meanings. Thoughts reside in the uses we make of public and private systems of signs. To be able to think is to be a skilled user of these sign systems – that is, capable of using them correctly. Hence, assessing students' scientific thinking, during formative assessment, would be framed as assessing their correct use of scientific language and other sign systems.

The methodological concern regarding the *unit of analysis* is addressed by a discursive view of learning, as it is by other sociocultural views of learning. One way to study the cultural aspects of learning is to adopt the unit of analysis of identity (see Chapter 14). One way to study social aspects of learning is to adopt the unit of analysis of human action (Wertsch 1991), rather than focusing on the unit of analysis of concepts, linguistic and knowledge structures, and attitudes (as often found in psychology), although they might be used in an analysis of human action. In adopting human action as the unit of analysis, recognition is given to the fact that some activities are so highly contextualized, and dependent on the situation, that a distinction cannot easily be made between cognitive knowledge and skills, the context and the activity a person is engaged in. For example, to describe a formative assessment activity, we cannot separate individuals from their activities and the contexts in which they take place. That is, to understand the formative assessment activity we have to consider the context in which it occurs. In this way, sociocultural and discursive views of learning address the integration of cognition, affect and conation, where constructivist approaches do not (Gilbert 1997: 228).

In a discursive approach to learning, all *three aspects* of 'mind' (cognition, affect and conation) can be taken into account, rather than each being studied in isolation, as has been the case in more reductionist approaches in psychology. A discursive view of mind asserts that to understand the mind is to study social interaction, not the biological brain operation of an individual. Harré and Gillett (1994) state the need to move away from a focus on the individual as a rational subject and look at a broader framework to understand meaning and rule-following.

To add emphasis to the notion that communication, mental processes and conation are linked, Wertsch (1991) uses the notion of 'voice' (after Bakhtin 1986 for example), meaning the speaking personality, the speaking consciousness. The notion of 'voice' is concerned with the wider issues of a speaking subject's perspective, conceptual horizons, intentions and worldview. It always exists in a social milieu – that is, not in isolation from other voices. Voices produce utterances – a notion used by Bakhtin to focus on the situated action of language-in-use, rather than on objects that can be derived from linguistic analytic abstractions. Bakhtin's notion of utterance is linked with that of voice as an utterance can only be produced by a voice.

Considering how voices engage with one another is important to a discursive view of mind (Wertsch 1991), for it is only when two or more voices come into contact (for example, when the voice of a listener responds to the voice of a speaker) that meaning comes into existence. And during the formative assessment process, the teacher and students share their meaning-making and respond through their actions to improve learning. Taking into account both voices reflects a concern for 'addressivity' – the quality of turning to someone else. In the absence of addressivity, an utterance does not exist. Addressivity is not inherent in the unit of language (for example, word or sentence) but in the utterance. The notion of addressivity means that: 'utterances are not indifferent to one another, and are not self-sufficient; they are aware of and mutually reflect one another' (Bakhtin 1986: 91, quoted in Wertsch 1991: 52).

Therefore, utterances involve both a concern with who is doing the speaking and a concern with who is being addressed. A teacher, in giving feedback to a student about their learning, is concerned with speaking the voice of the scientist and how to phrase what they say for a learner of science. Utterances are inherently associated with at least two voices – the speaking voice may indicate an awareness of the addressee's voice. Bakhtin's concept of 'dialogicality', meaning more than one voice, is useful to Wertsch (1991). Human communicative and psychological processes are said to be characterized by a dialogicality of voices. That is, when a speaker produces an utterance, at least two voices are heard simultaneously. If human communication is characterized by a dialogicality of voices, then understanding is dialogic in nature. That is, to understand another's utterance is to orientate oneself with respect to it. There are different sorts of dialogues: face-to-face, inner dialogue, parody, and social languages within a single national language. Dialogicality is illustrated in the work of Scott (1999) who analysed classroom talk in terms of the authoritative and dialogic nature of the discourse in the classroom.

Bakhtin (1986) also made a distinction between social languages (for example, 'teen speak') and speech genre (for example, military commands, everyday greetings and farewells). He saw the 'speech genre not as a form of language but as a typical form [a type] of utterance' (Wertsch 1991: 61). Wertsch also distinguishes between social languages and speech genres in that social languages relate to the different social groupings, whereas speech genres relate to 'typical situations of speech communication' (1991: 61).

Social languages and speech genres appear to be hierarchically used. Wertsch (1991: 124) uses the term of 'privileging' to refer to 'the fact that one mediational means, such as a social language or genre can be viewed as being more appropriate or efficacious than others in a particular social setting'. For example, in the science lesson, 'curriculum science' is privileged over 'children's science'. Formative assessment plays a role in giving students feedback as to acceptable social languages and speech genre. And in being hierarchical, there is a use of power in formative assessment.

One of the main criticisms of a discursive approach is its inability to explain retention and memory, for it does not focus on mental activity (Augoustinos and Walker 1995). In highlighting or foregrounding the social, the individual aspects are hidden or backgrounded. While teachers and students may attend to the social situatedness of formative assessment in the classroom, assessment regimes in most education systems focus on individual achievement and cognitive development.

A strength of a discursive view of learning and meaning is that it allows us to, more readily than the other sociocultural views, give consideration to the notion of 'power'. If language is seen as a form of social practice and if meanings are seen as socially constructed, then what counts as coherent or meaningful depends very much on the power relationships, rather than on an absolute truth (Drewery and Winslade 1997). Seen in this context, power is not the 'possession' of particular persons but is constituted in positions occupied by subjects in discourses. This is important in assessment tasks where the power relations between teacher and student are influential on pedagogical and learning outcomes. Foucault's notion of surveillance and other techniques of power (Gore 1998) might be a useful start from which to theorize about power in formative assessment as a subtle form of social control.

If formative assessment is viewed as a social and discursive practice, then the implications (Gipps 1999) are that formative assessment can only be fully understood if: the social, cultural and political contexts in the classroom are taken into account; formative assessment is seen as a social practice, constructed within social and cultural norms of the classroom; the cultural and social knowledge of the teacher and students are seen as mediating their responses to assessment; formative assessments are viewed as value-laden and socially constructed; teachers and students are seen as being in a process of negotiation when engaging in formative assessment; and the way language is used in formative assessment is determining of the learning outcomes in the science lesson. Importance is also given to students understanding the use of language in the science classroom to make assertions, argue a case, or demonstrate supporting evidence (Driver and Newton 1997) as well as to the relationship between the teacher and student if the issue of power is to be acknowledged.

Concluding comment

Theorizing about formative assessment as a social and discursive practice has highlighted: the role of language and communication in formative assessment; the centrality of meaning; viewing the context not as the background but an integral part of formative assessment; a focus on the 'mind', rather than the 'brain'; formative assessment as an intentional activity; the nature of the partnership and the power relationship between the teacher and students inherent in the formative assessment process; and the units of analysis that enable the interrelationships of cognition, affect and conation to be studied. Viewing formative assessment as both a discursive and sociocultural practice will be a fruitful theoretical position for future research.

Acknowledgement

I wish to thank Bronwen Cowie for her discussions and feedback on this chapter.

References

Augoustinos, M. and Walker, I. (1995) *Social Cognition: An Integrated Introduction*. London: Sage.

Bakhtin, M. (1986) *Speech Genres and Other Late Essays* (C. Emerson and M. Holquist, eds). Austin, TX: University of Texas Press.

Bell, B. and Cowie, B. (1997) *Formative Assessment and Science Education* (research report of the Learning in Science Project (Assessment)). Hamilton, NZ: University of Waikato.

Bell, B. and Cowie, B. (1999) Researching formative assessment, in J. Loughran (ed.) *Researching Teaching: Methodologies and Practices for Understanding Pedagogy*. London: Falmer Press.

Bell, B. and Cowie, B. (in press) *Formative Assessment and Science Education*. Dordrecht: Kluwer Academic Publishers.

Bell, B. and Gilbert, J. (1996) *Teacher Development: A Model from Science Education*. London: Falmer Press.

Black, P. and Wiliam, D. (1998) Assessment and classroom learning. *Assessment in Education*, 5(1): 7–74.

Carr, M. (1998) 'Early childhood technology education', unpublished DPhil thesis. University of Waikato, Hamilton, New Zealand.

Cowie, B. (1997) Formative assessment and science classrooms, in B. Bell and R. Baker (eds) *Developing the Science Curriculum in Aotearoa New Zealand*. Auckland: Longman Addison Wesley.

Cowie, B. (in press) 'Formative assessment in science classrooms', unpublished DPhil thesis. University of Waikato, Hamilton, New Zealand.

Cowie, B. and Bell, B. (1996) Validity and formative assessment in the science classroom. Paper presented to the Symposium on Validity in Educational Assessment, Dunedin, New Zealand, 28–30 June.

Cowie, B. and Bell, B. (1999) A model of formative assessment in science education. *Assessment in Education*, 6(1): 101–16.

Drewery, W. and Winslade, J. (1997) The theoretical story of narrative therapy, in G. Monk, J. Winslade, K. Crockett and D. Epston (eds) *Narrative Therapy in Practice: The Archaeology of Hope*. San Francisco: Jossey-Bass.

Driver, R. (1989) Students' conceptions and the learning of science. *International Journal of Science Education*, 11(5): 481–90.

Driver, R. and Newton, P. (1997) Establishing the norms of scientific argumentation in classrooms. Paper presented to the European Science Education research Association Conference, Rome, 2–6 September.

Driver, R., Asoko, H., Leach, J., Mortimer, E. and Scott, P. (1994) Constructing scientific knowledge in the classroom. *Educational Researcher*, 23(7): 5–12.

Edwards, D. (1991) Categories are for talking: on the cognitive and discursive bases of categorisation. *Theory and Psychology*, 1: 515–42.

Gilbert, J. (1997) 'Thinking "other-wise": re-thinking the problem of girls and science education in the post-modern'. Unpublished DPhil thesis. University of Waikato, Hamilton, New Zealand.

Gipps, C. (1994) *Beyond Testing: Towards a Theory of Educational Assessment*. London: Falmer Press.

Gipps, C. (1999) Sociocultural aspects of assessment. *Review of Research in Education*, 24: 355–92.

Gore, J. (1998) Disciplining bodies: on the continuity of power relations in pedagogy, in T. Popkewitz and M. Brennan (eds) *Foucault's Challenge: Discourse, Knowledge and Power in Education*, pp. 231–51. New York: Teachers College Press.

Harlen, W. and James, M. (1996) Creating a positive impact of assessment on learning. Paper presented to the American Educational Research Association Annual Conference, New York, April.

Harré, R. and Gillett, G. (1994) *The Discursive Mind*. London: Sage.

Hennessy, S. (1993) Situated cognition and cognitive apprenticeship: implications for classroom learning. *Studies in Science Education*, 22: 1–41.

Lave, J. and Wenger, E. (1991) *Situated Learning: Legitimate Peripheral Participation*. Cambridge: Cambridge University Press.

Lemke, J. (1990) *Talking Science: Language, Learning, Values*. Norwood, NJ: Ablex.

Nuthall, G. (1997) Understanding student thinking and learning in the classroom, in B. J. Biddle, T.C. Good and I. Goodson (eds) *The International Handbook of Teachers and Teaching*. Dordrecht: Kluwer Academic Publishers.

O'Loughlin, M. (1992) Rethinking science education: beyond Piagetian constructivism toward a sociocultural model of teaching and learning. *Journal of Research in Science Teaching*, 29: 791–820.

Resnick, L. (1991) Shared cognition: thinking as a social practice, in L. Resnick, J. Levine and S. Teasley (eds) *Perspectives on Socially Shared Cognition*. Washington, DC: American Psychological Association.

Rogoff, B. (1995) Observing sociocultural activity on three planes, in J. Wertsch, P. Del Río and A. Alvarez (eds) *Sociocultural Studies of Mind*. Cambridge: Cambridge University Press.

Sadler, R. (1989) Formative assessment and the design of instructional systems. *Instructional Science*, 18: 119–44.

Salomon, G. (1993) *Distributed Cognitions: Psychological and Educational Considerations*. New York: Cambridge University Press.

Salomon, G. and Perkins, D. (1998) Individual and social aspects of learning. *Review of Research in Education*, 23: 1–24.

Scott, P. (1999) An analysis of science classroom talk in terms of the authoritative and dialogic nature of the discourse. Paper presented to the National Association of Research in Science Education, Boston, USA, April.

Vygotsky, L. (1978) *Mind in Society: The Development of Higher Psychological Processes* (M. Cole, V. John-Steiner, S. Scribner and E. Souberman, eds). Cambridge, MA: Harvard University Press.

Wertsch, J. (1991) *Voices of the Mind: A Sociocultural Approach to Mediated Action*. Cambridge, MA: Harvard University Press.

Wertsch, J., Del Río, P. and Alvarez, A. (1995). Sociocultural studies: history, action and mediation, in J. Wertsch, P. Del Río and A. Alvarez (eds) *Sociocultural Studies of Mind*. Cambridge: Cambridge University Press.

4   National evaluation for the improvement of science teaching

Björn Andersson

Introduction

In Sweden, the parliament (Riksdag) and the government determine the national objectives and guidelines for childcare and the school system. Rules are set out in the Swedish Education Act, curricula and various regulations. It is the duty of the National Agency for Education to work actively to ensure that objectives and guidelines are followed. Therefore the Agency carries out follow-ups, evaluation, development, research and supervisory work.

One main component of the evaluation work is national testing each year of students' knowledge and skills in Swedish, mathematics and English. The testing is carried out in Grades 5 (11–12 years) and 9 (15–16 years) in the comprehensive school, and for some courses at upper secondary school (Grades 10–12). The testing is mandatory for Grade 9. Results are reported to the Agency. The purpose of this programme of testing is to assist teachers and schools with judging if goals for the three subjects have been obtained, and with grading the students against national criteria.

Another important component of the evaluation is an in-depth study every third year of the extent to which the goals for other subjects have been obtained. This programme started in 1989 and has focused on Grade 9, but Grades 5 and 12 have also been involved. Most subjects of compulsory school education have been studied and generally 3 per cent of the students in a certain grade have been sampled.

Science has been part of this programme from the outset. In 1989 only Grade 5 was tested with an emphasis on biology. In 1992 Grade 9 was included with the areas matter, ecology and the human body. Again in 1995 only Grade 9 was included, then with the areas energy, temperature and heat, and optics. In 1998 Grades 5, 9 and 12 were all included, this time in a thematic context, namely, 'the state of the world'.

A problem of balance

As indicated, the main purpose of the evaluation programme that started in 1989 is to find out the extent to which curriculum goals are attained. However, another purpose is to carry out the work in such a way that it stimulates teachers and other actors in the school system towards improvement. The small project group at Göteborg University working with the science subjects has been particularly concerned with finding an appropriate balance between these two purposes. Little by little the group has evolved a 'philosophy' that involves playing down the evaluation aspect somewhat, placing more and more emphasis on the possibilities that exist, thanks to assessment, of influencing teaching in a positive way (Andersson *et al.* 1996). This may be seen as an example of a recent trend in assessment, observed by Gitomer and Duschl (1998: 796). They state: 'Whereas traditional models of assessment placed the highest priority on providing valid information concerning the normative and absolute achievement of students, assessment reform has placed at least equal value on the role of assessment in improving instructional practice'. They also note that: 'to date, however, examinations of consequences [of assessment] have only addressed issues of instructional practice peripherally' (p. 802).

The experiences and insights that have led to this philosophy, and examples of how it is put into practice, are described below.

Some methodological problems

The subjective route from national goals to test questions

Investigating the extent to which curriculum goals have been attained involves handling several difficult problems. One of these has to do with the fact that anyone making an evaluation has to interpret and operationalize national goals that are formulated in rather general terms. It is a question of subjective appraisals, which means that one problem is the extent to which a project group evaluates the teaching that has actually taken place in schools – the teachers may have interpreted the national goals differently. This problem can be partially solved by having regular discussions with a reference group of teachers and by letting teachers assess suggestions for test questions, among other things, with regard to their degree of difficulty and relevance in relation to their own teaching. In this way, some link-up with teaching practice is achieved but, in fact, it is the interpretation of the national goals made by a select few that steers the assessment, which complicates the evaluation of the results obtained.

An uncontrolled experiment

Another methodological complication is the fact that teaching that is followed by a national assessment is not a controlled experiment. There is no untaught control group to compare with. In principle, it is therefore impossible to draw the conclusion that good results depend on the teaching. On the other hand, less good results always motivate improvements.

Would a little help influence the results?

Another thing to consider is that, in a national evaluation, students are set to answer rather difficult questions individually and in a short time, often without preparation. If one is confronted with similar questions in everyday life, the normal thing to do is to consult reference books and maybe also talk things over with friends and acquaintances. In this way, one would obtain answers that, with a little consideration, one could understand and account for. If a project group had plenty of time and economic resources, they could find out what students can achieve with a little help, and possibly obtain a different picture of their knowledge potential than that revealed with more conventional methods.

Taking both general and subject-specific goals into consideration

Another problem of interpretation is connected with the fact that school teaching is directed by both general and subject-specific goals, which together are intended to be a whole. How should the general goals influence the test situation and test content? Take, for example, the self-evident general goal that it should be possible to use one's school knowledge in various situations in the future, such as gaining insight into a social question with scientific aspects and forming an opinion. A test situation in line with this could be to read an article in a newspaper, understand what it is about, and work out the pros and cons until one reaches an independent point of view, either on one's own or in a group. Other test situations are to study a radio or TV programme. It appears that, in general, this type of test is relatively unusual in school. Most of the teachers carry out subject teaching which certainly aims at providing the students with information that they can use in various situations in the future, but they usually assess this with short tasks that are very specific to the subject and therefore do not reflect realistic future situations where scientific knowledge might be used. A project group could break new ground here by using tasks that correspond better than the teachers' evaluation methods to the curriculum as a whole. In this situation, the project group and the teachers would differ in their assessment practice, a fact to consider when evaluating the students' responses.

The problem of generalization

Regardless of the tasks one finally selects, one is faced with a generalization problem when it comes to assessment. One can always create a large number of tasks in an area, as well as many contexts and types of task, but one has to select a limited number. If the students answer these well or badly, can one then say that their knowledge in that area is in general good or bad? One way of trying to master this problem is to relate the results obtained to international research on students' conceptions and difficulties in understanding. If other researchers with other methods have found similar conceptual problems, statements about Swedish students could gain greater validity. Another way is to take up relatively few areas of school science but to shed light on them with a relatively large number of different tasks.

Evaluating results – what criteria formulated by whom?

One consequence of the methodological problems discussed above is that the evaluation of results obtained is not a simple and obvious process. The primary role of the project group in this connection is to create conditions for others to evaluate. The proper thing is to describe the different stages in the work as clearly as possible – what decisions have been made and why, and what uncertainties exist.

There is a problem in deciding what is meant by 'good' and 'bad' results. One can think about this from two quite different points of departure. One is the goals set up, which one naturally hopes most students will reach. The other is the assumption that, before teaching, students know very little science. Within this framework, the result that 30 per cent of the students in a school year answer a question correctly may be seen as a sign of considerable success.

Evaluation is a delicate and sensitive task. Teachers, headteachers and other responsible people may feel that they are under attack and become locked in defensive positions, or they may think that the results are good and feel satisfied. Neither reaction leads to the development of teaching.

Developmental validity

Finding out to what extent curriculum goals are attained is of course important. However, both the methodological and social problems mentioned are good reasons for not overemphasizing the evaluation aspect of national assessment. After all, results considered good or bad rest, from a methodological point of view, on somewhat uncertain ground. This fact is no reason for not trying to improve this ground. But the uncertainty must be taken into consideration when deciding if goals have been attained or not. This insight has led us to play down the evaluation aspect somewhat when reporting results, and to put greater emphasis on the fact that national assessment may be a good way to build up knowledge that could contribute to school development. We have introduced a concept for this – namely, 'developmental validity' (Andersson *et al.* 1996). An assessment has good developmental validity if it stimulates the thinking and actions of the teachers and other actors concerned in such a way that it results in attempts to improve teaching.

In other words, development of teaching is a possible consequence of assessment. Therefore, developmental validity may be seen as a type of consequential validity, a concept introduced by Messick (1989).

Developmental validity may also be seen as a type of systemic validity, introduced by Fredriksen and Collins (1989). Systemic validity expresses how an assessment facilitates educational practices that promote desired learning. Teaching in the classroom is certainly an example of such an educational practice. Gitomer and Duschl (1998: 795) emphasize the point that: 'assessment validity requires attention to both an assessment's construct validity and the consequences of its use. Attending to only one of these validity aspects can lead to poor assessment and educational practice'.

From philosophy to practice

Qualitative approach

Our striving towards developmental validity is expressed in various ways. One is to include as many open-ended tasks as economic resources allow. It is often a question of trying to formulate a number of categories that describe different ways of thinking in relation to a particular task. The insights into the students' ways of thinking induced by qualitative analysis may lead to ideas about improvements of teaching both in general and in detail.

We have been inspired to take a qualitative approach by the work of Ros Driver in the Assessment Performance Unit (APU) Science Project (Johnson 1988; Black 1990) and the Children's Learning in Science Project (CLISP)

(CLISP 1987a, 1987b). The CLISP in particular demonstrates how one might use knowledge of students' conceptions, obtained through assessment, as a significant element in the development of new teaching sequences.

Evaluation for developing knowledge rather than control

If a system of national evaluation is made permanent, it may lead to the teachers starting to teach in order to obtain good test results, particularly if the approach is quantitative and schools are compared with each other. This may have an inhibitory effect on the creative development of teaching. The risk of this happening in the Swedish system is small, from a general point of view, since only 3 per cent of all students in a particular year are included in each evaluation. In addition, as far as science is concerned, different content areas have been included on different occasions.

Reporting

In view of our philosophy we regard our reports as an important instrument for increasing knowledge and awareness of school science teaching and learning. In line with this, the following elements are included in the reports:

- Discussion of methodological and assessment problems in national evaluation.
- Discussion of national goals and how these may be interpreted.
- Discussion of the content in commonly-used teaching material.
- Discussion of why a selected content area (for example, energy or ecology) has an important place in school teaching.
- Description and analysis of international research results concerning students' conceptions and learning difficulties in the area subjected to evaluation.
- Definition of the goals that guide the evaluation.
- Description of how the students have answered, task by task, with a fair number of examples of students' answers.
- Discussion, task by task, of the significance of the students' answers, particularly to teaching.
- Overall discussion of new possibilities for teaching in the area evaluated.
- Discussion, when motivated, of more general questions (for example, the integration of science subjects as opposed to separate subject teaching).

Detailed examples where we have tried to achieve developmental validity are provided in the next section.

Theme: 'The state of the world' – an overview

Background and aims

In the current curricula for Swedish comprehensive and upper secondary schools it is pointed out that the students should be able to orientate themselves in a complex world with a large flow of information and a rapid rate of change. It is further stated that an important task of schooling is to provide overview and structure, and that an international perspective is important to be able to see one's own reality in a global context and to create international solidarity. In the Education Act it is stated that each and every person working within school is to promote respect for our common environment. All this is easier said than done, and one may certainly wonder to what extent the stated intentions are realized.

To shed light on discussions of these issues, an evaluation was made on the theme 'The state of the world' as part of the National Education Agency's evaluation programme for 1998 (Andersson *et al.* 1999). Pupils in Grades 5 (11–12 years) and 9 (15–16 years) at the compulsory comprehensive school and in Year 3 at the upper secondary school (18–19 years) took part. The evaluation had a dual purpose:

- To stimulate deeper discussion about the selected theme. The classical questions of *didaktik* apply: What should the teaching contain, for what reasons, and how can the teaching be done?
- To shed light on students' knowledge, skills and attitudes in relation to the theme, and how these are developed during their school years, taking the curriculum and the syllabus as the point of departure.

Content, methods and sampling

The following aspects of the selected theme have been studied:

1 Population growth
2 Energy questions
3 The greenhouse effect and the role of the ozone layer
4 The global water cycle
5 Biological diversity
6 Rich and poor
7 Global dependence and trade patterns
8 Students' views of the future of the world and possibilities of influencing it
9 What the poster 'Earth at night seen from a satellite' says about the state of the world
10 The individual as a local actor in the world

As far as the first eight aspects are concerned, between 200 and 450 students in each school year completed various tests inquiring into their knowledge, understanding and attitudes. The tasks were distributed *via* the internet. The selection was national but not randomized. It included schools from different regions in Sweden. The relatively small number of students is explained by limited economic resources and the fact that one main purpose of our project has been to stimulate deeper discussion of the selected theme.

Both open questions, to which students write their own answers, and multiple-choice questions have been used. The written responses are analysed qualitatively. Categories and other details in the analysis are not decided in advance but formed through interaction with the actual responses.

Students were interviewed in pairs about how they understood the picture 'Earth at night seen from a satellite'. More than 20 pairs per school year (3, 5 and 9) were interviewed. 'The individual as a local actor in the world' is a problem-solving test in which the student has to decide about the dilemma of whether to buy 'certified organically grown, more expensive bananas or normal, cheaper ones' Working in groups, the students search for information from different sources about how different types of bananas are cultivated, examine and evaluate this information, make an independent choice and motivate it. Somewhat more than 80 students per school year (3, 5 and 9) took part. The students were allowed to use a total of eight lessons, spread over a few weeks, to solve the banana problem.

Remarks about developmental validity

Teaching separate science subjects is a dominant pattern in Swedish schools. Therefore, the choice of a thematic approach for the evaluation, as well as the content of the theme, was made as an attempt to challenge this pattern, and hopefully provoke school development. The issue for debate is whether traditional subject matter teaching is enough when the aim is to help students to orientate themselves in the complex world of today, with a large flow of information and a rapid rate of change.

It is also worth noting that the methods chosen for the evaluation are quite diverse, hopefully stimulating teachers to try new approaches when evaluating their own teaching.

What is the greenhouse effect?

Let us now look at one of the aspects of the theme in more detail, namely the 'greenhouse effect'. The students were given the following question to answer individually and on paper.

We speak of the greenhouse effect in many different contexts. Describe in your own words what the greenhouse effect is.

The question was included in a test of knowledge ('Test 1') with 14 questions, half open, half multiple-choice. The answers were categorized. For each category below, the first number in brackets refers to the percentage of students answering in the specified way from Year 9 in the comprehensive school (n = 201), whereas the second number refers to the corresponding proportion from Year 3 in the upper secondary school (n = 222) (i.e. Year 12). Each student is classified into one category only. The figures included below are schematic representations of the students' mental models, beginning with the ozone effect (Model 2) and moving on to models concerned with the greenhouse effect (Models 1, 3, 4 and 5). They will be commented on later.

A Not answered/don't know (27; 14)

B Confusion with the 'ozone effect' (12; 10)

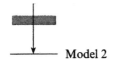

Model 2

Example: 'It is when poisonous gases that are let out thin the ozone layer and in this way increase the amount of radiation that can get in from the sun and space. This makes it warmer and ice, especially at the north and south poles, melts.'

C Only the results of, and/or the causes of, the greenhouse effect or its enhancement are described (15; 10)

Example: 'The greenhouse effect means that it gets warmer and the ice in the polar areas melts and that the water level rises by 70 metres.'

D Association between (more of) something (in the atmosphere) and warming (7; 6)

Model 1

Example: 'Carbon dioxide from fossil fuels that is let out into the air forms a "lid" over the earth that makes the average temperature rise.'

E Heat does not come out/bounces back because of a barrier (13; 19)

Model 3

Example: 'I don't know for sure, but I think that there are lots of gases that lie like a roof round the earth. It gets warm and the heat can't come out. In the end things can get so bad that the poles melt and the earth is flooded.'

F Reflection of solar radiation (heat) is blocked by something (what comes in does not come out, is kept behind, etc.); same word for 'input' and 'output' (13; 24)

Example: 'When the sun's rays come into the "earth layer" but not out because of all the pollution.'

Model 4

G Inflow and outflow are different (described with different words); outflow is stopped/reduced (1; 5)

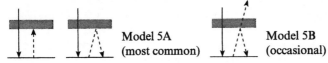

Model 5A (most common)   Model 5B (occasional)

Example: 'Some gases, like CO_2, form a layer round the earth that acts so that the solar energy that penetrates down through the atmosphere to earth is not reflected entirely. Some of the heat energy "bounces" back down to the earth's surface and heats up the earth. The gas becomes like the glass in a greenhouse that keeps the heat in.'

H Other (13; 12)

Discussion of the answers to the greenhouse task

This rather detailed example can be used to illustrate the claim made above that the insights into the students' ways of thinking gained by qualitative analysis may lead to ideas for improvements of teaching. It is suggested in the project report that teachers could, for instance, start the subject area by allowing small groups to discuss and work out a description of what the greenhouse effect is and then to report this to the whole class. The task is reasonable as this effect is a subject of discussion and comment in the media. One may expect at least some of the models described above to appear in the groups' reports. The teacher, or perhaps other students, will then have a reason for challenging each model. If, for instance, Model 4 is proposed, a natural challenge is to ask why the radiation gets through in one direction but not in the opposite one. If the student claims that the heat or outgoing radiation is stopped by a barrier then there is reason to wonder whether the earth ought not to have become overheated already. There would have been a 'filling up' with heat all the time, and greenhouse gases such as water vapour and carbon dioxide have, of course, existed in the atmosphere for a long time. To be able to realize that this objection is justified the student should be aware of the concept of conservation of energy.

The effects on society of reducing carbon dioxide emissions

Test 1 was followed by a test that consisted of questions concerning how one should regard the threat of climatic change caused by humankind's emission of greenhouse gases and what effects a reduction of carbon dioxide emission would have on society. First of all the participants discussed all the questions in pairs. Then they answered individually. The reason for this procedure was that we wanted to make it easier for the students to become acquainted with the different questions, which are about judging complex situations and may be seen from different points of view.

The test about what effects a reduction of carbon dioxide emission would have on society began with information about sources of carbon dioxide emission and about typical emissions per person and year for industrialized countries (typically 10–20 tonnes) and developing countries (a few tonnes). The test then continued as follows:

> Researchers and other experts believe that the rate of emission should be about 1 tonne per person and year to prevent the greenhouse effect from getting out of control. There is no consensus among the experts, but many believe that it is high time to make adjustments.
>
> Imagine yourself taking part in a world conference about what the world's countries will have to do in this situation. Five suggestions have been put forward for the industrialized countries and five for the developing countries. Which suggestions for the industrial countries will you vote for? Which for the developing countries?
>
> *Industrialized countries should*: (A) Cut down their emissions drastically to about 1 tonne per person and year; (B) Cut down their emissions quite drastically to a few tonnes per person and year; (C) Cut down their emissions a little; (D) Keep to the present emission level; (E) Be allowed to emit as much as they want.
>
> *Developing countries should*: (A) Not be allowed to emit more than about 1 tonne per person and year; (B) Be allowed to emit a few tonnes per person and year, but not more; (C) Be allowed to emit a number of tonnes per person and year, but not as much as the industrialized countries do; (D) Be allowed to emit as much per person and year as the industrialized countries do; (E) Be allowed to emit as much as they want.

A summary of the students' answers is given in Table 4.1. The response alternatives have been combined as follows:

> Industrialized countries: drastic limitation (A+B), little or no limitation (C+D+E)

Developing countries: drastic limitation (A+B), little or no limitation (C+D+E)

Table 4.1 How should the emission of carbon dioxide per person and year be limited in developing countries and industrialized countries? Percentage distribution of students among various alternatives, Years 9 and 12

	Year 9 (n = 309)	*Year 12 (n = 328)*
Drastic limitation for both developing and industrialized countries	73	77
Drastic limitation only for developing countries	13	7
Drastic limitation only for industrialized countries	9	11
Little or no limitation for both developing and industrialized countries	5	6

The students who chose drastic limitation for industrialized countries were given a follow-up question:

How many years should be allowed to pass before the reduction is fully effected?

Just over 60 per cent stated a maximum of 10 years. Among the rest, most answered a maximum of 25 years.

After the students had selected the emission alternatives, they were presented with the following question:

What would be the consequences of carrying out the alternatives you have chosen for industrialized countries and developing countries?

The students' answers were categorized. A number of sectors of the surrounding world were identified as main categories (A–F). An answer was sometimes allocated to two or more main categories. The results of the categorization for the part of the question referring to industrialized countries are given in Table 4.2. When several consequences are mentioned in an answer, this usually means that they are listed. A minor proportion (15 per cent in Year 9 and 17 per cent in Year 12) contain chains of consequences – for example, drastically reduced car driving will result in the car industry not being needed, which in turn will lead to a reduction of steel production.

Table 4.2 Consequences of various emission alternatives for industrialized countries. Review of the sectors affected and the percentage of students in each year referring to each sector in their answers

Category	Year 9 (n = 318)	Year 12 (n = 334)
A Social sector (lower standard, changed labour market, protests)	19	28
B Transport (less car driving, more public transport)	23	19
C Environment/health (less emission, better environment)	23	12
D Industry/manufacturing/research (less production, closures, 'environment friendly' research/production)	17	16
E Energy (transition to alternative fuels, reduction of fossil fuels, saving)	11	15
F Economy (adjustments are expensive)	10	16
Consequences expressed in general terms (e.g. 'there will be problems')	17	16
Other	12	25
Not answered	15	11

The general picture is that the students have few main categories in their answers (on average one, the calculation being based on the total number of students asked). This picture becomes even more accentuated if we look at the answers referring to the developing countries.

The answers to the consequences test and developmental validity

Collective breadth may stimulate the individual development of knowledge

The answers just described give insight into the students' ways of thinking and lead to suggestions for improvements of teaching. The following is proposed to the reader of our project report.

It is obvious that the students take the threat of climatic change seriously. When faced with different alternatives, they advocate a drastic reduction of carbon dioxide in a rather short time for industrialized countries and a low level in terms of what developing countries should be allowed to emit. They indicate rather few consequences of these drastic measures for each type of country. This is a little disappointing, but there is also a hopeful element in our picture of the results – the students as a group demonstrate a broad understanding when it comes to stating the consequences (see Table 4.2). This provides ideas for a teaching approach: small groups of students can work on a problem similar to the one about the consequences of various emission alternatives for the industrialized and developing countries, and then present their findings to the whole class. Working on their own, students' individual contributions are perhaps small, but if a number of them each do their bit, then the perspective widens. When the whole class enters into the process, the consequences may multiply and branch out into different aspects of the world around them. In other words, the collective breadth that exists in a class may stimulate the individual development of knowledge and help the students to see the world as a web whose parts depend on each other in various ways.

Wider considerations – the nature-technology-society (NTS) system

The students' answers to the consequences test are used in the project report as a point of departure for discussing the more general problem of how best to help students orientate themselves in today's world. The following remarks are made in the project report.

It is likely that the students' radical views about the limitation of carbon dioxide emission may be partly due to the fact that they, as individuals, are not aware of all the consequences of such a reduction (see Table 4.2). It is a question of being aware that a good 80 per cent of humankind's energy supply is made up of oil, coal and gas and understanding that this is a prerequisite for the well-being and continued development of industrialized and developing countries over the next few decades. One should also know which technical systems emit carbon dioxide. One example is the combustion engines in 500 million cars, another is power plants which generate electricity, which are responsible for a third of the annual world consumption of oil, coal and gas. Further, it is a question of understanding the world as a web of dependence. A drastic reduction in carbon dioxide emission would have repercussions throughout the web because it would affect the economy, trade and industry, the infrastructure, social institutions and the environment.

All these understandings and insights may fall between the chairs in a system where the dominant mode of teaching is subject by subject. A thematic approach, taking the NTS system into consideration might be more appropriate for understanding the urgent problems of today, such as the enhancement of the greenhouse effect.

Other studies

As was mentioned above, an important aspect of our striving for developmental validity is relating, when possible, results of evaluation to research concerning students' conceptions and learning difficulties. When it is a question of human–atmosphere interactions, it is noted that interesting studies have been conducted concerning the greenhouse effect and its enhancement by Boyes and Stanisstreet (1993), Francis *et al.* (1993), Dove (1996), and Rye *et al.* (1997). Students' understanding of the depletion of the stratospheric ozone layer has been studied by Dove (1996), and by Boyes and Stanisstreet (1998).

It has been possible to carry out the project in such a way that a contribution to this field of research is made (Andersson and Wallin in press).

An opportunity to renew the content of teaching

We have asked the students who participated in the evaluation to assess the tests included from different points of view. They think that the theme 'The state of the world' is important, both with reference to knowledge and decision making. The girls in Year 9 at the comprehensive school and Year 3 (i.e. Year 12) at the upper secondary school are more interested in this than the boys. The students state that they have not learned much at school about what the test questions deal with. This shows that the theme 'The state of the world' is an area that the students care about and are motivated to tackle, but which is not brought out clearly in the teaching they receive at present. The area is in line with central goals of the Swedish school system. In other words, the theme 'The state of the world' stands out as an excellent opportunity to renew the content of teaching. This insight is perhaps the most important result of the evaluation.

Final remarks: have we succeeded?

A philosophy for national evaluation has been formulated in this chapter, and examples have been provided of how this philosophy has been put into practice. The question is, have we succeeded? Do the evaluations of 1992, 1995 and 1998 have good developmental validity – i.e. do they stimulate the teacher in particular to reflect on his or her teaching and attempt to improve it? The answer is that we do not know. There are, however, two signs that we are on the right path. One is that members of the National Education Agency's field organization have observed that our reports are known and read by teachers. Thanks to these reports, teachers are considered to be aware of students' conceptions and learning difficulties in the areas investigated. The other sign is that the reports quite often are prescribed texts in teacher training. 'Fine', one may think, but in a wider perspective this is only a small contribution to the major problem of improving science education in school. So much remains to do.

Acknowledgement

The research reported in this chapter has been financed by the Swedish National Agency for Education.

References

Andersson, B. and Wallin, A. (in press) Students' understanding of the greenhouse effect: societal consequences of reducing CO_2 emissions and why ozone layer depletion is a problem. *Journal of Research in Science Teaching*.

Andersson, B., Bach, F. and Zetterqvist, A. (1996) *Nationell utvärdering 95 – åk 9. Energi i natur och samhälle (NA-SPEKTRUM, nr. 18)*. Mölndal: Göteborgs Universitet, Inst. för Ämnesdidaktik.

Andersson, B., Kärrqvist, C., Löfstedt, A., Oscarsson, V. and Wallin, A. (1999) *Nationell utvärdering 98 – tema 'Tillståndet i världen' (NA-SPEKTRUM, nr. 21)*. Mölndal: Göteborgs Universitet, Inst. för Pedagogik och Didaktik.

Black, P. (1990) APU science: the past and the future. *School Science Review*, 72(258): 13–28.

Boyes, E. and Stanisstreet, M. (1993) The 'greenhouse effect': children's perceptions of causes, consequences and cures. *International Journal of Science Education*, 15(5): 531–52.

Boyes, E. and Stanisstreet, M. (1998) High school students' perceptions of how major global environmental effects might cause skin cancer. *The Journal of Environmental Education*, 29(2): 31–6.

CLISP (1987a) *Children's Learning in Science Project: Approaches to Teaching the Particulate Theory of Matter*. Leeds: Centre for Studies in Science and Mathematics Education, University of Leeds.

CLISP (1987b) *Children's Learning in Science Project: Approaches to Teaching Plant Nutrition*. Leeds: Centre for Studies in Science and Mathematics Education, University of Leeds.

Dove, J. (1996) Student teacher understanding of the greenhouse effect, ozone layer depletion and acid rain. *Environmental Education Research*, 2(1): 89–100.

Francis, C., Boyes, E., Qualter, A. and Stanisstreet, M. (1993) Ideas of elementary students about reducing the 'greenhouse effect'. *Science Education*, 77(4): 375–92.

Fredriksen, J.R. and Collins, A. (1989) A systems approach to educational testing. *Educational Researcher*, 18(9): 27–32.

Gitomer, D.H. and Duschl, R.A. (1998) Emerging issues and practices in science assessment, in B.J. Fraser and K.G. Tobin (eds) *International Handbook of Science Education*. Dordrecht: Kluwer Academic Publishers.

Johnson, S. (1988) *National Assessment: APU Science Approach*. London: HMSO.

Messick, S. (1989) Validity, in R.L. Linn (ed.) *Educational Measurement*. Washington, DC: American Council on Education and the National Council on Measurement in Education.

Rye, J., Rubba, P. and Wiesenmayer, R. (1997) An investigation of middle school students' alternative conceptions of global warming. *International Journal of Science Education*, 19(5): 527–51.

5

Learning to teach science in the primary school

Hilary Asoko

Introduction

Science is an increasingly important component of the primary school curriculum across much of the world. These first encounters with the subject may have a long-term impact on children's interest in, and attitudes to, science and have the potential to provide a useful basis of knowledge, understanding and skills. There is, of course, considerable variation between countries in terms of curriculum content and emphasis, reflecting local and national traditions, aims and priorities. However, in all countries teachers are the key to realizing curriculum aims, and the quality of the science education which children receive rests, ultimately, with them.

Typically, primary teachers are generalists, teaching all subjects, and many find their understanding of science challenged by the demands of the curriculum which they are expected to teach. Teachers' lack of subject knowledge in science has been documented and frequently identified as a barrier to implementation of curriculum reform and to pupil progress (see for example Wragg et al. 1989; Alexander et al. 1992; Summers 1992; Ofsted 1994; Harlen et al. 1995). Teachers who lack knowledge and confidence may attempt to avoid or minimize their difficulties through a variety of strategies, including avoidance of topics, heavy reliance on texts, and overemphasis on practical activity which, over time, may result in an impoverished science education for children (Lee 1995; Harlen and Holroyd 1997). Osborne and Simon (1996) have discussed some pragmatic solutions to the problem of lack of expertise within the existing teaching force. However, sustained improvements in primary science will depend on improved teacher capability. This has implications for both initial and in-service education of teachers and raises some fundamental questions such as: what knowledge is needed to teach a particular science topic and how best can that knowledge be developed? Given limited time, where should initial training focus its efforts and what is better left for future professional development?

In this chapter the question of teacher knowledge of science will be discussed in the context of initial teacher education in the UK. Here, primary teachers are trained through a variety of routes, one of which is a 38-week postgraduate course. This attracts well-qualified students who have completed 13 years of schooling and at least 3 years of higher education. However, like their counterparts on other courses both in the UK and elsewhere, the majority are not highly qualified in science and may not have studied it for some years. Many of them have found their own education in science uninspiring and uninteresting and approach the teaching of it with apprehension, particularly those aspects which they have never studied or which they found difficult, often despite at least 5 years of science study at secondary school. Training thus needs to address student attitudes to science as well as knowledge and practice, since without positive attitudes and a belief in themselves as science learners and science teachers, students are unlikely to develop enthusiasm, interest and understanding in children.

The knowledge utilized by teachers has been categorized by Shulman (1987) and includes knowledge of the science curriculum, the content appropriate to it, and the pedagogy necessary to teach it. The category of 'pedagogical content knowledge', which relates to the ways to represent a subject and make it understandable and accessible to others, clearly links subject knowledge and more general pedagogical knowledge, and this raises a number of issues. Should, for example, the science and the pedagogy be taught separately and integrated later? Is it possible to identify and teach 'pedagogical content knowledge' or does this develop from classroom experience? Studies of changes in teacher knowledge of science as a result of professional development programmes suggest that subject knowledge and pedagogy can develop hand in hand in a mutually interdependent manner, though this development characteristically takes some considerable time (Smith and Neale 1989; Bell and Gilbert 1996; Rosebery and Puttick 1998). Student teachers have little time. Unlike experienced teachers they may also be struggling with generic pedagogical issues (such as classroom management) simultaneously with developing their teaching of not one, but several, subjects. What they need to learn, when they need to learn it, and how and by whom it should be taught are important questions.

In most countries two partners, a college or university and one or more schools, contribute to the training of teachers (Moon 1998). Developing subject knowledge is normally seen as the responsibility of the higher education partner, but it is in the classroom where this knowledge is put to the test. The tension between providing students with strategies to cope with the demands placed upon them in their early experiences of teaching and stimulating the curiosity and awareness necessary for continued professional development has been described by Geddis and Wood (1997). It is particularly pronounced when students are learning to teach a subject about which they themselves are unsure, as is often the case with science. Positive experiences, which may result from students being given prescriptive teaching models, may raise confidence but it is through recognizing and confronting the difficulties and dilemmas of practice that the development of autonomy and self-reliance will best be stimulated.

Calderhead and Shorrock (1997), exploring the complexity of learning to teach, consider that during initial training students are 'learning to manage activities rather than becoming expert in particular subject matter and the pedagogy associated with it' (p. 208). Other studies, with a more specific focus on science teaching, have explored student perceptions of their own development, the ways in which their subject knowledge and pedagogy interact and change, and the development of pedagogical reasoning (John 1991; Bennett and Carré 1993; Geddis 1993; Lederman *et al.* 1994; Peterson and Treagust 1998). Smith's (1999) study of five science-specialist primary students describes a situation in which knowledge, including subject knowledge, was drawn on, challenged and changed in response to teaching tasks.

However, although student teachers frequently consider their school experiences to be the most influential aspect of their training, few studies of student teacher development in science have included observation of classroom practice and those that have rarely consider issues related to the teaching of specific content. Consequently we know very little about the ways in which school experience interacts with and influences subject knowledge and pedagogy, and have little empirical base on which to make decisions about the content and structure of the courses we provide. Despite an extensive literature on subject knowledge and pedagogical content knowledge, it is not at all clear, given a specific context for teaching, what kind of knowledge is needed, how it is deployed and how it develops as a result of teaching (McNamara 1991; Cochran and Jones 1998).

In an attempt to explore these issues within a specific context, a number of students on a one-year postgraduate training course were observed and interviewed as they taught a sequence of science lessons over a period of five weeks during their first teaching attachment. None of the students observed were science specialists. Within the teaching attachment they taught the full curriculum to children aged between 7 and 10. The science to be taught related to the broad topic of 'forces'.

As would be expected, the progress made by the students and the contexts in which they were working varied considerably. Nevertheless, four interrelated aspects of practice were consistently influenced or constrained by the subject knowledge of the students:

- the balance between process and content;
- the use of practical work;
- classroom talk and the development of explanations;
- the ability to take account of, and respond to, children's thinking and to use their existing experience.

Aspects of the classroom experience of one of these students, Kathy, illustrates these issues. Her story as described here draws upon her written planning and reflections on her teaching, classroom observations, and transcripts of interviews and classroom interactions.

Kathy's story

Kathy held a first degree in religious studies and a masters degree in European environmental policy. She had studied biology to advanced level and chemistry to General Certificate of Secondary Education (GCSE) level in school but had not studied physics since the age of 14. Having attended sessions on primary science teaching in the university, as well as observing and participating in science activities in school, she felt 'daunted and excited' about the prospect of teaching science to a class of 9- and 10-year-olds.

With the help of published materials, including a national scheme of work (QCA 1998), and in consultation with the class teacher, Kathy developed her teaching plans for a five-lesson sequence of 1 hour 15 minutes per week. The first two lessons allowed the introduction or revisiting of some ideas and techniques which provided a basis for the introduction of the main conceptual focus of the work, the force of friction. Within this context, Kathy also intended to develop children's abilities to carry out a scientific investigation. Her plans for the final three lessons (see Box. 5.1) suggest that the exploration of a phenomenon (an object sliding on different surfaces) was intended to provide a context for the introduction of an explanatory idea, the force of friction, which was new to the class. This idea was then to be drawn upon in the context of an investigation related to a 'real life' problem within children's experience.

It is always easy to criticize aspects of observed or reported practice and therefore it should be stressed from the start that Kathy's science lessons, and her reflections on them, were impressive for a student at this stage of training. In her classroom the management of the children was never an issue and the atmosphere was calm and purposeful. The children enjoyed their work and were keen to participate, and the class teacher had no concerns about Kathy's competence. Kathy was very self-critical and keen to consider ways to improve her performance. As such, issues arising from one lesson were, as far as possible, dealt with in the next.

Box 5.1   Kathy's learning objectives

Lesson 3: Investigate on which surfaces objects slide more easily.
Objectives: Pupils should be able to decide what evidence to collect, to predict what will happen and to plan a fair test. Pupils should be able to make and record useful measurements.

Lesson 4: Complete forces investigation and interpret results, introducing friction.
Objectives: Pupils should learn that friction is a force that opposes movement and slows things down.

Lesson 5: Investigate which shoes grip the best on a tiled surface.
Objectives: Pupils should be able to plan a fair test. Pupils should be able to gather information on the amount of force needed to make a shoe slip. Pupils should be able to explain results in terms of forces.

Lesson 3: sliding matchboxes

In the second lesson of the sequence children had used a piece of elastic, tied between the legs of a chair, to investigate the relationship between the stretch of the elastic and the distance travelled by a matchbox propelled across the floor. In the third lesson a similar arrangement was to be used to compare the distance travelled by the matchbox on three different surfaces. Since part of the classroom floor was tiled and a corner was carpeted, this appeared, to Kathy, to provide the contrast between rough and smooth which she needed. An intermediate surface was provided by pieces of matting. Since the carpet was fixed to the floor, Kathy organized three workstations in each of the three different areas. Children made one set of three measurements in each spot and then moved on to use a different surface. Unfortunately, both Kathy and the class teacher, who had provided help with organizing the resources, overlooked the fact that the children were also using elastic of varying tensions and thus, when the results were collated in a whole class discussion, the expected relationship was not consistently apparent. While some children had found that the matchbox travelled further on the floor, as expected, other groups had recorded greater distances on the mat or the carpet. Kathy could not, therefore, use the results obtained as she had intended. Instead she focused children's attention on the differing results, and asked for suggestions as to why these might be so before ending the lesson.

Lesson 4: introducing friction

Building on the mistakes of the previous week, Kathy involved the children in a careful consideration of the experimental set-up and encouraged a constructively critical approach to the collection of the evidence. The investigation was repeated as a demonstration, with children taking and recording measurements and ensuring that the test was carried out appropriately. This time the results supported the prediction which most children had made at the beginning of the previous lesson, that the box travelled furthest on the smooth surface and least far on the roughest surface. Up to this point the work in both lessons had emphasized the procedural aspects of the practical work: the need for repeat readings, control of variables and so on. Kathy now needed to make sense of these results, for the class, in terms of the forces acting, especially friction – the main focus of the whole sequence of teaching. She attempted to do this through a series of questions, interspersed with direct statements and supported by a written summary. Children were then asked to draw a picture of a training shoe and indicate on it the forces acting if it was sliding across the floor. This, together with a 'newspaper article' about accidents caused by slipping on floors provided a link to the final lesson of the sequence.

Lesson 5: testing shoes

In this lesson Kathy intended that everything introduced in the preceding weeks would contribute to the planning and execution of a test to compare the force needed to make different shoes slide. Children were expected to use their knowledge of forces, in particular friction, to explain the results and to speculate on the effect of factors such as the material of the sole and possibly the mass of the shoe. The class tackled the work with enthusiasm, but the relationship between the experimental results and the explanation proved difficult for Kathy to deal with, leading to a discussion based heavily in the everyday world of shoes and 'grip', with little reference to the ideas of forces and friction.

Issues arising from the teaching

From the start Kathy felt much more confident about the procedural aspects of the science than the conceptual. This was reflected in the emphasis in her lesson plans, both in terms of time and objectives (see Box 5.1). Her ability to utilize opportunities arising in the classroom when she felt confident was demonstrated by the way in which she dealt with the problem which arose in lesson three. Although she had failed to spot a crucial variable in setting up the investigation, and the activity therefore 'went wrong', Kathy was able to use this to advantage to focus children's attention on flaws in the experimental design and the reasons for apparently contradictory results. Her confidence and knowledge in this area enabled her to recognize and exploit a learning opportunity.

In contrast, she had not fully realized the work she needed to do in relating the practical activity to the ideas about friction which she wanted to introduce. This became evident in the second half of lesson four where, in trying to make the link between the observed events and the scientific idea, she first appealed to the class:

Kathy: . . . on the smooth surface the box went further didn't it, and on the rough one it slowed down and it didn't go so far? Does anyone know, some of you might know but I'm not sure, what's the force called that we've been looking at? What's the force called that slows things down? . . . Does anyone know? . . . Slows things down and makes them stop?

Not surprisingly, this did not result in the answer Kathy hoped for! Instead children offered other ideas, including gravity and resistance, which were acknowledged but not explored, and Kathy resorted to giving the answer herself:

Kathy: The word we're looking for today, OK is friction [writes on board] . . . Anyone ever heard the word friction used anywhere else?

A child suggested 'friction burns' and Kathy picked up this idea, related it to sliding down ropes and asked:

Kathy: What causes your hands to be sore? . . . Ian?
Ian: Gravity.
Kathy: Not gravity is it, well, I know gravity makes you come down, but what is it that makes your hands sore?
David: When you slide it like burns your hands.
Kathy: Yes, it does burn your hands doesn't it. Why? Rachel?
Rachel: You're going down the rope fast.
Kathy: Good, yes. Lynne?
Lynne: The rope rubs your hands.
Kathy: Yes, the material rubs against your hands and makes your hands hot and it also hurts, OK. But friction is the word we use. If we moved that box and there was no friction, that matchbox would continue moving. OK? Friction is a force which slows things down or makes them stop.

She then asked:

> *Kathy:* Your books on the table aren't moving at the moment. Why aren't they moving? ... Tom?
> *Tom:* The weight holds them down.
> *Kathy:* Yes, that's one answer, that's true. What else is stopping them moving? What else do you think might be stopping them moving?
> *Pupil:* [inaudible].
> *Kathy:* Yes, sort of. Someone else?
> *Paul:* Friction.
> *Kathy:* Why? How?
> *Paul:* Friction sort of pulls them back.
> *Kathy:* Sort of isn't it. There's not much friction is there between them and the table, because the table is smooth. The table sort of holds them in place, doesn't it? What I want you to do now is to copy down, very quickly in your science books, I want you to put the title 'friction' and then we're going to copy down a note.

This interaction epitomizes the difficulties faced by non-specialist students trying to use knowledge with which they themselves have only recently become acquainted and which has not been consolidated. Although Kathy in one sense 'knew' the science, in that she could articulate a textbook definition of friction and had some understanding of the effects of forces on moving objects, she had problems in relating this knowledge either to the real world of phenomena, events and children's comments or to the science world of forces and their effects. The links between the phenomena which are being discussed and the ideas to be explored needed to be made explicit but Kathy had not fully realized this or recognized the consequent demands on her as the teacher. On the basis of their classroom experience children could be expected to relate the motion of the matchbox to the nature of the surface. Indeed, to the majority of the class this relationship was obvious before carrying out the activity. They also shared an awareness of relevant situations, such as sliding down ropes or on ice. However, the explanatory idea, friction, does not arise unproblematically from experience but must be 'talked into existence' (Ogborn *et al.* 1996). It was Kathy's responsibility to do this, but she did not. As a result, she had to abandon the discussion in favour of copying notes which, though scientifically correct, probably meant little to the class. In effect she achieved little more than the labelling of phenomena as examples of friction. As she commented:

> There was a gap wasn't there because we kind of went down the fair testing road, which was fine, but then it needed bringing back to what we were testing in the first place and then, unpacking all those things [about forces]. It's a bit like you've been doing all this stuff and now

we're going to stick a label on it, instead of here's what we're learning now you can look for it in what you're doing.

This last comment also indicates Kathy's recognition that an alternative way of teaching would be to introduce the idea of friction at an earlier stage and then provide opportunities to explore the implications of it.

Second, despite her acknowledgement that it was important to respond to and utilize children's ideas, Kathy found this difficult to do in practice. In teaching other subjects she felt this was not such a concern because:

> I can see where it could go but in this I think if he said that, what does it mean?

This difficulty in interpreting children's responses in science meant that Kathy was less able to follow up opportunities to extend, develop or challenge children's understanding of forces in general and friction in particular. In addition, as she had not anticipated children's thinking or considered the previous knowledge or everyday experiences on which they might draw, she had to respond spontaneously to any ideas expressed, and this generated feelings of insecurity:

> I not only occasionally felt ill-equipped to challenge pupils' misunder-standings, I also felt unnerved by the most able pupils! Indeed I felt particularly challenged by the brightest child in a class who raised questions I had not anticipated, and introduced language that was not straightforward.

Third, in trying to relate the idea of friction to everyday experiences and to children's thinking, spontaneous responses were likely to cause confusion rather than clarity. Kathy readily accepted this, for example in relation to her unplanned introduction of the example of the books on the table:

> I'm trying to get them to think about their experiences of things but that was a bit of a tangent, wasn't it really . . . that came from nowhere in relation to what they were doing. They'd been looking at moving things and then all of a sudden, with no preparation at all, I ask them to look at stationary things when we haven't really clarified what happens with moving things. Poor things!

A recurring theme in Kathy's comments on her teaching relates to the difficulty of communicating and explaining ideas she herself had only just begun to think about:

> In preparation for teaching forces I researched the topic and attended university lectures related to forces. Despite this I felt as though I had just 'grasped' the concepts and at the outset of my teaching I did not

feel wholly confident to explain these ideas to others either inside or outside the classroom.

I had not fully consolidated my learning . . . and this created problems during my early lessons on forces. For instance, hesitancy and reluctance to use appropriate language for fear of error limited my communication skills in class. It also proved difficult to expound ideas in alternative ways when they needed further clarification and I found it difficult to invent reliable analogies.

As mentioned earlier, a factor behind many of the difficulties Kathy faced was the relationship between phenomena and explanations in this context. This was brought home to her in the fifth lesson in which she intended children to think about the factors which affect friction by exploring the forces needed to move shoes. As she said:

> . . . all those shoes, and those children coming up with all those ideas about shoes and in the end I just thought where's the friction gone! Where's the friction in this? It's about shoes!

Doing, seeing and talking science

The study of which Kathy's story forms a part arose from pragmatic concerns about the training of teachers in science and the nature of the knowledge which is most needed, particularly in areas such as forces, which students typically find difficult both to learn and to teach. Inevitably, each student in the study faced their own personal difficulties and dilemmas in the classroom. However, in terms of the content of the teaching two issues were common to all students and likely to be reflected in their teaching of other topics. In different ways, both limit the conceptual understanding which children could develop as a result of teaching.

First, although students defined their teaching in terms of the content areas to be covered, in practice they emphasized process issues over content. A number of factors probably contributed to this, including the traditional emphasis on practical work in science in the UK, a belief that children enjoy practical work and learn best by doing, and an assumption that this will lead unproblematically to the desired conceptual learning. These beliefs and assumptions in essence relate to views about the nature of science and about learning and may be difficult to change (Gustafson and Rowell 1995), especially if they are reinforced by existing practice in the school setting. In addition students, like teachers, may emphasize process simply because it seems easier. As Kathy commented:

My intention wasn't to swamp the knowledge with something that was easier but I have to admit that I found it easier to teach that because I've done that myself . . .
My intention really was to build their skills in investigation alongside learning about friction . . . but if you're trying to do both and you're not entirely clear about how the science knowledge is going to come through, which I obviously wasn't in that last lesson, then you've got lost in the process.

Second, although all students had attempted to ensure that they understood the relevant science concepts, they needed to learn to apply what they knew both to 'see the science' and to 'talk the science' in relation to the activities they had selected. Kathy's comment about 'how the science knowledge is going to come through' reflects her recognition of this.

'Seeing' the science, both when planning and in the opportunities which arose in the classroom, was necessary in order to:

- recognize the relevance, or otherwise, of events, phenomena, and children's comments and questions;
- generate links between related phenomena, especially those within children's experience or provided by practical explorations;
- distinguish between a description of an event or phenomenon, and an explanation which draws on scientific ideas and understanding;
- generate links between newly introduced science concepts and phenomena, events and existing scientific knowledge;
- evaluate the potential and limitations of, for example, activities, analogies and resources in relation to the topic.

Being able to 'see' the science makes it possible to 'talk' science in a way which can generate interest and support understanding by explicitly making the links described above within the framework provided by the activity. Students could rely on published materials and advice regarding activities to use and generally gave considerable thought to planning and preparation related to 'doing science', such as the provision and organization of resources. However, they paid much less attention to thinking about what to say. As a result, they learned to manage the physical, rather than the mental, activity of children and found difficulty in encouraging consideration of the ideas with which they wanted to deal. Typically, a feature of whole class interaction was time spent in question and answer sequences during which students attempted to extract from children the information which they were in fact trying to teach and needed to explain. Ogborn *et al.* (1996: 2) point out that 'beginning teachers are supposed to learn by example how to explain, often without being conscious of doing so'. The dialogue patterns typical of primary classrooms, termed 'Socratic argument' (Boulter and Gilbert 1996), involve teachers in collecting and reshaping ideas contributed by the class towards a predetermined end. Sizmur and Ashby (1997) observed experienced teachers using this pattern together with a 'model building' approach which used analogies of various kinds to develop conceptual understanding. However, to be successful, this strategy demands a confidence and knowledge of the subject matter and of children's thinking which students may not yet possess. They therefore have difficulty in identifying useful models and analogies and in weaving children's comments into a coherent 'story'.

Developing science subject knowledge in practice

The experience of grappling with the teaching of an unfamiliar topic for the first time has the potential to exemplify and clarify for students a number of broad issues about the teaching of science. These include the role of practical work, the limitations of 'discovery learning', influences on children's thinking and the development of conceptual understanding.

Important though these are, students are typically more concerned with the immediate challenges of teaching topic X to class Y. They can prepare themselves, as Kathy did, by reading up on the science, using resource materials for guidance and discussing plans with more experienced teachers and tutors. However, when implementing their plans in the classroom, students are dependent on their own resources. Their success in terms of promoting children's learning depends on their ability to capitalize on the opportunities, both planned and unplanned, which arise. The contribution of their teaching experience to their own professional development involves identifying not only the successes, but, more importantly, the difficulties and missed opportunities which occur. In the bustle of the classroom the novice teacher may be unaware, or unable, to take notice of these.

Ideally, experienced observers can provide subject-specific feedback and support. However, class teachers responsible for students may be unable to fulfil this role if they are themselves unsure about teaching science. Without specialized support and feedback in the classroom, how then can students begin to develop their teaching of specific content?

One possibility might be to explore the subject-specific routines (Frost and Glauert 1999) which teachers, and teacher educators, develop in relation to specific topics. These routines include the conversations which can be stimulated by the activities or experiences which form a focus for teaching. They represent pedagogical content knowledge in action and are elaborated and developed with experience. As frameworks they provide security and confidence but they can also be modified to suit particular circumstances.

Students have no such routines of their own and may be tempted to imitate the actions of others with little thought. However, explicit consideration of the knowledge which underpins, and is exemplified through, these routines may make them both practically useful and professionally informative. In particular, a focus on the talk which is generated might help students to begin to plan their own interactions with children more effectively. Examples of the interactions of both novice and experienced teachers within specific contexts, together with opportunities to consider the features of different types of explanation (Ogborn *et al.* 1996) and aspects of teacher interaction which can support conceptual learning (Asoko 1993) might also be of assistance.

Conclusion

The success of primary science depends, ultimately, on the quality of the teaching which children receive. We owe it to our students, and to the children they go on to teach, to prepare them as well as we can for the challenges they will face. Initial teacher education is inevitably limited in what it can achieve, not only because of the restricted time into which so much must be compressed, but also because much of a teacher's professional learning must be derived from experience in the future. Teaching is an enormously complex activity and initial training provides a foundation, not a finished product. Knowledge, attitudes and beliefs inform a teacher's practice, are expressed through it and may be challenged or changed as a result. 'Good' classroom teaching, by whatever criteria that is defined, is a dynamic process, influenced by and responsive to a multitude of factors of varying degrees of significance. Subject knowledge is clearly one such factor. Teachers whose understanding of science is weak will inevitably be limited in what they can achieve, but the knowledge they need differs from that needed to pass examinations. Teachers need to understand science in ways appropriate to teaching. At primary level it is likely that this means a broad, interconnected, qualitative understanding of important scientific ideas, closely linked to everyday events and phenomena, and embedded within and exemplified through practice.

As a result of working with Kathy both she and I have a better understanding of the knowledge needed to teach about friction. We can both, if we choose, use this to inform our future teaching routines, in particular the ways in which we select activities which provide opportunities to talk about issues of importance for children and students respectively. Further studies of students' early attempts at teaching, across a range of topics, could both inform and enhance teacher education programmes as well as elucidating more clearly the relationship between subject knowledge and pedagogy.

References

Alexander, R., Rose, J. and Woodhead, C. (1992) *Curriculum Organisation and Classroom Practice in Primary Schools.* London: HMSO.

Asoko, H. (1993) First steps in the construction of a theoretical model of light: a case study from a primary school classroom. *Proceedings of the Third International Seminar on Misconceptions and Educational Strategies in Science and Mathematics Education.* Ithaca, NY: Cornell University.

Bell, B. and Gilbert, J. (1996) *Teacher Development: A Model from Science Education.* London: Falmer Press.

Bennett, N. and Carré, C. (eds) (1993) *Learning to Teach.* London: Routledge.

Boulter, C. and Gilbert, J. (1996) Texts and contexts: Framing modelling in the primary science classroom, in G. Welford, J. Osborne and P. Scott (eds) *Reseach in Science Education in Europe: Current Issues and Themes.* London: Falmer Press.

Calderhead, J. and Shorrock, S.B. (1997) *Understanding Teacher Education.* London: Falmer Press.

Cochran, K.F. and Jones, L.J. (1998) The subject matter knowledge of pre-service science teachers, in B.J. Fraser and K.G. Tobin (eds) *International Handbook of Science Education.* Dordrecht: Kluwer Academic Publishers.

Frost, J. and Glauert, E. (1999) Research into pedagogy in primary science, *Publication of the 4th summer conference for teacher education in primary science: 'The Challenge of Change',* University of Durham.

Geddis, A.N. (1993) Transforming subject-matter knowledge: the role of pedagogical content knowledge in learning to reflect on teaching. *International Journal of Science Education,* 15(6): 673–83.

Geddis, A.N. and Wood, E. (1997) Transforming subject matter and managing dilemmas: a case study in teacher education. *Teaching and Teacher Education,* 13(6): 611–26.

Gustafson, B.J. and Rowell, P.M. (1995) Elementary pre-service teachers: constructing conceptions about learning science, teaching science and the nature of science. *International Journal of Science Education,* 17(5): 589–605.

Harlen, W. and Holroyd, C. (1997) Primary teachers' understanding of concepts of science: impact on confidence and teaching. *International Journal of Science Education,* 19(1) 93–105.

Harlen, W., Holroyd, C. and Byrne, M. (1995) *Confidence and Understanding in Teaching Science and Technology in Scottish Primary Schools.* Edinburgh: Scottish Council for Research in Education.

John, P.D. (1991) A qualitative study of British student teachers' lesson planning perspectives. *Journal of Education for Teaching,* 17(3): 301–20.

Lederman, N.G., Gess-Newsome, J. and Latz, M.S. (1994) The nature and development of pre-service science teachers' conceptions of subject matter and pedagogy. *Journal of Research in Science Teaching,* 31(2): 129–46.

Lee, O. (1995) Subject matter knowledge, classroom management and instructional practice in middle school science classrooms. *Journal of Research in Science Teaching,* 32(4): 423–40.

McNamara, D. (1991) Subject knowledge and its application: problems and possibilities for teacher educators. *Journal of Education for Teaching,* 17(2): 113–28.

Moon, B. (1998) *The English Exception? International Perspectives on the Initial Education and Training of Teachers*, Occasional Paper No.11. London: Universities Council for the Education of Teachers.

Ofsted (Office for Standards in Education) (1994) *Primary Matters*. London: HMSO.

Ogborn, J., Kress, G., Martins, I. and McGillicuddy, K. (1996) *Explaining Science in the Classroom*. Buckingham: Open University Press.

Osborne, J. and Simon, S. (1996) Primary science: past and future directions. *Studies in Science Education*, 26: 99–147.

Peterson, R.F. and Treagust, D.F. (1998) Learning to teach primary science through problem-based learning. *Science Education*, 82(2): 215–37.

QCA (Qualifications and Curriculum Authority) (1998) *Science: Teacher's Guide*. London: QCA.

Rosebery, A.S. and Puttick, G.M. (1998) Teacher professional development as situated sense-making: a case study in science education. *Science Education*, 82(6): 649–78.

Shulman, L.S. (1987) Knowledge and teaching: foundations of the new reform. *Harvard Educational Review*, 57: 1–22.

Sizmur, S. and Ashby, J. (1997) *Introducing Scientific Concepts to Children*. Slough: NFER.

Smith, D.C. and Neale, D.C. (1989) The construction of subject matter knowledge in primary science teaching. *Teaching and Teacher Education*, 5(1): 1–20.

Smith, R.G. (1999) Piecing it all together: student teachers building their repertoires in primary science. *Teaching and Teacher Education*, 15(1): 301–14.

Summers, M. (1992) Improving primary school teachers' understanding of science concepts: theory into practice. *International Journal of Science Education*, 14(1): 25–40.

Wragg, E.C., Bennett, S.N. and Carré, C.G. (1989) Primary teachers and the National Curriculum. *Research Papers in Education*, 4(3): 17–37.

Managing science teachers' development

6

Justin Dillon

Introduction

Research into learning processes is *only* useful if teachers are able to make use of new ideas in their lessons. And the gap between research and implementation is a wide one to bridge. Without an understanding of how teachers develop and how that development is managed, the findings of many of the studies reported in the rest of this book will be of little use. There *are* examples of research findings influencing curriculum design at a national or regional level, but curriculum change on its own is not necessarily the most satisfactory method of improving classroom practice. Empowering teachers to develop their own understanding about students' learning and to try out their ideas for improvement are, as many of the authors of this volume would agree, more likely to succeed.

Teacher development is a management responsibility. Research into teacher development has built up a useful body of knowledge but what we lack is a critical understanding and a theory of the management of teacher development. This chapter argues, with the aid of an empirical study, that research into the management of teacher development is as essential as research into student learning. In this chapter I draw on research in schools in England to critique some existing models of teacher development management and to argue for a more appropriate model. Through studying the micropolitics of different school science departments, a picture of the complexity of managing teacher development emerges. The analysis of the data, and the theoretical perspective taken throughout the research, derives from the work of Hoyle (1982) and Ball (1987, 1991). The research was co-supervised by John Head and Ros Driver.

A review of the research literature in this field (Dillon, in preparation) indicates that there are many factors that might encourage successful teacher development, including:

- initial disturbance or dissatisfaction;
- time to reflect on existing strategies;
- an evidence base of successful teaching strategies based on models of learning;
- a source of new ideas;
- an opportunity to work with colleagues;
- coaching and mutual support;
- appraisal;
- encouragement from managers;
- a feeling of personal growth;
- a sense of ownership of innovation.

However, it appears to me that few, if any, of these factors are present for many teachers. Furthermore, this appears to be the case in many other countries around the world. What is presented later in this chapter is a series of empirically derived issues that raise questions about any notion held by policymakers, researchers or teacher educators that teacher change is likely to be systematic, fruitful or, indeed, achievable. Data from my own study (Dillon, in preparation) will be used to illustrate why I have a deep sense of concern that many of the good ideas in the rest of this book might have minimal impact on tomorrow's students. The implications of these findings stand in bleak contrast to the optimism frequently displayed by researchers into learning processes.

Management and the English context

The main thrust of government change in England has been on the curriculum and on assessment, as if they were the major influences on what teachers do in classrooms. These changes have been influenced by policy borrowing between countries including Australia, South Africa, New Zealand and the USA. In England, the introduction of a national curriculum, nationwide testing and rigorous inspection have had major impacts on many aspects of life in schools, particularly on management practices. Moves towards more accountability in education have led to measures, often borrowed from business management, aimed at improving schools – for example, appraisal, target setting, total quality management and performance management.

How can we make sense of what happens as policy becomes practice? Management usually involves one or more people getting their own way sooner or later – the social practices of interacting, deciding, influencing and negotiating. Micropolitics, as Ball (1991: 190) writes, involves establishing a 'set of analytical tools – power, goal diversity, ideological disputation, conflicts, political activity and control – which can be employed in specific settings towards the understanding of social practices'. Micropolitics recognizes that interaction between individuals and between individuals and institutions can usefully be interpreted as being manifestations of issues concerned with power and control: 'micropolitics is a system for making sense of the complexity of organisational life' (Ball 1991: 189). Reay (1998: 179), writing about the English education scene, argues that the: 'current political and discursive climate requires an analysis which stresses the influences of the structural just as strongly as the more familiar emphases on the agency of individual teachers'. The key issue here is the importance of individual teachers' relationships with individual institutions.

Most English secondary schools operate a hierarchical management structure with a headteacher, deputy headteachers, senior teachers and heads of department (HoDs). Usually, all management positions are advertised nationally although internal, unadvertised promotion is possible. It is not unusual for a teacher with five years' experience to consider themselves ready for promotion to a post of responsibility. Such posts usually merit higher salaries, and often involve a reduction in teaching hours.

Science departments usually include biologists, chemists and physicists, although some schools maintain separate departments for each science. As science departments are large, often around ten teachers, it is common to find science staff with paid responsibilities for aspects of departmental management (for example, assessment, or for a particular stage of the curriculum).

The HoD, once seen as the lead professional, has traditionally had a range of tasks, responsibilities and roles. The majority of the tasks during the 1970s and 1980s were administrative, however the job of the HoD has changed and a greater emphasis on teacher development, as a means to raise standards, has emerged. Turner (1996) asks whether the roles and tasks of a subject HoD in secondary schools in England and Wales is 'a neglected area of research' and comments that 'ERIC [Educational Resources Information Centre] searches have revealed a fragmented literature which can be considered to be prescriptive and empirical, making little attempt to link with or be informed by available theoretical ideas' (p. 204). Turner adds that 'there is a dearth of literature relevant to the HoDs influence on classroom processes' (p. 215). The absence of practitioner understanding and use of the limited ideas about teacher development has created a vacuum into which governments have been able to impose narrow, technicist standards for heads of department.

The Teacher Training Agency (TTA – a government body) has produced 'standards' that 'set out the knowledge, understanding, skills and attributes' that 'define expertise in subject leadership and are designed to guide the professional development of teachers aiming to increase their effectiveness as subject leaders' (TTA 1997: 2). 'Key outcomes of subject leadership' include 'teachers who: work well together as a team; support the aims of the subject . . . [and] are dedicated to improving standards of teaching and learning' (p. 4). Training for middle management (i.e. the layer between senior management and classroom teachers) has reflected the move away from skills, such as time management, towards person management.

The setting of national standards for HoDs reflects a particular model of teacher development. The standards are borne out of a perception that improvements were needed in middle management in schools. The school inspectorate, the office for Standards in Education (Ofsted) reported that 'about one-fifth of schools have weaknesses in middle management which frustrate developments'. Other points to emerge from Ofsted inspections were that:

- too many HoDs take the narrow view that their responsibility is for managing resources rather than people;
- the quality of curriculum development within a subject department is dependent upon the energy and leadership of the HoD and varies considerably; and
- monitoring to see that agreed procedures are being used and evaluated to discover their effects on the performance of pupils is poorly developed.

(quoted in OHMCI 1997: 1)

The model of teacher development management implicit here is that HoDs and their staff agree what to do then implement changes in their teaching; HoDs monitor the use of new strategies and their evaluation and, as a result of the whole process, pupil performance rises. This model of teacher development and its management seems to ignore what we already know about teachers and teaching.

Teacher knowledge

Teacher development implies changing teacher knowledge, thinking and practice. Schön (1987), who was influenced by thinkers as diverse as Tolstoy, Dewey, Piaget and Wittgenstein, developed an epistemology of action, of 'knowing-in-action'. Carter (1992: 110–11) summarizes the major lines of thinking about teacher knowledge in the field to have emerged in recent years:

- teachers' knowledge is practical and 'contextualized' in the sense that it is knowledge of the common dilemmas teachers face in classroom life;
- teachers' disciplinary knowledge affects how teachers organize instruction and represent the curriculum to students;
- teachers' knowledge is task-specific and event-structured;
- teachers' knowledge is constructed and invented from repeated experience in accomplishing tasks or close approximations of tasks in a domain.

For Schön, knowledge resides in performance (and therefore is non-propositional) and is highly individual. Knowledge-in-action is built up in two ways: reflection-on-action (systematic and deliberate thinking back over one's actions or 'feedback') and reflection-in-action, 'a process with non-logical features, a process that is prompted by experience and over which we have limited control' or 'backtalk' (Munby and Russell 1992: 3). Russell and Munby (1991: 164–5) refer to reflection-in-action as 'hearing' or 'seeing' the process differently; I would argue that this empowers teachers by giving them greater awareness. Thus teachers, particularly beginners, are encouraged to engage in systematic reflection (sometimes couched in terms such as 'evaluate your lesson') as well as being given opportunities to practise teaching skills such as identifying problems that children have and adapting their teaching strategies during lessons.

Much of the literature about teacher education focuses on reflection-on-action (for example, Baird *et al.* 1991). Reflection-on-action 'involves careful consideration of familiar data' whereas 'reflection-in-action presents the data . . . in a novel frame' (Russell and Munby 1991: 164–5). Erickson points out that, 'by far the most common and problematic issue identified by all of Schön's critics is the dichotomy that he establishes between a "technical rationality" and a "reflective" approach to problem solving in a practice setting' (Erickson 1988: 196). The normative standards of the TTA, while playing lip-service to the reflective practitioner model, actually drive teachers towards technical rationality. Clandinin (1992), in the context of preservice teachers, describes a much more individual and empowering process – that of narrative inquiry which leads, through reflection, to the development of 'personal practical knowledge' (p. 125). In telling stories of teacher education, Clandinin wishes to: 'highlight the tensions between personal and institutional narratives, between university and cooperating teachers' stories and student teachers' stories, and through these stories to foster reflection on the ways individuals and institutions construct teacher education' (p. 136).

The major responsibility for 'highlighting the tensions' or for driving practising teachers towards the norm seems to lie, in most schools, with the HoD. What is missing from the literature is much by way of 'reflection on the ways individuals and institutions construct teacher education' (Clandinin 1992: 136). Without that knowledge, any attempt to improve learning will founder on the rocks of the great barrier of implementation.

Models of teacher development

Studies of teacher development, which might be expected to inform management practices, have tended to focus on aspects of the process or on outcomes. Models of teacher development have generally failed to take into account personal aspects of the developed and the developer. The complexity of the contexts that science teachers find themselves in necessitates a more detailed and individual approach to teacher development than has often been the case. A notable exception is the work of Beverley Bell and John Gilbert, who promote a social constructivist view of learning as teacher development.

The New Zealand science teachers in Bell and Gilbert's study were involved in a three-year research project, 'Learning in Science'. The researchers provide a holistic model of teacher development involving professional, social and personal development (Bell and Gilbert 1996). *Professional development* involves new knowledge and skills – the development of pedagogical content knowledge (Shulman 1987) or the application of a psychological theory of learning. *Social development* relies on the development of an awareness of the value of collaborative learning and working. *Personal development* involves a transition from acceptance of an aspect of teaching as problematic to a feeling of empowerment resulting from the success of new strategies in a supportive environment. What is not made explicit, however, are the implications of the model for teacher managers and the extent to which HoDs can make use of such models.

One of the major thrusts of my argument is that individuality and individualism are paramount to developing an understanding about how and why HoDs assist in the development of their teaching staff. Bell and Gilbert's normative model of teacher development reflects the importance of the individual in the process of teacher development. But any normative model involving human agency and institutional context walks a tightrope. As Gunter (1997: 110) cautions: 'the management of institutions can be improved, but the borderline between having an agenda of options and presenting a prescription is so blurred that it is easy to slip into the latter rather than participate in the debate about the former'.

What is needed, if teacher development is not to slip into prescription is an understanding and a valuing of the contexts within individual teachers and their managers' work. With the guidance of John Head and Ros Driver, I engaged in a small-scale study of individual middle managers' roles and responsibilities.

The research

The research, briefly described here, was based on the premise that individual HoDs themselves can identify some of their needs and can evaluate the likely success of strategies. A group of nine middle managers in science departments, chosen to provide a wide range of school situations, experience and style, were 'active partners' in the research process, the major function of which was to research the effectiveness of a variety of strategies in their own context. One step in this process was the identification of the contexts within which the participants operated.

Sample

The number of participating schools was chosen because it was thought that nine would provide data from a variety of contexts (see below) while allowing for drop-outs. Consideration was given to their gender; experience of management; school location (inner city vs. suburban) and the perceived school success (as indicated by Ofsted reports, league table positions, value added scores, etc.).

The majority of the participants were already known to me. As Ball (1987: 178) argues in *The Micro-Politics of the School*:

> I needed a degree of trust from my respondents. I needed them to take me into their confidence. I wanted them to share their folk-knowledge of their institution with me. In some respects I was operating close to the level of gossip and personal criticism – the informal aspects of organisation, which are ritually referred to but rarely analysed in organisational theory.

Data collection

A preliminary phase of interviews and informal discussions with inspectors, advisers, senior managers, HoDs and teachers took place over a period of about three years. These are not reported on in any detail here. A series of themes emerged from the analysis of those interviews and these formed the basis of the interview *aide-mémoire* for HoDs during the second phase of data collection, which took place over a period lasting from 1995–8. The data required were collected predominantly through semi-structured interviews about what participants did, why they took certain actions and how they evaluated their success. All interviews were tape-recorded and transcribed. A range of school and departmental documentation was collected, usually volunteered by the participants to illustrate their practice.

Recent inspection reports were available for all the schools in which the participants worked. They provided a variety of data, which informed the study. For example, they commented on a school's context, examination performance, relative levels of attainment, resource provision, leadership and management issues, and on individual departments. In England, inspection reports are public documents and are available on the internet.

Analysis

The interview transcripts were analysed using progressively focused coding techniques (Glaser and Strauss 1967) to establish categories which formed the basis of an analysis involving 'fragmenting' the data (Strauss 1987). The transcripts were broken down into large 'thematic chunks' and pattern coding (Miles and Huberman 1994: 69) was used to identify emergent themes. The 'constant comparative' method of data analysis used (Ball 1991: 182–7) was chosen because of the potential for initial research to produce ideas and questions which could inform further data collection and analysis. As the research developed, the use of 'progressive focusing' (Ball 1991: 173) was used to identify themes and patterns in the data. Strauss (1987: 17) refers to coding 'beginning to yield conceptually dense theory' and this would be a good description of the process that was undertaken.

Issues in the management of teacher development

In the light of the research outlined above, and other studies not specifically referred to here, various factors such as time, evidence, encouragement and feedback, might be expected to encourage successful teacher development. However, for many teachers, few, if any, of these factors are present.

Initial disturbance or dissatisfaction

Teachers in Davis' study (1996) and in Bell and Gilbert's (1996) research were able to move forward only after realizing that they were dissatisfied with their teaching. Dissatisfaction can come through direct or indirect feedback from students, criticism by colleagues or inspectors, or through reflection. However, in a climate of managerialism and accountability, in which salary advancement might depend on successful appraisal, teachers are under pressure to deny that they have problems.

Another problem faced by teacher developers is that in departments which have experienced staff, successful students and an established social structure, it is very difficult to create a sense of dissatisfaction with existing practice. Creating constructive dissatisfaction is not a skill that is taught to most managers. It requires confidence on the part of the teachers, trust in their manager and time to stop and think.

Time to reflect on existing strategies

'Reflective thinking . . . involves (1) a state of doubt, hesitation, perplexity, mental difficulty, in which thinking originates, and (2) an act of searching, hunting, inquiring, to find material that will resolve the doubt, settle and dispose of the perplexity' (Dewey 1933: 12).

One of the most common problems facing middle managers is that the majority of their time in school is spent not managing but teaching and administering. There is an air of busyness in English schools: lessons are short, transfers between lessons involve maximum simultaneous upheaval, morning and lunchtime breaks are rushed, and meetings are held at the end of the day when people are most tired. The ethos lies somewhere between a Victorian workhouse and a 1960s Detroit car factory.

For many teachers, and especially managers, stress caused by lack of time is just part of the job. Management activities are more likely to be disrupted by teacher absence, short-term crises or time constraints, than by other 'businesses'. Anne, one of the HoDs that I worked with, graphically illustrated the busyness and stress characterizing her role:

> Oh God, today has been a really bad day. I've been in tears today. That hasn't happened for a long time. It's been horrible. I've just felt that all day today I have been like ... I get strings of children sent to me consistently for behaviour ... I'd been on the go since eight this morning ... consistently following up cases of bad behaviour, right, I taught two lessons this morning and then I observed Gerard after break. And that wasn't too bad and then it started really badly about 12.00 p.m. and I spent the whole of my own lunchtime dealing with this awful class and all they were saying was what rights they had. Ah, you know, the street talk and none of them owned up to this and it made me feel sick.

The busyness that characterises English schools has its effects on the amount of time available for staff development. As Mike, another HoD that I worked with explained:

> It has become a major problem that the ten staff have ten views plus feedback and I haven't put my targets in for this year. In fact I haven't seen the managers this year. So I've seen everybody else but not the managers. That is a problem ... lack of time.

An evidence base of successful teaching strategies based on models of learning

If lack of time to manage in school is limited, there is also limited time to collect ideas about good practice outside school. Despite efforts to identify good practice at classroom, department and school level, the existing knowledge base is highly contested and strategies for measuring effectiveness are either too simplistic or too unreliable to be more than starting points in teacher development work.

Lack of time to find out about new ideas limits the discourse of middle managers to repeating the rhetoric of their own managers: targets, performance, appraisal and improvement. Managers' abilities to describe what is required in concrete terms at anything more than a general level ('students on task'; 'safe environment') can lead to frustration on the part of teachers who are vague about what is required and on the part of managers who feel helpless to provide real help.

A source of new ideas

'Better teaching', according to Baird, involves the teacher knowing more, being more aware and making better decisions – all in all, being more 'metacognitive'. Improving teaching involves 'fundamental change in one's attitudes, perceptions, conceptions, beliefs, abilities and behaviours' (Baird 1992: 33). Evidence from another study (Dillon *et al.* 2000) indicates that teachers' sources of information about good practice are limited and have diminished with the demise of many of the local advisory teachers and teachers' centres.

An opportunity to work with colleagues

Teachers in a recent study (Dillon *et al.* 2000) expressed a great desire to talk to teachers from other schools and saw the potential benefits of collaboration. Teachers felt that opportunities for professional development were limited and, though useful, hardly likely to make a major impact on their performance. However, teachers usually work in isolation from their colleagues. Lesson preparation and marking, two of the major non-classroom based tasks, are invariably carried out solo and often at home. Participants in my study reported that with the increase in administrative tasks, more detailed assessment practices and a prescriptive curriculum, the time and motivation to work collaboratively have diminished.

Coaching and mutual support

Joyce and Showers' (1988) meta-analysis of the effectiveness of in-service education showed that success depends on *long term*, classroom-focused coaching involving feedback. However, I found little evidence that teachers watch each other frequently or systematically, and when they do it is often part of a formal, short term, appraisal system. As one HoD, Anne, put it:

> The plan . . . was that each member of staff was observed twice by two separate people . . . I'd be looking at doing it termly. And really, if everybody was involved then it's a case of doing one and maybe being looked at once. I started off by doing 'buddy pairs' . . . so that you saw and watched somebody else so that the two of you can work together. Then you can change the 'buddy pairs' . . . Or you might say, I can't work out how to . . . do Science 1,[1] the investigative work, you might match up with somebody then who'd be a bit stronger.

Appraisal

Appraisal of teachers by managers became statutory in England in the 1990s although it has not had the impact that was originally hoped. Formal appraisal usually involves focused observation and other data-gathering followed by discussion. In reality, because HoDs teach for the majority of the week, the opportunities for appraisal are limited. The idea of mutual observation is also becoming more common although the time constraints for teachers without significant responsibility are even greater than for HoDs. Mike, one of the HoDs in my study, said:

> I try to observe everybody at least once a year formally. There's the book monitoring: you can see what the sort of standard of the students' work is. There's the homework setting and the defaults from that. And I think you can pick up more when people put in no defaulters than when they put in a whole list. And so it's a question of saying, well didn't you get any defaulters last week? And then, if they say no, you say, well what did you set, you know, have you collected it in, got it marked. Why are you getting no defaulters and I'm getting about half a dozen?

Teachers are able to deploy a range of strategies to block, deny or distort feedback from the rare observations that they receive from inspectors or other colleagues. Ironically, the changes in the curriculum and the assessment policies in England, which have failed to shake the reliance on memorization as a learning strategy, have failed to create much dissatisfaction in teachers' own practice. Teachers are in danger of becoming resistant to criticism as a strategy for maintaining professional pride. One of the interviewees, Alan, an experienced HoD, was questioned on his forthcoming inspection:

> Well, senior management say they're going to get all the 'top bods'[2] in to tell us what to do but I think some of us, and I think myself

included, are saying 'well you know, we'll do what we can but we're going to carry on doing our proper job and not let Ofsted get in the way too much'.

The issue of being told 'what to do' by local education authority staff is a concrete example of the 'discursive working of the new managerialism' (Reay 1998: 188). It is as though education is a Russian doll, with Ofsted (which controls the national inspection system), local education authorities, heads, HoDs and teachers being seen as separate dolls each constrained by the rigidity of the biggest doll.

Encouragement from managers

Evidence from research carried out a few years ago into the success of teacher education (Adey *et al.* 1995) indicated the importance of support from senior management in a school. Getting the balance right between support and pressure is a key aspect of teacher development. Now, however, changes in the role of the HoD seem to have shifted the balance more towards pressuring rather than supporting. HoDs are now 'proxy-managers', carrying out school policy (and government policy) at a distance and using appraisal as a means of quality assurance. As one of the HoDs indicated, the period of adjustment for this process has been minimal, the training variable and the penalties for failure high:

> [we] are more accountable than [we] ever were before. Changes are taking place . . . overnight and we're having to . . . implement them more or less as we speak and there are so many changes that people are threatened by that . . . especially the young teachers.

A feeling of personal growth

Huberman's (1989) work with Swiss teachers indicates that those who were allowed to engage in 'tinkering' with resources and teaching styles were likely to be 'satisfied' later in their career. Huberman identified other factors that, it might be argued, were predictors of teacher satisfaction – the ability to 'make small spontaneous role shifts when one began to feel stale' (quoted in Ruddock 1992: 166) and satisfaction in recognizing that they had a significant impact on student learning. In the light of the issues raised above, many teachers' opportunities for personal growth appear to be limited. Teachers, particularly in small schools, are faced with increasing isolation and pressure, which are more likely to result in feelings of inadequacy rather than growth.

A sense of ownership of innovation

Until recently it was taken for granted that teachers needed to feel committed to change for it to be implemented. Some research has questioned that necessity (Adey *et al.* 1995). However, personal control over the change process should be a desirable situation if only on democratic rather than psychological grounds. Ownership can be exerted through a range of strategies from physical ownership of resources to active participation in decision making.

Gold and Evans (1998: 22) express the view that 'excessive micropolitical activity within a school may be indicative of blocked or ineffective decision-making routes'. They go on to say that 'whatever the cause of the excessive micropolitical activity, those with management responsibilities within a school need to be aware when they are overactive and to make some basic decisions about whether to use or ignore the unofficial structures'. However, it must be borne in mind that: 'Decision-making is not an abstract rational process which can be plotted on an organisational chart; it is a political process, it is the stuff of micro-political activity' (Ball 1987: 26). This position does not seem to be recognized by those giving advice to HoDs (see for example Gold 1998).

Gender

The issue of gender in management, which was not one of the factors listed earlier, has been studied but is still little understood. As more women become managers and more men become managed, there is a continuing need to appreciate the gender issues involved. My feeling is that research into gender issues needs to focus more than it has upon providing rich descriptions and critical analysis of the situations in which women find themselves as managers. Stereotypical views of women as managers are still too common. One of my participants articulated a view that is rarely found in the literature:

> I'm very careful how I deal with the men 'cos I think . . . and I'm not saying this in front of you in any way to insult male populations, but I feel that with men you've got to be careful. They're not used to women managing them a lot of the time and um . . . and I don't want to ruin their egos. I don't want to denigrate them and make them feel small. But sometimes they see me with the kids and how strong and tough I am with them. Not necessarily succeeding, but I am tough with them and I suppose maybe they feel a little bit threatened by that . . . So I do, I do deal with the men differently, the women I tend to have a great relationship with. They just accept everything. I have no problems.

Another female HoD, Kelly, spoke of the differences between men and women:

> I think women tend to be more flexible and more adaptable in terms of what they're prepared to accept and do and sometimes see alternative viewpoints, though there are obviously still some women who see something and decide on it. But I think, generally speaking, there are big disadvantages having a woman because quite a few of them have got young children and so they have the commitment to childcare that men don't always have.

Final comments

I have argued that research into the management of teacher development is essential if the work done on understanding student learning is to be effective. Our knowledge of how individual teachers develop in schools is tenuous and ill-defined. I have outlined, from the literature, a range of factors that might be considered important in maximizing individual teacher development. However, using the findings of my own in-depth work, it seems clear that substantial barriers stand in the way of progress. Teachers with management responsibilities often lack the time to reflect on existing strategies; the evidence base of successful teaching strategies based on established models of learning is weak; sources of new ideas and opportunities to work with colleagues are few and far between; and, most importantly, the current climate of accountability in schools, which is designed to raise standards, actually serves to create a climate of stress and suspicion.

What can other countries learn from this work? The message is clear: models of teacher development that are based on simplistic, normative, technicist ideas are unlikely to be effective. Teacher development needs support from managers but if teaching is complex then managing teachers is even more so. Teachers and their managers need to see development as multi-faceted, progressive and dependent on individual personalities, psychology and politics – both macro and micro. These lessons apply in education systems where there are few middle managers as well as in those, like England, where there are many.

Management is partly about confidence as well as competence. The inadequate training that HoDs receive, the lack of time that they have to manage, the ethical dilemmas facing them, the pressure on them from parents, heads, inspectors and colleagues all conspire to make the job difficult, unsatisfactory and impossible to finish. The job of the head of science is possibly the most demanding of all middle managers and there is little sign that this will change in the future.

Notes

1 This refers to a particular section of the National Curriculum followed in Anne's school.
2 i.e. staff from the local education authority who have a role in monitoring standards in schools.

References

Adey, P.S., Dillon, J.S. and Simon, S.A. (1995) School management and the effect of INSET. Paper presented at the European Conference on Educational Research, Bath, 14–17 September.

Baird, J.R. (1992) Collaborative reflection, systematic enquiry, better teaching, in T. Russell and H. Munby (eds) *Teachers and Teaching: From Classroom to Reflection*, pp. 33–48. London: Falmer.

Baird, J.R., Fensham, P.J., Gunstone, R.F. and White, R.T. (1991) The importance of reflection in improving science teaching and learning. *Journal of Research in Science Teaching*, 28(2): 163–82.

Ball, S.J. (1987) *The Micro-Politics of the School*. London: Routledge.

Ball, S.J. (1991) Power, conflict, micropolitics and all that, in G. Walford (ed.) *Doing Educational Research*, pp. 166–92. London: Routledge.

Bell, B. and Gilbert, J. (1996) *Teacher Development: A Model from Science Education*. London: Falmer.

Carter, K. (1992) Creating cases for the development of teacher knowledge, in T. Russell and H. Munby (eds) *Teachers and Teaching: From Classroom to Reflection*, pp. 109–23. London: Falmer.

Clandinin, D.J. (1992) Narrative and story in teacher education, in T. Russell and H. Munby (eds) *Teachers and Teaching: From Classroom to Reflection*, pp. 124–37. London: Falmer.

Davis, N.T. (1996) Looking in the mirror: teachers' use of autobiography and action research to improve practice. *Research in Science Education*, 26(1): 23–32.

Dewey, J. (1933) *How We Think: A Restatement of the Relation of Reflective Thinking in the Educative Process*. Chicago: Henry Regnery.

Dillon, J. (in preparation) Unpublished PhD thesis. King's College London.

Dillon, J., Osborne, J., Fairbrother, B. and Kurina, L. (2000) *A Study Into the Professional Views and Needs of Science Teachers in Primary and Secondary Schools in England*. London: King's College London.

Erickson, G. (1988) Explorations in the field of reflection: directions for future research agendas, in P.P. Grimmett and G.L. Erickson (eds) *Reflection in Teacher Education*, pp. 195–205. New York: Teachers College Press.

Glaser, B.G. and Strauss, A.L. (1967) *The Discovery of Grounded Theory*. Chicago: Aldine.

Gold, A. (1998) *Head of Department: Principles in Practice*. London: Cassell.

Gold, A. and Evans, J. (1998) *Reflecting on School Management*. London: Falmer.

Gunter, H. (1997) *Rethinking Education: The Consequences of Jurassic Management*. London: Cassell.

Hoyle, E. (1982) Micropolitics of educational organizations. *Educational Management and Administration*, 10: 87–98.

Huberman, M. (1989) Teacher development and instructional mastery. Paper presented at the international conference on 'Teacher Development: Policies, Practices and Research', Toronto, Ontario Institute for Studies in Education, February.

Joyce, B. and Showers, B. (1988) *Student Achievement through Staff Development*. New York: Longman.

Miles, M.B. and Huberman, A.M. (1994) *Qualitative Data Analysis*. London: Sage.

Munby, H. and Russell, T. (1992) Frames of reflection: an introduction, in T. Russell and H. Munby (eds) *Teachers and Teaching: From Classroom to Reflection*, pp. 1–8. London: Falmer.

OHMCI (Office of Her Majesty's Chief Inspector of Schools) (1997) *Subject Management in Secondary Schools: Aspects of Good Practice*. London: Ofsted.

Reay, D. (1998) Micro-politics in the 1990s: staff relationships in secondary schooling. *Journal of Education Policy*, 13(2): 179–96.

Ruddock, J. (1992) Practitioner research and programs of initial teacher education, in T. Russell and H. Munby (eds) *Teachers and Teaching: From Classroom to Reflection*, pp. 124–37. London: Falmer.

Russell, T. and Munby, H. (1991) Reframing: the role of experience in developing teachers' professional knowledge, in D.A. Schön (ed.) *The Reflective Turn: Case Studies In and On Educational Practice*, pp. 164–87. New York: Teachers College Press.

Schön, D.A. (1987) *Educating the Reflective Practitioner: Toward a New Design for Teaching and Learning in the Professions*. San Francisco: Josey-Bass.

Shulman, L.S. (1987) Knowledge and teaching: foundations of the new reform. *Harvard Educational Review*, 57(1): 1–22.

Strauss, A.L. (1987) *Qualitative Analysis for Social Scientists*. New York: Cambridge University Press.

TTA (Teacher Training Agency) (1997) *National Standards for Subject Leaders: Annex*. London: TTA.

Turner, C.K. (1996) The roles and tasks of a subject head of department in secondary schools in England and Wales: a neglected area of research. *School Organisation*, 16(2): 203–17.

7 Status as the hallmark of conceptual learning

Peter Hewson and John Lemberger

Introduction

Conceptual change has been an influential idea in science education for more than two decades. Yet for many, the term 'conceptual change' means *only* that one conception replaces or supersedes another; following Hewson (1981) we refer to this as *conceptual exchange*. While any definition of conceptual change must necessarily include the prototypical notion of conceptual exchange, we argue that focusing exclusively on conceptual exchange has limited the opportunities for understanding the full range of conceptual learning. This is so because *status*, an idea built on a conceptual change foundation, can illuminate deep conceptual learning, whether or not it involves conceptual exchange. Such an expanded view has much to contribute at a time when reformers are advocating deep understanding of significant science content, and exploring different approaches, such as modelling and argumentation, that emphasize rational approaches to science learning. In short, we suggest that status is the hallmark of conceptual learning.

What is status?

Status has grown from conceptual change roots. The most widely cited theory of conceptual exchange (or 'accommodation') is that of Posner *et al.* (1982). Their theory focuses on a competition between different conceptions and specifies four conditions for accommodation to occur. The competition may spark *dissatisfaction* with an existing conception. In order for a competitor to be successful, it has to be *intelligible*, initially *plausible*, and suggestive of a *fruitful* research programme. Hewson (1981) drew a distinction between dissatisfaction and the three conditions for success: intelligibility, plausibility and fruitfulness. Dissatisfaction with current conceptions arises when people recognize that they are not as plausible or as fruitful as originally thought – i.e. dissatisfaction is a psychological response to the other, epistemological, conditions. Drawing on the common notion of status as social power, Hewson (1981) suggested that, analogously, status could refer to the intellectual power of a conception for a person considering or holding it. He proposed that the status of that person's conception rises or falls to the extent that its intelligibility, plausibility, and/or fruitfulness respectively increases or decreases within the person's conceptual ecology. Falling status may then lead to dissatisfaction, a psychological state not to be confused with status itself.

Thorley (1990) expanded the status construct. While affirming the essence of Hewson's (1981) original version, his analysis reveals a greater complexity of the components of status and blurs some of its sharp distinctions. It demonstrates that, while originally intelligibility, plausibility, and fruitfulness were portrayed as forming a unidimensional sequence, intelligibility and plausibility each have a multidimensional character. While the essences of intelligibility and plausibility are captured respectively by 'representability' and 'reality/truth', both also have a consistency dimension that makes it impossible to draw clearly distinct boundaries between them, even though the endpoints of the continuum are readily distinguishable. Table 7.1 presents a set of categories, adapted from Thorley (1990), that we used for analysing status in the following example of genetics learning. Categorizations of the empirical data presented in all the following status analyses are included in brackets. The explicit inclusion or exclusion of an element of status is indicated, respectively, with a + or – sign. For example, (+PROMISE) indicates that a conception was regarded as having promise, and (–PAST EXPERIENCE) indicates that it was not consistent with past experience.

Empirical evidence of status-related conceptual learning

Empirical evidence of status-related conceptual learning was found in a study of a Madison-area senior high school genetics course (Lemberger 1995). Here, students' conceptualizations were driven by status considerations; they cannot be characterized as conceptual exchange, but rather as conceptual *expansion*. The course, an elective genetics class in the school's science curriculum, used a model-building, problem-solving approach in order to provide students with some of the experience of working in a scientific research laboratory. The philosophy, early design and development of the course are fully described in Johnson and Stewart (1990).

Briefly, at the start of the course the teacher presented students with Mendel's simple dominance model of genetic inheritance. A computer program, Genetics Construction Kit (GCK) (Jungck and Calley 1985), simulated populations of fruit flies that were used to demonstrate how simple dominance works in a population of organisms. Students, working in

Table 7.1   Status analysis categories (from Thorley 1990)

Intelligibility: representational modes

INTELLIGIBILITY ANALOGY	Analogy or metaphor used to represent conception
IMAGE	Use of pictures or diagrams to represent conception
EXEMPLAR	Real-world exemplar of conception
LANGUAGE	Linguistic or symbolic representation of conception

Plausibility: consistency factors

OTHER KNOWLEDGE	'Reasoned' consistency with other high-status knowledge
LAB EXPERIENCE	Consistency with laboratory data or observations
PAST EXPERIENCE	Particular events consistent with conception
EPISTEMOLOGY	Consistency with epistemological commitments
METAPHYSICS	Reference to ontological status of objects, or metaphysical beliefs about how the world really is
PLAUSIBILITY ANALOGY	Another conception or phenomenon is invoked as analogous to the first conception or phenomenon

Plausibility: other factors

REAL MECHANISM	Causal mechanism invoked

Fruitfulness

POWER	Conception has wide applicability
PROMISE	Looking forward to what new conception might do
COMPETE	Two competing conceptions are explicitly compared

research groups of three or four, were required to decide, through computer-simulated crosses of fruit flies, which of the two alleles was dominant. After the students had gained competence in this task, the teacher used GCK to provide new populations of fruit flies not operating under the rules of simple dominance. GCK produced phenotypic data that conflicted with the expectations of Mendel's model – i.e. the data were anomalous. Students were expected to revise Mendel's model of simple dominance to explain the data generated by GCK from these other crosses. In order to do so, students had to recognize anomalous data, become dissatisfied with currently held conceptions of genes, and revise old conceptions or develop new ones to explain the anomalies. To assist model revision, the teacher introduced the following representation of models (exemplified with the simple dominance model):

- Model objects and their frequency in the model (for example, different alleles in the population = 2, variations per trait = 2).
- Inheritance pattern (for example, when alleles 1 and 2 interact, 1 is dominant and 2 is recessive).
- Matching of allele combinations (genotypes) to variations (phenotypes) (for example, [1,1] and [1,2] code for variation A).
- Outcomes of all possible crosses expressed in both genotypes and phenotypes (for example, variation A × variation B produces variation A [1,1] × [2,2] = [1,2]).

To revise a model, students changed the frequency of objects in the model and/or the inheritance patterns. They could then carry these changes through into genotype–phenotype matching and the detailing of all possible cross-outcomes in the model.

A solution to the problem posed by anomalous phenotypic data required students to pay attention to several features of the data including:

- number of variations of a trait in the population;
- outcomes of crosses between individuals with different variations; and
- numerical ratios of variations produced in different crosses.

Understanding a model of inheritance means matching each of these features to the model as previously outlined. Without this understanding, a person would not be able to identify phenotypic data in a new population as anomalous. Once an anomaly had been identified, two general problem-solving strategies were available. Empirically, a person could generate more data by crossing selected individuals; this could be done with varying degrees of systematicity. Conceptually, a person could construct different models of inheritance and use these to explain existing data, or predict future data. The quality of these models could be a major factor in influencing whether crosses were random or systematic. A final component of successful problem-solving would be the ongoing evaluation of various steps along the solution path as the basis on which further steps are taken. We claim that this evaluation is best understood in terms of status consideration.

The first and second rounds of problem-solving used populations governed, respectively, by co-dominant and multiple alleles inheritance patterns. The following empirical data is drawn from the second round. The first problem-solving round served as a necessary prelude to the second, because it provided both a relatively straightforward example of problem-solving and another model of inheritance (co-dominance) to accompany Mendel's model. Understanding features of this round will help in interpreting the empirical data.

Anomaly recognition for the co-dominance round required that students held a beginning conception of gene expressed as '2 alleles with 1 dominant over 2; combinations [1,1] and [1,2] both produce phenotype (A); combination [2,2] produces phenotype (B)' – the Mendel (or simple dominance) model. No matter what combination of the two alleles the parents provide, no more than two phenotypic variations (A and B) can be expressed in the offspring. Thus, when a third phenotypic variation (C) appeared, this counted as anomalous data. By the end of the co-dominance round the students had resolved the anomaly by explaining the third variation as the product of the heterozygous combination of alleles [1,2]. This model was supported by an expanded gene conception constructed by the students as a result of the problem-solving process (Lemberger 1995) and expressed as '2 alleles with 1 dominant over 2; combinations [1,1] and [1,2] both produce phenotype (A); combination [2,2] produces phenotype (B); *or* 2 alleles with neither 1 nor 2 dominant over the other; combinations [1,1], [1,2] and [2,2] produce different phenotypes'. Students commonly referred to the second, co-dominant, part of this conception as the Dwarf model. This expanded gene conception is capable of explaining field populations with either two or three phenotypes.

Multiple alleles

The following data are from one group in this classroom, the Womendel group, consisting of Rita, Anna and Jean. At the end of the previous (co-dominance) round the group was able to solve problems with two and three phenotypic variations. To do this they had expanded their conception of 'gene' to encompass both Mendel and Dwarf models; both of these are two-allele models. The problem in the new, multiple alleles, round involved four phenotypic variations. A successful solution of the problem required a further expansion of their gene conception to include a multiple alleles model, i.e. '3 alleles: interactions between alleles are either simple dominant or co-dominant'. Note that this is a 3-allele model. In what follows this is termed the *targeted conceptual expansion*. The group's path to a solution of the multiple alleles problem is summarized in Table 7.2.

Table 7.2 Summary of episodes, tentative conceptions and status elements used in multiple alleles problem-solving round

Episodes	Tentative conceptions	Status elements
Anomaly recognition and initial problem construction	2 alleles: 1 dominant over 2, *or* 2 alleles: neither dominant over the other	Fruitfulness (−POWER)
Generating two-allele models to be explored and accepted or rejected based on elements of status	2 sets of paired alleles: one pair from each parent	Fruitfulness (+PROMISE) Plausibility (−METAPHYSICS) Fruitfulness (−POWER)
	2 alleles: allele interaction dependent on gender of parent	Fruitfulness (+PROMISE) Fruitfulness (−POWER)
	3 alleles: offspring receives only 1 allele from each parent	Fruitfulness (+PROMISE) Not explored, but see next episode
	1 or 2 alleles: offspring receives 1 or 0 alleles from each parent	Fruitfulness (+PROMISE) Plausibility (−METAPHYSICS) Fruitfulness (−POWER)
Accepting the necessity of more than two alleles	3 or 4 alleles	Fruitfulness (+COMPETE) Plausibility (+P ANALOGY) (+OTHER KNOWLEDGE)
The three allele/four allele dilemma	3 alleles: all act in simple dominant fashion	Fruitfulness (−PROMISE)
	3 alleles: all act in co-dominant fashion	Fruitfulness (−PROMISE)
	4 alleles: all act in simple dominant fashion	Fruitfulness (+PROMISE) (−POWER) (+COMPETE)
	4 alleles: all act in co-dominant fashion	Fruitfulness (−PROMISE)
Constraints imposed by ontology	3 alleles: interactions between alleles are either simple dominant or co-dominant	Plausibility (−METAPHYSICS) Intelligibility (+LANGUAGE) Fruitfulness (+PROMISE)
The intelligibility problem	3 or 4 alleles: some interact in simple dominant fashion *and* some interact in both simple dominant and co-dominant fashion	Intelligibility (+IMAGES) Plausibility (+LABORATORY EXPERIENCE) Fruitfulness (+POWER)

Anomaly recognition and initial problem construction

The students inspected the initial field sample and immediately noticed that they had four variations of wing shape: gull, jammed, blistery, and balloon.[1] Since their current gene conception could not explain four phenotypic variations, they regarded four variations as an anomaly, and interpreted the problem as one of imagining a gene that could produce four variations of wing shape. They began work by crossing fruit flies from the field population They had no model in mind, but hoped one would emerge from the data they were generating. After a few crosses nothing had emerged, and the group had little idea what a new model might look like. As Rita commented, 'We can't think of much of anything'.

The teacher talked with the group about reworking their old models of simple dominance and co-dominance by changing model parameters such as number of alleles per population or number of alleles per individual. The teacher's influence shows in this end-of-day journal entry for 16 February 1994: 'We began Model 2 [multiple alleles]. There are 4 variations per trait. We are having problems imagining what the allele (i.e. gene) would be like. After crossing 2 homozygous parents for each variation we are seeing some similarities to both the Dwarf and the Mendel model'.

Status

The group members accepted that their current expanded conception of gene was not consistent with four variations of wing shape. Implicit in their determination is their unstated conception of 'gene', namely '2 alleles: 1 dominant over 2 *or* 2 alleles: neither dominant over the other'. Also, their representation of the problem at this stage was partial: they focused on the anomalous number of variations, but did not address the patterns of cross data. That came later. Their recognition of the anomaly was a status judgement: the lack of power of their conception demonstrated to them its lack of fruitfulness; this created dissatisfaction and the need to look for a different solution (–POWER). The group didn't exchange their conception of gene for another (at this point, they had no alternative), nor did they abandon the models their gene conception supported. Instead the group, guided by their teacher, sought to expand their conception of gene to include a third model with an inheritance pattern that could explain observations beyond the status boundaries of their current gene conception.

Generating 2-allele models to be explored and accepted or rejected based on the elements of status

The group began to consider the number of alleles needed to explain four phenotypes while continuing to collect cross data, and proposed and rejected four different ideas (see Table 7.2). First, Rita suggested that offspring should get 2 alleles from each parent. Anna, however, objected that 'you don't get 2 alleles from each parent'. The basis for the objection is that meiosis determines that each parent contributes only 1 allele per trait to its offspring. Second, the group wondered if the phenotypic expression of alleles as [2,1] could be different than [1,2], the order indicating that it mattered which parent had contributed the allele. This was rejected because the group thought 'it would be too hard a problem'. Third, the group suggested adding a third allele (3) to the population. They wondered if this was possible and decided it was, while recognizing that each child could only have 2 alleles, one from each parent. Before exploring this further, they were distracted by a fourth suggestion from Jean: an allele might be absent. This would allow them to get four variations with [1,1], [1,2], [1] and [2]. Rita objected, probably because her understanding of meiosis required that each parent contribute an allele, and Anna, after doing some figuring, couldn't get it to explain the cross data.

Status

The first suggestion promised to explain the four variations (+PROMISE). Anna, however, objected because '2 alleles from each parent' didn't appear plausible to her. Contributing 2 alleles per trait wasn't how the world worked (–METAPHYSICS). Anna also added that she didn't believe the model had the power to resolve the anomaly – i.e. it wasn't fruitful (–POWER). The second suggestion promised to explain four variations (+PROMISE), but it was rejected because it couldn't solve the details of the problem – i.e. the cross patterns (–POWER). The third suggestion – multiple alleles in the population – was promising (+PROMISE), but not explored because the group's attention was drawn elsewhere. The fourth suggestion – the absence of an allele – held immediate promise for one requirement (it provides four variations) (+PROMISE). It was, however, rejected on the grounds of both plausibility (it isn't consistent with the high status conception of meiosis) (–METAPHYSICS) and fruitfulness (it lacks power to explain other allele combinations) (–POWER). These cases point to an emerging pattern: the suggestions all have some promise, pointing to their potential fruitfulness with one aspect of the solution (number of variations). There were, however, objections (some not well developed) over other aspects of the solution on both plausibility and fruitfulness grounds.

Accepting the necessity of more than 2 alleles

The group members now conducted a bewildering array of crosses to determine the dominant allele, but without success: they concluded that none was dominant. Looking for patterns, they had classified crosses as Dwarf or Mendel. They did not see this as evidence that some alleles might be acting in both dominant and co-dominant fashion, depending on which alleles they were interacting with. The group then turned its attention to another aspect of the problem: the need to explain four variations. On 16 February 1994 Jean suggested adding a third and fourth allele 'How about this? You have 1, 2, 3, and 4. 1 is most dominant. 2 is dominant over 3 and 4, but not to 1. 3 is dominant over 4, but not 2. Any one individual could only get two alleles total'. However, after a number of frustrating crosses that left them unable to explain the four variations, they began to question their commitment to the idea of more than two alleles. Jean, however, reminded the group of an analogous situation, human hair colour: 'Well, look at hair colour. You can have red hair, brown, black, blond. It can be 2 numbers, 2 alleles, but there can be like 4 numbers to code for that allele'.

Status

The group began considering 3 and 4 alleles because it could not see a way to explain four variations with 2 alleles. The lack of explanatory power (–POWER) of their current gene conception ('2 alleles: both interact in dominant fashion *or* 2 alleles: both interact in co-dominant fashion') lowered its status in this problem domain. At this point the group was considering four possible expansions of their gene conception: number of alleles (3 or 4) × inheritance pattern (simple or co-dominant). Although none contained all elements of the targeted conceptual expansion needed to solve the problem, the group continued to work with them because they seemed to be the most attractive alternatives (+COMPETE) based on the considerations mentioned earlier. Jean strengthened the plausibility of the 3/4 allele ideas by mentioning an analogy the group was familiar with, human hair colour (+P ANALOGY).

The 3/4 allele dilemma

At this point the group had not decided if 3 or 4 alleles were needed to explain the four observed variations in wing type. They looked first at the '3 alleles: all act in simple dominant fashion' possibility and tried to determine which allele was dominant. Finally Jean pointed out that this task was

irrelevant because four variations by the interactions of three simple dominance alleles was simply not possible: 'You're never going to get a new one
[i.e. fourth variation]. You're going to get the same three [variations] over
and over again'.

Here's how the three variations (A, B, C) would be created by 3 simple
dominance alleles: A by [1,1] or [1,2] or [1,3]; B by [2,2] or [2,3]; and C by
[3,3]. Apparently forgoing the '3 alleles: all act in co-dominant fashion'
possibility, the group turned again to the '4 alleles: all act in simple dominant fashion' idea. They quickly calculated all of the possible genotypes using
4 alleles. There are ten genotypes, and interaction by simple dominance
rules yields the four variations the group was looking for: A by [1,1] or [1,2]
or [1,3] or [1,4]; B by [2,2] or [2,3] or [2,4]; C by [3,3] or [3,4]; and D by [4,4].

The group were now left with the task of determining the order of
dominance. Their working model predicted there must be 1 allele that would
be dominant over all the others (a 'solid' dominant). The search for the
solid dominant, however, was unsuccessful and the group reconsidered co-
dominance. Jean, however, objected because 3 co-dominant alleles yielded
too many variations (6: i.e. [1,1], [2,2], [3,3], [1,2], [1,3] and [2,3]), whereas
2 co-dominant alleles yielded too few (3: i.e. [1,1], [2,2] and [1,2]). The group
had to explain four and only four variations and Jean couldn't imagine how
to eliminate the extra two: 'It would be impossible ... we need a fourth
[allele] if we're going to stick with 2 alleles per individual'.

The group had acquired some pieces to the puzzle. These were, however,
somewhat unreliable because the group hadn't always paid careful attention
to whether parents had been homozygous or heterozygous. This problem
arose because they considered the variations (for example, ballooned, blistery,
etc.) to be names of the alleles rather than phenotypes produced by the
interaction of 2 alleles. As a result they believed that jammed was dominant
to ballooned and blistery was dominant to gull. They also believed that
jammed and blistery produced jammed, blistery and gull (an obvious co-
dominance result, but apparently held in abeyance by the group because
of the low status of co-dominance at this point). Subsequent crosses were
contrary to these results and the group finally realized that many of the crosses
were worthless because they had not been careful about the underlying
genotypes of the variations.

Status

Jean's insight that 3 simple-dominance alleles will not interact to produce
four variations lowered the status of the '3 alleles: all act in simple dominant fashion' possibility, because they could not see how it would explain
their data (−PROMISE). The '4 alleles: all act in simple dominance fashion'

possibility seemed to the group more likely since it provided a way to account for four and only four variations (+PROMISE). The cross predictions made by the 4-allele possibility, however, failed to materialize (–POWER) and its status fell. Possible ideas involving co-dominance ('3 alleles: all interact in co-dominant fashion' and '4 alleles: all interact in co-dominant fashion') had low status because they yielded too many variations (–PROMISE). The group was finally left with '4 alleles: all act in simple dominant fashion' *not* because it solved their problem, but because it held the highest status within the group. In other words, it was consistent with their beliefs about meiosis (+OTHER KNOWLEDGE) and not as unattractive as other possibilities (+COMPETE).

Constraints imposed by ontology

While making crosses the group found results resembling interaction of both simple dominant and co-dominant alleles. The targeted conceptual expansion '3 alleles: interactions between alleles are either simple dominant or co-dominant' had not emerged in the group's thinking probably because one member, Jean, held a strong assumption about allele interaction that precluded the possibility. The constraint emerged when the researcher (JL) asked Jean about the variations that could be explained using the Dwarf and Mendel models separately and together. Jean remonstrated with him: 'Right . . . But you can't combine the two! There's no way you can combine Mendel and the Dwarf models. I just think you can't combine them here, because for Mendel [1,1], [1,2] and [1,3] will all be the same. [2,2] and [2,3] would all be one variation'.

Further probing did not get Jean to back down; it also revealed the reason for her insistence: a need for consistency in the behaviour of the alleles. Jean didn't see how an allele (say 1) could relate to another allele (say 2) in a simple dominant/recessive fashion and to yet another allele (say 3) in a co-dominant fashion.

What I'm saying is, if you take a 1 from one parent, it's either going to be dominant or it's not. Looking at it all by itself and not with its partners you have to see how it relates. You can't just say, either here it's dominant and here it's not. You can't say, it might be [dominant, for example] if this [the allele it's paired with] is something, or it might not be. It either is or it isn't *on its own*' (italics added).

The researcher pushed for a further interpretation.

Researcher: So if 1 can play by the rules that it's dominant/recessive, then what?
Jean: 2 and 3 have to as well.

Even though Jean was adamant, the question started Rita and Anna thinking:

Rita: What if, can you use some of Mendel and some of – OK, what if a [1,1] is the same as a [1,2], but not the same as a [1,3]? I don't know. I'm just trying to . . .

Researcher: Well, if say 1 is playing by Mendel's rules . . . does that mean that the 2 and the 3 have to play by the dominance rules?

Jean: Like 1 is dominant, but 2 doesn't have to be dominant over 3? Is that what you're saying?

Researcher: Why should it be?

Jean: Well, wait. OK 1's dominant, then [1,1], OK. [1,1], [2,2], [3,3]. If you have a [1,2] or a [1,3] it equals a 1. If you have a [2,3] it equals – then you'd have a 1 and a 2 and a 3.

Anna: That would work.

Jean: There'd be a way to get four different things.

The sudden insight that 'that would work' very rapidly collapsed all resistance to the mixed model. The group began immediately to review the cross data to see if this idea could explain what they were seeing. The results were promising enough for Jean to comment, 'We gotta combine Mendel and Dwarf'. She suggested a nascent model: 'How about this? We have 3 alleles. A [1,1] for something (i.e. variation A). A [2,2] for something. A [3,3] for something. And any of the mixed is the fourth'.

Status

Initially, the targeted conceptual expansion held low status within the group because it was inconsistent with how Jean believed alleles worked (–METAPHYSICS). It seems likely that Anna and Rita had not thought of the idea and Jean had never verbalized it because she had not seen it as a viable alternative. With respect to status issues, intelligibility was involved, because getting Jean to articulate her position along with her reasons allowed her views to be examined in greater detail than before (+LANGUAGE). Hearing Jean's objections, the group was able to isolate the problem without having to abandon the whole conception. When the idea was made public during the interview, Anna quickly saw how it might explain the four variations (+PROMISE) and the group decided to test the idea. They began with the suggestion of using 3 alleles in the population. The focus of their thinking had to shift from the nature of the individual allele to the nature of the relationship between any 2 alleles. This proved to be a major conceptual hurdle for the group to overcome.

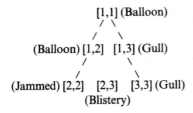

[1,1] (Balloon)

(Balloon) [1,2]   [1,3] (Gull)

(Jammed) [2,2]   [2,3]   [3,3] (Gull)
        (Blistery)

Figure 7.1   The triangle model 1 is dominant to 2, 3 is dominant to 1, and 2 and 3 are co-dominant. The group determined that [1,1] and [1,2] coded for balloon, [1,3] and [3,3] coded for gull, [2,2] coded for jammed and [2,3] coded for blistery.

The intelligibility problem

Even with a clear idea to test, it was still hard going. It proved tricky to decide which allele combination belonged to which variation and which alleles were acting in a dominant or co-dominant fashion. The intelligibility problem had to be overcome before they could fully describe their model. Towards the end of one class period the teacher asked the group if they had been able to identify crosses to back up their new model. They hadn't, partly because they hadn't been able to construct an intelligible representation of the model for themselves, and partly because they were still struggling with hidden alleles in heterozygous dominant genotypes. The frustration of the group is expressed in their journal entry for 17 February: 'Today we still don't have a model yet and aren't sure of how to combine the Dwarf theory and the Mendel model, but we think it is necessary to explain the four variations. We've thought about having 3 or 4 alleles but we don't know. We're extremely frustrated!!!'

The teacher solved the intelligibility problem by introducing 'the triangle model' (see Figure 7.1) as a way for the group to represent their model.

The teacher worked through a series of test crosses with the group until all the phenotypes were assigned genotypes. The teacher pointed out that there should be no cross that couldn't be explained with the triangle. The teacher then had Jean pick a troublesome cross and use the triangle to explain it. In addition to the triangle, the teacher and students also used another representation, the Punnett square, to assign genotypes to phenotypes.

Status

Identifying or constructing a coherent representation of the conception is an important aspect of intelligibility (+IMAGES). The group could hardly make status judgements about a complex conception until they had a way to represent it. The triangle model helped the students organize the complex array of genotypes and phenotypes. Once organized, the students were able to explain even seemingly anomalous crosses (for example, where the parents and offspring do not share any common phenotypes!) The ability of the targeted conceptual expansion to explain cross data (+POWER) and the representation of the conception (triangle model) (+IMAGES) helped raise the status of this elaboration to where it became an accepted part of the group's gene conception.

Conclusion

We argue that status – a construct originating in conceptual change theory – is the hallmark of all forms of conceptual learning. Coming to a deep understanding of a conception, whether or not this involves overcoming a contradictory competitor, still means grappling with the conditions of intelligibility, plausibility and fruitfulness that define a conception's status. Specifically, the goal of the empirical study reported here was not conceptual exchange. There was no fundamental paradigm characterizing student knowledge and beliefs that was antithetical to the desired outcomes of the curriculum. On the contrary, the purpose of the curriculum was to expand a simple dominance model of genetic inheritance into a family of closely related models through a problem-solving approach. The modifications to existing models of genetic inheritance consisted of defining the boundary conditions of their applicability and adding complementary models to the family rather than exchanging existing models for new ones. In other words, the study was not about prototypical conceptual change. It did, however, demonstrate that students necessarily used status considerations in identifying anomalous phenotypic patterns in their data and in evaluating the merits of different models proposed to remove these anomalies. Status is indeed a hallmark of the deep conceptual learning experienced by these students.

Status as an idea that applies to cases of both conceptual exchange and conceptual expansion speaks to a long-standing debate about prior knowledge in learning, and instructional responses to prior knowledge (see for example Scott *et al.* 1992). Too often, the debate is oversimplified as a dichotomy between viewing prior knowledge as either positive or negative. Is prior knowledge problematic, riddled with misconceptions, and in need of exchange? Many have viewed conceptual change approaches as the way to address this unhappy state of affairs. Or is prior knowledge essential in learning, the stuff from which new knowledge is constructed, the foundation that supports learning (Smith *et al.* 1993)? From such a perspective, the notion that existing knowledge can be replaced is suspect. Status, however, provides a range of criteria for evaluating the suitability of prior knowledge, pointing to a dependence on the circumstances in which prior knowledge is used. The example of genetics learning demonstrates that status considerations were integral to the students' deliberations. They used status in identifying the limitations of their initial conception of gene, in expanding it, and in constraining the ways in which it was expanded. A dichotomy of prior knowledge being either right or wrong drastically misrepresents the example.

In identifying status as a hallmark of conceptual learning, we recognize that it is not sufficient. To illustrate one of several other factors that facilitate conceptual learning, we note the importance of the teacher in creating and sustaining an intellectual and social environment that fostered and shaped the work of the students. She did so by taking on a variety of roles such as curriculum designer, instructor and facilitator. Without her taking on these roles, her students were unlikely to have produced a successful multiple alleles model.

Knowledge of status enhances curriculum design. The teacher designed her genetics curriculum with explicit attention to different components of status. First, intelligibility. Among other examples, the triangle model introduced by the teacher organized the many crosses conducted by the group so that they were able to see how the Mendel and Dwarf patterns were interwoven with each other. Next, plausibility. Students used their knowledge of meiosis in evaluating the plausibility of various models. Absent of attention to meiosis in the curriculum, they would not recognize the implausibility of a parent providing 2 alleles to a child. Finally, fruitfulness. Students were able to test the fruitfulness of their models by predicting the outcomes of proposed crosses and using GCK to test their predictions. In other words, knowledge of status, particularly as elaborated in Thorley's (1990) status analysis categories (see Table 7.1), can ensure that teachers include a range of tasks in their curriculum that engage students in considering the different components of status.

Status also improves formative assessment aspects of instruction, as discussed by Bell and Black in this volume (see Chapters 3 and 18). In reflecting on the difficulties students have with any given topic, teachers can use status analysis categories as a source of hypotheses about these difficulties, and can plan instructional interventions with these in mind. While initially such reflection is likely to happen outside class, in time it becomes part of a teacher's repertoire of practice that can be used in class. A classroom poster expressing the major components of status in question form would greatly enhance this possibility.

Note

1 These are purely descriptive terms; their meaning does not influence problem-solving.

References

Hewson, P.W. (1981) A conceptual change approach to learning science. *European Journal of Science Education*, 3(4): 383–96.

Johnson, S.K. and Stewart, J. (1990) Using philosophy of science in curriculum development: an example from high school genetics. *International Journal of Science Education*, 12(3): 297–307.

Jungck, J. and Calley, J. (1985) Strategic simulations and post-Socratic pedagogy: constructing computer software to develop long-term inference through experimental inquiry. *The American Biology Teacher*, 47: 11–15.

Lemberger, J. (1995) 'Conceptual change and problem solving', unpublished doctoral dissertation. University of Wisconsin-Madison.

Posner, G.J., Strike, K.A., Hewson, P.W. and Gertzog, W.A. (1982) Accommodation of a scientific conception: toward a theory of conceptual change. *Science Education*, 66(2): 211–27.

Scott, P.H., Asoko, H.M. and Driver, R.H. (1992) Teaching for conceptual change: a review of strategies, in R. Duit, F. Goldberg and H. Niedderer (eds) *Research in Physics Learning: Theoretical Issues and Empirical Studies*, pp. 310–29. Kiel: IPN.

Smith, J.P., diSessa, A.A. and Roschelle, J. (1993) Misconceptions reconceived: a constructivist analysis of knowledge in transition. *Journal of the Learning Sciences*, 3(2): 115–90.

Thorley, N.R. (1990) 'The role of the conceptual change model in the interpretation of classroom interactions', unpublished doctoral dissertation. University of Wisconsin-Madison.

8 Analysing discourse in the science classroom

Eduardo Mortimer and Phil Scott

Introduction

In recent years the influence of discursive or sociocultural psychology (see for example Wertsch 1985a; Harré and Gillett 1994) on research in science education has been reflected in a gradual development of interest in studies of how meanings are developed through language and other semiotic means in the classroom. This 'new direction' for science education research (see Solomon 1994; Sutton 1996) signals a move away from studies focusing on individual student's understandings of specific phenomena towards research into the ways in which understandings are developed in the social context of the science classroom (Duit and Treagust 1998).

In this chapter we present a new approach to analysing and characterizing the ways in which classroom discourse mediates the development of meaning and understandings between teachers and students. We refer to this approach as the 'flow of discourse' analytical framework.

It is often the case that teaching approaches in science education are equated with the kinds of practical activity that teachers and students engage in. It is our view that the teacher and student talk 'around' these activities is at least as important in establishing scientific knowledge in the classroom as the activities themselves. We therefore believe that it is of fundamental importance in thinking about science teaching to have the analytical tools for reviewing and identifying the different kinds and patterns of *classroom talk*.

The 'flow of discourse' framework has been developed through reference to Vygotskian and neo-Vygotskian perspectives on teaching and learning (see for example Bakhtin 1981; Wertsch 1985b; Vygotsky 1987) and is part of an established and continuing line of research work (Mortimer and Machado 1996; Scott 1997a, 1998; Mortimer 1998).

Theoretical foundations of the 'flow of discourse' analytical framework

A fundamental tenet of Vygotsky's perspective on development and learning is that higher mental functioning in the individual derives from social life (Vygotsky 1978: 128). In the first instance language and other semiotic mechanisms provide the means for scientific ideas to be talked through on the social or intermental plane and following the process of internalization, language provides a tool for individual thinking.

The 'flow of discourse' framework follows a Vygotskian approach in focusing on the ways in which classroom talk can mediate student learning of science concepts. Much of that talk is directed and guided by the teacher, but we are also interested in the ways in which students' contributions can influence (and possibly redirect) the flow of classroom discourse. We are concerned with the multiple ways in which classroom discourse can develop to make scientific knowledge available to students on the intermental plane and to enable them to develop personal understandings of that knowledge.

Given this focus of interest, our analysis is based on the *utterances* of teacher and students as they interact within the social context of the classroom. Bakhtin (1986: 71) considers the utterance to be 'the real unit of speech communication' and maintains that 'speech can exist in reality only in the form of concrete utterances of individual speaking people'. Such a perspective is in contrast to those linguistic analyses which focus on words and sentences, which according to Bakhtin 'Belong to nobody and are addressed to nobody' (1986: 99).

Bakhtin also draws attention to the fact that different modes of discourse are used in different parts of society, and refers to these as *social languages*. For Bakhtin a social language is 'a discourse peculiar to a specific stratum of society (professional, age group, etc.) within a given system at a given time' (Holquist and Emerson 1981: 430). Thus social languages would include a dialect used in a particular geographical area, or a particular form of professional jargon, or indeed the ways of talking about the natural world, which are termed *science*.

Bakhtin makes a further distinction between *speech genres* and social languages. According to Bakhtin 'a speech genre is not a form of language, but a typical form of utterance' (1986: 87). What differentiates social languages from speech genres is that the former are tied to classes of speakers and the latter to classes of speech situation. Thus, different speech genres include: everyday genres of greeting; genres of table conversation; everyday storytelling; genres of classroom discourse.

In the 'flow of discourse' framework Bakhtin's concepts of social language and speech genre are drawn upon as tools for analysing classroom discourse. In the science classroom, at least two different social languages, the 'scientific' and the 'spontaneous/everyday' (Vygotsky 1987) are represented and interact as ideas and phenomena are talked about by teacher and students. This, of course, can lead to teacher and students talking about the same phenomenon in quite different ways. In addition, the interactions between students and teacher are inevitably mediated, and restricted (Wertsch 1998) by those distinctive and accepted patterns of discourse which constitute the speech genres of the classroom. Our aim is to draw upon these conceptual tools of utterance, social language and speech genre in characterizing both the *content* and *patterns* of *interaction* in the flow of discourse of the classroom.

Wertsch (1991: 93–118) makes further use of the concept of speech genre in discussing the notion of 'heterogeneity of verbal thinking' and suggests that the various forms of mediational means be viewed not as some kind of single undifferentiated whole, but rather in terms of the diverse items that make up a *toolkit*. He draws on the concepts of Bakhtinian (Bakhtin 1986) 'speech genres' and Wittgensteinian (Wittgenstein 1972) 'language games' in elaborating the toolkit analogy and suggests:

> When the notion of heterogeneity is coupled with a Bakhtinian approach to meaning, I argue that speech genres are good candidates for the tools in the heterogeneous mediational tool kit . . . children do not stop using perspectives grounded in everyday concepts and questions after they master these [scientific] forms of discourse. Different speech genres are suited to different activity settings or spheres of life.
>
> (Wertsch 1991: 118)

Following this perspective, the different social languages and speech genres which are rehearsed on the intermental plane of the classroom offer the means for developing a range of distinctive modes of personal thought: a whole kit of mediational tools. One of us has drawn upon this idea of the heterogeneity of verbal thinking in analysing classroom discourse in terms of a 'conceptual profile of matter'. This conceptual profile is used to categorize the different voices that arise in classroom discourse during teaching about the particulate model of matter (Mortimer 1995, 1998).

The notion of heterogeneity is also useful because it helps avoid treating modes of thinking in isolation from ways of talking. Saying that different social languages 'are specific points of view on the world, forms for conceptualising the world in words' Bakhtin (1981: 292) provides a warning against treating students' ideas as if they were solely individual constructs, independent of the language used to express them, and against treating language simply as a channel or conduit for communicating ideas.

From the perspective set out above, learning science involves internalizing (Vygotsky 1987), and developing competence in using, the social language of science. However, it must be recognized that internalization cannot simply involve direct transfer of 'ways of talking' from social to personal planes; there must be a step of personal interpretation or personal sense-making. In simple terms, individual learners must make sense of the talk which surrounds them and in doing so relate it to their existing ideas and ways of thinking. This sense-making step can involve significant conceptual and ontological challenges for the learner (see Leach and Scott 1995). Learners must *reorganize* and *reconstruct* the talk and activities of the social plane. In this respect Vygotskian theory shares common ground with *constructivist* perspectives in recognizing that the learner cannot be a passive recipient of knowledge and instruction.

Having introduced the principal theoretical ideas informing this work, we now turn our attention to the analytical framework itself.

The 'flow of discourse' analytical framework

The main features of the 'flow of discourse' framework can be summarized as follows. First, the framework is based upon an *interpretative* approach (see for example Edwards and Mercer 1987; Barnes and Todd 1995) which aims to characterize emerging *patterns in the flow of discourse* in science lessons, in terms of both *teacher and student utterances*. The analysis is made over a *continuous timeline* (which might be limited to a short episode within a single lesson or extend over a sequence of lessons). The analysis is concerned with the ways in which *conceptual themes or content* are made available and developed on the intermental plane of the classroom.

Aspects of the 'flow of discourse' analytical framework

The 'flow of discourse' analytical framework addresses three aspects of classroom discourse.

The content of the discourse
This first aspect of the analytical framework focuses upon the content of student utterances and is operationalized in terms of whether or not those utterances *match* the intended conceptual learning goals set by the teacher. As part of the analysis, each student utterance is therefore taken as either:

• 'student utterance matches the intended learning goal'; or
• 'student utterance does not match the intended learning goal'.

For example, it might be the case that a teacher sets the goal for a sequence of lessons as 'to establish an explanation for air pressure phenomena based on differences in air pressure'. During the lessons the teacher asks the class to explain how a rubber suction cup can stick to a smooth surface (a door). One student responds that 'the air inside the suction cup sticks it to the surface'. Such a response would *not* match with the teacher's intended learning goal. Here the student draws upon an alternative *theme* (that of the air inside the suction cup making it stick) in responding to the question. Another student responds that 'the suction cup tries to hold onto the surface'. Here the student's explanation is framed in anthropomorphic terms; this mode of explanation is characteristic of an alternative, everyday *genre*. This aspect of the analysis refers to conceptual learning goals, which are set by the teacher at the outset of a unit of teaching.

The form of the utterances
This aspect of the framework focuses upon the form of student and teacher utterances and is framed in terms of three categories: description, explanation, and generalization. These categories are defined as follows:

- *Description:* involves statements of what is directly observable or is generally taken to be the case.
- *Explanation:* involves importing some form of model or mechanism to account for a specific phenomenon.
- *Generalization:* involves making a description or explanation which is independent of any specific context.

The categories can be illustrated through the 'rubber suction cup' example:

- *Description:* the rubber suction cup sticks to the smooth surface when it is pressed down.
- *Explanation:* the rubber suction cup sticks to the door because the air pressure on its outer surface is greater than that on the inside.
- *Generalization:* differential air pressures create a net force.

In passing from description through explanation to generalization there is a change in focus: from the here and now of 'what happens' when the rubber suction cup is pressed down; to an explanation of what happens drawing upon the scientific conceptual tool of air pressure; and to a statement which applies to a whole range of different phenomena. As defined here, the move from description, to explanation, to generalization involves a progressive 'decontextualization of mediational means' (Wertsch 1985b).

We recognize that approaches to defining the above categories (description, explanation, generalization) have been, and will continue to be, the subject of academic debate. For example, reference to 'what is directly observable' (in defining 'description') is likely to prompt questions about the extent to which the process of observation is conceptually driven. At this point in the development of the framework, we do not intend to enter into such philosophical debates. We do, however, anticipate that the socioculturally based perspectives

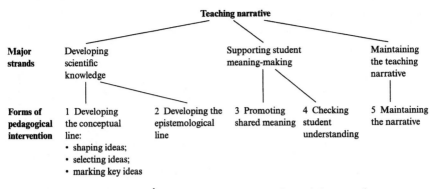

Figure 8.1 The teaching narrative: major strands and forms of pedagogical intervention

drawn upon in developing the framework will provide a useful alternative approach to these matters and this will be addressed in a later paper.

The patterns in the flow of the discourse

This aspect of the analysis focuses on the patterns of teacher and student utterances in the flow of the discourse; it is concerned with characterizing the typical patterns of interaction or speech genres which constitute the discourse.

When teachers are engaged in talk with students in the classroom, the most common pattern of interaction is described as I-R-F (see for example Edwards and Mercer 1987), where *I* corresponds to the *initiation* of the dialogue by the teacher (normally by means of a question); *R* is the student's *response*; and *F* is the *feedback* from the teacher.

In the analytical framework presented here we expand upon the I-R-F pattern by including additional elements to characterize the flow of the discourse. The principal focus is on the form of teacher interventions as the teacher regulates and guides the discourse. Attention, however, is also paid to those utterances made by students which cannot be classified as 'responses' to the teacher and which can have an influential effect on the flow of discourse.

The nature of teacher interventions

This aspect of the analysis is based on an existing scheme (Scott 1997b, 1998) in which five categories of teacher or pedagogical intervention have been identified. These five forms of pedagogical intervention are grouped into three major strands: developing scientific knowledge; supporting student meaning-making; and maintaining the teaching narrative (see Figure 8.1).

The *teaching narrative* can be thought of as a teaching 'performance' mediated by talk, through which scientific ideas are introduced and explored on the intermental plane of the classroom.

The first strand of the teaching narrative consists of those teacher interventions directed towards making scientific knowledge available on the intermental plane and is subdivided into 'Developing the conceptual line' and 'Developing the epistemological line' of the narrative.

Developing the conceptual line involves teacher interventions to make scientific ideas available. These include: 'shaping ideas' (where the teacher might introduce new ideas, guide students through the steps of an explanation by means of a series of instructional questions, paraphrase students' utterances or differentiate between utterances); 'selecting ideas' (where the teacher might select a student utterance, retrospectively elicit a student utterance or overlook a student utterance); and 'marking key ideas' (where the teacher might repeat an utterance, ask a student to repeat an utterance, enact a confirmatory exchange with a student, authorize a student utterance, pose a rhetorical question or use a particular intonation of voice).

Developing the epistemological line involves teacher interventions aimed at introducing students to aspects of the *nature* of the scientific knowledge (such as the generalizability of scientific explanations) which is being taught.

The second strand of the teaching narrative consists of those interventions directed towards making the science point of view available to *all* of the students in the class and checking the meanings and understandings that they subsequently develop. It is subdivided into 'promoting shared meaning' and 'checking student understanding'.

In *promoting shared meaning* the teacher might: present ideas to the whole class; share individual student ideas with the whole class; share group findings with the whole class; or jointly rehearse an idea with a student in front of the whole class. In making interventions to *check student understanding* the teacher might: ask for clarification of student ideas; check individual student understanding of particular ideas; or check consensus in the class about certain ideas.

The third and final strand involves those interventions where the teacher provides a commentary on the unfolding 'science story' with a view to helping students follow the development of that story. In *maintaining the narrative* the teacher might: state aims/purposes for the next part of the narrative; look ahead to anticipate possible outcomes; review progress of the narrative; or refocus discussion. These various interventions to maintain the narrative help establish lines of *continuity* (Mercer 1995) in the discourse from one part of a teaching sequence to another.

An important point to bear in mind in considering these various strands of the teaching narrative is that a single teacher intervention can serve more than one goal or purpose. For example, the teacher asking a student to repeat an idea can serve the function of 'marking a key idea' and also 'promoting shared meaning'. Wertsch (1998: 32) makes the general point when he argues that 'mediated action typically serves *multiple* purposes . . . multiple goals, often in interaction and sometimes in conflict, are typically involved'.

The flow of discourse analysis grid

The three aspects (content, form, pattern) introduced above constitute the analytical elements of the 'flow of discourse' framework and each utterance made by the teacher and the students is categorized, wherever possible, and represented on an analysis grid (see p. 135).

The grid is arranged in upper and lower sections. If the *content* of a student utterance matches the intended learning goal then it is marked (by student identity) in the upper part of the grid. If the *content* of a student utterance does not match the intended learning goal then it is marked in the lower part. Each student utterance is also classified according to *form* as either a description, explanation or generalization. The *nature* of teacher (and student) interventions as they influence the *pattern* in the flow of discourse are marked in the central part of the grid.

Having introduced the 'flow of discourse' analytical framework we now turn our attention to applying it to a particular classroom episode.

An analysis of one teaching and learning sequence taken from a high school classroom

The episode which is presented here is taken from a Brazilian high school chemistry lesson (students aged 15–16), and focuses on talk between the teacher and a group of students about the spontaneous dissolution and diffusion of potassium permanganate in water.

In the teaching approach taken, the lessons usually began with observation of a phenomenon, followed by small group work in which the students were asked to discuss some aspect of what they had seen.

This particular episode (Mortimer and Machado 1996) occurred in a lesson which was part of a unit entitled 'What substances are made of'. The class had observed the spontaneous dissolution of a crystal of potassium permanganate in water and the students were then asked to work in their groups to explain what they had seen.

Basic aspects of the particulate nature of matter (distribution and motion of particles) had been introduced to the class in earlier lessons. The teacher's *goal* for this lesson was to account for the dissolution of the potassium permanganate in terms of the motion of the particles in solution and to thereby move towards establishing the intrinsic motion of particles as a central feature of the particulate model of matter.

Analysis

The sequences of classroom discourse which are presented below were collected on audiotape and later transcribed and analysed. The analysis suggests that the overall episode can be divided into three phases.

Phase A: why does the whole solution become coloured?
At the start of the episode the teacher sits next to a group of students. He initiates the interaction with the students by asking them why the whole solution becomes coloured. In posing this instructional question the teacher makes a substantive input in *describing* the key features of the phenomenon:

1 *Teacher:* Why class? Why is it ... when I leave ... Why is it, that when I leave the crystal of permanganate still, without any movement, after some time, the whole solution became coloured?
2 *Student 5:* Because it is soluble in water ...
3 *Teacher:* It is soluble in water. But why? What happens?
4 *Student 1:* The particles mix ...
5 *Student 4:* Ah, the permanganate goes looking ...
6 *Student 5:* ... like the breaking of the permanganate particles.
7 *Student 3:* How do I say that then?
8 *Student 4:* ... because the permanganate is, kind of, goes looking for particles.
9 *Student 1:* ... they go and mix themselves.
10 *Teacher:* Looking for? How do you mean? Is it intelligent?
11 *Student 4:* Yeah [laughter from the other students].

Several attempts are made by the students to explain the phenomenon. Student 5 suggests that the solution becomes coloured 'because it [the permanganate] is soluble in water'. This is a macroscopic *explanation* which is *not* consistent with the intended teaching goal (see Table 8.1). The teacher responds (Turn 3) with an instructional question (iq) to *shape* the flow of discourse, 'But why? What happens?' Student 1 introduces an explanation (Turn 4) based on particles, which is consistent with the intended view, but makes no explicit reference to motion of particles. Student 4 offers an explanation drawing on an inappropriate anthropomorphic *genre* (Turns 5 and 8). In Turn 10, the teacher *selects* and *checks* Student 4's response (overlooking the suggestion from Student 1 in turn 9) and challenges what Student 4 said by questioning the genre he was using: 'Looking for? How do you mean? Is it intelligent?' Student 4's response 'Yeah' creates some amusement among his fellow students.

Table 8.1 Flow of discourse analysis grid A(i)

		1	2	3	4	5	6	7	8	9	10
Matches goal	Generalization										
	Explanation					S1			S1		
	Description	T									
		T shape, iq		T shape, iq		Genre			Genre		T select, check
Does not match goal	Generalization										
	Explanation		S5			S4	S5		S4		
	Description										
	Turn	*1*	*2*	*3*	*4*	*5*	*6*	*7*	*8*	*9*	*10*

Note: S = student; T = teacher, iq = instructional question

Student 4 then refers to his drawing on a piece of paper and describes what can be seen. The teacher looks on:

12 *Student 4:* For example, this part is coloured isn't it? [pointing to the drawing]
13 *Teacher:* Hum.
14 *Student 4:* Then the permanganate, it . . . will mix with the water. Here it is mixed [student explains using the drawing as a support]. Then as it dissolves, it takes up the parts that are not yet mixed and . . .
15 *Teacher:* How does it take up?
16 *Student 5:* It's like breaking the particles.
17 *Teacher:* What is needed in the particles, for it to take up?
18 *Student 3:* I think the particles go . . . get broke down.
19 *Teacher:* Well look here. Are you saying that the particles leave here and come over here?
20 *Student 4:* This is the grain . . .

Student 4 develops his point of view and offers an explanation which is macroscopic in focus (Turn 14). The teacher responds with a *shaping* question: 'How does it take up?' Student 5 refers to particles: 'It's like breaking the particles' and the teacher *selects* the particle notion in *rephrasing* her initial question: 'What is needed in the particles, for it to take up?' She follows this up in Turn 19 when she introduces the idea of particle motion and asks, 'Are you saying that the particles leave here and come over here?' In posing this instructional question the teacher makes a significant intervention in attempting to introduce the conceptual theme of 'particle motion' to the discourse (see Table 8.2).

Table 8.2 Flow of discourse analysis grid A(ii)

		12	13	14	15	16	17	18	19	20
Matches goal	Generalization									
	Explanation									
	Description								T	
			T prompt		T shape, iq		T select, shape		T shape	
Does not match goal	Generalization									
	Explanation			S4		S5		S3		
	Description	S4								S4
	Turn	*12*	*13*	*14*	*15*	*16*	*17*	*18*	*19*	*20*

Note: S = student; T = teacher; iq = instructional question

Phase B: there is space . . . but how do you explain . . . ?

Student 5 initiates this second phase by posing a question relating to the space between the particles:

21 *Student 5:* There is space isn't there, between the particles?
22 *Student 4:* . . . then it takes up the parts . . .
23 *Teacher:* Why do you think it exists?
24 *Student 4:* . . . then it takes up the parts . . .
25 *Student 5:* Because if it didn't exist, the permanganate would not dissolve, it would occupy its space and the water occupies its own space.
26 *Teacher:* . . . its own space . . .
27 *Student 5:* Because two bodies cannot occupy the same space . . .
28 *Teacher:* . . . the same space . . .
29 *Student 3:* It's the same thing.
30 *Teacher:* Yeah. Ok? How do you explain the fact that a particle of permanganate comes up from down there and comes up here even though I did not shake anything?

Student 5 *initiates* a new phase in the episode by posing her question (Turn 21) which introduces to the discourse the idea that there is space between particles. Student 4 persists with his macroscopic explanation (Turns 22 and 24), but the teacher *overlooks* this in *selecting* and focusing attention on what Student 5 has said: 'Why do you think it [space between particles] exists?' In Turns 26 and 28, the teacher makes *shaping prompts* to Student 5 as she develops her explanation, which is consistent with the teaching goal. In Turn 27 Student 5 supports her explanation with a

Table 8.3 Flow of discourse analysis grid B(i)

		21	22	23	24	25	26	27	28	29	30
Matches goal	Generalization										
	Explanation					S5					
	Description	S5									T
		student initiates	T select, shape				T shape, prompt		T shape, prompt		T shape, iq
Does not match goal	Generalization							S5			
	Explanation		S4		S4						
	Description										
	Turn	*21*	*22*	*23*	*24*	*25*	*26*	*27*	*28*	*29*	*30*

Note: S = student; T = teacher; iq = instructional question

general statement: 'two bodies cannot occupy the same space'. The teacher then intervenes to refocus attention on the motion of the particles (Turn 30) (see Table 8.3).

Student 3 (Turn 31) refers to 'water' and another student mentions 'density'. Neither of these ideas contributes to the intended learning goal and the teacher attempts to move the discourse towards the intended learning goal by repeating her question (Turn 35):

31 *Student 3:* Would it be the same thing as the . . . in water?
32 *Teacher:* Same thing?
33 *Teacher:* Density?
34 *Student 5:* They don't have . . .
35 *Teacher:* How do you explain a particle all the way from the bottom of the grain going all the way to the top of the thing?
36 *Student 5:* This here is a liquid . . .
37 *Student 4:* Thrust . . .
38 *Student 5:* . . . this here is a liquid and a liquid does not have a definite shape. Isn't that so? That there is movement of particles.
39 *Teacher:* There is movement of particles . . .
40 *Student 5:* And there is space. So, because there is movement and space between the particles, the tendency is for one not to stay in the same place. They therefore mix themselves.

Student 5 focuses attention on the liquid in Turn 36 and develops her explanation by introducing 'movement of particles' in Turn 38. The teacher (Turn 39)

Table 8.4 Flow of discourse analysis grid B(ii)

		31	32	33	34	35	36	37	38	39	40
Matches goal	Generalization										
	Explanation								S5		S5
	Description				T	S5					
			T check	T check		T shape, iq				T select, mark	
Does not match goal	Generalization										
	Explanation	S3									
	Description										
	Turn	*31*	*32*	*33*	*34*	*35*	*36*	*37*	*38*	*39*	*40*

Note: S = student; T = teacher; iq = instructional question

selects and *marks* this key idea by repeating it. Student 5 then continues, offering a full explanation based on particle movement and space between particles – an explanation which is entirely consistent with the intended goal of the teaching (see Table 8.4).

Phase C: does that seem reasonable?
Following Student 5's explanation, the teacher turns to the rest of the group and again *marks* this key idea by posing the rhetorical question 'Does that seem reasonable?' In this way she lends authority to Student 5's voice.

41 *Teacher:* Do you agree with that? Does that seem reasonable?
42 *Student 4:* I didn't understand . . .
43 *Teacher:* Explain it to them Student 5.
44 *Student 5:* Since there is space between the particles and since the particles have energy, they will move and they will move and they will . . . move and mix themselves . . .
45 *Teacher:* Does that sound reasonable? Does it?
46 *Teacher:* So from that, what do we understand so far? How do you understand the make-up of particles from this experiment?
47 *Student 5:* That the particles have energy and there is space between them.
48 *Teacher:* This means . . . that these substances are made up of particles and the particles . . .
49 *Student 5:* . . . have energy.
50 *Teacher:* . . . have energy. What energy is this?
51 *Student 5:* Kinetic.

Table 8.5 Flow of discourse analysis grid C(i)

		41	42	43	44	45	46	47	48	49	50
Matches goal	Generalization						T	S5	T	S5	
	Explanation				S5						
	Description										
		T mark	S4 query	T share, mark		T mark	T shape, iq		T mark, share	Mark, share	T shape, iq
Does not match goal	Generalization										
	Explanation										
	Description										
	Turn	*41*	*42*	*43*	*44*	*45*	*46*	*47*	*48*	*49*	*50*

Note: S = student; T = teacher; iq = instructional question

Student 4 does not understand and the teacher asks Student 5 to explain to the rest of the group, thereby lending authority to Student 5's explanation and *promoting shared meaning*. Student 5 repeats the explanation and the teacher once more *marks* this key idea by posing the rhetorical question, 'Does that sound reasonable?' In Turn 46, the teacher extends the focus of the discourse by posing an instructional question about the *general* 'make-up of the particles'. Student 5 responds with a *generalized* statement in Turn 47: 'the particles have energy and there is space between them'. As Student 5 makes this statement the discourse has reached the teacher's intended goal. The teacher rephrases and summarizes (Turn 48) what Student 5 has said and *jointly rehearses* this final generalized statement with Student 5 (turns 48, 49, 50, 51), thereby *marking* its acceptability and making it available to all students (see Table 8.5).

Overview of the analysis

In looking back over the analysis of the episode, it is apparent that most of the teacher utterances are 'pedagogical interventions' *in response* to students' statements as she guides the development of the conceptual line of the discourse (shaping, selecting, marking key ideas). Thus, Student 4's anthropomorphic explanation is challenged and discounted, while Student 5's reference to particles (Turn 17) is selected and retained in the discourse.

The teacher does make a small number of 'substantive interventions' where she introduces a new conceptual theme to the discourse. These substantive interventions are limited to: Turn 1 (description of the phenomenon); Turn 19 (focusing attention on particle motion, which is repeated in Turns 30 and 35); Turn 46 (moving the discourse towards a generalized statement about the intrinsic motion of particles).

In this way, the teacher provides the opportunity for students to state their points of view, while at the same time prompting and guiding the flow of the discourse towards the intended learning goal. In other circumstances (possibly when introducing new ideas), it is quite likely that the same teacher would teach in such a way that the ratio of 'substantive' to 'pedagogical' interventions is higher and less time is spent in eliciting and responding to student ideas.

Overall, during the episode, there is a progressive shift in the discourse from phenomenon, to particle explanation, to a generalized statement about the intrinsic motion of particles. The intended teaching goal is reached, in the sense that the scientific explanation is made available on the intermental plane. What, of course, is not known is the extent to which individual students were able to internalize and make sense of that explanation. Student 4's reaction in Turn 42 'I didn't understand' suggests that the ideas developed by the teacher and Student 5 may not have been understood by all.

Final comments

In this chapter we have presented, and exemplified the application of, a framework for analysing the flow of discourse in classroom situations. It is our belief that the framework helps to make visible patterns in the flow of discourse and the ways in which language frames the process of meaning-making in the science classroom.

The episode presented for analysis extended over little more than a few minutes. However, the framework lends itself equally well to analysing patterns in the flow of discourse over whole lessons, or sequences of lessons. In this episode a progressive shift in the discourse towards a generalized statement relating to the particle model was identified. In other episodes, it is quite possible that the flow of discourse will be in the reverse direction, from generalized statement to specific phenomena. The framework is based on no assumptions about what might constitute 'effective teaching'; it simply affords the means for analysing different pedagogical interactions.

An important and novel feature of this approach to analysing classroom talk is the fact that the framework brings together the analysis of patterns in the flow of discourse with the content of the discourse and the form of utterances. Other approaches to discourse analysis have tended to focus on forms of teacher intervention, irrespective of the content or theme of the discourse (see for example Edwards and Mercer 1987). Our position is significantly different in that we are interested in how teachers can work with their students to make specific scientific knowledge available on the intermental plane of the classroom, and to support them in coming to an understanding of that knowledge. We are not interested in, for example, studies of the frequency of use of certain kinds of interventions by teachers *per se*, but wish to analyse how different patterns of intervention impact on the development of knowledge in the classroom.

What might be the practical importance of this kind of approach to discourse analysis? In short, we consider that the ability to manage classroom discourse is absolutely central to the teacher's art, but that this is an aspect of pedagogical subject expertise (Shulman 1986) which frequently passes unnoticed in analysing teaching practice. Furthermore, we believe that the analytical tools presented here offer a useful and effective means for talking and thinking about how classroom discourse can support development of knowledge and meaning-making.

The point has been made earlier that interactions between teachers and students are inevitably mediated and restricted (Wertsch 1998) by those distinctive patterns of discourse which constitute the speech genres of the classroom. It is our view that teachers can only begin to develop and extend the range of speech genres which they draw upon in the classroom when they become aware of the nature of their present performance. Through working with teachers to identify examples of different patterns of discursive flow in different thematic contexts, we believe that we can help teachers to reflect on their own practice and to become explicitly aware of the different ways in which language can be framed in the classroom to support student learning.

References

Bakhtin, M.M. (1981) *The Dialogic Imagination: Four Essays by M.M. Bakhtin.* Austin, TX: University of Texas Press.

Bakhtin, M.M. (1986) *Speech Genres and Other Late Essays.* Austin, TX: University of Texas Press.

Barnes, D. and Todd, F. (1995) *Communication and learning revisited: Making meaning through talk.* Portsmouth: Boynton/Cook.

Duit, R. and Treagust, D. (1998) Learning in science – from behaviourism towards social constructivism and beyond, in B.J. Fraser and K.G. Tobin (eds) *International Handbook of Science Education.* Dordrecht: Kluwer Academic Publishers.

Edwards, D. and Mercer, N.M. (1987) *Common Knowledge: The Development of Understanding in the Classroom.* London: Methuen.

Harré, R. and Gillett, G. (1994) *The Discursive Mind.* Thousand Oaks, CA: Sage.

Holquist, M. and Emerson, C. (1981) Glossary, in M. Holquist and C. Emerson (eds) *The Dialogic Imagination: Four Essays by M.M. Bakhtin.* Austin, TX: University of Texas Press.

Leach, J. and Scott, P. (1995) The demands of learning science concepts: issues of theory and practice. *School Science Review*, 76(277): 47–52.

Mercer, N.M. (1995) *The Guided Construction of Knowledge*. Clevedon: Multilingual Matters.

Mortimer, E.F. (1995) Conceptual change or conceptual profile change? *Science and Education*, 4(3): 267–85.

Mortimer, E.F. (1998) Multivoicedness and univocality in classroom discourse: an example from the theory of matter. *International Journal of Science Education*, 20(1): 67–82.

Mortimer, E.F. and Machado, A.H. (1996) A linguagem numa aula de ciencias. *Presenca Pedagogica*, 2(11): 49–57.

Scott, P.H. (1997a) Teaching and learning science concepts in the classroom: taking a path from spontaneous to scientific knowledge. Paper presented at an international seminar held at Universidade Federal de Minas Gerais, Belo Horizonte, Brazil, March.

Scott, P.H. (1997b) 'Developing science concepts in secondary classrooms: an analysis of pedagogical interactions from a Vygotskian perspective', Unpublished PhD thesis. University of Leeds.

Scott, P.H. (1998) Teacher talk and meaning-making in science classrooms: A Vygotskian analysis and review. *Studies in Science Education*, 32: 45–80.

Shulman, L.S. (1986) Those who understand: a conception of teacher knowledge. *American Educator*, 10(1): 9–15, 43–4.

Solomon, J. (1994) The rise and fall of constructivism. *Studies in Science Education*, 23: 1–19.

Sutton, C. (1996) The scientific model as a form of speech, in G. Welford, J. Osborne and P. Scott (eds) *Research in Science Education in Europe*. London: Falmer.

Vygotsky, L.S. (1978) *Mind in Society: The Development of Higher Psychological Processes*. Cambridge, MA: Harvard University Press.

Vygotsky, L.S. (1987) *The Collected Works of L.S. Vygotsky, Volume 1*. New York: Plenum.

Wertsch, J.V. (ed.) (1985a) *Culture, Communication and Cognition: Vygotskian Perspectives*. Cambridge: Cambridge University Press.

Wertsch, J.V. (1985b) *Vygotsky and the Social Formation of Mind*. Cambridge, MA: Harvard University Press.

Wertsch, J.V. (1991) *Voices of the Mind: A Sociocultural Approach to Mediated Action*. London: Harvester Wheatsheaf.

Wertsch, J.V. (1998) *Mind as Action*. New York: Oxford University Press.

Wittgenstein, L. (1972) *Philosophical Investigations*. Oxford: Blackwell & Mott.

Section 2

REVIEWING THE ROLE AND PURPOSE OF SCIENCE IN THE SCHOOL CURRICULUM

Rather than focusing on empirically testable questions, the chapters in Section 2 consider issues concerning the role and purpose of the science curriculum. In some senses, it may be argued that science education has made significant strides since the 1960s. In many countries, science is no longer a subject preserved for a minority of academic students, with study of the separate sciences strongly differentiated by gender. Instead, programmes including all the main sciences are increasingly offered to all students through the years of compulsory schooling. Yet, in many senses, the curriculum itself remains fundamentally unchanged and the content would be easily recognizable to any child of the 1950s. Thus, Peter Fensham, in Chapter 9, returns to the neglected issue of content to examine the theoretical perspectives available for framing decisions about the content of science courses. Reviewing contemporary attempts to specify content through national curricula, he suggests that these methods are based on a bureaucratic and rationalist notion of the curriculum in which accountability, rather than any consideration of its value for the child, is the driving ideology. Drawing instead on the German idea of *Bildung*, he argues for a science curriculum whose content is determined by the needs of the child. This, he thinks, would open up the ideas of sequence and progression to produce a curriculum more relevant to the child of today.

Criticisms of the bureaucratic, rationalist model and, in particular, the homogenizing influence of TIMSS (the Third International Mathematics and Science Study) are the driving imperatives of the work Svein Sjøberg discusses in Chapter 10. Drawing on small-scale but extensive work from 20 countries, he begins by showing the obvious, but often neglected, point that children differ in their needs and in their experiences that might contribute to their learning of science. Hence the results from any uniform international assessment framework must be of questionable value. What Sjøberg's data show is that the interest in science varies considerably both between the developed world and the developing world, and between genders. His evidence would suggest that the interests of the two genders are still largely and universally stereotypically divided, and that the science curriculum has failed to address this issue. Thus, although 'science for all' may have become more prevalent across the globe, science is still essentially a subject whose content is biased against the interests of girls. Using his data, Sjøberg shows revealingly how rewriting the science curriculum from a frame that relates to girls' interests dramatically changes their potential interest in learning science. This work has important messages for any future curricula if girls and women are not to remain the 'missing half' in science.

The remaining chapters in this section focus primarily on epistemological issues in the science curriculum. In Chapter 11, Richard Duschl focuses on the notion of epistemic goals, arguing that science education is in need of radical change. He argues that science education should seek to develop understanding not only of *what is known* but also of *how we have come to know it*. For if science is, as many scientists would wish to claim, epistemically privileged, a science education that ignores the social, cognitive and epistemic practices of science leaves its pupils with an incomplete understanding of science. Moreover, it is the epistemic dimension which is essential to developing young people's (and hence the future public's) understanding of science. Duschl argues that such a transformation requires a focus on the data 'texts' of science and the manner in which they are used to develop scientific ideas. Drawing on his own research, he shows how changes in the design of instructional sequences and learning environments could promote the refinement and development of scientific language and understanding. However, as he points out, such a revolution requires a fundamental change in the nature of activities undertaken in the science classroom.

Edgar Jenkins develops a similar theme in Chapter 12. He begins by pointing to the increasing emphasis on science in contemporary society as evidenced by the growth of 'interactive' science centres, popular books about science, and the expanding coverage of science in the media. Moreover, he suggests, science has been transformed from an activity driven by disinterested curiosity to one driven ever more strongly by technological needs and market requirements. Science can no longer, therefore, be detached from the values and priorities of the society in which it is embedded. What then, he asks, of the science that is studied in schools? Here he notes the evidence from many countries that pupils' interest in science declines during their school careers, and that this is reflected in a marked decline in the numbers choosing to pursue further study. Jenkins argues that the school science curriculum is in need of some radical revision and turns his attention to the school science laboratory and the activities demanded of pupils. He begins by questioning approaches that emphasize the acquisition of skills, arguing that they are rooted in an image of school science as pre-professional training. Drawing on notions of situated learning, he makes a case for activities which are more genuinely investigative and provide a context of action in which pupils are able to see and grasp the salience of scientific knowledge. Like Duschl, he sees that such approaches would provide an opportunity for developing understanding of the epistemic dimensions of science.

The attention of Steve Norris and Connie Korpan in Chapter 13 also focuses on epistemic aspects of the science curriculum. They argue that some of the idealist arguments of latter-day constructivists pose significant epistemological dilemmas for science teachers. For, in suggesting that science teachers portray science as a set of ideas which bear no necessary relation to reality, they inevitably trespass on the substantive claims of scientific knowledge as found in textbooks and other sources. Here science makes claims about the nature of reality, and to teach science in the manner advocated by the radical constructivists would require a fundamental rewrite of the texts of science. Norris and Korpan maintain that, while plural views should not be avoided when the appropriate occasion arises, views about the nature of science should not be allowed to determine first-order claims about the nature of reality.

Finally, in Chapter 14 Glen Aikenhead develops the notion of science as a cultural border crossing. Science education, it has been suggested, is a process of enculturation into science. Yet many young people grow up in a culture where the ideas and discourse of science seem foreign or unfamiliar. Confronted with such an alien culture, one response is shallow and superficial mechanistic learning, leading to little understanding of the content or the discourses and practices of science. One curricular response is to seek to develop meanings and understandings in some depth, so that students assimilate the models and ideas of western science. However, its failing is that it seeks to assimilate pupils into science rather than recognizing the value of their own cultural identity. Instead, Aikenhead argues for a third way in which science education is seen as a culture-making process. Here, exposure to the subculture of science as one of several ways of knowing encourages the student to see ideas about the world as cultural constructions. Such an approach would, while recognizing the value and importance of western science, help students to appreciate the legitimacy and value of other ways of knowing, including their own. In this context, the role of the teacher becomes more that of a cultural negotiator engaged in a process of *acculturation* – helping the child to recognize the strengths and weaknesses of western science in comparison to other ways of knowing – rather than *enculturation* into a singular dominant worldview. While he recognizes that this perspective will not be readily accepted, Aikenhead offers a fresh and radical perspective on what it might mean to teach and learn science.

9 Providing suitable content in the 'science for all' curriculum

Peter Fensham

Introduction

Rosalind Driver's doctoral study at the University of Illinois with Professor Jack Easley (Driver 1973) was one of a few studies before 1980 that inspired a striking shift in research interest among science educators – namely, to the study of students' alternative conceptions in science (see Pfundt and Duit 1994). Furthermore, the use of clinical interviewing by these pioneers to elicit their research data shifted the dominant styles of science education research from experimental and survey studies of science teaching to more qualitative research studies, involving relatively small numbers of learners or case studies of individual science classrooms. Gunstone *et al.* (1988) have, for instance, described their experience of these shifts.

This explosive interest in alternative conceptions of science in the 1980s led to a recognition that the 'science' of science education was in some sense problematic (Fensham 2000). A plethora of these studies found that school learners hold ideas about science (often tenaciously) that are contrary to those intended in school science. Nevertheless, the overwhelming response to these findings was not to question the suitability of such science for most learners. Rather, the consequences (with some positive outcomes for practice) have been a body of research into pedagogical strategies, such as conceptual conflict. A few authors, in isolated papers among the alternative conceptions studies and at several European conferences, have drawn conclusions directed at the content of science in the school curriculum; but these have not been generally adopted anywhere.

Another example of the tendency to slip easily into pedagogy and leave the content issues unresolved occurred when some of us at Monash University, Melbourne, edited a book, *The Content of Science*. Most of its chapters are more related to the subtitle, *Towards a Constructivist Approach to its*

Teaching and Learning than to the issues of content itself (Fensham *et al.* 1994). A notable exception was the chapter by White (1994) who, in setting out some properties of science content, argued that a *theory of content* is overdue – a task also recognized by Chevallard (see Chapter 2).

As an outcome of this body of research there is now a considerable body of knowledge of pedagogy in science education, although much still needs to be done before this knowledge is a standard feature of most science classrooms. One common implication of this body of research, if scientific concepts are to be understood by learners, has been that the dictum *less content, more learning*, must be applied.

Simultaneously, in the early 1980s as this research paradigm gathered momentum, country after country began to recognize the importance of what became known as the 'science for all' movement. This called for school science to be moved from the position where it entered the school curriculum in the senior secondary years, with its content chosen for the small minority of the cohort who were being prepared and selected for further study in the sciences, to occupy a position in the general educational curriculum where its content should have meaning and usefulness for all students.

The challenge of 'science for all' is well summarized by the four goals in the Canadian report of this movement, *Science for Every Citizen: Educating Canadians for Tomorrow's World* (Science Research Council of Canada 1984: 3):

- to develop citizens to participate in political and social choices in technological society;
- to train those with special interest in further studies in science and technology;
- to provide appropriate preparation for modern fields of work;
- to stimulate intellectual and moral growth in students.

Possibilities for change

Two basic aspects of school science need to be changed if it is to respond to society's demand for 'science for all'. These are: (i) the science to be learned (the *content*); and (ii) its manner of teaching (the *pedagogy*). Once either or both of these are determined, two other aspects become important for widely successful learning: the affective climate in which the teaching/learning occurs (the *motivation*); and the way learning is recognized (the *assessment*). These features are not independent of each other. For instance, the content to be learned ought to influence how it is taught (the pedagogy), and certainly how it is recognized (the assessment). Motivation for learning is affected by how it is recognized (the assessment), and can, in turn, be affected by both what is to be learned (the content) and how it is taught (the pedagogy).

In this chapter, I am directing attention to how the content for 'science for all' should be determined, because compared to other areas of research interest, the issues of content have lacked attention. For the great majority of learners who will not go on to science related careers, the case for the content of their science learning in school must be built on learning outcomes that will be sustained by their lives in society as citizens, in the world of work, and in their personal life (Goals 1, 3 and 4 in the Canadian report). In the first part of this chapter, I shall review several approaches to defining these outcomes in content terms, relating them where possible to research studies. In the second part I shall consider two ways of providing criteria for choosing the content to match these outcomes.

Approaches to defining content

The expert definition of important science

The first approach to redefining the content for school science draws on the expertise of the community of scientists and/or of those educators engaged in the determination of the school science curriculum. For example, Project 2061 in the USA began by asking about 100 scientists to list the important knowledge in their respective fields that all students should be given the chance to know in school (AAAS 1990). Similarly, the National Curriculum project in England and Wales appointed a committee of science educators (Ros Driver was a member) to address a similar question (National Curriculum Council 1989). The result of this approach, in almost every case, has been proposals that increase the range and extent of the content for school science. The compass of science content is extended beyond the traditional conceptual content of physics, chemistry and biology to include earth and space sciences and applications of science and technology, as well as various versions of the nature of science and technology. For instance, the National Academy of Science (1996) in the USA recommended eight content areas: science as inquiry; physical sciences; life science; earth and space science; science and technology; science in personal and social perspectives; history and nature of science; and unifying concepts of science. Other versions of this broad range were the 17 content strands for the National Science Curriculum in England and Wales, and the eight benchmarks for scientific literacy from Project 2061 (AAAS 1993) in the USA. Extensions of the range of content in these ways are indicative of intentions that, when science is for *all* learners they need more than the conceptual terms and principles of the basic physical and biological sciences. Although it is probably true that the authors of these proposals did regard some (perhaps even much) of that conceptual detail as dispensable in order to accommodate their broader interpretation of relevant science, clear proposals for large-scale deletions were not made.

Consequently, in becoming curricula in practice, there was only a pragmatic reduction in the range of content in the 1990s rather than any principled excision. The result was the retention of much of the traditional content with little new material. Hence, the science content, which is now intended to be covered by all students in the compulsory years, exceeds what was previously expected for all but a minority of students – ignoring the previously cited dictum of better learning and a disastrous recipe for 'science for all'.

In these new curricula, it has also been recommended that science teaching should now begin in the initial years of schooling (the primary or elementary levels). Previously in those years it had only been present in most countries in a nominal sense, depending in practice very much on the enthusiasm of the teachers at these levels, most of whom lacked a knowledge of science and the confidence to teach it. During the 1990s the implementation of this recommendation led, for example, in England and Wales, New Zealand, Australia, Korea, Canada, Norway and some states in the USA to the specification of detailed conceptual and preconceptual content for teaching / learning. In some of these cases, external testing of these young learners has also been introduced (reinforcing only the teaching and learning of the types of content these tests are able to measure). Research evidence is now appearing that shows that this trend to elaborate and test the science content is itself restricting the range of pedagogies that even the confident teachers feel able to use.

One notable exception to this detailing of the range of science content is Denmark – a country also concerned about the weak state of its students' learning of science, particularly in the first six years of schooling. In keeping with its traditions of *Didaktic* 'democracy in schooling' and the professional role of teachers, the new Danish curriculum for these years does not specify the science content to be learned. Rather, it outlines some scientific 'working methods and ways of thinking' which teachers and their students should practise together in contexts drawn from the 'near surroundings', the 'distant surroundings' and 'human interactions with nature' (Møller Anderson *et al.* 1995). A trial with almost 100 schools gave the curriculum planners confidence that when these methods and ways of thinking form a regular part of students' experience, sound science content will be learned. In this curriculum, conceptual knowledge emerges from the investigations, rather than being pre-specified as content to be learned in isolation from its purposes in science. There are definite advantages to this approach that could well be heeded by other countries, particularly those listed above, as each is now faced with the daunting problem of developing the scientific knowledge of their primary teachers when they are also under pressure to raise literacy, numeracy and information technology standards.

Maintenance of essential science knowledge

A second approach to defining content was developed when the project team responsible for the Third International Mathematics and Science Study (TIMSS) decided to test all students in the final year of secondary schooling for what it termed 'mathematical and scientific literacy' (MSL). Defining the content of MSL became a matter of interesting debate (Orpwood and Garden 1998). The two questions initially addressed were:

- What concepts and skills do students retain by the end of schooling? How much is enough? If it is not enough, where are the serious shortfalls?
- What attitudes and beliefs about mathematics and science do students and teachers hold at the end of these post-compulsory years?

For MSL, the recall of science content from a small number of topics, studied in the earlier years and considered to have ongoing significance, was to be stressed, but with some attention being given to societal impact, reasoning, social and historical developments and attitudes. The development of such tests was then disrupted by a paper by Atkin and Helms (1993) who had been independently commissioned by TIMSS to prepare a conceptual framework for MSL. They asked two very different questions:

- If MSL is analogous to language or cultural literacy, do citizens need to know science in the same sense that one needs to know one's mother tongue?
- Is the ability to use scientific knowledge in the way one uses language essential for adequate functioning and responsible citizenship?

Atkin and Helms answered their questions in the negative, and hence suggested that TIMSS, for its MSL population, should focus rather on intellectual and social history, practical reasoning and habits of mind. International evaluation juggernauts do not find it easy to respond to radical suggestions for new directions. Not surprisingly, TIMSS made only minor changes to its test development, continuing to emphasize the recall of content knowledge taught in earlier years (26 items) compared with reasoning and social utility (6 items). The contexts for these latter six questions were nuclear reactors, Chlorofluorocarbons (CFCs), biological control, high heels and floors, industrial creativity and a new paint for bridges. Each context had quite varying social, economic and political consequences, and relevance across the participating countries – an aspect TIMSS acknowledged but could not accommodate, because of its commitment to a test made up of common isolated items.

The findings from TIMSS, for students who had ceased their study of science for one, two or more years, clearly confirmed that forgetting of science knowledge begins *before* they leave school. One study of these students indicated, furthermore, that they had only a limited sense of the generalizability or relevance of their science knowledge (Fensham 1998a). Thus much of the learning of school science still appeared to be, as White (1988) observed, isolated fragments of knowledge that students did not link or anchor to relevant aspects of their lives. Such learning is particularly susceptible to forgetting.

The TIMSS evidence of students' inability to recall science they have learned in school is simply consistent with the evidence from the now popular surveys of public knowledge which reveal the low state of passive residual knowledge of science held by adult citizens, regardless of how much science they studied at school and how long ago (Durant *et al.* 1989; Miller *et al.* 1996). Although adults who have studied more science at school generally score a little better, these findings offer a poor prognosis for the learning outcomes of contemporary students when the new school science curricula are even more crowded – unless, that is, great leaps forward can be made in enabling learning coherence, and ways can be found to reinforce learning through assessment.

Coherence and linkage of science learning
In the last decade, curriculum design for science education has directly addressed this urgent problem of providing coherence – what might be called a long-lasting 'glue' for the knowledge developed by school science. One is the approach of the 'concepts in real world contexts' of the Dutch *PLON* physics project and of *Salters' Science* and *Salters' Chemistry* in England. The other is the 'curriculum as story' approach of which the science materials of the Curriculum Corporation in Australia for the compulsory years, and the chemistry materials of *Salters' A Level Chemistry* in England are good examples. The effective implementation of these designs in the classroom provides a range of 'contexts' and 'stories' which are integral components of the essential content, providing a framework that gives salience and relevance to the concepts. However, their acceptance has been difficult for many science teachers who have been strongly socialized into believing the content of the sciences consists of definitional abstract concepts, with the use of associated algorithms for application to standard, closed problems. Furthermore, both 'context' and 'story', as components of the content for learning, have personal and experiential qualities that make them inherently difficult to assess in external examinations, especially at senior levels.

Practical science knowledge-in-action

A third, albeit indirect, means of exploring features of a possible content for school science emerges from the studies of the public understanding of science, pioneered by Layton and his colleagues at Leeds. These studies contrast markedly with the surveys of passive, residual science knowledge referred to previously (Layton *et al.* 1993; see also Chapter 12). In the Leeds studies, groups in society were identified who had an urgent need to know some science, such as parents of Down's syndrome babies or old age pensioners who wanted to reduce their heating costs. Individual members in each case were interviewed about the knowledge they had acquired in order to cope with their compelling circumstances. One outcome from these interesting case studies is a set of criteria for what has become known as *practical science knowledge-in-action*. This knowledge has:

- pressing relevance to the persons concerned;
- stood the test of personal experience;
- been related to other social knowledge;
- a trustworthy source;
- been translated into a form that communicates differently from the way it is stated formally in science.

Some of these criteria are difficult for school science content to match. Only very occasionally is it likely that a class of students will share an urgent need to know, or that much of the balance between science knowledge and other related social knowledge can be explored in school science. However, it may be that 'compelling interest' could be used as a classroom counterpart to 'urgent need'. Sjøberg (see Chapter 10) shows, from his international studies of students' interest, that providing a focal question to explore, rather than the usual domain name, can dramatically alter the response to science content. For example, the generally low interest in studying 'Sound and Acoustics' changed to a clear positive interest in 'How birds and animals make music'.

A fourth approach, linking the acceptance of content knowledge with the trustworthiness of the source, has been insufficiently recognized in school science education. For instance, socioscientific decision making is now regularly listed among the desirable outcomes for scientific literacy. Reports have, however, begun to appear in the literature suggesting that persons make their decisions about socioscientific and sociotechnical issues as a result of their trust of the source of the relevant scientific information, or their identification with the social values of one of the opposing groups (see for example Gaskell 1994). These findings also downplay individuals' science knowledge and emphasize the social aspects of such knowledge. Yet most students at school, without access at home to scientific expertise, *have* to trust their science teachers about what they should learn, and what knowledge in particular is needed for the rites that society will use to accredit their school learning. Students also have the right to expect their teachers will conscientiously endeavour to engage their interest and to assist them in such learning. The undermining of this trust, either deliberately or unintentionally, through a curriculum that lacks any apparent relevance can be destructive of the further learning of science for students. In contrast, studies of classrooms where extended open-ended project work is given a central place as content in school science, suggest that the partnership required between teacher and learners can build very positive trust.

The more the assessment of learning in the separate subjects of a school curriculum is an individual matter, the more the social element of trust is obscured. Yet, outside of school we all recognize that it is not necessary for every individual to learn everything. Each of us develops a network, large or small, of persons we know and trust to have the knowledge that we, on occasion, need. Such shared trust about scientific knowledge is very evident among groups concerned with or involved in a socioscientific issue. Not all of them need to know the science of the issue, but they *do* need to know someone who does know. If networks of this sort were possible in school science its task of being 'science for all' would be easier.

Aikenhead (1992) developed a curriculum for mid-secondary science around decisions relating to the issues of car driving and alcohol consumption, and reported positively of its contribution to increased rationality in classroom discourse. The high personal motivation this socially important issue has for students of this age in Canada, and its relative scientific simplicity, may have made this intended outcome possible. However, many important socioscientific issues are so complex (holistic or multivariant) that no one group of scientists can investigate or report the totality of the relevant information. It would be indigestible for school students and the general public if they did. Commonly, when community and political decisions are required, the scientific studies are incomplete, so that sectional information is offered by opposing groups of scientists. Each group's information may be well founded as far as it goes, but their perspectives differ because they value dissimilar aspects of the issue. In the face of such complexity, it is quite wishful to think that any school science we can imagine would enable complete rational differentiation. Thus, in 'science for all' the content needs to emphasize the interdependence between scientific inquiry and personal and social values, as well as the emphasis on the logic and rationality of scientific argumentation advocated in the next section.

Finally, much more could be done about the fifth approach to translating formal scientific language into forms that are understood outside of school. Language researchers, with an orientation to functional grammar, like Halliday and Martin (1993), have many insights to offer, as have Layton (1993) and Gardner (1994) with their penetrating case comparisons of science and technology.

'Higher order' reasoning in science

A fourth approach to the determination of content blossomed in the 1990s. It shifts the definition of content from an extensive knowledge of the concepts of science to so-called 'higher order' scientific reasoning. For example, Kuhn (1993) has argued that the weight of important detailed conceptual knowledge in science courses is so great that its acquisition by most students is impossible. As an alternative learning outcome she has proposed *scientific argumentation* as a fundamental and powerful capability for all students to acquire. This is a particular example of Olson's (1994) claim that understanding a discipline like science requires the ability to participate in its discourses. The reports of studies about implementing this claim in individual classrooms are increasing, but nowhere are they yet systemically prescribed as part of the curriculum. Furthermore, although the theories underpinning this emphasis on discourse are substantial, they are also contested (see Chapter 3). Some socially orientated theories give little or no weight to individual cognition, and hence studies based on them seek only to implement shifts in the classroom discourse. This research literature about science discourses in classrooms sidesteps two important questions that are asked by others who see schooling as a process of teaching (learning) individuals:

• How much conceptual knowledge does an individual student need in order to engage meaningfully in these higher order discourses?
• Will practice and participation in higher order reasoning lead to and/or deepen an individual's conceptual understanding?

In the current OECD/PISA (Organization for Economic Cooperation and Development/Programme for International Student Assessment) science project, equal emphasis is given to the testing of students near the end of compulsory schooling for conceptual understanding and for four priority scientific process skills. These skills are identified as:

• recognizing scientifically investigable questions;
• identifying evidence/data needed in a scientific investigation;
• drawing or evaluating conclusions; and
• communicating valid conclusions.   OECD/PISA (1999)

The Science Group of OECD/PISA argue that these are not a 1990's reinvention of a set of the 1960s/70's science processes that were decontextualized and concept free. Thus in these new tests, students will be required to demonstrate these skills in relation to contexts made up of actual massmedia reports about science. In answering a series of items about each report students will have to draw on their conceptual or procedural science knowledge. This is a brave attempt (compared with TIMSS's reliance on isolated, multiple-choice conceptual items) to offer, internationally, a form of assessment that simulates two or three of the criteria of practical science knowledge-in-action that were discussed in the previous section. This is largely uncharted water at the research level with only a few ambiguous soundings to guide the PISA group, but its testings may well, in the next few years, help to further our understanding of the challenge of 'science for all' – a task the TIMSS project has notably failed to do.

Future projections about content

One of the last things Ros Driver (with some colleagues) did in science education was to initiate a series of seminars among British science educators in which they were asked to consider what the next new phase in school science might be like. This imaginative and morale-boosting enterprise led to the publication of the report *Beyond 2000: Science Education for the Future*, edited by Millar and Osborne (1998). The report also acknowledges that the changing curricular position of science (to 'science for all') has not been accompanied by a corresponding change in content, and three of the report's ten recommendations (recommendations 4, 5 and 6) address the content issue:

4 The curriculum needs to be presented clearly and simply, and its content needs to be seen to follow from the stated aims (*also suggested*). Scientific knowledge can best be presented as a number of key 'explanatory stories'. In addition the curriculum should introduce young people to a number of important ideas about science.
5 Work should be undertaken to explore how aspects of technology and applications of science currently omitted could be incorporated with a science curriculum to enhance 'scientific literacy'.
6 The science curriculum should provide young people with an understanding of some key ideas about science, that is, ideas about the ways in which reliable knowledge about the natural world has been, and is being, obtained.

(Millar and Osborne 1998: 14, 19, 20)

Some specific suggestions about new content are made for each of these recommendations, stemming from the broad principles the participants are trying to articulate. Other recommendations are clearly aimed at recovering directions evident in curriculum development in the UK before the imperatives of the National Curriculum became so totally dominant. For example, curriculum debate and materials in England in the 1980s helped to shape the idea that school science should be addressed through science-technology-society issues. However, the designation of technology as a separate key learning area stopped these mutually beneficial interactions.

Considerations of the future have also played a part in the development of a new science curriculum for the state of Queensland in Australia. Its project team was very aware that to try to implement their vision for the future immediately would invoke great bewilderment and resistance among teachers. Accordingly, they settled for modest changes in the existing content, including some clear exclusions. One new strand of content, 'Science as a way of knowing', was included in an introductory manner so that, it is hoped, it will inspire a group of enthusiastic teachers whose advocacy will enable this strand to have a much more central place as content in the next revision of school science. The shift from science as a body of knowledge to science as a way of knowing is rooted in the need to emphasize higher order reasoning in science (see previous section).

Criteria for choosing content

Curriculum emphases

Since the choice of content for 'science for all' can be approached in at least several ways, some clear criteria for choice are needed. Based on analyses of a large number of North American science curriculum materials, Roberts (1982) defined seven curriculum emphases. He deliberately used the word 'emphasis' (rather than purpose) because, he argued, if students are to become aware and confident that their learning of science does have a coherent, meaningful purpose, and is not just isolated pieces of information, this purpose must be given explicit and repeated emphasis over a reasonably sustained period of learning. In other words, the curriculum for any one semester or year of study should relate to only two or three emphases, with other purposes of science education having less prominence during that time.

Roberts (1988) further developed the concept, indicating among other things how an emphasis influences the choice of content, and the roles of the teachers and students. Later, Roberts (1995) himself described a new junior secondary curriculum in Alberta, Canada, that very explicitly matched content with emphasis. Of his other curriculum emphases, 'solid foundation', 'correct explanation' and 'scientific skill development' all relate to the content in most traditional courses, while the 'structure of science' foreshadowed the increasing interest internationally in open-ended practical problem solving, and in higher order reasoning as aspects of the nature of science. Some more recent curriculum materials relate to additional emphases, three of which I have identified as 'science in application', 'science as nurturing', and 'science through technology' (Fensham 1997).

The idea of different emphases for school science at different levels of schooling makes good sense to teachers. When they are asked to choose two or three from the list of ten (Roberts' seven and my own three) for their level of learners, there is usually quite remarkable agreement about at least the first two. For example, 'everyday coping' and 'science as nurturing (environment) are regularly chosen for the first three years, 'self as explainer' in the next three years and 'science technology decisions' in the later secondary years. This finding suggests more use could be made of this conception in designing curriculum and choosing its content.

Roberts (1988) stressed that each emphasis will include conceptual content if it is to remain true to science. A year earlier, Millar and Driver (1987) had powerfully debunked what, in hindsight, was an erroneous but influential example of different emphases for school science – that of process – that emerged from the great curriculum project period in the 1960s and 1970s. This had led to a division between an emphasis on conceptual science for secondary school science and an emphasis on so-called science 'processes' for the elementary or primary years.

In 1988 the Science Committee of the National Curriculum in England and Wales, in an embracing review of the whole curriculum of schooling for the 11 compulsory years in these two countries, found itself responsible for determining school science across both the primary and the secondary years. Hitherto, separate science curriculum projects had more confined tasks – the science for the primary years, for the junior secondary years, for examination courses in chemistry or physics or biology, etc. – situations that can accommodate different emphases. Furthermore, the Science Committee then found itself constrained by the beguilingly attractive, although educationally nonsensical position, taken by the National Curriculum as a whole, that there should be a progression in the learning of similar content from the point of entry to school until eleven years later. To facilitate the comparability of the development in the ten key school subjects (science being one of these), the committee for each learning area was provided with a matrix to fill. The columns of this matrix were to be content or process strands (based on a fallacious notion that they can be resolved), and the rows, the progression through ten levels of learning in each strand. Learning, as defined by this framework, was then to be externally tested periodically during the years of compulsory schooling.

This bureaucratic view of schooling was politically motivated by economic rationalist views of education in which accountability was a driving concept. Its structural matrix for the total curriculum, and for each of its component subject areas, was compatible with what has been described as a 'cultural restorationist' ideology. It was, however, incompatible with the various curriculum emphases that were emerging in England and Wales for the different levels of schooling, such as STS (science, technology and society) in junior secondary schools, science through practical technology and science for supporting the environment in the primary schools, and 'concepts in context' for secondary physics and chemistry.

The Science Committee made a brave but short lived attempt to work within (or perhaps to subvert) the constraints by first suggesting for the matrix 21 content strands for the columns, and then reducing them to 19. Accordingly, it is not surprising that the 190 content targets that this matrix presented seemed impossible for teachers, particularly those in primary schools. This reaction provided the opportunity for further pruning, and by 1991 the matrix for England and Wales had been simplified to four strands, three of which were familiar as traditional conceptual knowledge in the biological, chemical and physical sciences. The fourth strand, 'working scientifically', was the remnant of earlier strands that together related to the nature of science and the study of empirical enquiry, but was now quite like the limited notion of science processes that Millar and Driver (1987) had so broadly criticized.

A simplified form of the content matrix then began to appear in other countries, like New Zealand, Australia, Singapore and South Korea, where similar bureaucratic ideologies were in the ascendancy. The AAAS (1993) in the USA also used an extended matrix form to set out its content suggestions for the *Benchmarks for Scientific Literacy*, with eight distinctive strands that have also been largely reduced to the familiar and traditional when modified for implementation as a state curriculum. The fundamental differences in all these countries between the human and physical resources for teaching science in the primary and the secondary years are so marked and so well documented, that it is hard to comprehend how the notion of seamless progression, in and across these levels of schooling, was ever seriously proposed and slavishly imposed. Fortunately, other countries in Europe, North America and Asia have embarked on reforms of their science curriculum which are making use of criteria that are more compatible with the notion of distinctive curriculum emphases.

Didactical analysis

In the 1990s educational researchers from the Anglo-American curriculum tradition began conversing with colleagues in continental Europe with its traditions of Didaktiks (see Hopmann and Riquarts 1995 and the *Journal of Curriculum Studies* 1995, 27(1)). The reports of these meetings have clarified some differences in these traditions that have interesting consequences for research and important implications for curriculum content. I believe these differences are poorly understood, at least in the English-speaking educational world. To appreciate them, the meaning contained in the German word, *Bildung*, in an educational context, has to be understood. One of the useful metaphors for its meaning is the formation of the whole person; another is the nurturing of a plant from seedling to full flower. Such views of school education have not usually been recognized to any substantial extent in the Anglo-American curriculum tradition, with its strong emphasis on an education system as the source responsible for education (rather than the teacher working in the Didaktik tradition).

Some of the important differences between these conceptions for the determination of content are well stated in the first three of the five sets of questions about content that Klafki sets out in his didactical analysis for teacher education (see Hopmann and Riquarts 1995: 324):

1   What wider or general sense or reality does this content exemplify and open up to the learner? What basic phenomenon or fundamental principle, what law, criterion, problem, method, technique or attitude can be grasped by dealing with this content as an 'example'?

2   What significance does the content in question or the experience, knowledge, ability, or skill to be acquired through this topic already possess in the minds of the children in my class? What significance should it have from a pedagogical point of view?

3   What constitutes the topic's significance for the children's future?

4   How are the contents structured (which have been placed in a specifically pedagogical perspective by questions 1, 2 and 3)?

5(a) What fact, phenomena, situations, experiments, controversies, etc. (i.e. what intuitions) are appropriate to induce the child to ask questions directed at the essence and structure of the content in question?

  (b) What pictures, hints, situations, observations, accounts, experiments, models, etc., are appropriate in helping children to answer, as independently as possible, their questions directed at the essentials of the matter? What situations and tasks are appropriate for helping students grasp the principle of the content by means of the example of an elementary 'case', and to apply and practise it so that it will be of real benefit to them?

Sets 4 and 5 are familiar in both traditions as questions dealt with in subjects like 'methods of teaching' or 'pedagogics'. The first three sets are much less commonly addressed in the Anglo-American curriculum tradition, where the intended curriculum with its detailed content and sequence is usually provided for the teacher by the education system, through its curriculum body and/or examination board. The application of the first three sets of questions, in educational systems that are seeking 'science for all' provides criteria that can considerably assist the choice of content for school science. For example, Set 1 and Set 3 would require traditional science topics to only be justifiable because they exemplify *a fundamental principle, a general sense*, or *a common technique*, both for the learner now and for their future. Perhaps the answers to questions like these are what the Project 2061 or the National Academy of Science were seeking when they included content strands called 'Common themes' and 'Unifying concepts of science'?

It is certainly instructive and challenging to insert various familiar school science topics like series and parallel circuits, laws of reflection and energy flow in food chains, into the questions of Set 1. For example, what do chemical equations exemplify in science? One answer, often overlooked by chemistry teachers in their concern to impart algorithms for balancing, or calculating a yield, is the conservation of matter. This conservation principle (or more popularly, 'You can't get something from nothing, and you can't get nothing from something!') is knowledge of immense practical importance for society's conservation of resources and its recognition of the pressing issue of waste materials.

If answers of worth can be given to these questions, they serve to identify big ideas in the sciences that have wide application and hence are important content to be taught/learned (see Recommendation 6 above in Millar and Osborne 1998). The questions in Set 2 press for answers that make up a range of content for learning (experiences, knowledge, abilities and skills) and open the ideas of sequence and progression in learning to a variety of outcomes, which are more likely to find responses among all learners than the narrowly conceptual progressions have so far been able to do. Finally, Set 3 serves to remind us that, in the case of 'science for all', it is the future beyond school, not next week, next term or next school year, that needs to be the target for competent and confident learning.

Conclusion: urgency and resistance

In this chapter, I have argued that the content of school science must change. Its conceptual content must be more selective, and taught in a manner that gives these powerful ideas coherence and linkage. There ought not to be the same emphasis, and hence the same sort of content, at the different levels or stages of schooling, and the content to be learned must have some future significance if the intentions of 'science for all' are to be furthered. Some possible ways of defining what the change in content might be have been reviewed.

However, it is important to note that even when there appear to have been clear directions for this change, there has been strong resistance from powerful groups. Indeed, at the upper secondary level attempts to change the content have often been defeated or short lived. Defeat of content reform at the senior secondary levels has a knock-on effect to the lower levels of schooling, because of the academic status the senior sciences (particularly chemistry and physics) hold as prerequisite subjects for entry to highly competitive, tertiary courses. It is, therefore, not easy for schools and teachers to define the content of what seems to be the same subject lower in the school in radically different ways.

Hart (1995), Blades (1997) and Fensham (1998b) have all reported the intense struggles that have ensued when serious attempts have been made to reformulate the content of senior secondary sciences with another emphasis than that of the introductory conceptual emphasis they were given in the great reforms of the 1960s – when these subjects were only concerned with the preparation of students with an interest in further scientific studies. Blades uses an allegorical story about a kingdom in which children are disappearing (dropping out of school science) to present, in a powerful way, how interest groups align initially to support finding the children, and then realign to thwart the quest for them, indicative of the tinkering at the edges that is all that remains of so many attempts to reform the content of school science.

In some countries, recognition of the difficulty of reforming the senior secondary curriculum has led to alternative approaches being used to allow content, seen as more appropriate for 'science for all', to be available as curriculum. Two Australian states developed an STS science and an environmental science in the late 1970s as alternative senior sciences, but, in each case these were not mandatory or acceptable for entry to the old and high-status universities. Not surprisingly they have languished with only a few schools offering them to small numbers of students. On the other hand, Thailand, as early as the late 1970s, had defined two mandatory years of biological and physical science for senior students who had chosen to be in the humanities stream in their academic schools. Israel has now taken similar action by requiring all 'non-science' students in their senior years to study an STS-type science subject. The Netherlands in 1998 introduced 'Public understanding of science' as a new subject in Grade 10 to be taken by *all* students, including those who have chosen to continue with science in these senior years. The vision for this subject was to present the big ideas in science and technology in historical, philosophical, economic and societal contexts. De Vos and Reiding (1999) have reported some of the difficulties (not from obstructive sources) that curriculum developers face in embodying such an alternative view of science content in a designated curriculum, and in developing textbooks. There are important lessons to be learned from each of these approaches to reform as the search for the content of school 'science for all' continues.

References

AAAS (1990) *Science for All Americans*. Washington: American Association for the Advancement of Science.
AAAS (1993) *Benchmarks for Scientific Literacy*. Washington: American Association for the Advancement of Science.

Aikenhead, G.S. (1992) Logical reasoning in science and technology. *Bulletin of Science, Technology & Society*, 12(3): 149–59.

Atkin, M. and Helms, J. (1993) Getting serious about priorities in science education. *Studies in Science Education*, 21: 1–20.

Blades, D.W. (1997) *Procedures of Power & Curriculum Change*. New York: Peter Lang.

De Vos, W. and Reiding, J. (1999) Public understanding of science as a separate subject in secondary schools in The Netherlands. *International Journal of Science*, 21(7): 711–20.

Driver, R. (1973) 'The representations of conceptual frameworks in young adolescent science students', unpublished PhD dissertation. University of Illinois, Urbana.

Durant, J., Evans, G. and Thomas, G. (1989) Public understanding of science in Britain: the role of medicine in the popular presentation of science. *Public Understanding of Science*, 1: 161–82.

Fensham, P.J. (1997) Continuity and discontinuity in curriculum policy and practice: case studies of science in four countries, in K. Calhoun, R. Panwar and S. Shrum (eds) *Proceedings of 8th Symposium of IOSTE*, vol. 2, *Policy*, pp. 32–6. Edmonton: IOSTE Conference Committee.

Fensham, P.J. (1998a) Student response to the TIMSS test. *Research in Science Education*, 28(4): 481–9.

Fensham, P.J. (1998b) The politics of legitimating and marginalizing companion meanings: three case stories, in D.A. Roberts and L. Östman (eds) *Problems of Meaning in Science Curriculum*, pp. 178–92. New York: Teachers College Press.

Fensham, P.J. (2000) Science content as problematic: issues for research, in *Proceedings of the Second ESERA Conference* (Rosalind Driver Memorial Lecture), Kiel, September. Dordrecht: Kluwer Academic Publisher.

Fensham, P.J., Gunstone, R.F. and White, R.T. (1994) *The Content of Science: Towards a Constructivist Approach to its Teaching and Learning*. London: Falmer.

Gardner, P.L. (1994) The relation between technology and science: some historical and philosophical reflections. *International Journal of Technology and Design Education*, Part I, 4: 123–53; Part II, 5: 1–33.

Gaskell, P.J. (1994) Assessing STS literacy: what is rational? In K. Boersma, K. Kortland and J. van Trommel (eds) *7th IOSTE Symposium, Papers Part 1*, pp. 309–20. Endrecht: IOSTE Conference Committee.

Gunstone, R.F., White, R.T. and Fensham, P.J. (1988) Developments in style and purpose of research on the learning of science. *Journal of Research in Science Teaching*, 25(7): 5–13.

Halliday, M.A.K. and Martin, J.R. (eds) (1993) *Writing Science: Literacy and Discursive Power*. London: Falmer.

Hart, C. (1995) 'The story of a curriculum document for school physics', unpublished PhD thesis. Monash University, Clayton.

Hopmann, S. and Riquarts, K. (eds) (1995) *Didaktik and/or Curriculum*. Kiel, Germany: I.P.N.

Kuhn, D. (1993) Science as argument: implications for teaching and learning scientific thinking. *Science Education*, 77(3): 319–37.

Layton, D. (1993) *Technology's Challenge to Science Education*. Buckingham: Open University Press.

Layton, D., Jenkins, E., Macgill, S. and Davey, A. (1993) *Inarticulate Science? Perspectives on the Public Understanding of Science and Some Implications for Science Education.* Driffield: Studies in Education.

Millar, R. and Driver, R. (1987) Beyond processes. *Studies in Science Education,* 14: 33–62.

Millar, R. and Osborne, J. (1998) *Beyond 2000: Science Education for the Future.* London: Nuffield Foundation.

Miller, J.D., Pardo, R. and Niwa, F. (1996) *Indicators of Scientific Literacy and Attitude to Science and Technology: A Comparative Study of Canada, the European Union, Japan and the United States* (paper for 'New Indicators for the Knowledge-based Economy'). Paris: OECD.

Møller Anderson, A., Schnack, K. and Sørensen, H. (eds) (1995) *Science: Natur/ Teknik, Assessment and Learning.* Copenhagen: Royal Danish School of Educational Studies.

National Academy of Science (1996) *National Science Education Standards.* Washington: National Academy Press.

National Curriculum Council (1989) *Science: Non-statutory Guidance.* London: National Curriculum Council.

OECD/PISA (1999) *Measuring Student Knowledge and Skills: A New Framework for Assessment.* Paris: OECD.

Olson, D.R. (1994) *The World on Paper: The Conceptual and Cognitive Implications of Writing and Reading.* Cambridge: Cambridge University Press.

Orpwood, G. and Garden, R.A. (1998) *Assessing Mathematics and Science Literacy* (TIMSS Monograph no. 4). Vancouver: Pacific Educational Press.

Pfundt, H. and Duit, R. (1994) *Bibliography: Students' Alternative Frameworks and Science Education,* 4th edn. Kiel, Germany: I.P.N.

Roberts, D. (1982) Developing the concept of 'curriculum emphasis'. *Science Education,* 66: 243–60.

Roberts, D.A. (1988) What counts as science education? in P.J. Fensham (ed.) *Developments and Dilemmas in Science Education,* pp. 27–54. London: Falmer.

Roberts, D.A. (1995) Junior high school science transformed: analysing a science curriculum policy change. *International Journal of Science Education,* 17(4): 493–504.

Science Research Council of Canada (1984) *Science for Every Citizen: Educating Canadians for Tomorrow's World* (summary of Report no. 36). Ottawa: Supply and Service.

White, R.T. (1988) *Learning Science.* Oxford: Blackwell.

White, R.T. (1994) Dimensions of Content, in P.J. Fensham, R.F. Gunstone and R.T. White (eds) *The Content of Science: Towards a Constructivist Approach to its Teaching and Learning,* pp. 255–62. London: Falmer.

10 Interesting all children in 'science for all'

Svein Sjøberg

Introduction

International comparisons put one's own national contexts and educational choices in a wider perspective – a perspective from which one may better be able to see one's own curricula with new eyes and with a more open mind for alternatives. In this way, the comparisons may open up the potential for greater variety and for possible inspiration from outside. But international comparisons may also have the opposite effect. They may – often indirectly or unintentionally – have the effect of restricting choices and of providing a pressure to harmonize science teaching towards universal standards for content as well as teaching methods and assessment. This kind of criticism may be raised against the large-scale studies by the IEA (International Association for the Evaluation of Educational Achievement). The most recent IEA study is TIMSS (Third International Mathematics and Science Study; reported in, for instance TIMSS 1996, 1997, 1998). However, smaller and less ambitious comparative studies may supplement the large-scale studies. Such studies may provide other sorts of information that may give clues and ideas for the improvement of science education. In this chapter, I will present some results from a study of this sort, the SAS (science and scientists) study.

Background, rationale and aims

There is broad agreement that all teaching should 'build on' the interests and experiences of the child. But the simple and obvious fact is that *children are different.* They do not have the same experiences when they meet school science, nor do they have the same interests. There are differences between pupils in the same class, in the same school, or the same nation. And there may be systematic differences between girls and boys. There are certainly large differences between children in different countries. Growing up in rural Africa is different from growing up in London, and growing up in Tokyo is different from growing up in New York. In the light of this, the striking similarity of science curricula and textbooks becomes problematic.

The intention of this study was to shed light on some of the issues that may be important for an informed discussion of culture, gender and science education. The results may be used for comparisons between the interests of the pupils and the actual contents of curricula, textbooks and exams. Another purpose of the study was networking and capacity building, with a special focus on engaging female researchers from developing countries in joint research. These aims emerge from the context of the development of the study. The three researchers, Jane Mulemwa from Uganda, Jayshree Mehta from India and Svein Sjøberg from Norway are jointly involved in international cooperation and development. Details about the project, its development, the questionnaire, participation and main results are available (Sjøberg 2000). Presented here are some of the findings from our work.

The instruments

The research instrument is a questionnaire consisting of seven items, designed to explore the interests of children, their experiences, their perceptions of science, their hopes, priorities and visions for the future. The questions cover aspects that are relevant for the science curriculum. In addition, a questionnaire to be filled in by the researcher was also developed.

The items in the pupils' questionnaire were based on research instruments used in previous research, by this author and by others. Prior to this work, these items have been used in only one country or in comparisons between similar countries in the North. Therefore, we undertook a long process of adopting the instruments to this new cross-cultural context. Piloting of the instruments was then done in the countries of the three researchers.

The pilot testing provided experiences from three different continents, and was the basis for the process of refining and developing the items. We had in mind to make an instrument that could, in principle, be used in all parts of the world. However, in each culture, there will be words, phrases and even contexts that may seem strange for the kids. For instance, few children in industrialized countries have experience with 'making bricks' or 'carrying water on the head'. Similarly, few children in developing countries are likely to have much experience with computer games and video recorders. Hence, the final instrument is a compromise, and it should be seen and understood in this light. A brief description of the items referred to in this chapter is provided below.

Item 2: out of school experiences – what I have done

This item is an inventory of a total of 80 activities that may have a bearing on the teaching and learning of science. It has also been used in previous research in a slightly different form (Lie and Sjøberg 1984; Whyte *et al.* 1987). Care was taken to sample a large variety of activities, with a broad cultural diversity. There are three possible responses to each activity in the inventory: 'Often (many times)'; 'Seldom (once or twice)'; and 'Never'.

Item 3: things to learn about

This item is a similar list to that in Item 2, and is used in some of the above mentioned studies. It is an inventory of possible topics for inclusion in the science curriculum. A total of 60 topics are listed. Care has been taken to put similar scientific *content* into different *contexts*. The rationale behind this is to explore whether different contexts, or different perspectives, appeal in another way to different groups of pupils or different cultures. The pupils responded by simply ticking a 'Yes' to each topic they would like to learn about.

Item 5: science in action

'Science' may mean different things to different pupils, and the word may trigger different emotions, or provide different associations. This item is a list of such possible word associations, and the pupil is invited to indicate the ones that they find suitable. This item is meant to elicit some attitudes to science and some perceptions about what science may or may not contribute to.

Item 6: scientists at work

The task of 'draw a scientist' has been used in research for a long time in different formulations and with slight modifications (Mead and Metraux 1957; Krajkovich and Smith 1982; Chambers 1983; Kahle 1987; Kjærnsli 1989; Matthews 1996). The purpose of such an item is to elicit the image of scientists held by the learner. It may be argued that this item simply begs the presentation of stereotypes. In the research reported in this chapter, different approaches were used to counteract this happening, such as asking the students to draw two scientists, or by sorting cards with drawings. In our version, we asked the respondents to draw a scientist *at work*, and also to add something *in writing* on what scientists do and issues they work on. This may have been a story or just a list of key words.

Item 7: writing – 'Me as a scientist'

This last item may be seen as an extension of the previous one. Pupils were invited to put themselves in the position of being a scientist, being free to work and to do research on what they find important and interesting. Here, they were able to express their own interests, concerns and priorities. Previous research has indicated interesting differences between the priorities of girls and boys (Kjærnsli 1989).

Target population and organization of the study

It was decided that the questionnaire should be administered to the class in each country with the most 13-year-old children. In most countries, this is towards the end of the primary stage, which often means that a large proportion of the age cohort is still at school. In most countries it is also an age before which selection, curricular choices and streaming have taken place.

Since the involvement of new researchers from developing countries was an important aim, the project group decided that it was unrealistic to be very strict on sampling, since this requires the existence of reliable educational statistics plus resources for travel and other forms of communication. Modest funding also permitted only the reimbursement of basic expenses for the researchers in the participating countries, limiting the extent of the sample and the work. Hence, care should be taken in attempts to generalize to national populations. However, interpreted with caution, we believe that the results may shed light on some important aspects regarding differences and similarities based on culture as well as gender.

More than 60 researchers from nearly 30 countries have shown an interest in the study, and today (mid 2000) we have data files from 21 countries, collected by some 30 researchers. The total number of pupils in the data files is 9350. The participating countries (and numbers in brackets) are: Australia (116), Chile (410), England (906), Ghana (270), Hungary (312), Iceland (647), India (1038), Japan (531), Korea (269), Lesotho (312), Mozambique (307), Nigeria (813), Norway (1483), Papua New Guinea (204), Philippines (201), Spain (280), Sudan (300), Sweden (193), Trinidad (317), Uganda (176), USA (265). In this chapter a few examples of results are presented and the findings and implications discussed.

What I have done: relevant experiences

For this item (Item 2) we tried to sample activities from a wide range of contexts that we found might be of value for learning science. We tried to

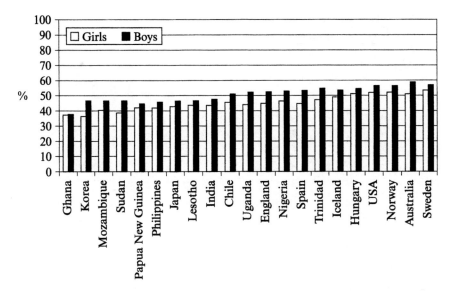

Figure 10.1 What I have done: mean percentage responding positively to 80 items. Countries are sorted in ascending order of total frequency.

balance relevant activities from different continents and cultures, and we also tried to find activities that would be representative of girls as well as boys. A test for the degree of success in this respect is to look the total picture that emerges from the data. We therefore made a composite score with the sum of all responses. The results are given in Figure 10.1, country by country and separately for girls and boys, as a total percentage of all the activities that children indicated they had undertaken – i.e. overall children in Ghana indicated they had undertaken 38 per cent of the activities on the list.

As we can see, the means of all countries fall within a rather narrow range from 38 per cent (Ghana) to 56 per cent (Sweden). Furthermore, there is no systematic difference between types of country, developing and developed countries emerging with similar values and in a rather mixed order. For all countries, however, there is a difference in favour of the boys. The difference is, however, not very large, and may of course indicate that we have been better in sampling boys' activities in the item.

The pupils' experiences can be analysed or grouped in various ways. Here some simple results are presented as illustrations (see Figures 10.2–10.4). The data are given for girls and boys, and the countries are sorted according to the total frequency.

On Figure 10.2, we have developing countries at both extremes. On the low end of the spectrum are some Asian countries, while children in Africa

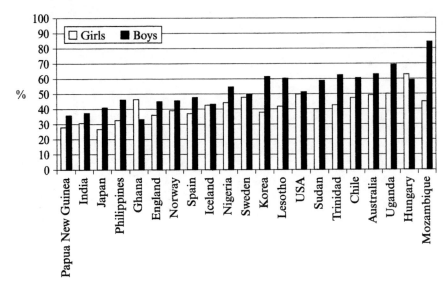

Figure 10.2   What I have done: percentage for each country indicating the children have made toys from wire, wood or another material. Countries are sorted in ascending order of total frequency.

report much higher activity. A possible explanation may be that in Africa, children (mainly boys) are, in some countries, extremely skilful in making toys out of metal wire. These skills and experiences may be an untapped resource for education in science and technology. We note that boys in all countries have more experience in this area. Girls, on the other hand, have a corresponding (and much stronger) domination in activities relating to the use of textiles (weaving, knitting, making clothes, etc.).

Activities like 'Using ropes and pulleys to lift heavy things' (see Figure 10.3) are often rather close to the curriculum contents in mechanics in most countries. It is likely that children with these experiences may have an advantage in learning the principles of classical, simple mechanics. We noted the extreme gender differences on this item in most countries. It is also noteworthy to see that this kind of experience is a type of shared experience across countries (for boys). The same pattern is obvious in a range of similar activities. There is no doubt that boys may have an experiential advantage in learning mechanics in most countries.

Several types of skill are developed in playing with different sorts of building kits (see Figure 10.4). Development of manipulative skills is an obvious one, and probably also the ability to follow detailed instructions with patience and concentration. Such skills are important in at least some practical laboratory situations in science. The percentages on this item

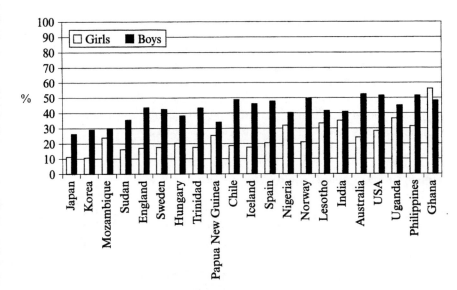

Figure 10.3 What I have done: percentage who indicated they have used rope and pulley mechanisms to lift heavy things. Countries are sorted in ascending order of total frequency.

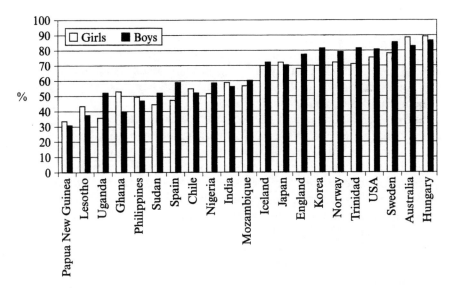

Figure 10.4 What I have done: percentage who indicated that they had played with building kits (i.e. Lego). Countries are sorted in ascending order of total frequency.

varied between countries, the mean ranging from less than 40 per cent to nearly 90 per cent. The highest averages are in general found in the more developed countries. This is not surprising, since such kits are by definition sold in shops. We also note that countries like Korea and Japan come out rather high on this activity, in contrast to the very low responses to the two previous topics. It seems that Korean and Japanese children score relatively higher on indoor (and urban?) activities. An interesting aspect with this topic is that it is rather gender neutral in most countries.

Things to learn about: the overall picture

Item 3 consists of a list of 60 possible topics to learn about. Pupils simply ticked the ones they liked. These items have been assembled to show different ways of approaching science content, bearing in mind different cultures as well as possible gender differences. These items may be presented one by one, or grouped in a variety of ways. For an overview, we may look at the overall picture by compositing the scores. The results are given in Figure 10.5, sorted by the total frequency.

As can be seen, the variation on this sum is much larger than the similar sum on the question about children's experiences. Means for the countries range from only 30 per cent (Japan) to more than 70 per cent for several countries.

As researchers, we noted an interesting grouping of countries. Children in rather rich countries indicate a low or moderate interest in learning science topics, with the Nordic countries Norway, Sweden and Iceland among the lowest – but considerably higher than Japan! Children in developing countries, on the other hand, appear to be interested in a very high proportion of the science items on the list.

The gender differences on the total sum were not large in any country, with Korea as an exception. But there seems to have been an interesting pattern: in most of the developed countries, the difference was 'in favour' of boys, while the difference in most developing countries was in favour of girls. A tentative explanation for these observations may be the following: in developing countries, education is a 'luxury' and a privilege, a resource that only a few children have access to. The motivation to learn and to study is high both for girls and boys. But, since access to education is often denied to the girls, for them education and learning may be perceived as being even more of a 'luxury'. Hence, they may indicate an eagerness to want to learn about most things on our list!

The overall picture given above may be supplemented by responses to Item 5. For the question 'Science is: interesting, exciting?' we get the results shown in Figure 10.6.

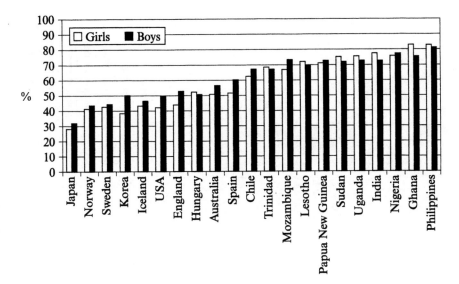

Figure 10.5 Things to learn about: children's 'interest to learn' different topics as a mean percentage of 60 items. Countries are sorted in ascending order of total frequency.

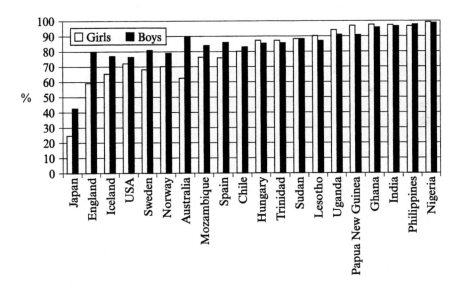

Figure 10.6 Science in action: percentage of responses that indicated science was 'interesting' or 'exciting'. Countries are sorted in ascending order of total frequency.

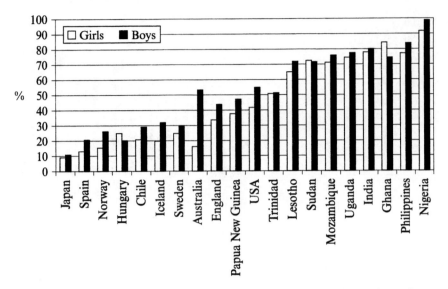

Figure 10.7   Science in action: percentage who indicated that 'science is easy to understand'. Countries are sorted in ascending order of total frequency.

Figure 10.6 reinforces the impression that Japanese pupils indicate a remarkably low interest in science, in particular the girls. In fact, the Japanese girls' response to this item (25 per cent) is much less than the half of any other group in the study! Similarly, the Japanese boys' response is also less than the boys' response in any other country.

Additionally, it is interesting to note that the average response for children in most rich countries was considerably lower than the interest expressed by children in developing countries. There is the same gender profile as above: in developed countries, the boys' responses were much higher than the girls', while the opposite pattern (to a lesser degree) was the case in developing countries. The explanation for these differences may be similar to that suggested previously.

The response to the question from Item 5 as to whether science is 'easy to understand' shows that only 10 per cent of Japanese children find it easy (see Figure 10.7). This response is interesting in the light of the fact that Japanese children usually emerge as the most successful in international comparisons on science achievement such as TIMSS. These data also show that in most rich countries, children do not find science to be very easy, in particular girls. Again, most of the developing countries had rather high scores, the children indicating that they find science easy to learn. It is hard to judge, however, whether this is a realistic assessment of their own learning, or whether it is a reflection of their positive attitude towards learning science.

Interesting topics: some examples

The simplest level of reporting is to provide data for girls and boys from each country. This section includes a number of graphs of such data. They are all sorted by the arithmetic difference between boys' and girls' scores. It is important to keep in mind that we have chosen the *arithmetic* difference as our 'criterion' for gender stereotyping. This means that countries with small numbers (like Japan) for both genders will produce low differences. If we had chosen the *ratio* between the responses of boys and girls as the criterion, the results would look very different: Japan and Korea would come out as the most gender stereotyped countries in the children's responses for most items. This should be borne in mind when looking at the data.

The topics represented in Figure 10.8 ('the car and how a car works') are related to technology. We note the extreme male dominance on these topics. The same pattern was found in a series of similar topics. We also noticed that the interest among Japanese children for such topics was extremely low compared to all other countries. As mentioned, if the ratio had been chosen as the criterion, Japan would have come out as the most extreme (for each girl wanting to learn about the car there are six boys). We also noted that the gender difference for these items was very high in the Nordic countries (in this case Sweden, Norway and Iceland). This was a general pattern, and I will return to this towards the end of the chapter.

Figures 10.9 ('AIDS: What it is and how it spreads') and 10.10 ('What to eat to be healthy') show the level of interest in learning about aspects of human biology, and, as the reader shall see, reveal a rather different pattern of responses. For both these topics, the overall interest is (not unexpectedly) much higher in developing countries. These countries also have rather small gender differences. In most developed countries, these topics come out as girls' interests. Again, we find that Nordic countries are among the extreme with regards to gender differences.

Learning about the rainbow (see Figure 10.11) can be seen as an example of optics, but it also has elements of aesthetics and possibly of fantasy and wonder. We see that the responses were very gendered: this is a prime example of 'girls' interest' in science, although the score was also rather high for boys! The high (but gendered) response was noteworthy for Japan, at least when compared to the Japanese responses to most items relating to 'pure' science, and in particular to modern technology.

'The possibility of life outside earth' (see Figure 10.12) can be seen as belonging to 'proper science', but it also contains elements of speculation, uncertainty and science fiction that are seldom found in science curricula. In fact, this particular topic seems to be the most popular of all the 60 topics in this study. It is also noteworthy to see that it was popular among girls as well as boys in all nations. The response from Japan was not overwhelmingly high, but was much higher than on most other topics.

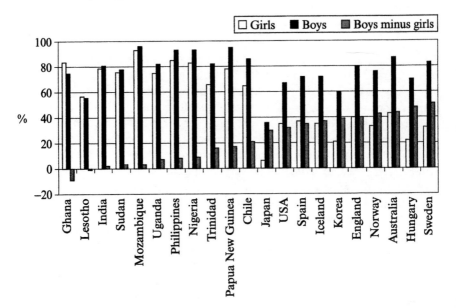

Figure 10.8 Percentage of children who indicated that they would like to learn about 'the car and how it works'. Countries are sorted by frequency for gender difference.

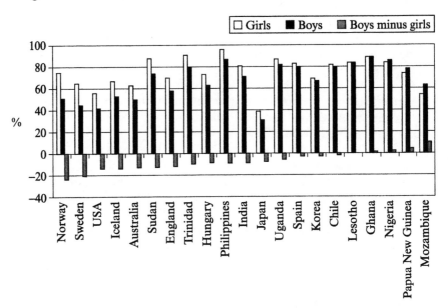

Figure 10.9 Percentage of children who indicated an interest in learning about 'AIDS: What it is and how it spreads'. Countries are sorted by frequency for gender difference.

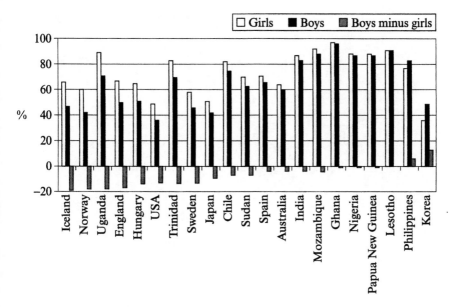

Figure 10.10 Percentage of children who indicated an interest in learning about 'what to eat to be healthy'. Countries are sorted by frequency for gender differences.

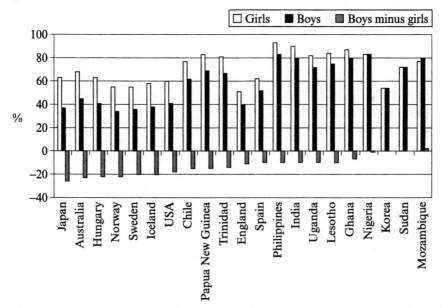

Figure 10.11 Percentage of children who indicated an interest in learning about the rainbow: what it is and why you can see it. Countries are sorted by frequency for gender differences.

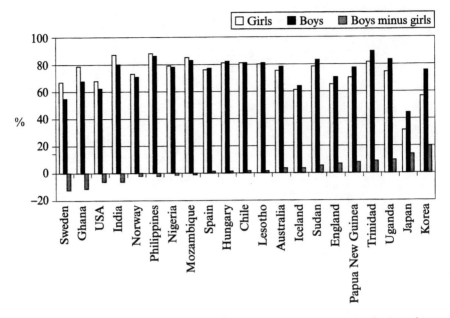

Figure 10.12   Percentage of children who indicated an interest in learning about 'the possibility of life outside earth'. Countries are sorted by frequency for gender differences.

Things to learn about: an example of further analysis

The wealth of information in the SAS material may be used in many different ways. Here is an indication of how one may go a little beyond the mere data. The examples that follow show how we have used the data in the national context of Norway.

A dominating political and educational concern in Norway, as in other Nordic countries, is *gender* equity. Another key equity-based concern is that of geographical background and social class, two issues that often coincide. The concern about *cultural* and *ethnical* equity has only recently become an issue, since Norway until recently has been a country with a rather small proportion of the population from ethnic minorities. This picture is, however, rapidly changing due to immigration.

There is a national concern to make curricula that are fair for these various groups. In particular, there is a strong concern for a *local* curriculum, and for a *gender fair* curriculum. (In science this would mean a curriculum that does not favour boys.) Concerns about class and gender equity may in practice be in conflict with each other, and they also have different interest groups promoting them. The Norwegian SAS data can be used to shed light on at least some aspects of this issue.

In the Norwegian study, therefore, pupils were sampled from two very different sub-populations: one population was the pupils in the richest part of the country, the wealthy suburbs of the capital, Oslo. The other population area was the county of Finnmark in the extreme North. By most statistical indicators, these two parts of the country represent extremes of level of education, income, and employment. The climate in the South is comfortable, with moderate winters and mild summers, lots of sunshine, and seldom any extremes. The climate in the North is extremely harsh, including a long winter with permanent darkness and temperatures that drop to –50 degrees Celsius. Growing up in these two places represents extremes in a Norwegian context. Therefore it might be expected that children in these areas will have very different life experiences, hopes and aspirations. It might also be expected that they may demonstrate very different profiles of interest in learning science. We wanted to shed light on the relative importance of the geographical (i.e. in part the social) and the gender aspects for the debate about the nature of the science curriculum.

Therefore, the data on pupils' interests was analysed from these two perspectives (Myrland 1997). The total sample of pupils (N = 1500) was divided into four groups by gender and by geographical location (North/South). The results were surprising. Although there were some differences between pupils in the South and North, these differences were very small compared to the differences between girls and boys. On the particular topics, as well as on different aggregates of data, the overall pattern was that when it comes to interest in science topics, it seems that 'girls are girls' and 'boys are boys', independent of their social and geographical backgrounds.

This result is a strong indication that a debate over equity in the science curriculum should focus more on gender differences and less on other aspects. It is, of course, important not to over-generalize from this conclusion; the results are from Norway and they relate only to the contents of the science curriculum!

Same science – different approaches

Taking the gender perspective further, it is evident from the data presented previously that there are some dramatic differences between the interests of girls and boys. It might seem that the data lead one to conclude that biology is a girls' subject, and physics is a boys' subject. Such a conclusion is not very productive, and it will certainly not help us in making *all* science knowledge attractive to all kinds of learners. Rather, there is another possible way to resolve the concern for a more gender fair curriculum.

In the list of possible topics to learn about, 'the same' science content was put in different contexts. A topic like 'acoustics' may be approached in

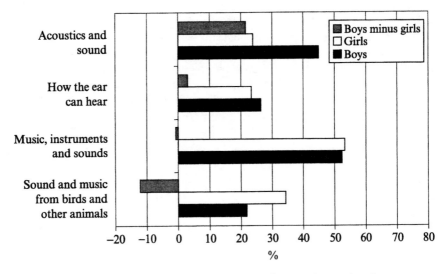

Figure 10.13 Popularity of different approaches to the topic of 'acoustics' (sorted by gender difference, N = 1500)

different ways in a school setting. Possible topic names may be: 'Acoustics and sound', 'How the ear can hear', 'Music, instruments and sounds', or 'Sound and music from birds and other animals'. Figure 10.13 shows the popularity of these topics among Norwegian pupils. The results are sorted by the difference between girls and boys. As we can see, the first topic come out as 'male', and the last as 'female', with the in the middle topics as rather gender neutral.

A similar approach was used for topics that may be classified as 'optics'. Again a similar pattern can be seen showing that changing the context may change the 'gender profile' of the science content (see Figure 10.14).

Several comments can be made on such data. For these science topics, we see that the 'popularity' varied strongly with the associated context, for girls as well as for boys. When a topic is related to life (human or animal), aesthetics or personal issues, the context seems to appeal more to girls; aspects that relate to earth science are also popular among girls. These results are not very surprising. They support general statements about the interest profiles of girls and boys in many countries. The advantage of this study is, however, that it has provided data that take us beyond general statements. In this way, it may actually be productively used in debates about the curriculum. Or it may be communicated to textbook authors, who in most countries have some freedom in choosing different approaches and contexts, even within a given national curriculum. Results like these may, of

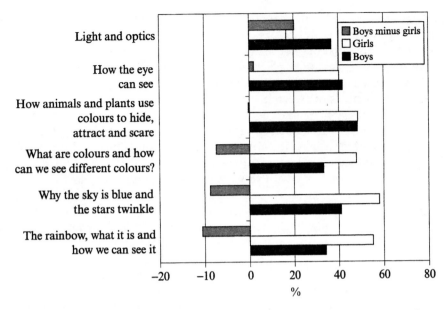

Figure 10.14 Popularity of different approaches to the topic of 'optics' (sorted by gender difference, N = 1500)

course, also be of value to student teachers or practising teachers. Such data may sensitize them to the fact that children can be rather different, and that as teachers they have different options and possibilities in the presentation of science concepts and ideas. If student teachers get involved in collecting data themselves, the ownership may of course be much stronger.

Drawing and writing about science and scientists

The last two items of this research do not lend themselves to straightforward coding. In Item 6, the pupils made drawings of scientists at work, and complemented this with some writing about what they think scientists do. In Item 7 they were free to write about what they would like to do themselves if they were scientists. Since responses have been made in many different languages, the project as such has not been able to code and interpret this material in a thorough way. Some national studies have, however, been published in different languages.

The following is therefore a more qualitative and tentative description of the impressions from looking through the material (with some 9350 children's drawings!).

For the rich, industrial countries, the data seem to support similar published research (see previous references). The researcher was drawn mainly as male. Only girls (but not many) seemed to think of a scientist as female. The researcher was often placed in stereotypical laboratory contexts and often depicted as a bald-headed, bearded man with a lab coat, test-tubes and other symbols of research.

As many researchers have noted, the 'draw a scientist' test actually begs for stereotypes of this nature, so care should be taken not to over-generalize from the mere drawings. But the free writing that accompanied the drawings provided additional information. An analysis of the Norwegian sample (Kind 1996) showed that, with very few exceptions, only boys' drawings and writing may be classified as 'science fiction' (boys 6 per cent; girls 1 per cent). Some pupils envisaged the scientist as a cruel and gruesome person (boys 11 per cent; girls 2 per cent). For instance, among the examples given were cruel experiments on animals. From the writing about 'me as a scientist', the Norwegian data showed the clearest difference for topics classified as 'technology' (boys 36 per cent; girls 0 per cent!). Twice as many girls, however, saw themselves doing research in medicine and health (girls 37 per cent; boys 18 per cent). Also, for the topic of 'environment/pollution', the girls predominated (girls 15 per cent; boys 9 per cent). These results are similar to Norwegian findings a decade ago (Kjærnsli 1989). Kjærnsli also noted that 18 per cent of the girls but only 2 per cent of the boys were inclined to do research that could help other people.

A similar pattern seems to emerge from drawings and writings in other industrialized countries in the reported study. Basically, the image drawn was very much the standard stereotype, but also with a certain (but not very high) percentage of the crazy or mad scientist. It is, however, interesting to note that very few pupils in western countries explicitly wrote that they wanted to help other people – or that they thought scientists actually help other people.

Most of these data were in a stark contrast to writings and drawings from pupils in developing countries. They saw the scientist as a very heroic person. Scientists were often seen to be brave and intelligent, portrayed as helping other people, curing the sick, and improving the standard of life for everybody. They were also often seen as helping the poor and underprivileged, aspects that are *never* mentioned in responses from pupils in the West. In developing countries scientists are seen as the servants and the heroes of society.

Hence, the image of the scientist is indeed very different in the developed and the developing parts of the world. This is not the place to discuss whether the views of the children are 'correct' or not. But their images, whether they be real or fantasy, surely must influence their motivation to engage in science. To a certain extent it must also determine what kind of pupils feel at home with the culture of science, and who will feel alienated or hostile. This may also indicate that the perceived 'values of science' or its 'subculture' may be seen as very different in diverse parts of the world. Although school science is often characterized as 'western science', and based on a western 'worldview', these data indicate that children from non-western countries have a much more positive image of the culture of science than most children in the West have. These findings may be a challenge for discussions about the possible match or mismatch between the subculture of science and the cultures of children in different countries (see Chapter 14).

Gender equity in the Nordic countries: a paradox?

TIMSS has reported large gender differences in achievement in the Nordic countries. For instance, of nearly all the 50 countries in TIMSS, Denmark has the second largest difference in score between boys and girls in science at age 13 – only being 'beaten' by Israel. Also at the age of 19, the gender differences in scores were remarkably high in four participating Nordic countries (Finland did not take part in TIMSS). The gender difference was also reflected in the later choice of subjects, Denmark and Norway having the lowest proportion of girls among their physics pupils (in Denmark, 20 per cent, and in Norway, 26 per cent).

The SAS study provides details that elaborate this overall picture. We documented large differences in the *interest* to learn science. Other SAS data also indicated large differences in *values* and *priorities*, such as in the ranking of factors that are important for children in their choice of job (Item 4, not presented in this chapter). Girls are more 'person-orientated' than boys: they want to 'help other people' and to 'work with people instead of things', while boys are more orientated towards making money and obtaining personal benefits.

The Nordic countries often consider themselves the 'world champions' of gender equity, and the issue has been a major political concern since the mid-1970s. Much has been accomplished, and the overall picture is undoubtedly rather positive. In my country, Norway, legal barriers were removed a long time ago, and laws against discrimination and unequal pay are in operation. Female participation in politics and the labour market is among the highest in the world. Even textbooks in all subjects have to pass a gender equity test before they may be used in schools. In the education system, girls and women dominate the overall picture, with some 56 per cent of tertiary students being female.

The Nordic achievements regarding gender equity are also visible from an analysis of official statistics. In the UNDP's (United Nations Development Programme) *Human Development Report*, the five Nordic countries are close to the top of the indices constructed to measure gender equity (UNDP 2000). The 'gender empowerment measure' includes measures of participation in education, politics and professional life, along with equity in salaries, etc. The five Nordic countries came out on top of this list of 150 countries: Norway (1), Iceland (2), Sweden (3), Denmark (4) and Finland (5).

However, the percentage of women in science and engineering is very low in the Nordic countries – lower than in most parts of the world. And the enrolment has actually gone down in the last few years. This issue is of great political concern. The reason does not seem to be the girls' lack of ability or lack of self-confidence! Rather, it would seem that even very able girls are turning their backs on science and engineering. The choices seem to be rather deliberate, based on value orientations and emotional and personal factors. Some of the underlying values are indicated above, such as the girls' high person orientation and relatively low orientation towards money and careers. If this is correct, it suggests that we should pay more attention to the underlying values, ideals and ideologies in science education. Textbooks as well as classroom teaching carry implicit (sometimes also explicit) messages about the nature of the subject and its underlying values. If we believe that these values are not strictly determined and logically deduced from the subject itself, then we should analyse, discuss and possibly reconsider how these messages can be altered.

Science educators have drawn our attention to the fact that the culture of science is alien to people from non-western cultures (see Cobern and Aikenhead 1998 and Chapter 14). I would argue that pupils in western societies may also feel alienated by what they perceive as the culture, ethos and ideals of science, as well as the possibly frightening uses and misuses of science and technology in modern societies. Hence, a cultural 'border crossing' may be required of many pupils in western society as well. Concepts and perspectives taken from these kinds of cultural approaches might be used to understand why so many young people – in particular girls – choose not to take science in countries that have actually removed most visible barriers for girls to enter the sciences.

Some conclusions from the SAS study

It is evident from this study that children in most parts of the world come to school with a rich variety of relevant *experiences* that could, and should, be utilized in the teaching and learning of science at school. This study does not indicate whether this resource is actually used in a systematic way or not, but it may indicate how this might be done.

The *interest* in learning seems to be much higher in developing countries than in the rich and technologically well-developed countries. An explanation for this may be that education in developing countries is largely seen as a privilege that everybody strives for, while many pupils in developed countries see school as a tedious duty that is imposed on them. The same perspective may explain the strong interest in science expressed by girls in developing countries: girls in these countries often have even less access to all sorts of education than boys have, and therefore learning science may be seen as a very positive option.

The *profile* of experiences and interests does, however, vary strongly between countries. This fact should call for caution when it comes to 'importing' foreign curricula and foster a sceptical resistance to the pressure to 'harmonize' science curricula across the globe. Data from projects like SAS help by providing a basis for deliberation about curricular priorities.

It is also evident that the *profile* of experiences, as well as interests, is very different for girls and boys in most countries. In general, the gender differences in interests are greater in developed countries than in developing countries, both when summed over all topics and when studied separately. Gender differences are very high in some North European countries and Japan, an aspect that has been discussed a little previously. If gender equity in science education is a national concern, it is important to analyse possible biases in the curricula, textbooks and classroom teaching.

The *image* of science and scientists is more positive among children in developing countries than in the developed countries. Children in the developing countries seem to be eager to learn science, and for them, scientists are the heroes. This is in marked contrast to at least a significant part of the children in the developed countries, who often express sceptical and negative attitudes in their responses to several of the questions. The notion of the crazy or mad scientist is often found in developing countries. Very few children in developed countries envisage the scientist as a kind, human and helpful person, whereas this is often the image of scientists in developing countries.

This study does not tell which image is closer to 'reality'. But many of the data do indicate that science has a problem with its public image in many developed countries. Why? One possibility is that this may be a result of a low public understanding of science – even of dis-information from the media. Many scientists adhere to an explanation like this. But there is another possibility: it may be an indication that many young people have a rather well informed sceptical attitude towards aspects of modern society. Maybe their doubts are based on real fears about an unknown future that scientists may lead them into? This study does not answer these questions.

References

Chambers, D.W. (1983) Stereotypic images of the scientist: the draw-a-scientist test. *Science Education*, 67(2): 255–65.

Cobern, W.W. and Aikenhead, G. (1998) Culture and the learning of science, in B. Fraser and K.G. Tobin (eds) *International Handbook of Science Education*. Dordrecht: Kluwer Academic Publishers.

Kahle, J.B. (1987) Images of science: the physicist and the 'cowboy', in B.J. Fraser and G.J. Giddings (eds) *Gender Issues In Science Education*. Perth: Curtin University of Technology.

Kind, A. (1996) 'Barns oppfatning av vitenskap og forskere – en analyse av tegninger' ('Pupils' perceptions of science and scientists – an analysis of drawings), term paper in science education. University of Oslo.

Kjærnsli, M. (1989) 'Elevers forestillinger om forskning og forskere' ('Pupils' ideas about science and scientists'), master's thesis in science education. University of Oslo.

Krajkovich, J.G. and Smith, J.K. (1982) The development of the image of science and scientists scale. *Journal of Research in Science Teaching*, 19: 39–44.

Lie, S. and Sjøberg, S. (1984) *Myke jenter i harde fag?* (Soft girls in hard science?). Oslo: Universitetsforlaget.

Matthews, B. (1996) Drawing scientists. *Gender and Education*, 8(2): 231–43.

Mead, M. and Metraux, R. (1957) Image of scientist among high school students. *Science*, 126(3270): 384–90.

Myrland, K. (1997) 'Norske 13-åringers oppfatninger om naturfag og forskere innen naturfag' ('Norwegian 13-year old pupils' ideas about science and scientists'), master's thesis in science education. University of Oslo.

Sjøberg, S. (2000) 'The SAS (science and scientists) project: development and results', Acta Didactica 1/2000, Institute for Teacher Education and School Development. University of Oslo.

TIMSS (1996) *Science Achievement in the Middle School Years*. Boston, MA: TIMSS International Study Center.

TIMSS (1997) *Science Achievement in the Primary School Years*. Boston, MA: TIMSS International Study Center.

TIMSS (1998) *Mathematics and Science Achievement in the Final year of Secondary School*. Boston, MA: TIMSS International Study Center.

UNDP (2000) *Human Development Report 2000*. New York and London: Oxford University Press.

Whyte, J., Kelly, A. and Smail, B. (1987) *Girls into Science and Technology: Final Report in Science for Girls*. Milton Keynes: Open University Press.

11

Making the nature of science explicit

Richard Duschl

Introduction

The traditional curriculum approach to science education has been one that stresses 'knowing'. An interpretation of traditional curriculum practices in science education is that the process asks 'What do we want students to *know* and what do they need to *do* to *know* it?' The 'hands-on' approach, as practised in the majority of schools, embodies this dictum. The tasks students do are done in the service of attaining either conceptual goals or process goals. The overall goal is acquisition of what scientist's *know*. Very little time, if any, is typically given over to examining and discussing the nature of the problem being investigated, to developing higher level reasoning skills, to engaging in the argumentative discourse of science, or to exploring the assumptions and beliefs held by the investigators. In short, the contexts in which science is 'done', the how and why of science, the construction and evaluation of knowledge claims, the places where the concepts and processes are shaped and take on meaning, are missing. This chapter sets out an argument for a radical change in science education. The proposal is to adjust curriculum, instruction and assessment models so that epistemic goals can have a more prominent standing in science education. The intention is to adjust and realign the dominance of learning concepts and process skills in science education.

When pupils learn about what is known, without also learning how we have come to know it, and why this belief or conceptual scheme is better than another belief, it eliminates any chance of students understanding the social, cognitive and epistemic dynamics that make science an objective way of knowing. My argument will hinge on making the nature of science explicit in science classrooms. This, in turn, requires a focus on conversations about the data domains when the ways of knowing are forged – a position that requires a change in the activity structures of classrooms. The lever of change is student discourse and instructional designs that examine critically the symbiotic relationship between evidence and explanation. When students are given opportunities to examine, discuss and argue which data-gathering strategies one might use, which measurements should be repeated and which data to use for analysis, the nature of science is made more explicit. When students are given opportunities to examine the selected data for patterns, and debate which of several alternatives would be the best way to model and represent the data, and finally, to consider which of several alternative explanations would best account for the evidence, then, in addition, the nature of science is made more explicit.

Designing learning environments that both engage and empower learners in the construction and, importantly, the evaluation of transformations of evidence to explanation is the goal. Having evaluation as a curriculum goal requires a shift in priorities away from (but not divorced from) conceptual goals. Simply put, time must be made available for learners to engage in 'speaking together' – activities which the teacher directs toward developing an understanding of the criteria used to conduct evaluations of, for example, the design of experiments, the composition of models, the evidential support of explanations and the fidelity of data.

The need for school science programmes to focus on the various public understandings of the nature of science (i.e. our images of how science *can* be a reliable and rational way of knowing that *can*, within select ethical and moral limits, answer questions, solve problems, and generate explanations) is an important educational goal. Such a goal is a strong theme in *Young People's Images of Science* (Driver *et al.* 1996) and is framed by three aspects of science deemed essential for a public understanding:

- understanding some aspects of science content;
- understanding the scientific approach to enquiry;
- understanding science as a social process.

The critically important message is that science education should be embedded in problem/subject contexts that afford opportunities for students to examine, discuss and engage in the epistemological, social and political bases by which scientific knowledge claims are advanced. The challenge is to design instructional sequences and learning environment conditions that help pupils become members of epistemic communities. The recommendation by Driver *et al.* (1996) is to explicitly address two aspects of the nature of science: namely the epistemological basis for conducting scientific inquiry, and the decision making process embedded within the social enterprise of doing and reporting science. The focus of this chapter will be on the first aspect – the epistemological basis.

The grounds on which we base our decisions about the acceptance or rejection of scientific knowledge claims are deeply tied, as Driver *et al.* (1996) fully recognize, to epistemological issues. Such issues shape and determine

'what counts'. The proposal put forth by Driver *et al.* is that the epistemological basis for making scientific knowledge claims needs to be addressed
explicitly and not merely implicitly in classrooms. Grandy (1997: 51) con-
curs and argues compellingly for a science education in which students
'develop the skills to participate in the epistemic interchanges that take place
in scientific communities'. But he also recognizes how important it is for
'the classroom community [to] have the appropriate features of an objective
epistemic community'. I agree strongly with these positions and my work
in examining how to address epistemic goals through the SEPIA (Science
Education through Portfolio Instruction and Assessment) project represents
a starting point for understanding how to design learning environments to
support epistemic communities of pupils (Gitomer and Duschl 1995; Duschl
and Gitomer 1997; Gitomer and Duschl 1998; Duschl *et al.* 1999a).

Hence, while I agree with the aim to explicitly teach epistemic issues, I am
less in agreement with the recommendations that Driver *et al.* (1996) propose for making epistemic issues explicit. The three strands of curriculum
emphasis proposed by Driver *et al.* to explicitly establish an epistemological
basis for scientific knowledge claims include: 'evaluation of evidence'; 'evaluation of theories'; and 'the generation and evaluation of predictions from
theories'. The emphasis on evaluation is critically important because it
signals the need to create instructional sequences and activities that develop
students' sense of the standards, rules, or criteria used for determining what
counts. But equally important is the emphasis on the generation of ideas
and information. Since only the last strand incorporates the notion of generation, the three curriculum strands are incomplete. A fourth epistemic
strand I propose would be the evaluation of data domains or data texts
that generate or give rise to evidence and to theory. The dialectic between
data and theory, observation and theory, and fact and theory has long been
recognized by philosophers of science as the foundation for understanding
the nature of science. This dialectic needs a more prominent place in our
science classrooms. Research is now needed on how to design learning
environments such that the curriculum, instruction and assessment models
function in tandem to engage students and teachers in the investigations and
conversations that are characteristic of epistemic communities.

My approach in this chapter will be one that considers two dynamic
elements that Ros Driver felt were essential to learning about the nature
of science – the epistemic basis for enquiry (Driver *et al.* 1996) and the role
of argumentation in science learning environments (Newton *et al.* 1999; Driver
et al. in press). The first section of the chapter presents the results of the
Driver *et al.* (1996) research on pupils' images of the role of observation and
evidence. Next we turn to the topic of data dialectics. Here I argue for, and
give examples of, changes in the design of instructional sequences and learning environments that promote the refinement and extension of scientific

language around data domains or data texts. The chapter finishes with recommendations for future research on understanding the important role language and argumentation must play in the design of learning environments that seek to explicitly address the nature of science.

Pupils' images of the nature of science

Focusing science instruction on the evaluation of knowledge claims is, as previously, discussed, a sound recommendation. The focus on moving from evidence to explanation is appropriate as well. What we must be concerned about is the size of the steps we take. There are, I would argue, three important transformations in moving from the raw data of observation, investigation and experimentation to the theories and explanations that account for the data. These three transformations are preceded by decisions (informed by theoretical commitments and ideas) about what data to collect. Transformation 1 is evaluating what raw data become the selected data or evidence. Transformation 2 is evaluating how the evidence can be manipulated to locate patterns and models in the selected data. Transformation 3 is evaluating how the patterns and models fit, or do not fit, scientific theories and explanations. This complex relationship between evidence and explanation, or observation and theory, in science warrants an explicit examination of three domains of criteria:

1 criteria for assigning data to one of four categories: fact, artefact, irrelevant or anomalous;
2 criteria for identifying and representing patterns/models in selected data;
3 criteria for generating theories or explanations to account for the patterns/models.

An explicit approach to the nature of science will be one that examines the relationship between data, observation, fact and theory, and develops a sense of the criteria used to evaluate these relationships. The data texts of science result from the various and sundry ways we observe, collect, select, represent, model and explain our investigations of, and inquiries into, the material world. An epistemic focus for science education will foreground the development of criteria to be used in the evaluation of data texts. Developing in students an understanding of the criteria for deciding what counts, while certainly grounded in executing investigations, is honed through activity structures that promote student discourse; in particular argumentation discourse.

I think it is important for us to recognize that, each and every time we embark with students of all ages on scientific inquiries in various contexts, we face the problem of needing to make an epistemological break with common sense. I will elaborate on this idea in the next section but mention it now to set the stage for an interpretation of the research on pupils' images of the nature of science. While fully recognizing that sense perception observations are still an important part of science, the historical record makes it very clear that the practices of science with respect to evidence gathering, data acquisition and observation have moved steadily away from sense perception observations and common sense explanations, towards instrument and theory-driven observations and the development of scientific explanations. Science is the domain of inquiry that takes us beyond our senses and into the realms of reasons and reasoning, and models and modelling. The data texts of science have become more complex.

Thus, it is interesting to note that while the observational practices of science have come to rely less and less on sense perception, and more and more on theory-driven observations, the research by Driver *et al.* (1996) informs us that a concomitant shift has not taken place in the kind of science presented to learners in schools. The data reported by Driver *et al.* (1996) on students' understanding of the nature of science indicated that there is a strong disposition among pupils to characterize good science as that which involves direct perceptual evidence. For instance, in the findings of the topic 'Purpose of scientific work', the results suggest that students think investigations are done in order to see or make a phenomenon happen. Empirical testing for young students was seen 'as a simple process of observation from which outcomes are obvious' (Driver *et al.* 1996: 84). For the topic 'Nature and status of scientific knowledge' results indicated that students believed that the inquiry involved in experimentation relates cause to effect where a comparison of conditions can be made as they affect an outcome.

The results on students' views of the nature of explanation in science indicates that students view theories as entities that show how to relate variables and believe that 'the aim of the empirical evaluation is to "prove" or demonstrate that the stated variables do in fact influence the phenomenon in question' (Driver *et al.* 1996: 94). Most compelling though is the result reported for 'Warrants for belief' which showed a belief across ages 'that reliable knowledge is necessarily based on direct perceptual evidence' (p. 98).

The finding that students have such a strong dependence on perceptual evidence is critically important for researchers and educators to consider. The importance resides in the fact that such a reliance on sense perceptions as the basis for reliable science runs counter to transformation of observation acts in twentieth-century science. There is a tension between the data texts. Over the years, scientists, as Shapere (1982) puts it, have 'learned how to learn'; observational processes and evidence-gathering practices have come to rely less and less on sense perception information and more and more on evidence derived from complex instruments, technological devices, experimental designs and inferential reasoning practices (Shapere 1982; Duschl

1990). Thus, the finding by Driver *et al.* (1996) that students do not understand the relationship between theory and evidence is significant because is suggests that the relationship between theory and observation, and the relationship between evidence and data, is unexamined in classrooms. Conversations about the data texts are missing. Making the nature of science explicit to pupils will, I propose, require the design of instructional sequences and learning environments that facilitate an epistemic break with common sense. The contexts for engaging in epistemic breaks are the data texts of science. The process will engage pupils in sustained and frequent conversations at each of the transformation stages as data becomes theory. The enterprise, however, will require teachers to become better listeners to and analysers of the arguments put forth by pupils.

Data dialectic approaches

The dialectic between data and theory is a missing conversation in most science classrooms (Duschl 1990; Hodson 1990; Chinn and Brewer 1993; Grandy 1997). The dialectics of theory telling us what are the significant facts, and of facts telling us what are the significant theories, involve, as the history of science shows, complex processes. Over time there are refinements and extensions to the tools and instruments employed to generate data, and to the discriminating language 'talking science' used to talk about and evaluate the data:

> Man's environmental niche was originally constrained by his sensory apparatus plus the discriminations in perceptions that could be coded into ordinary language. This niche has been considerably broadened by science. The instruments of science can best be seen as refining and extending human sensory apparatus, and scientific languages as refining and extending the discriminations that can be coded into ordinary language.
>
> (Ackerman 1985: 127)

Over time, the cumulative effect of these refinements and extensions has created a break from common-sense perceptions and common-sense explanations, or what Ackerman refers to as the epistemological break with common sense. The educational path to understanding the nature of science is a path that requires an epistemological break with common sense, or what I refer to as a boundary crossing from sense perception 'folk explanations' to theory-driven science explanations (Duschl *et al.* 1999b). The evidence from Driver *et al.* (1996) presented above, suggests that in spite of years of science education, we have failed in helping our pupils make this epistemic break and boundary crossing.

I would maintain that the problem lies with the imbalance in instruction between the use of scientific instruments and the opportunities to use and develop a discriminating scientific language. As advances in scientific tools and instruments have been extended and refined and been brought to classrooms for pupils to use, the extension and refinement of that discriminating language in the data texts has lagged far behind. While science education curriculum efforts have been responsive in getting tools, techniques and instruments that extend human sensory apparatus into the hands of learners and teachers, these same curriculum efforts have been much less successful in creating instructional contexts for developing the scientific languages that refine and extend the discriminations that can be coded into ordinary language (Lemke 1990). In other words, discussion, debates and arguments about understanding what counts, or more generally the discourse practices of science of an epistemic community, are missing from our instructional sequences.

Consider, for example, the gap between scientific instruments and scientific language in classrooms which use computer programs to import data visualization techniques. In 1997 I completed the GLOBE (Global Learning and Observation to Benefit the Environment) instructor training course held at Middle Tennessee State University in the USA. The goal of the program is to recruit and involve classrooms of students, worldwide, in the gathering of data that can be used to model and monitor climatic change and the effects on the environment (Rock *et al.* 1997). To this end, scientists have written a set of data-gathering protocols for students and teachers to use.

Participants are also provided with access to the computer database on climate and weather. In the GLOBE program (Rock *et al.* 1997), computer generated models of global climate or weather data are presented in the form of contour colours, each colour being representative of a range of the variable (i.e. red for high temperatures and blue for low). The computer files allow students to compare and contrast one day with another, or one year with another. Patterns and trends can be proposed to determine, for example, if global warming is taking place. Students can also have access to Landsat (a satellite used to conduct land cover studies) photographs generated by four bands of electromagnetic radiation. All of this is done on a global, hemispheric or regional scale, but not on a local scale. The resolution of data does not permit local modelling.

One element of the program is the need to recruit teams of older students (Grade 12) to establish new ground-based data-gathering sites in order to expand the data input and thus the data modelling capabilities. Data on minimum/maximum daily temperature, cloud cover and precipitation are collected on a daily basis and reported on the internet to NASA/NOAA (National Aeronautics and Space Administration/National Oceanographic and Atmospheric Administration) computers. Data on soil profiles and tree canopy coverage, along with stream studies of flora and fauna are reported annually or seasonally. Thus at the one end we have the students examining the finished polished models of evidence and at the other end we have students inputting raw data. An exciting program at face value, since it seems to have the necessary elements of doing science. But a closer examination of the classroom-level activities reveals that the dialectical processes of going from data to evidence are left unattended. In the GLOBE program, at the time of my training, there were no instructional strategies for talking about data and its relationship to theory. There were no activities that engaged students in the construction or evaluation of the data models. These were simply downloaded on the computer. This is a significant shortcoming of the program in my opinion. (The year after my training, the National Science Foundation and NASA announced funding for educational research and development for the GLOBE program. I do not know if the refinements to the program now include explicit steps to discuss the data texts.)

The GLOBE program is a clear case where scientific instruments have extended our human sensory apparatus. But it is also an example of how drastically the data domains have been modified through the data modelling process. The refinement and extension of the scientific language is lost and thus the epistemic break with common sense is jeopardized. The computer visualizations are not presented as data models but as sense perception information to be used by students to learn facts and concepts about climate and weather. The data gathering and reporting, while clearly innovative and carefully designed, is at best a short-term motivating device. Sustained inquiry over the course of an entire school year will require engagement in the transformations of data to evidence, evidence to patterns/models, and patterns/models to theories and explanations. The proper deployment of visualization techniques in science classrooms will involve the employment of instructional designs that make the link between data and data visualizations a topic of discussion and a focus of evaluation. For a forward-thinking application of visualization techniques in classroom see Edelson *et al.* (1999).

The point, therefore, is that there are important steps between obtaining the raw data of observation and acquiring the theory-informed selection of evidence used to make visualization models. According to Grandy (1997: 49–50) in a critique of constructivist practices in the science classroom:

> What is missing are the epistemic connections that relate theory to supporting data, to conflicting theories, to anomalous data, to equivocal data . . . what can be taken as data and what is disqualified, what is strong evidence and what is weak evidence, is always judged against the background provided by the community's experience with the theories, the data domain, and the instruments in question . . . the demarcation between what counts and what does not . . . is critical to the ongoing enterprise.

In other words, the epistemic break with common sense, the boundary crossing, requires the refinement and extension of the discriminating language.

In school science, the enterprise of addressing epistemic connections is about carefully designed learning sequences that engage students in both investigations and colloquia or conversations around the investigations. The idea of colloquia in science classrooms is taken from Lansdown *et al.* (1971). Grounded in Vygotsky's theory of learning (that meaning is obtained through language), colloquia are 'speaking together' opportunities that begin with 'a pooling of observations, getting a collection of facts into the arena, so to speak, to make individuals aware of common data seen from different viewpoints. This is the beginning of speaking together' (Lansdown *et al.* 1971: 120). In the SEPIA project the 'speaking together' takes place during assessment conversation activities. These can occur as either whole class or small group (n = 3 or 4) activities. Briefly, an assessment conversation begins with the selection of student work that displays relevant ideas and information. The student work comes from investigations that, by design, promote a diversity of student responses. Nothing seems to shut down argumentation in a science classroom more than all students doing the same investigation, employing the same tools and methods, with the expectation of obtaining the same outcome. In the next step of an assessment conversation the students' ideas and information are publicly shared (for example, displayed on an overhead projector, or copied and distributed to student groups) and discussed. Over time, the goal of these discussions is to promote the refinement and extension of scientific language and thinking along three cognitive dimensions: metacognitive/conceptual, notational/representational and epistemological. This tripartite approach to 'speaking together' follows Gardner's (1991) argument that higher-level thinking involves acquisition and coordination of several systems. Among these are the notational, epistemological and conceptual systems of the domain. For Gardner, to engage in higher-level thinking is to employ notational, epistemic and conceptual systems that support or frame reasoning within the domain.

Other examples of 'speaking together' models are the reciprocal teaching discussion groups used in Brown and Campione's (1994) 'community of learners'; the Knowledge Integration Environment computer platform (Bell *et al.* 1995; Linn *et al.* 1999); and the Knowledge Forum/CSILE (Computer Supported Intensive Learning Environment) computer platform used in classrooms (Scardamalia *et al.* 1994). In each case, the goal of the 'speaking together' opportunities is to make thinking visible for teachers and pupils. Within this discovery/discussion/debate learning environment, Gardner's conceptual, representational and epistemological constructions can be realized.

Learning to learn: observational changes in science

The subjectivity or objectivity attached to an observational act is determined by the confidence one holds in the theoretical frameworks that define the observational events. The claim is that the transition from sense perception observation to theory-driven observation is a necessary condition to cross the boundary from common-sense folk explanations to theory-driven scientific explanations (Duschl *et al.* 1999b). Explicitly teaching the nature of science will engage students in boundary crossings or epistemological breaks that explore how we have learned to learn. The crossover from sense observation to theory-driven observation is certainly dependent on a special curiosity and a special environment that supports curiosity. This curiosity leads us to seek and use tools and texts to develop non-obvious 'how and why' explanations. What comes to count as a theoretically relevant observational event depends largely on our theories about the source, transmission and reception of information and evidence (Shapere 1982; Duschl 1990). So in the case of an MRI (magnetic resonance imaging) scan, our theories of tissues, of electromagnetism, of the non-invasive effect of electromagnetic waves on tissues, of how the absorption and reflection of those waves reveals the structure of different tissues, and of how the digital display of received waves represents tissue sections, all contribute to an observational event.

Ackerman (1985) argues that the examination of the development and refinement of data domains presents a way to establish the objectivity of science through a process he calls 'epistemological breaks with common sense'. His argument is based on a dialectical process between theory and fact that gives rise to legitimated facts, or what he calls the 'hard data' of science. Legitimated facts emerge from the refinement and extensions of instruments and techniques within research groups. For Ackerman, the exchange of scientific information within such groups is the 'crucible within which scientific progress takes place' (1985: 54). The scientific information of importance is the knowledge distributed or embedded in the instrument and data domain contexts. As mentioned above, as we refine our human sensory apparatus with instruments and tools, we generate new data domains. These new data domains are subjected to refinements and extensions in our discriminating language. As members of the research group scrutinize the data texts, a dialectic between fact and theory takes place with neither theory nor fact having precedence.

The dialectical focus is the data domain. The development of scientific instruments, according to Ackerman, serves the purpose of refining the human sensory apparatus. Thus, he writes, there is a 'role of instrumentation in fixing the limits of data domains and in locating the facts within them' (Ackerman 1985: 128). Now you may be asking at this point, 'How can this be accomplished in science classrooms? Why can't we have this dialectic in classrooms?' We can, if we think of classrooms as the research group cru-cible and students as the researchers scrutinizing data texts. Here I will pause the discussion of Ackerman for a moment to answer the last question by examining some of the research reported by Richard Leher and Leona Schauble and revisiting Lansdown's idea of importance of colloquia in science instruction.

For the past six years or so Leher and Schauble (in press a) have been working collaboratively with teachers to understand ways to bring model-based reasoning about conceptual systems and data texts to elementary classrooms. Their work demonstrates that children and teachers can co-ordinate instructional sequences that promote discourse on data. In the text, *Children's Work with Data* (Leher and Schauble in press b), each of the teachers presents a chapter on how children in their classrooms have engaged in conversations on data. Contrary to extant deficit models of chil-dren's reasoning abilities, the 7- to 9-year-old children display the statistical language of central tendencies. They are engaged in refining and extending the language of data texts through the use of graphic representations for displaying data and the use colloquia and presentations for debating and attaching meaning to the displays. Leher and Romberg (1996) report on the developmental steps children follow in learning to 'ask questions of data'. Initially, children do not think you can ask questions of data. In this pro-gramme of research, the boundaries between mathematics and science edu-cation are blurred. The contexts for doing science and doing mathematics are frequently situated design contexts, like modelling the function of the elbow (Penner *et al.* 1997) or problem-solving contexts like gathering data on the distribution and frequency of fruit flies in a school to determine the source of the pests (Leher and Schauble in press b). In each instance, the investigation facilitates the colloquium on science concepts in the design of the elbow and the colloquium on data representation in the investigation of fruit flies in the school.

As mentioned earlier, the coupling of investigation with colloquium (Lansdown *et al.* 1971) is very similar to the assessment conversation in the SEPIA project. Consider the following exchange during an assessment con-versation in a seventh-grade science classroom with children aged 11–12. Like all assessment conversations, the colloquium or 'speaking together' session is preceded by an investigation. In this case students were provided with a variety of food substances, instructed to use their senses to describe the food substances, and then asked to classify each food as either an acid or a base. Next the students were asked to individually draw in three differ-ent frames (a model of an acid; a model of a base; and a model of mixing acid and base together).

The evening before the assessment conversation activity the teacher, Mr D, sorted and selected seven samples of students' work from the two classes of students working with the Acids and Bases Unit. He had colour transparencies made of the students' work. If the student was in the classroom, he had them come to the overhead projector to explain their models. His goals were to share the diversity of models students had made, and to provide feedback on representations of 'models that explain'. As is typical of students at this age, when asked to draw a model that explains many will just depict the items used in the activity (for example, slices of lemon) and not get at the epistemic structures. During the lesson a variety of explanations (appearing in bold text in the extract beneath), and challenges to explanations (appearing in italic text) occur. Students' names are represented by the capital letters in quotes, for example, 'Y'.

Field notes: 5th period, 5 June 1997
The first drawing displayed on the overhead was by 'Y' (7th period). Mr D asks the class if the words help to know what 'Y' is trying to say. 'Does the use of words help?' The students say yes. Mr D encourages the students to begin making changes on their own drawing using the ideas from the work he is showing. Here the student is commenting on the assertion in the drawing that '**carbon makes acids burn**'. Again Mr D asks if the words help. One student responds '*Not really because someone may think carbon is a base*'. Mr D presents this as a theory about acids. Mr D talks through the drawing pointing out the symbols and keys used to depict carbon and fat. 'Y', in the mixing acid and base together frame, states acid and base mixed together make a salt.

The next picture put on the overhead projector is 'A's. It is the first abstract drawing. Comments by Mr D at the beginning of class indicate he has made a decision about the order he wants to show the pictures. 'A's frustration from the day before now gives way to some level of excitement. She begins to describe her picture: '**The spikes are**' – she struggles for the right word which is finally offered by a classmate as '**tangy**'. Mr D reinforces the use of a drawing to capture the feeling an acid has on the tongue. (There was some discussion the day before about taste (flavour) and taste (texture).) 'A' then starts to describe the pits ('holes') on the surface of the acid particle and begins to try and use some of her encyclopaedic knowledge. The day before, 'A' had come to class with three pages of handwritten notes obtained from her reading of the *Encarta* CD-ROM entries on acids and bases. 'Molecules' comes out, 'hydrogen' is used but it is not presented in a manner that suggests she sees the connection between the terms.

'A' then begins to describe her base – a plain rectangle to depict 'dull'. Mr D states it is like a brick. 'Foundation to a building' is heard. 'A' then describes how her mixing acid and base drawing, labelled with the word 'neutral', is a composite of the two drawings, the wavy lines being like water which is '7.0 on pH, little bit of acid and little bit of base'. (This is the first of what will become many references to acids and bases coming together in such a way that properties of each are preserved – this idea of physical properties being preserved is a major and important theme of the lesson.)

The next drawing is by 'L' (7th period). She provides sentence descriptions of her drawing of acids and bases. Her theory is '**carbon is made up of oxygen and carbon and when combined it has a burning chemical change**'. '**Carbon dioxide sticks to tongue and causes it to burn.**' '**A base has no carbon dioxide causeing [*sic*] it to not bubble and sting.**' 'A' is intrigued by yet another alternative idea. Mr D ties it to a previous lesson and emphasizes the idea of a chemical change. 'L' also shows acids and bases coming together to make salts. (Mr D was absent on Monday and the substitute or replacement teacher let some students go to the library to get information on acid and bases. One item introduced was acid + base = salt.) One student can be heard to ask if the salt is NaCl, 'A' says to her that the Na is an acid and the Cl is the base because they are + and –.

The next the class is shown 'B's (7th period) picture. Yet another theory: '**fumes cause sour, tingling comes from air bubbles. Air pressure pushes on the base to make it thick and moisture makes it feel wet**'. Labels are used.

Next is 'P's picture – he is absent. This drawing is the first to use colours and shapes to depict the properties of acids and bases. Mr D asks the class, 'What do you see?' 'Bright and citrusey' (words from word bank), 'Base is dull', 'Uses sharp edges', 'Zingy – zing around'. Mr D highlights some marks in the drawing that are not that visible to establish that the yellow jagged things are moving around. The idea of energy is raised and someone comments that the lines look like lightning bolts. 'A', trying to assimilate this drawing with her knowledge, is heard to say, 'energy to give and energy to take'. The interesting feature of the drawing is how 'P' has taken some of the features of the acid model and base model to draw the model of acids and bases mixing together. One student says, 'They don't really combine completely'. 'A', drawing on her *Encarta* knowledge says, 'Which is part of the English theory'. One student then provides an analogy to cookies: '**It's like when you make cookies, you can't see all the parts but you can see some**'. Students are now calling out all sorts of ideas and brainstorming: 'part solution, part mixture'.

We can see from this description of the assessment conversation the wide-ranging comments pupils will bring to the colloquium. One interesting feature of this lesson was the students' enthusiastic responses to the abstract representation by 'P'. Here, I would argue, is a kind of epistemological break. Whereas the majority of students' models of neutralization could be classified as concrete representations of the objects employed (for example, slices of lemon, tongues, jars of milk), it was a surprise to see how the abstract drawing engaged the students. The conversation to assess the various models the students produced brought to the discourse not only creative representations of neutralization but also a diversity of sources of evidence. From the comments of students it was possible to assign sources of evidence to one of several categories: from the portfolio of work each student kept; from previous lessons in other units, days or weeks earlier; from the investigation itself; from outside the classroom (for example, *Encarta*); and from personal opinion. Tracking the evidence found in student discourse, it is possible to ask questions such as:

- What is the frequency of use of each category?
- What trends in the frequency of use exist over the course of the unit?
- What learning environment factors promote the use of one kind or form of evidence over others?
- How do the argumentation strategies of students evolve and develop?

Argumentation and the establishment of epistemic communities

The broadening of science studies in this century, from the exclusive domain of philosophy of science, to an integration of perspectives from philosophy, history and sociology of science, has challenged perspectives about what should count as the basic unit for doing science. The established or received view of the individual scientist as the unit or agent of conceptual change is being replaced by a view that has communities of scientists as the fundamental unit of change. Hull captures the essence of the changes that are taking place among philosophers when he writes, 'The objectivity that matters in science is not primarily a characteristic of individual scientists but of scientific communities' (1988: 4). Ackerman (1985), you will recall, says the crucible of scientific progress is the research group.

Longino (1994) is another philosopher of science who advocates locating objectivity in the group dynamics of communities of scientists. One example she gives of consensus-building toward scientific knowledge is the peer review processes that occur in scientific communities – for example, publishing in refereed journals, conference presentations, and grant funding reviews. Longino lists four conditions that a community must meet in order for a consensus to qualify as knowledge:

1 There must be publicly recognized forums for the criticism of evidence, of methods, and assumptions about reasoning.
2 There must be uptake of criticism. The community must not merely tolerate dissent, but its beliefs and theories must change over time in response to the critical discourse taking place within it.
3 There must be publicly recognized standards by reference to which theories, hypotheses and observational practices are being evaluated, and by appeal to criticism relevant to the goals of the inquiring community.
4 Finally, communities must be characterized by equality of intellectual authority.

These guidelines, as Grandy (1997) suggests, are well worth considering in the design of learning environments that seek to promote epistemic communities within which it is possible to explicitly teach the nature of science.

The emerging perspective for philosophers of science is that the objectivity of scientific claims is borne out of the arguments and debates that occur between different factions of investigators seeking a consensus about knowledge claims, methodological claims and aims of scientific inquiry. Ackerman (1985), citing from Ravetz's *Scientific Knowledge and its Social Problems* (1971), also proposes that social processes are involved in converting individual research to scientific knowledge. He identifies two stages: one is the journal referee system, and the other is the practice of citing earlier work in a field when writing individual research reports.

Lansdown *et al.* (1971) make remarkably similar claims in their suggestion that science education needs to be coordinated between investigation and colloquium. According to Longino (1994), the epistemic criteria used to forge a consensus opinion, or challenges to a consensus opinion, are established at many different levels of inquiry by members of inquiring communities. The size of membership and the beliefs of members change as the scientific claim moves from the private confines of the 'lab' to the public corridors of scientific conferences, proceedings and refereed publications. The excerpt from Mr D's classroom shows how this happens with students thinking about models of neutralization prior to any formal instruction.

Promoting colloquia in epistemic contexts

The research clearly suggests that the way to format the explicit teaching of epistemic goals is through the implementation of sustained instructional sequences that provide forums for investigation, colloquia and argumentation. Such an approach allocates significant instructional time in terms of weeks rather than days to studying a scientific context. This, in and of itself, is a radical change for many science education programmes. The additional allocation of time affords opportunities for learners to investigate, construct and evaluate both the knowledge claims and criteria used to answer a question, solve a problem, or pose an explanation or model.

Given the opportunity, guidance and support, children of all ages are capable of writing and telling epistemic stories that progress from data to theory. One challenge to teachers is locating motivating contexts to conduct an inquiry and then designing an age-appropriate sequence to execute the inquiry. Here is where our research needs to be done. The research by Leher and Schauble (in press b) demonstrates that within a motivating context, children are capable of working from data, using that data to locate patterns in data, and then interpreting the patterns to generate explanations of the patterns. The activity of science is an iterative process of moving back and forth between evidence, models and theory. Doing science in classrooms and in other learning environments is basically about getting children to produce models and then evaluate the fit of the model with evidence and theory stories. We need to do research on the pedagogical practices, the design of learning environments, and formative assessment strategies that facilitate students' epistemological breaks with common sense.

The history of science reveals that scientific knowledge and methods are frequently modified, adapted, and at times abandoned. A necessary condition of inquiry is providing learners with experiences that exemplify this responsive feature of science as a way of knowing. Investigation and colloquium formats are the way to go. In the face of new evidence, new observational techniques, and/or new theoretical perspectives, scientists and students will respond by subjecting established knowledge and methods to critical evaluation. Science as a way of knowing is responsive. The responsive nature of knowing is driven by the need for the ideas, beliefs and claims of scientists and students to be consistent with or cohere with the evidence and beliefs posed by other members of the inquiry community. In other words, there is a drive to 'get it right'. Science as a way of knowing values and seeks coherence – claims and techniques from one community of scientists cannot ignore the claims and techniques from another community of scientists. Thus, two critical goals of understanding the nature of scientific inquiry are developing in our students an awareness:

- of the commitments held by members of scientific communities 'to get it right';
- of the processes and events that cause scientific communities to change commitments.

But let us not underestimate the complexity of instruction that is committed to investigation, colloquium and argumentation. The knowledge demands on teachers are quite significant, for the teacher must have a clear sense of the conceptual, notational and epistemological trajectories they wish to move students along. Our research needs to be conducted with teachers and focused on learning how to design instructional sequences that link investigation with colloquium. What is common to all inquiries is that responsiveness and change should be encourage at each and every step. Questions like 'How do you know?', 'Is there a better way or a different way to do this?', 'How would you explain this to someone not in this class?', 'Is there an investigation you can think of that would help us decide between the two ideas we are discussing?', 'Is there anything you have found that does not fit?' and 'What would you change?' can be applied to each of the general transitions of moving from evidence to explanation.

Our designs of learning environments reverse the science curriculum goal question that opened this chapter by asking 'What do we want students to *do* and what do they need to *know* to *do* it?' Rhetorically, the shift is simple. At the level of the classroom, however, the shift is quite dynamic. When the doing becomes the construction and evaluation of models, explanations, experiments and arguments, very different curricular, instructional, and assessment dynamics are required to support and motivate students' efforts. Conducting research on the dynamics listed below is critically important to achieve the goals of explicitly teaching the nature of science and, in turn, to develop a public understanding of science. The dynamics are:

- There is a need to blur the boundaries between curriculum, instruction and assessment. The teacher should be empowered to alter the path of the curriculum and of instruction in light of judgements made from the assessment of students' understandings, skills, ideas and habits of mind, to name but a few.
- The learning environment must stimulate and nurture learners' development, evaluation and communication of scientific information, hence the desire to link investigation with colloquium and argumentation discourses.
- There needs to be a set of criteria and goals, clearly understood by the teacher and developed in pupils, to both direct and make transparent the evaluation of the scientific claims, in particular epistemic criteria and goals.
- Formative assessments should be a primary role of the teacher – i.e. coordinating feedback on student products, representations and ideas, or being a provocateur or 'devil's advocate'. Listening on the part of the teacher, and learning to listen to students in different ways is so very important.
- Students should be held accountable for the quality of products and ideas they present. Claims and positions should be backed up with evidence, reasons and warrants. Hence, colloquium and argumentation sessions on prior work and ideas (their own as well as those of other students in the class or community of inquirers) is also very important.

The way forward requires a radical shift in how we conduct research, how we design curriculum, instruction and assessment models, how we educate teachers to teach science and how we conceptualize the organization of the science curriculum. I have argued here for an approach to science that requires a significant amount of engagement and monitoring on the part of the teacher. Here are some of the changes we need to consider:

- *Change 1*: Starting in science methods classes, beginning teachers should be engaged in the design, implementation and evaluation of instructional sequences that promote inquiry and examine data texts. The emphasis on planning and teaching should shift from single lessons to units. New teachers should begin the process of developing expertise in science teaching by learning how to refine and extend scientific language along three cognitive dimensions: metacognitive/conceptual, notational/representational and epistemological. The unit developed in the methods class should be taught during the student teaching experience, evaluated and refined. The beginning teacher would make this unit a part of their pedagogical profile.
- *Change 2*: School science programmes should change to accommodate the expertise of teachers, not teachers to the expectations of school programmes. The full inquiry unit that teachers develop should follow them to whatever school and whatever grade level they teach. Only then will expertise in explicitly teaching data texts and the epistemic nature of science be developed.
- *Change 3*: The year-long science curriculum at each grade level should allocate, at a minimum, six to eight weeks for teachers to implement the full inquiry/investigation-colloquium units. During these units the number of science terms and concepts taught would be drastically reduced in order to facilitate development of the metacognitive/conceptual, notational/representational and epistemological dimensions that constitute the language of science.
- *Change 4*: Criteria for selecting teachers to be a member of staff should include consideration of the full inquiry/investigation-colloquium units they could teach or would be willing to learn to teach. This would guarantee that over the course of several years, students would engage in life science, physical science, earth science, modelling, explaining, designing, experimenting, etc., and data-text driven units of instruction.
- *Change 5*: In-service teacher education and classroom based research would focus on understanding the pedagogical, learning environment and assessment challenges teachers and students encounter during the full inquiry/investigation-colloquium units. The conversations and research would be directed to understanding engagements in data texts and epistemological breaks with common sense. For these specific units, the task of teaching would be highly domain specific. Teachers and researchers would

come together because they are interested in learning how to teach the epistemic sequence of moving from data to explanation while using colloquia, investigations, and assessment conversations along the way. Then, and only then, will a teacher begin to develop the complex set of skills and understandings needed to implement instruction coordinated around investigations and colloquia. Then, and only then, will we begin to develop an understanding of the age-appropriate curriculum, instruction and assessment models to use with pupils. Then, and only then, will we shift science education from knowing what there is to know to learning and evaluating how we know and why we believe what we know. Then, and only then, will a science education begin to promote a public understanding of science. The way forward requires a radical reconceptualization of the research we do in science education.

References

Ackerman, R.J. (1985) *Data, Instruments and Theory: A Dialectical Approach to Understanding Science*. Princeton, NJ: Princeton University Press.
Bell, P., Davis, E. and Linn, M. (1995) The 'knowledge integration environment': theory and design, in *Proceedings of the Computer Supported Collaborative Learning Conference*. Mahwah, NJ: Erlbaum.
Brown, A. and Campione, J. (1994) Guided discovery in a community of learners, in K. McGilly (ed.) *Classroom Lessons: Integrating Cognitive Theory and Classroom Practice*. London: MIT Press.
Chinn, C. and Brewer, W. (1993) The role of anomalous data in knowledge acquisition: a theoretical framework and implications for science instruction. *Review of Educational Research*, 63(1): 1–50.
Driver, R., Leach, J., Millar, R. and Scott, P. (1996) *Young People's Images of Science*. Buckingham: Open University Press.
Driver, R., Newton, P. and Osborne, J. (in press) Establishing the norms of scientific argument in classrooms. *Science Education*.
Duschl, R. (1990) *Restructuring Science Education: The Role of Theories and Their Importance*. New York: Teachers College Press.
Duschl, R. and Gitomer, D. (1997) Strategies and challenges to changing the focus of assessment and instruction in science classrooms. *Educational Assessment*, 4(1): 337–73.
Duschl, R., Ellenbogen, K. and Erduran, S. (1999a) Understanding dialogic argumentation among middle school science students. Paper presented to the American Educational Research Association Annual Meeting, Montreal, 19–23 April.
Duschl, R., Deak, G., Ellenbogen, K. and Holton, D. (1999b) Developmental and educational perspectives on theory change: to have and hold, or to have and hone? *Science & Education*, 8(5): 525–41.
Edelson, D., Gordin, D.N. and Pea, R.D. (1999) Addressing the challenges of inquiry-based learning through technology and curriculum design. *The Journal of the Learning Sciences*, 8(3&4): 391–450.

Gardner, H. (1991) *The Unschooled Mind: How Children Think and How Schools Should Teach*. New York: Basic Books.

Gitomer, D. and Duschl, R. (1995) Moving toward a portfolio culture in science education, in S. Glynn and R. Duit (eds) *Learning Science in Schools: Research Reforming Practice*. Mahwah, NJ: Erlbaum.

Gitomer, D. and Duschl, R. (1998) Emerging issues and practices in science assessment, in B.J. Fraser and K.G. Tobin (eds) *International Handbook of Science Education*. Dordrecht: Kluwer Academic Publishers.

Grandy, R. (1997) Constructivisms and objectivity: disentangling metaphysics from pedagogy. *Science and Education*, 6(1&2): 43–53.

Hodson, D. (1990) A critical look at practical work in school science. *School Science Review*, 70: 33–40.

Hull, D. (1988) *Science as Process*. Chicago: University of Chicago Press.

Lansdown, B., Blackwood, P. and Brandwein, P. (1971) *Teaching Elementary Science: Through Investigation and Colloquium*. New York: Harcourt Brace Jovanovich.

Leher, R. and Romberg, T. (1996) Exploring children's data modeling. *Cognition and Instruction*, 14(1): 69–108.

Leher, R. and Schauble, L. (in press a) Modeling in mathematics and science, in R. Glaser (ed.) *Advances in Instructional Psychology V5*. Mahwah, NJ: Erlbaum.

Leher, R. and Schauble, L. (in press b) *Children's Work with Data: Modeling in Mathematics and Science*. New York: Teachers College Press.

Lemke, J. (1990) *Talking Science: Language, Learning and Values*. Norwood, NJ: Ablex.

Linn, M., Bell, P. and Hsi, S. (1999) Using the Internet to enhance student understanding of science: the knowledge integration environment. *Interactive Learning Environments*, 1(6): 4–38.

Longino, H. (1994) The fate of knowledge in social theories of science, in F.F. Schmidt (ed.) *Socializing Epistemology: The Social Dimension of Knowledge*. Lanham, MD: Rowman & Littlefield.

Newton, P., Driver, R. and Osborne, J. (1999) The place of argumentation in the pedagogy of school science. *International Journal of Science Education*, 21(5): 553–76.

Penner, D., Giles, N., Leher, R. and Schauble, L. (1997) Building functional models: designing an elbow. *Journal of Research in Science Teaching*, 34(1): 1–20.

Ravetz, J.R. (1971) *Scientific Knowledge and its Social Problems*. Harmondsworth: Penguin.

Rock, B.N., Blackwell, T.R., Miller, D. and Hardison, A. (1997) The GLOBE Program: a model for international environmental education, in K.C. Cohen (ed.) *Internet Links for Science Education: Student-Scientist Partnerships*. New York: Plenum.

Scardamalia, M., Bereiter, C. and Lamon, M. (1994) The CSILE Project: trying to bring the classroom into World 3, in K. McGilly (ed.) *Classroom Lessons: Integrating Cognitive Theory and Classroom Practice*. London: MIT Press.

Shapere, D. (1982) The concept of observation in science and philosophy. *Philosophy of Science*, 49: 485–525.

12

'Science for all': time for a paradigm shift?

Edgar Jenkins

> My major bias is the hope that a repeat of previous science
> education reforms can be avoided. My other bias is to stay
> clear of science education reform proposals contradictory
> to a democratic society and the welfare of young people
> and the current practice and ethos of science.
>
> (Hurd 1998: 14–15)

As the new millennium begins, it is doubtful whether science and science education have ever had so much academic, political and public attention or commanded such resources. School science curriculum reform is a global phenomenon, with change in the form and/or content of science courses often being allied to the specification of standards, goals or levels of attainment that students should achieve at particular stages of their schooling. In many countries, the study of science is now mandatory throughout compulsory schooling, although, more commonly, the opportunity to study science is available to only a proportion of the school population and the curriculum shows a marked differentiation between boys and girls.[1] Comparative studies of school science education have flourished, the outcomes including both international comparisons of student achievement and a wealth of detail about matters such as how science is organized and taught, the textbooks used, the qualifications of teachers and the attitudes of students towards science (see for example, Black and Atkin 1996; Robitaille 1997; Solomon and Mariano 1999). It is evident that more students are studying science than at any time in history and that much more is known than hitherto about the science education that they receive.

Beyond the world of schooling, science is promoted to a wider public via interactive science centres, museums and 'exploratories' – which seek to engage the attention of visitors by means of 'hands-on' activities and challenging visual, tactile or other experiences. The development of such centres is also a global phenomenon. As Persson (1996: 55) has somewhat cryptically noted, 'the sheer number of science centres indicates that something is going on'. His estimate in 1996 was that such centres attracted 'in excess of 100 million' visitors worldwide and that some of them were among the top tourist attractions in the countries concerned. However, despite an overt commitment to inquiry and exploration, interactive science centres are principally concerned to promote an understanding and appreciation of science. They rarely challenge or interrogate aspects of the scientific endeavour, and the few attempts that have been made to do so have led to considerable political difficulties with funding agencies or other interested parties (Macdonald 1996, 1998; West 1996; Gregory and Miller 1998).

Attention should also be drawn to the rapid growth of books which seek to promote and popularize science, some of which have become international best sellers, and to the increasing attention being given to science in the broadcast media. Not all of this attention is necessarily supportive of science, partly because journalistic practices and values do not always coincide with those of the scientific community, notably its emphasis upon peer review prior to publication. Nonetheless, a series of environmental, ecological, medical, genetic, health, dietary, agricultural or other problems and issues has ensured that some aspects of science have been given a high, and not always brief, profile in both the printed and the broadcast media. Like their parents, pupils at school cannot escape from the role that science has come to play in the modern world, nor from the consequences that flow from it.

That role has led some commentators to refer to a new system of knowledge production, arising from what Ravetz (1990) has referred to as the 'merger of knowledge with power'. The new system, at this stage complementing rather than displacing the old, emphasizes the generation of knowledge within the context of application, involves different and more fluid institutional research structures, and seeks validation in such notions as utility and marketability rather than the more traditional peer reviewed publication (Gibbons *et al.* 1994).

> ... Science has changed its ends. It is no longer the old science of the last few centuries ... Contemporary science is worldly in every sense of the word and quite different in its essential character from the European science of the recent past ... the differences are apparent in all dimensions of scientific research, intellectual, instrumental and organisational. They are also revealed in the changed relations of science, technology and production.
>
> (Redner 1987: 15)

Given the commanding position and authority that science has come to occupy in the contemporary world, it is perhaps inevitable that it has been subjected to academic and other scrutiny and criticism. One result has been a lively controversy involving those, such as Gross and Levitt (1994) and Sokal and Bricmont (1998), who seek to defend science against what the former identify as the 'academic left'. There is also a scholarly community working within a critical and hermeneutic tradition which has mounted a challenge to many of the widely-held assumptions about how science is conducted and scientific knowledge generated and validated (for example, Latour 1987). This academic challenge, which should be distinguished from crude anti-science sentiments, is significant for school science education since it has helped to render 'antique' the understanding of science which 'explicitly or implicitly [has] provided coherence and security for generations of [science] teachers' (Ravetz 1989: 20).

Much the same lesson can be drawn from studies of the public understanding of science, especially from work which has explored the relationships between science and its various publics rather than attempted to quantify the understanding by an undifferentiated public of a number of scientific concepts (Layton *et al.* 1993; Irwin and Wynne 1996). Such work shows that science, as encountered by most people in their everyday lives, is rarely objective, coherent, well-bounded and unproblematic. Science beyond the laboratory turns out to be a messy business and, far from scientific knowledge being central to decisions about practical action, it is often irrelevant or, at best, marginal to it. Scientific knowledge is not encountered free of its social and institutional connections and scientific thought is often rejected as the yardstick by which to judge the validity of everyday thinking. In addition, ignorance of science on the part of adults may have nothing to do with intellectual ability and such ignorance may not always be seen as in need of remedy. The significance of this account of science is that it stands firmly at odds with the view of science commonly presented at school, where the discipline is well bounded, answers are secure, and uncertainty, doubt or debate are not admitted, save under severely limited conditions. School science reflects an endeavour that is essentially positivist, heroic, apolitical and more concerned with scientists of the past than with those of the present. It can, of course, be argued with considerable justification that much of science, and perhaps almost all of school science, *is* unproblematic. Accepting this, however, leaves students confronted with two seemingly conflicting, if perhaps overlapping, visions of science: one constructed and institutionalized in the school curriculum, and another which is much less secure and develops from their own, rapidly enlarging, experience of the social, physical and emotional worlds which they inhabit.

We should not be surprised, therefore, if the understanding of scientific phenomena promoted at school rarely transfers to the solution of problems in the out-of-school world. This is not simply a matter of two different perceptions of science or of 'situated cognition'. It also involves a failure on the part of those who lament the enduring nature of pupils' scientific misconceptions both to appreciate what is involved in applying existing knowledge to a new context and the adequacy of some of these misconceptions for coping with many aspects of everyday life. Addressing satisfactorily the coldness of a room by closing a door, double glazing one or more windows, or insulating the walls and ceiling does not require an understanding of cold as an absence of heat conceptualized in terms of molecular motion. Likewise, a fluid theory of heat is usually adequate for most heating engineers. To argue thus is in no way to devalue the power of the kinetic theory of heat or, more generally, to privilege functional or even commonsense knowledge above scientific understanding. It is simply an acknowledgement that natural phenomena can be understood at many levels and from a variety of perspectives, and that, in many everyday circumstances, scientific explanations may be over-sophisticated or even unnecessary as a basis for effective action.

What of the pupils who study science at school? At the risk of some overgeneralization among different educational systems, it seems clear that, for most pupils, interest in school science declines throughout secondary schooling. The reference to *school* science is significant since many of these same pupils are often quite positive in their attitudes to science beyond school and are very interested in, for example, cosmology, the nature of time and those aspects of science that impact, or seem likely to impact, upon their lives. In many industrialized countries, physics and chemistry have become relatively unpopular subjects for study, especially at the upper levels of secondary schooling, with enrolments in physics, in particular, often showing a marked gender bias in favour of boys. Attitudes are, of course, open to a variety of personal and other influences – for example, from parents, teachers, pupils' peers, schools and the broadcast and printed media, but much more needs to be known about the relative significance of these various influences and about how attitudes might be changed. For example, how are pupils' attitudes towards science affected by the kind of teaching they receive, or by the science curriculum to which they are exposed, and which of these factors is the more important?

At the start of a new millennium, therefore, those reflecting upon the future of school science education confront a complex picture, with a number of contradictory elements. Attendance at a growing number of interactive science centres is buoyant, and the publication of books that seek to explain and popularize science to the public constitutes something of a growth industry. Science figures prominently on radio and television, and more resources are available than ever before, including the internet, to support self-instruction in science and/or access to scientific information. In broad terms, interest in, and support for science remains high, although this support is not uncritical and it does not extend to all areas of science. Alongside this, commonly-held views about the way science is conducted and the authority vested in scientific knowledge, together with such notions as objectivity and truth, have been challenged as never before. That challenge comes not simply from the 'academic left' or from 'postmodernists' of one sort or another but increasingly from the experience of ordinary people as they grapple with issues that have a scientific dimension and are of concern to them. In such a context, the world proves to be much more complicated, uncertain and risky than school science encourages pupils to believe, and the power of science to explain, predict and control turns out to be severely limited.

It is possible, of course, to argue that, while both scholarly and popular understandings of the nature of science are undergoing profound shifts, the practice of science is not only insulated from these shifts but needs to remain so in the interests of science itself. High quality science sits uncomfortably with political controversy (Collingridge and Reeve 1986). In addition, as Poincaré observed almost a century ago: 'If the confidence that his methods are weapons with which he can fight his way to the truth were taken from the scientific explorer, the paralysis of those engaged in a hopeless task would fall upon him' (quoted in Heilbron 1983: 178).

To ignore the wider public and critical perceptions of science, however, seems unwise. Science needs widespread public understanding and support if it is to flourish and be seen as other than as a means of delivering the technological goods, whether these be new 'smart bombs' or more powerful ways of treating disease. As Asimov once observed (in Thomas and Durant 1987), where scientists are not understood, they run the risk of being persecuted.

Historically, secondary school science education has allied itself with academic science, the more so in those countries in which selection for secondary education has been, or is, the norm. Its function was essentially pre-professional and its content determined, however vicariously, by the academic scientific community. However, since science was first schooled in the mid-nineteenth century, the practice and ethos of science, its social context and public estimation have all been transformed. In addition, there is now a substantial research literature relating to the teaching and learning of science, notably that concerned with children's ideas about a range of natural phenomena and how these develop with age. For a variety of reasons that are important but lie beyond the scope of this chapter, school science education has either been slow to respond to many of these changes or has done so in ways that have accommodated innovation without weakening the traditional alliance with academic science. Something more radical and amounting to a paradigm shift is now needed. In this chapter, I discuss two aspects of school science education upon which attention might be focused in the first instance. These are the role of the laboratory and the need to accommodate within school science courses the uncertainty and risk commonly associated with science in the everyday world.

Revisiting the school laboratory

The science laboratory occupies a central and fundamental place in secondary school science teaching, a position that is both ideological and material. Unsurprisingly, therefore, it figures prominently in the research and professional literature of science education (for example Lazarowitz and Tamir 1994), and practical work conducted in a laboratory remains an important feature of current attempts to improve science teaching. Equally, there is no shortage of criticism of the role that the science teaching laboratory has come to play in school science teaching or of prescriptions for reform (for example Wellington 1998; Leach and Paulsen 1999). Science teachers see laboratory teaching as serving a variety of purposes, not all of which are easily reconciled. In addition to allegedly helping pupils to understand scientific concepts – i.e. as a support for learning, or to develop so-called scientific skills – practical work in the laboratory is seen as the means whereby pupils gain an insight into science's greatest mystery: its method. It is in the laboratory that things are 'found out', where ideas are tested and new knowledge ultimately validated. It is where, for many science teachers, the 'nature of science' can be demonstrated to, and experienced by, pupils. As Donnelly has shown, the teaching laboratory structures science teachers' work both literally and metaphorically and changing it 'would involve . . . changing much of the discursive, social and institutional system of science education as it is enacted within schools' (Donnelly 1998: 595).

The intention here is somewhat more modest. It is to direct attention to the emphasis upon skill acquisition in the practical teaching of science and to suggest that this seriously misrepresents science by reducing a highly imaginative and creative activity to little more than a series of algorithms. To put the claim more succinctly, it is argued that practical work in school science commonly short changes both pupils and science itself. As a corollary, it is suggested that more effort is needed to engage pupils in learning activities in science that are both genuinely investigative and collaborative.

First, the issue of 'skills', reference to which has now become endemic in much of the discourse of school science education. A cursory survey of the literature reveals references to, for example, observation skills, practical skills, and skills such as hypothesizing, investigating and inferring. To a considerable extent, the emphasis on skill acquisition in the laboratory teaching of science is a consequence of an imposed need to assess pupils' competence at practical science. It is also sustained by the belief that science is a practical subject and that, as a result, pupils must be taught, and acquire, the relevant practical skills needed to work in a scientific manner. However, such emphasis reflects a number of assumptions not only about teaching and learning but also about science and, more widely, about the nature and purpose of education. More particularly, it sustains a performance curriculum and an outcomes-led approach to teaching and learning, and it presents science as little more than an aggregation of skills. It is as if to be good at observing, hypothesizing and so on is the guarantee of scientific excellence.

The weaknesses in the skills or, to use other fashionable and ill-considered terms, competence or process, approaches to education are substantial. If there are generic skills, they are unlikely to relate to such activities as observing or hypothesis-making. What is seen depends upon many factors, including who is looking and what is being sought. Hypothesizing is not simply a matter of guessing, and a scientific hypothesis is a particular kind of supposition, the framing of which requires knowledge and understanding of the relevant scientific concepts.[2] It is also important to ask who determines the skills to be taught and assessed, and to be clear about the contribution they can make to pupils' understanding of science. Beyond all this, however, are two broad and difficult questions. The first is whether such an approach can ever help pupils capture something of the wonder of science and gain some insight into the intellectual and imaginative immensity of its achievements. A good case can be made for claiming that much of school science trivializes science by atomizing it and reducing it to little more than a set of algorithmic procedures. It thus fails, because it does not seriously try, to introduce pupils to the claims of science upon the intellect, the emotions and the imagination, emphasizing instead the skills thought necessary to meet the ends of employers or to promote 'scientific literacy'.[3]

The second broad question is by no means new. This is whether a skills-based approach to laboratory science has more to do with scientific training than with scientific education, a question that can, of course, be extended, *mutatis mutandis*, to the curriculum as a whole. Distinctions can be drawn between training and education, and they are important, even if currently unfashionable. Training is intimately linked to a pre-established purpose determined by those responsible for the training. As a result it can claim to be relevant, skill- or practice-based and related to the employability or enhanced workplace competence of the trainee. The appeal of such an approach in a world dominated by accountability and a so-called 'scientific' approach to many aspects of life is obvious. In contrast, education, including scientific education, is imbued with a different set of values and purposes that are, and should be, open to contention. Education is inescapably about values in a sense that is different from training. As far as school science is concerned, it is surely about introducing pupils to the world of science itself, not as a set of skills or techniques, but as an imaginative and moral enterprise. It may thus be asked: how might school science, and laboratory teaching in particular, contribute to this end? The short answer seems to be by involving pupils in scientific studies that engage the hand and mind in investigating some aspect of the natural world, and thereby, contributing to their intellectual and moral development as citizens in a democratic community.

In her book, *The Pupil as Scientist?* (1983), and in much of her subsequent work, Ros Driver showed that pupils come to school with their own understandings of how and why things happen, or don't happen, in the natural world; that these ideas are often very resistant to change; and that many of them are at odds with accepted scientific explanations. There are two reasons for referring to this work in the present context. The first is simply to draw attention to the fact that young people *are* curious about natural phenomena and continue to develop explanatory ideas, tested against everyday experience, from an early age. It is this curiosity, allied with other qualities (notably imagination) that lies at the heart of any creative endeavour, and science is no exception. The second reason is to emphasize that for many pupils, as perhaps for most people, knowledge and understanding are more readily sought and acquired within the context of action, such as a scientific investigation, than in the context of passing an examination which is essentially a means to an end and not an end in itself. For many pupils, preparing for an examination is a vicarious purpose, derived directly, as they might judge it, from requirements set by the school and, more widely, by society itself. What is being argued here is that context is an integral part of thinking, not some kind of nuisance variable. Thinking is intricately interwoven with the context of the problem being addressed and problems are defined by the answers at the same time as the answers are helping to shape the problems. Anyone who has ever done any practical scientific investigation is likely to recognize the force of this view.

More generally, work of this kind offers a challenge to the traditional perception of schooling as an activity concerned with the teaching of abstract and universal ideas which can then be called upon for some specific, practical purpose. In Barbara Rogoff's words, it is a challenge to the 'Euro-American institution of schooling, which promotes an individually centred analytic approach . . . to tools of thought and stresses reasoning and learning with information considered on its own ground, extracted from practical use' (Rogoff 1990: 191). By integrating action and learning, by encouraging collaboration within and beyond the school, and, where appropriate, working or liaising with scientific experts, a well-framed science project offers a significant response to this challenge. It is perhaps worth pointing out that the method of training scientists, the PhD, is essentially an apprenticeship in which the student learns his or her craft in the laboratory of an expert scientist. It is also worth pointing out that most problem solving in the real world contrasts sharply with the problems presented in school examinations, assessments and teacher-assessed 'investigations'. These commonly seek to measure 'out of context' success and an understanding of general principles, while denying pupils access on demand to books, other databases and the advice of others, and disallowing the reshaping of the problems that the students are asked to address.

The educational case for involving pupils in scientific investigation, therefore, might rest on the general claim that such an investigation challenges the distinction between knowing and doing and encourages the development of knowledge and understanding for a particular purpose. Examples of successful work of this kind in school science are not difficult to find. Posch provides examples[4] from the international Environment and Schools Initiatives project which involved schools in about 20 countries. In Italy, five upper secondary schools cooperated to study the quality and degree of pollution of ground and surface waters in the surrounding communities (Posch 1993). The activities were coordinated by a group of students and teachers and financed by the communities on a contractual basis. The responsibilities of the students ranged from the selection and drawing of water samples and on-the-spot analyses, via a detailed chemical, bacteriological and micro-plankton analysis in their school laboratories, to reporting and discussing their results with the authorities. In a secondary school in Austria, 14-year-old students studied energy usage in four small villages. They designed a questionnaire, went from house to house in pairs, and sought collaboration and offered assistance in data collection. The students processed the data at school and produced a comparative analysis of the use of energy for each house and for each village. The results were presented by the students at a public event. This energy project was subsequently developed to involve a larger community. This increased complexity and scale made it necessary to look for partners and for external support. Links were established with the local primary school and the kindergarten, and both became involved in the work. The intention to influence the use of energy in the community led the school to establish formal links with the mayor and local council and to seek their support. An external energy expert was hired with funds provided by local government.

The outcome of investigations of this kind is knowledge which is not a reconstruction of existing knowledge, but knowledge that is new in the sense that it provides information about issues that was not hitherto available. It is of use to a particular, rather than a universal, audience and it is intended to underpin action and change. None of this reduces its scientific validity, although these are not criteria commonly associated with scientific understanding. Insofar as they are not, it is perhaps time to rethink what we mean by school science.

The two examples cited above illustrate both the interdisciplinary potential of project work and the commitment of the students to it. This commitment is fundamental to any successful science project and its absence is the reason why so many school science projects are regarded by pupils as contrived. The issue or problem being addressed has to be of real concern and interest to the pupils themselves. One teacher, reflecting upon his experience of conducting a project with a class of 13-year-old girls, wrote that his experience had made him more conscious of the need to involve pupils in the evolution of a project, 'giving them a chance to translate their values into action and to develop a sense of ownership of what they do'. The corollary of this is that pupils must be involved at every stage in shaping, defining, developing and monitoring their solution to the problem with which they are engaged.

There may also be a *consequence* of giving pupils a sense of ownership of their investigation. When a group of 16-year-old Austrian students were asked about what they had gained from their scientific investigation, they replied: 'We learned to co-ordinate, to talk and work with other people, to write articles. We found out that young people can do serious things respected by others' (Posch 1993: 43). This same group of students also took up a position when it came to grading their work. They felt that grades were a devaluation of their work, arguing that the real-life evaluation which they encountered (for example, the types of people they had met and with whom they had discussed their work) was incommensurate with formal grading. There are, of course, some interesting issues of a more general kind here about the assessment of project work in science.

The two examples also illustrate the development of dynamic links with agencies, organizations and individuals outside the school who have a legitimate interest in a problem and its solution. There are other examples where the students and their school have come to constitute the site of excellence and expertise on the basis of their school-based investigation and to be seen as partners in a wider enterprise. In a number of cases, schools are linked by e-mail or by satellite and are engaged not just in exchanging data but in genuinely collaborative and simultaneous investigations that involve them in framing and shaping of the problem to be studied. There are also a few, exceptional, schools in Finland and Australia where part of the curriculum is left flexible and open to accommodate the dynamic and particular requirements of projects derived from a commitment by the school as a whole to environmental education based upon local issues. Since many young people care passionately about environmental issues, such issues almost suggest themselves as the site of investigative work. However, it is important neither to ignore nor underestimate, on the one hand, young people's interest in a range of other issues having a scientific dimension such as those associated with health, hygiene, diet, medication and safety at home, in the streets or in the workplace, and, on the other hand, their deep commitment to internationalism and to making the world a better place in which to live. For most young people, understanding, including scientific understanding, needs to have a purpose beyond that of understanding for its own sake. As John Dewey observed, 'Understanding has to be in terms of how things work and how to do things. Understanding by its very nature is related to action, just as information, by its very nature, is isolated from action' (Dewey 1946: 49).

There is an important message here for current attempts to promote 'scientific literacy' and the public understanding of science. The need for a greater public understanding of science has been argued from a number of standpoints and for a variety of not always compatible motives. There is, however, a measure of agreement that such understanding must include some insight into the 'nature of science', a term that is commonly taken to refer to scientific methodology but to exclude, for example, the political economy of science.[5] Providing such insight, however, is a difficult task. There is a large, heterogeneous and scholarly literature in the history, philosophy and sociology of science which addresses the nature of science and scientific investigation. It offers no uniform account. Rather, there is:

> no well-confirmed picture of how science works, no theory of science worthy of general assent. We did once have a well-developed and historically influential philosophical position, that of positivism or logical empiricism, which has now been refuted. We have a number of recent theories of science which, while stimulating much interest, have hardly been tested at all. And we have specific hypotheses about various cognitive aspects of science, which are widely discussed but wholly undecided. If any extant position does provide a viable understanding of how science operates, we are far from being able to identify what it is.
>
> (Laudan *et al.* 1986: 142)

If this were not enough to give pause for thought to those who would have schools teach the 'nature of science', it would be well to recall the words of Peter Medawar, a Nobel prize-winning scientist:

> Science, broadly considered, is incomparably the most successful enterprise human beings have ever engaged upon; yet the methodology that has presumably made it so, when propounded by learned laymen, is not attended to by scientists, and when propounded by scientists is a misrepresentation of what they do. Only a minority of scientists have received instruction in scientific methodology, and those that have done so seem no better off.
>
> (Medawar 1982: 80)

The relevance of all this is that the engagement of pupils in scientific investigation allows them to sidestep much of the rhetoric about the nature of science ('metascience') and to confront, directly and personally, a number of metascientific issues that include the epistemological and the methodological. As several studies have reported, engagement in an independent investigation is related to the students' 'image' of science (Ryder and Leach 1999), stimulates changes in thinking and can develop important insights into the nature of scientific activity (Tyler 1992; Shapiro 1996). What aspects of a problem are to be addressed if, for example, a pupil wishes to investigate the rates of water flow at different points in a river, the change in leaf colour of trees during the autumn or explore the effect of background and siting on the visibility of road signs? How are the data to be obtained? It is not immediately obvious how to measure the rate of flow of water in the middle of a river or large stream, or how to monitor the rate of change of colour of the leaves of a tree. What confidence can be placed in the data obtained? How sensitive are the data to the methods and techniques used for their collection? How sensitive are they to the theoretical perspective of the data gatherer? Collecting scientific data is a theory-laden task and a set of quantitative readings taken from experimental apparatus cannot be considered independently of the interpretation to be put upon them. On what basis might some data be ignored or rejected while others are accommodated? How are conflicts between data to be dealt with? How are data best presented to inform or convince others who were not party to the original investigation? What is the role of other members of the group involved in a project in reaching a consensus about any aspect of the work being addressed?

Epistemological and related issues generally receive scant treatment in science education at any level within an educational system. Even graduate scientists are usually perplexed when asked how it is that error-prone and fallible human beings can create knowledge which, if the word 'true' is unacceptable, is at least (to borrow Ziman's 1984 term) 'consensible'.

What do scientists think they are doing when creating scientific knowledge and what sort of knowledge is being created? Medawar's answer to these questions is that science is about 'building explanatory structures, *telling stories* which are scrupulously tested to see if they are stories about real life' (Medawar 1982: 133). If pupils are to consider the sorts of issue that metascientists, as they are increasingly being called, are properly interested in, then engagement with investigatory science offers a rich vein to be mined and one which parallels that derived from contemporary research into the nature of the interactions between science and its publics. Such engagement would seem to be essential if science education is to contribute to the development of the informed democracy and the welfare of young people urged by Hurd (in the quotation at the head of this chapter) and, from a different perspective, by Longbottom and Butler (1999).

Engaging pupils with science in this way presents difficulties of various kinds, not least in systems of mass secondary education. Schools are concerned not with the generation of scientific knowledge but with its reproduction and transmission. In addition, pupils can command neither the scientific knowledge nor the intellectual, communal and other resources available to an expert scientist. To this extent, any school-based scientific investigation might easily be dismissed as ersatz. The response to these difficulties, however, is not to try to turn school teaching laboratories into research laboratories or to try to capture scientific investigation in some algorithmic or descriptive way. Rather, it is to acknowledge that schools can, and do, succeed in engaging pupils, for at least some of the time, with seminal questions of the kind indicated above. Such engagement does not require an exclusive commitment to the laboratory but it does demand a practical capability and an intellectual honesty that is not always evident in current attempts to teach pupils something about the nature of science. More is required than data gathering or mere monitoring, one of the weaknesses of many television- or internet-based projects, and, where appropriate, advantage needs to be taken of the opportunities present in a school to generate data over time. Albone *et al.* (1995) provide a number of examples of studies to which successive generations of pupils are able to contribute, including a longitudinal study of exercise tolerance in adolescent schoolgirls, a long-term ecology project and the gradual colonization of new pond.

Accommodating uncertain science

Reference has already been made to the changes that have taken place, most rapidly during the past half-century or so, in the relationships between science and industrial, military or commercial interests. The notion that natural science now stands pure and separate from all involvement with society is no longer tenable. In the USA, for example, over half of all research scientists are located in industry and, in Hurd's judgement, 'science and technology have become an integrated system and research is now more social than theory driven' (Hurd 1990: 413). Science is principally valued for its contribution to technology and economic growth, a valuation that is increasingly evident in the rationale underpinning science curriculum reform in many countries of the world. One of the difficulties of adopting such a rationale, however, is that it is precisely from this commitment to technology allied with economic growth that many of the problems confronting industrialized societies arise (as, of course, also do the benefits). In addition, as Ravetz has pointed out, 'the scientific expertise that *creates* an external problem is *not* usually adequate to its solution':

> Mechanical engineers, designing boilers that use radioactive fuel as a heat source, have no expertise in the chemistry of reprocessing or in the biological effects of radiation. Nor even do scientists using recombinant DNA techniques necessarily possess skills in pathenogenicity or in microbial ecology.
>
> (Ravetz 1987: 81)

The curriculum response to the commercialization and industrialization of science and its integration with technology has been principally the development of a range of science, technology and society (STS) courses and programmes. For the most part, STS materials have served the limited, if valuable, function of supporting and enriching otherwise conventional school science courses. To this extent, they can be seen as attempts to rescue science curricula in difficulty rather than as attempts to reshape school science education in any fundamental way. Their impact has generally been modest: '[STS courses] are valuable adjuncts to science teaching, but their integration into the hard-core technicality goes very slowly indeed' (Ravetz 1997: 9).

In addition, such courses have not impinged upon the technical and instrumental rationality and certainty of school science and have sometimes been seen as a means of improving the public perception of science rather than as offering an alternative curriculum, although there are some notable suggestions for more radical reform (see for example Cross and Price 1992). In Ziman's (1994: 22) estimation, each of the 'multiplicity of approaches to STS education' is:

> designed to bridge the gap, so to speak, along some particular sector of the moat surrounding 'valid' science. It [STS] tries to introduce the student to some particular aspect of science in its social context, and thus to complement and extend conventional science education in that particular direction.

There are, of course, many and formidable obstacles in the way of any major extension of school science to reflect a more accurate picture of science and its social relations in the modern world. They are, for the most part, obvious and are not rehearsed here. One question, however, deserves attention. How much *scientific* understanding of a conventional kind (as distinct, for example, from scientific attitudes, attitudes towards the scientific endeavour or technological competence) do pupils need to acquire at school as a basis of effective functioning as adult citizens in a democracy? One provocative answer to this question is 'Not very much'. A more cautious response is 'We do not know'. If, however, the question is to be addressed at all, and in terms that are other than platitudinous, then much more needs to be known about the ways in which such knowledge is acquired and deployed – i.e. about the nature of adult scientific literacy.

What seems clear is that something more radical than STS programmes or other attempts to 'humanize' school science is needed if school science education is to respond adequately to the position that science has come to occupy in the modern world and all that flows from it. Consider the following observation from the chairman and chief executive of Shell UK, plc, taken from the Shell website (undated):

> With issues as complex as the impact of human activity on the natural environment, the search for simple truths may obscure the uncertainty of reality.

Almost anything we do, consume, or are exposed to has some risks. We have to decide which risks require tackling, with what priority, in what way, to what extent, and at what cost.

The issues are not simple, and science matters.

Embedded in these few lines is a major issue for school science education. Given the limitations of STS courses, how are the 'simple truths' of school science and the 'uncertainty of reality' both to be accommodated? One response is to marginalize or compartmentalize the latter in STS programmes or in courses such as environmental science or ecology. The limitations of such an approach and its potential implications for traditional courses need no elaboration. An alternative approach suggested here is to restructure school science courses in a way that recognizes that science 'comes in an infinite variety of shapes and sizes' (ACARD 1986: 15), among which the following three broad categories might be identified:

- Basic/fundamental science: driven by curiosity and speculation about the natural world without thought of possible applications.
- Strategic science: a body of scientific understanding which supports a generic or enabling area of technological knowledge; a reservoir of knowledge out of which many specific products and processes may emerge in the future.
- Mandated science: the output of scientists and technologists in the context of bodies mandated to make recommendations or decisions of a policy or legal nature (for example, regulatory agencies, standard setting organizations, expert commissions) (Levy 1989: 41).

As already indicated, much present-day scientific effort is dedicated to the production of the second and third of these categories. In contrast, the content of school science courses and the prevailing emphasis in science education, at all levels, has been largely derived from the first category – i.e. 'insider' or 'high church' science, rather than science drawn upon for instrumental purposes.

Categories can be beguiling as well as useful, and it is important to note that more is involved here than some principle upon which a curriculum might be structured. The scientific research associated with each category is different because it is concerned with different kinds of research questions, different research methodologies and different criteria for validating the answers. As an example, fundamental science is concerned with questions of how and why. Does the pressure of an enclosed volume of gas increase as its temperature is raised? If so, is this the case for all gases? What is the quantitative relationship between the variables that prevails in these circumstances and how may it be explained? In contrast, much of mandated science is concerned with the construction of expert advice about a range of issues or the establishing of standards that can be enshrined in legislation or codes of practice. A related concern is that of risk assessment, an undertaking with a long history in a variety of fields such as chemical engineering and systems design. Risk assessment in contexts in which science is involved, such as BSE (bovine spongiform encephalopathy) or genetically modified foods, brings together the uncertainty and complexity of the real world in a way that school science, derived from the first of the categories above, seeks to avoid. Of the general importance of risk assessment, there can be little doubt: 'The question of "safety" is emerging as a great task for science, as a successor to the twin goals of knowledge and power that were articulated nearly four centuries ago in the Scientific Revolution' (Ravetz 1998: 12).

The importance of risk assessment to school science education derives not only from this wider authority but from the fact that it is in this context of uncertainty and complexity that most pupils encounter science-related issues outside school. As Feynman (1998: 17) has observed, 'We have to understand how to handle uncertainty'. What risks to health are associated with the use of, for example, mobile telephones, cannabis or the contraceptive pill, with living near a nuclear power facility or eating British beef, how are they assessed and perceived, and how significant are they? It is in this context, rather than in technological examples of the 'applications' of 'Category 1' science, that many pupils are likely to see science as both useful and relevant to their everyday lives. The case for accommodating a more generous view of science in the school curriculum is thus a strong one. Moreover it is one that points to a re-envisioning of the science curriculum for all, rather than the development of adjunct, supplementary or derivative courses in the 'public understanding of science', welcome though these may be (De Vos and Reiding 1999).

Conclusion

In the preceding sections, I have discussed two aspects of school science education upon which those seeking science curriculum reform might initially focus attention. At first glance, rehabilitating the creative and imaginative, and accommodating the uncertain within school science may seem to have little in common. Both, however, are concerned with using what is known to help understand the unknown, and with reasoning in the context of action and all that this implies (Brickhouse *et al.* 1992; Atkin and Helms 1993). It is not, of course, suggested that school science education should be concerned exclusively with work of the kind that has been suggested above. It will remain an important function of school science to help students acquire a basic understanding of what science has to say about a number of matters of widespread interest and great importance. Nonetheless, accommodating changes of the kind discussed above would, in many parts of the world, amount to something of a paradigm shift in school science education, despite considerable experience of laboratory-based project work and important curriculum developments such as 'ChemCom' in the USA and the Salters' initiative in the UK.

Central to that paradigm shift are changes in the aims of school science teaching and in the ways in which science is taught. Aims will need to become more student-centred, reflecting what studying science can do for the student rather than what the student may eventually be able to contribute to science. The challenge to much of the traditional pedagogy of school science is likely to be no less severe. Science teaching is dominated by work in the laboratory and characterized by an emphasis upon secure and known outcomes. In addition, there is some evidence that, while science teachers do not use a narrower range of pedagogical activities than some of their colleagues teaching other subjects, the approach to teaching individual scientific topics is often remarkably standardized (Donnelly *et al.* 1999). Much repetitive (and often outdated) laboratory work will need to be abandoned to make room for genuine collaborative scientific investigation, perhaps extending over several months. The problems of class organization and management are substantial but, as the evidence of some schools suggests, they are by no means insuperable. Familiarizing pupils with the role that science has come to play in, for example, standard-setting and regulation, will require new understandings of what it means to teach science, a greater use of pedagogies that are not laboratory based and the development of expertise in teaching about uncertainty and risk. The implications for assessment, especially of pupils' scientific investigations, are likely to be no less severe, and it will be important to pay more than lip-service to the notion that assessment should follow, and not determine, the curriculum. It will be no less important to acknowledge that pupils will have their own views of what constitutes science and that these, too, may need to be challenged.

My task in this chapter, however, has not been to offer a detailed prescription for science curriculum reform or to suggest how a number of substantial political, practical and other problems might be overcome. Rather, I have sought to contribute to an ongoing debate about the role of science in the education of young people growing up in the early years of the new millennium.

Notes

1 It is important to recognize that what constitutes 'science' varies between countries. In some contexts, for example, science includes subjects such as geography and history.
2 This raises interesting questions about the currently fashionable notion of a 'fair test' and some of the practical activities undertaken with younger children. For

example, determining which of a number of paper towels will absorb the most water, while it may a worthwhile exercise for other reasons, does not address the important scientific question of why the absorbency differs.

3　In 1993–4 a new curriculum was introduced into the first stage of Dutch secondary education, 'Application, Skills and Connectedness'. It promotes knowledge 'related to everyday life and ... meaningfully embedded in society ... Furthermore, the student is expected to use social and cognitive strategies such as researching, collaborating and expressing opinions' (Roelofs and Terwel 1999: 201). Where, here, are the triumphs of the scientific imagination?

4　For other examples, covering a range of scientific disciplines, see Albone *et al.* (1995).

5　This commitment to understanding the nature of science has statutory authority in the science component of the National Curriculum in England and Wales. For a critique of earlier versions of the attempt to codify and assess 'scientific investigation', see Donnelly *et al.* (1996).

References

ACARD (Advisory Council for Applied Research and Development) (1986) *Exploitable Areas of Science*. London: HMSO.

Albone, E., Collins, N. and Hill, T. (1995) *Scientific Research in Schools. A Compendium of Practical Experience*. Bristol: Clifton Scientific Trust.

Atkin, J.M. and Helms, J. (1993) Getting serious about priorities in science education. *Studies in Science Education*, 21: 1–20.

Black, P. and Atkin, J.M. (eds) (1996) *Changing the Subject: Innovations in Science, Mathematics and Technology Education*. London: Routledge/OECD.

Brickhouse, N., Stanley, W. and Whitson, T. (1992) Practical reasoning and science education: implications for theory and practice. Paper presented at the 2nd International conference on the History and Philosophy of Science in Science Teaching, Kingston, Ontario.

Collingridge, D. and Reeve, C. (1986) *Science Speaks to Power: The Role of Experts in Policy Making*. London: Falmer.

Cross, R.T. and Price, R.F. (1992) *Teaching Science for Social Responsibility*. Sydney: St Louis Press.

De Vos, W. and Reiding, J. (1999) Public understanding of science as a separate subject in secondary schools in the Netherlands. *International Journal of Science Education*, 21(7): 711–19.

Dewey, J. (1946) The challenge of democracy to education, in J. Dewey *Problems of Men*. New York: Philosophical Library.

Donnelly, J.F. (1998) The place of the laboratory in secondary science teaching. *International Journal of Science Education*, 20(5): 585–96.

Donnelly, J.F., Buchan, A., Jenkins, E.W., Laws, P.M. and Welford, G. (1996) *Investigations by Order: Policy, Curriculum and Science Teachers' Work Under the Education Reform Act*. Driffield: Studies in Education.

Donnelly, J.F., Jenkins, E.W. and Jenkins, I. (1999) *End of Award Report*, ESRC Grant No. R000236073.

Driver, R. (1983) *The Pupil as Scientist?* Milton Keynes: Open University Press.

Feynman, R.P. (1998) *The Meaning of it All.* London: Allen Lane.

Gibbons, M., Limoges, C., Nowotny, H. *et al.* (1994) *The New Production of Knowledge: The Dynamics of Science and Research in Contemporary Societies.* London: Sage.

Gregory, J. and Miller, S. (1998) *Science in Public: Communication, Culture and Credibility.* London: Plenum.

Gross, P.R. and Levitt, N. (1994) *Higher Superstition: The Academic Left and its Quarrels with Science.* Baltimore, MD: Johns Hopkins University Press.

Heilbron, J.L. (1983) The virtual oscillator as a guide to physics students lost in Plato's Cave, in F. Bevilacqua and P.J. Kennedy (eds) *Proceedings of the International Conference on Using History of Physics in Innovatory Physics Education.* Pavia: University of Pavia.

Hurd, P.deH. (1990) Guest editorial: change and challenge in science education. *Journal of Research in Science Teaching,* 27(5): 413–14.

Hurd, P.deH. (1998) *Inventing Science Education for the New Millennium.* New York: Teachers College Press.

Irwin, A. and Wynne, B. (eds) (1996) *Misunderstanding Science? The Public Reconstruction of Science and Technology.* Cambridge: Cambridge University Press.

Latour, B. (1987) *Science in Action: How to Follow Scientists and Engineers through Society.* Milton Keynes: Open University Press.

Laudan, L., Donovan, A., Laudan, R., Barker, P., Brown, H., Leplin, J., Thagard, P. and Wystra, S. (1986) Scientific change: philosophical models and historical research. *Synthese,* 69(1): 141–223.

Layton, D., Jenkins, E., Davey, A. and Macgill, S. (1993) *Inarticulate Science: Some Perspectives on the Public Understanding of Science and their Implications for Science Education.* Driffield: Studies in Education.

Lazarowitz, R. and Tamir, P. (1994) Research on using laboratory instruction in science, in D.L. Gabel (ed.) *Handbook of Research on Science Teaching and Learning,* pp. 94–128. London: Macmillan.

Leach, J.T. and Paulsen, A.C. (eds) (1999) *Practical Work in Science Education: Recent Research Studies.* Dordrecht: Kluwer.

Levy, E. (1989) Judgement and policy: the two-step in mandated science and technology, in P.T. Durbin (ed.) *Philosophy of Technology: Practical, Historical and Other Dimensions.* Dordrecht: Kluwer.

Longbottom, J.E. and Butler, P.H. (1999) Why teach science? Setting rational goals for science education. *Science Education,* 83(4): 473–92.

Macdonald, S. (1996) Authorising science: public understanding of science in museums, in A. Irwin and B. Wynne (eds) *Misunderstanding Science? The Public Reconstruction of Science and Technology.* Cambridge: Cambridge University Press.

Macdonald, S. (ed.) (1998) *The Politics of Display: Museums, Science, Culture.* London: Routledge.

Medawar, P. (1982) *Pluto's Republic.* Oxford: Oxford University Press.

Persson, P. (1996) Science centres: dedicated to inquiry and exploration. *Physics World,* 9(7): 55–6.

Posch, P. (1993) Research issues in environmental education. *Studies in Science Education,* 21: 21–48.

Ravetz, J.R. (1987) Uncertainty, ignorance and policy, in H. Brooks and C.L. Cooper (eds) *Science for Public Policy*. London: Pergamon Press.

Ravetz, J.R. (1989) Some new ideas about science relevant to education, in E.W. Jenkins (ed.) *Policy Issues and School Science Education*. Leeds: Centre for Studies in Science and Mathematics Education, University of Leeds.

Ravetz, J.R. (1990) *The Merger of Knowledge with Power: Essays in Critical Science*. London: Mansell.

Ravetz, J.R. (1997) Simple scientific truths and uncertain policy realities: implications for science education. *Studies in Science Education*, 30: 5–17.

Ravetz, J.R. (1998) 'Beyond the good and the true in science education', unpublished paper.

Redner, H. (1987) *The Ends of Science: An Essay in Scientific Authority*. Boulder, CO: Westview Press.

Robitaille, D. (ed.) (1997) *National Contexts for Mathematics and Science Education: An Encyclopaedia of the Education Systems Participating in TIMSS*. Vancouver: Pacific Educational Press.

Roelofs, E. and Terwel, J. (1999) Constructivism and authentic pedagogy: state of the art and recent developments in the Dutch national curriculum in secondary education. *Journal of Curriculum Studies*, 31(2): 201–27.

Rogoff, B. (1990) *Apprenticeship in Thinking: Cognitive Development in Social Context*. New York: Oxford University Press.

Ryder, J. and Leach, J. (1999) University science students' experience of investigative project work and their images of science. *International Journal of Science Education*, 24(9): 945–56.

Shapiro, B. (1996) A case study of change in elementary student teacher thinking during an independent investigation in science: learning about the 'face of science that does not yet know'. *Science Education*, 80(5): 535–60.

Sokal, A. and Bricmont, J. (1998) *Fashionable Nonsense*. New York: Picador.

Solomon, J. and Mariano, J. (eds) (1999) *Science in School and the Future of Scientific Culture in Europe*. Brussels: European Communities Commission, Director-General for Science, Research and Development.

Thomas, G. and Durant, J. (1987) Why should we promote the public understanding of science? in M. Shortland (ed.) *Scientific Literacy Papers*. Oxford: Department of External Studies, Oxford University.

Tyler, R. (1992) Independent research projects in school science: case studies of autonomous behaviour. *International Journal of Science Education*, 14: 393–411.

Wellington, J.J. (ed.) (1998) *Practical Work in School Science. Which Way Now?* London: Routledge.

West, R.M. (1996) ACS abandons negotiations with Smithsonian over science in American Life Exhibition. *The Informal Science Review*, 17: 9.

Ziman, J. (1984) *An Introduction to Science Studies: The Philosophical and Social Aspects of Science and Technology*. Cambridge: Cambridge University Press.

Ziman, J. (1994) The rationale of STS education is in the approach, in J. Solomon and G. Aikenhead (eds) *STS Education: International Perspectives on Reform*, pp. 21–31. New York: Teachers College Press.

13 Science, views about science, and pluralistic science education

Stephen P. Norris and Connie A. Korpan

It is assumed sometimes that study of the nature of science deepens and broadens science learning. At other times, it is assumed that study of the nature of science is neutral with respect to learning science, but helps foster other worthy educational objectives, such as democratic citizenship (see Chapters 9 and 12). Both of these assumptions seem to presuppose that what is taught about the nature of science is fully compatible with what is taught from the substantive content of science itself.

We shall argue that some views on the nature of science that are found in the science education literature compete with substantive science, either directly or by implication, and that science teachers must be ever alert to this possibility. In the worst case, they can directly contradict science and could interfere with, rather than promote, science learning and other worthy educational objectives. Characterized as ideas from the nature of science, they are advanced as being 'about' science, as if to suggest that they are outside the boundary of science. Yet, they cross the boundary in interesting and subtle ways, and trespass into the territory of science, thus inviting direct comparison with the substance of science itself.

The implication of the last claim is that statements about the nature of science should not be accepted or rejected without taking into account the implications for the acceptance or rejection of science itself. The upshot for science education is that science educators' long-standing commitment to teaching conventional science ideas and science interpretations often is incompatible with their more liberal approach to teaching ideas from the nature of science. This liberal view is a form of insufficiently critical pluralism: pluralistic in motivation and content, in that it advocates teaching a variety of views on the nature of science; insufficiently critical, because it fails to direct attention towards determining the compatibility of each of the views with science itself. We wish to endorse a pluralism tied to greater criticism. We shall suggest that, at the very least, if ideas from the nature of science that directly compete with science itself are to be a focus for instruction in science classes, then students should be taught to see competing points and to adjudicate among them. To fail to address the issue at this minimal level, we shall argue, is to provide a misleading education in science and to breach the public's trust in the science education community. On the other hand, to explore freely and deeply the tensions between substantive science, and some views on the nature of science, is to capitalize upon an opportunity with great educational potential for science students.

In the first section, we shall illustrate claims about the nature of science that we allege trespass upon the substantive content of science. The claims chosen speak to the ontology and objectivity of science. In the second section, we shall provide two examples of substantive science that could serve as the basis for science lessons. In the third section, we shall argue how the alleged trespassing claims about the nature of science are rightly interpreted as trespassers. We employ two strategies: a strategy that uses metalevel claims about science in order to convert claims belonging to the substantive content of science into claims that straightforwardly contradict the unconverted substantive claims; and a strategy that demonstrates that certain claims about science contradict the presuppositions of substantive scientific claims. Finally, we shall examine some of the implications for science education, and offer some suggestions that science teachers, who include in their science teaching statements that under our analysis would be defined as trespassing, might follow. The suggestions point to a way to make apparent the contradiction between substantive science and the intruding claims about science, and a way to judge the comparative credibility of the competitors.

Trespassing claims about the nature of science

There is a very long potential list of claims about science. We shall concentrate on those claims dealing with the ontology of science and the objectivity of scientific knowledge, because we have found many such claims that encroach into the territory of substantive science. There are other categories of statements that also can encroach. For example, claims about a narrative structure of science that equate science to literature and storytelling (Myers 1990; Norris 1995), and claims about theory choice as being wholly a matter of politically and culturally driven preference (see Hacking 1999, especially Ch. 3) are also potential trespassers. If the encroachment is of the same type as that described subsequently in this chapter, then it is likely that it also can be treated in the manner described herein.

Our primary targets are science education theorists who propound views about science that have as their logical consequences a contradiction with science or its presuppositions. The group of theorists we identify is a legitimate target, because their views are promoted in recent literature, and because their views present new challenges to science teachers, including a rhetoric that is seriously at odds with the substantive science that they aim to teach. The challenge is to understand the consequences of a view designed to alter how teachers conceive of their work, and to formulate an appropriate educational response.

Von Glasersfeld maintained that 'cognition serves the subject's organization of the experiential world, not the discovery of an objective ontological reality' (1995: 51). By this claim, von Glasersfeld means that 'what we ordinarily call "facts" are not elements of an observer-independent world but elements of an observer's experience' (1995: 14). The implication for science is that: 'the scientific method does not refer to, nor does it need, the notion of ontological reality. It operates and produces its results in the experiential domain of observers. Scientific knowledge, then, provides more or less reliable ways of dealing with experiences, the only reality we know' (1995: 117).

A claim similar to von Glasersfeld's is made by Staver (1998: 503), who says that: 'observations, objects, events, data, laws, and theory do not exist independently of observers. The lawful and certain nature of natural phenomena are properties of us, those who describe, not of nature, what is described'. Staver is motivated to avoid solipsism, and hopes to do so by 'remaining silent with respect to ontology' (1998: 508). He does not deny 'the existence of a world separate from and independent of our perception' (1998: 508), but does not affirm it either.

Taking a position similar to Staver's view that the objects of science are properties of us and not of a world independent of us, Wheatley (1991: 10) says that, 'knowledge originates in the learner's activity performed on *objects*. But objects do not lie around ready made in the world but are mental constructs'. Saunders (1992: 136) says that:

> any so-called reality is, in the most immediate and concrete sense, the mental construction of those who believe they have discovered and investigated it . . . what is supposedly found is an invention whose inventor is unaware of his act of invention and who considers it as something that exists independently of him . . .

We shall now illustrate substantive scientific claims from two areas of science that will serve as comparisons to the trespassing claims.

Illustrative substantive scientific claims

The first example that follows is based upon standard science textbooks. The second example, in the area of medical science, is intended to model the information that might be consumed and evaluated by an educated layperson on a matter important to health. Our intent is to present examples of substantive scientific claims in the form in which scientists might present them, in order that these claims can be compared to the claims about science illustrated in the previous section.

Example 1: The fossil record

Instruction on the fossil record is common in high-school biology curricula, being frequently integrated into a treatment of evolution and the evidence that there is for that theory. Descriptions in textbooks typically are liberally supplemented with photographs of a variety of fossils. Topics frequently include ones dealing with what fossils are, how they are formed, examples of fossils, and how the fossil record is engaged by scientists. We shall present excerpts from four widely used high-school biology textbooks describing substantive scientific knowledge for each of these topics.

What are fossils?

> Any . . . impression or remains of an organism that lived in a past age is called a fossil . . .
>
> (BSCS 1987: 753)

> . . . fossils [are] the mineralized remains or impressions of dead organisms . . .
>
> (Galbraith *et al.* 1993: 167)

How are fossils formed?

> There are many types of fossils, but most consist of the hard parts of the organisms, such as bones, shells, or wood. Sometimes these have survived unaltered; in other cases their molecules have been replaced by molecules of minerals, so they literally have become stone . . . Occasionally, an entire organism is found, preserved in glacial ice or permafrost for thousands of years. Less frequently, clay, tar, or peat bogs may preserve a complete specimen. Whole insects have been preserved in amber, the fossilized sap from ancient coniferous trees. Coal consists of the compressed remains of plants, and often complete leaves are found in it. More frequently, just a film of carbon remains . . .
>
> (Galbraith *et al.* 1993: 168)

What are examples of fossils?

Nelson's *Biology* (Ritter *et al.* 1993) contains photographs of fossils including that of a 'hominid fossil skull', a 'fossilized fish', and a 'pterodactylus fossil' (p. 97), and references to fossils of the sabre-toothed tiger, woolly mammoths, horses, birds, camels and petrified forests.

Biology Directions (Galbraith *et al.* 1993) contains photographs of 'the most complete fossil known of Albertosaurus found in Dinosaur Provincial Park near Drumheller, Alberta', a 'fossil of a fish from Wyoming', 'footprints of a dinosaur which walked in the Peace River Valley of Alberta' (p. 169), and 'Archaeopteryx [which] had characteristics both of reptiles and of birds' (p. 182), as well as many other fossils. There are references to fossilized whole insects preserved in amber, fossilized sap from coniferous trees (which is amber), the fossilized footprints of organisms in mud, and multiple references to fossils representing creatures that now are extinct.

Nuffield's *Biology* (Monger 1992), like the other texts, contains photographs of a sample of fossils, including those of an ammonite and of a footprint of an iguanodon (p. 310). The photographs also include those of a fossil horseshoe crab and of a present-day horseshoe crab; and of a fossil of a leaf from a ginkgo tree and of a leaf from a present-day ginkgo tree. The text accompanying the photographs includes the following:

> Something else we can learn from fossils is how much (or how little) different organisms have changed. The fossil of the horseshoe crab, which lived 350 million years ago, is not much different from the horseshoe crab of today, which is found living in shallow water along sandy and muddy shores along the east coast of North America . . . About 160 million years separate the fossil leaf of the ginkgo tree from the one living today.
>
> (Monger 1992: 311)

What is done with fossils?

Nelson's *Biology* (Ritter *et al.* 1993) speaks of the use of radioactive dating to determine the age of fossils, and of the conclusion from this research 'that life appeared about 3.5 billion years ago' (p. 99). In addition, it tells of the fact that scientists have been able to link fossils and the sedimentary rocks in which they are found, enabling them 'to establish a world-wide inventory of former life forms and their environments' (p. 99). In so doing, scientists are reported to have discovered that the 'oldest parts of the fossil record contain fossils of very simple organisms' and that fossils 'of more recent origin represent more complex organisms' (p. 100).

Biology Directions (Galbraith *et al.* 1993) reports that the teeth of mammals provide a more complete record than any specific bone and thus have been used extensively to reason about evolution in mammals. For example, one type of study involves graphing tooth size against the age of the fossil. A conclusion from such research is that the range in tooth size of mammals has increased as the present is approached.

Example 2: Poliomyelitis

According to medical science, poliomyelitis, or polio, is an infectious disease caused by a virus commonly found in sewage and untreated water. This disease is spread by the fecal-oral route. Once ingested, the virus travels through the digestive tract and infects the cells lining the intestine. Certain clusters of cells in the intestine, called Peyer's Patches, appear to support the initial infection. It is here that the virus replicates and produces thousands of new virus particles, or 'virions'. The virions are carried through the intestine and released into the sewage system to start the cycle anew.

Polio usually manifests itself in the form of a brief illness with sore throat, headache, fever and vomiting. Because the Peyer's Patches are closely associated with the body's immune system, the virus can sometimes migrate via the bloodstream to the central nervous system. Once infection in the central nervous system occurs, paralysis and sometimes death may result.

How resistant is the polio virus?
Killing the virus involves protein denaturation using physical or chemical means. The virus is resistant to cold, to desiccation and to acidic environments (Debre *et al.* 1955). The protein undergoes spontaneous denaturation and inactivation at high temperatures – the higher the temperature, the faster the rate of denaturation.

How does the polio virus replicate itself?
After passing through the stomach, the polio virus enters the intestine and attaches itself to host cells on the intestinal lining. Once inside the cell, the virus uncoats, and releases its genetic material into the cell's cytoplasm. This release serves to shut off the host RNA (ribonucleic acid) ensuring that the cell will die and break down, thereby allowing the progeny virus particles into the organism.

Why was there a polio epidemic in the twentieth century?
Ironically, improvements in waste disposal and widespread use of indoor plumbing may have helped the polio virus spread. Once sewage is dumped away from the drinking water supply, babies are much less likely to be exposed to the virus. Exposure to the virus during infancy is usually asymptomatic and moreover confers lifelong immunity. Because the virus was not totally eradicated by improved sanitation, exposure to it at some point is

almost inevitable and exposure after infancy is more likely to result in devastating illness.

Incompatibilities with science

The substantive content of science is carried in first-order statements, a sample of which we have exemplified from biology and medical science. The nature of science is carried in second-order statements, which are statements about first-order statements – some of which we have identified as the 'trespassers'. The logic of the relationship between first- and second-order statements is that the person making second-order statements is taking a perspective and entering a discourse that is outside of the discourse conducted at the first order. Therefore, discourse on the nature of science is usually thought to be conducted from a perspective outside of the substantive content of science. The idea of one discourse being conducted outside another discourse is meant to capture the presumption that they can proceed independently of each other, because the truth of statements in one has no bearing on the truth of statements in the other. Our aim is to challenge the presumption that the discourses of science and of the nature of science can always be kept separate in this way. To mount this challenge, we shall employ two strategies to show how the statements about science that previously we have called 'trespassing' encroach into the territory of substantive science.

In the first strategy, we shall show that the second-order trespassing statements imply alterations to substantive scientific statements resulting in new first-order statements that conflict with the original substantive statements of the first order. The conflict is induced by interpreting the original first-order statements in light of the second-order ones and then, based upon this interpretation, converting them. The effect of the strategy is to demonstrate that the first-order statements *of* science and the second-order statements *about* science were in conflict all the while, although the conflict was subtly hidden.

Our second strategy is to demonstrate that first-order statements of science carry as presuppositions the very ontological and epistemic claims that the trespassing statements deny. Science contains ontological and epistemic commitments, and to challenge these commitments puts one into direct confrontation *with* science, not simply with other views *about* science. Just as in the first strategy, the second strategy takes claims at the metalevel and situates them in direct contradiction with science itself. The upshot, in implementing either strategy, is to demonstrate that one cannot consistently hold both to science and to the trespassing claims about science that we have identified.

Our strategies are different from those usually employed to confront what are seen as offending statements about science. Usually, second-order statements are met by competing second-order statements. For example, Staver's claim that the laws of nature are properties of us might be met with the claim that the laws of nature are properties of the world independently of us. The effect of this approach is to keep the discourse at the metalevel. The strategy we employ has been adapted from Dworkin (1996) and from Nagel (1997), who recommend it as a mode of response to general subjectivist and sceptical claims, of which Staver's and the other trespassing claims are a subset. The idea is that scepticism about science can be countered effectively by showing that the sceptical challenge runs into the content and reasoning internal to the very field it challenges. The effect is to bring the second-order discourse down to the first order and to force it to compete at that level.

Strategy 1: Converting first-order claims

Let us convert some of the first-order statements in the examples in light of the second-order statements described previously. To begin, here are four first-order statements from Example 1:

1 Fossils are the remains or impressions of organisms that once were alive.
2 Most fossils consist of the preserved hard parts of organisms (teeth, shells, bones) or the mineralized replicas of these hard parts.
3 Archaeopteryx, the woolly mammoth, Albertosaurus, and the iguanodon are extinct species whose members once lived, and walked the earth or flew the earth's sky.
4 The death of an organism preserved as a fossil can often be dated, and, in general, organisms that lived more recently are more complex than those that lived more distantly.

Acting upon the views of Wheatley (1991) and Saunders (1992) we would reinterpret fossils and their origins to be mental constructs, as inventions that do not exist independently of the inventor. Taking, for example, Statements 1 and 3 and converting them according to this dictum, we arrive at statements like 1W(heatley)S(aunders) and 3WS:

> 1WS: It is a mental construct and invention of human beings that fossils are the remains or impressions of organisms that once were alive; fossils, and the organisms said to be their source, do not exist independently of human beings.

> 3WS: It is a mental construct and invention of human beings that archaeopteryx, the woolly mammoth, Albertosaurus and the iguanodon are extinct species whose members once lived, and walked the earth or flew the earth's sky; these were not creatures that existed independently of human beings.

The qualified Statement 1WS and the unqualified Statement 1 cannot both be true. Neither can Statements 3WS and 3 both be true. If fossils are mental constructions and inventions, then they cannot be creatures that once lived. By the same logic, if archaeopteryx and Albertosaurus are extinct species that once lived and walked the earth or flew the earth's sky, then they cannot be inventions of human beings, and vice versa. The science teacher teaching about fossils from the texts we surveyed, and also teaching about the nature of science, will run into difficulties if those views from the nature of science are Wheatley's and Saunders'. The teacher faces a task of reconciliation and explanation of incompatible statements that will be examined in more detail in the final section.

Others might counter that Wheatley and Saunders are making the far more modest claim that we construct ideas, concepts and theories, not that we construct the world, and that our conversions of Statements 1 and 3 into 1WS and 3WS are therefore unwarranted. According to this interpretation, the concept of fossils is a mental construct, a construction invented by human beings, and something that does not exist independently of human beings. Similar points might be made about the concepts of Albertosaurus and archaeopteryx, and about all concepts. If this is all that Wheatley and Saunders are saying, then they are simply asserting a truism that nobody disputes. There is an indisputable sense in which our concept of reality and our concepts of everything else are constructed by us. If this is their claim, then it is not incompatible with science, and our conversions would be unwarranted. However, it is the very triviality of this interpretation that makes it implausible that this is the claim they are actually making.

Alternatively, perhaps they are making the claim that we construct both the concepts and the objects that make up the classes to which these concepts refer. If so, then we need to examine whether they are talking about objects that are what Hacking (1999: 22) calls 'ontologically subjective'. Consider some objects and their associated concepts: water and the concept of water, hotels and the concept of a hotel, labour contracts and the concept of a labour contract, rabbits and the concept of a rabbit, ski resorts and the concept of a ski resort. Hotels, labour contracts and ski resorts are ontologically subjective, because they would not exist without human practices. Yet, they are real objects in the world, and we can have objective knowledge of them. For an ontologically subjective category, it is sensible to say that we construct both the object and the concept of the object. Water and rabbits are not ontologically subjective, however, because they do not depend for their existence on human practices (although the survival of rabbits might). Therefore, although the concepts of water and of rabbit are constructed by us, water and rabbits exist independently of us. If Wheatley and Saunders mean that we construct both objects and concepts, then their claim is true, only if it is restricted to ontologically subjective objects. As it happens, Wheatley and Saunders speak generally about the natural sciences, and do not limit their claim to ontologically subjective objects. Furthermore, the vast majority of objects in the natural sciences are not ontologically subjective. More to the point, in the examples we have been considering, fossils, teeth, shells, bones, woolly mammoths, iguanodons, and so on, are not ontologically subjective. Therefore, their general claim is inconsistent with large tracts of science, as our 1WS and 3WS conversions demonstrate.

If, as a final alternative interpretation, Wheatley and Saunders reject the distinction between objects and concepts, we must dismiss their claims as totally ambiguous. Without the distinction, we do not know how to take such statements as, 'objects do not lie around ready made in the world but are mental constructs' (Wheatley 1991: 10) or, 'what is supposedly found is an invention' (Saunders 1992: 136). Without further clarification from Wheatley and Saunders about their interpretations of objects and concepts, we maintain that 1WS and 3WS provide plausible interpretations of their claims.

Here is a sample of first-order statements from Example 2:

5 Poliomyelitis is an infectious disease caused by the polio virus.
6 The polio virus resists being killed by low temperatures, desiccation and acidification, but can be killed by high temperatures.
7 The polio virus genome consists of RNA.
8 Human beings infected with the polio virus can become ill, paralysed, and can die because of the infection.

Considering Staver's (1998) advice, we would say that the lawful and certain nature of the behaviour of the polio virus and its influence on human beings that is captured in Statements 5 and 6 are properties of us, not properties of what is described. Under this advice, we would convert the scientific Statements 5 and 6 into 5S(taver) and 6S:

5S: It is a property of human beings not of nature that poliomyelitis is an infectious disease caused by the polio virus.

6S: It is a property of human beings not of nature that the polio virus resists being killed by low temperatures, desiccation and acidification, but can be killed by high temperatures.

Statements 5S and 6S stand in direct conflict with the unqualified scientific Statements 5 and 6. In effect, 5S and 6S provide an alternative account of the world to the scientific account: 5S and 6S are statements about human beings, in contrast to Statements 5 and 6, which are not. As competitors, the pairs of statements invite comparison. From the scientific point of view, Statements 5 and 6 express truths about the world, about the existence of a virus and the pernicious way that it attacks the human body, about its remarkable resistance to counterattack, and about its persistence in the world in the face of the only known means of eradicating it. Statements 5S and 6S are not easily intelligible as explanations. What can it possibly mean to explain the etiology of an infectious disease on the basis of properties of us? We have acknowledged already in our example that human practices can contribute to the spread of infectious disease. However, no medical scientist believes that diseases are properties of human beings in the sense intended by Staver, or that diseases can be understood entirely as products of human practices. When Staver says that objects such as viruses do not exist independently of us, he means independently of our thinking. Epidemiologists predicate their research on the search for objects that would exist whether or not they were being mentally represented by humans. In effect, Statements 5S and 6S require that we cease to speak of viruses as objects in the world and speak instead of our perceptions and construals. The notion of making contact with and explaining events in the world is supposed to be expunged from the dialogue, although Staver has no difficulty making contact with human perception as an event in the world. A science teacher choosing to teach, as part of a nature of science lesson, something along the lines of Staver's view, must be prepared to deal with the thorny issues that arise – issues concerning the incompatibility between science and these other views, concerning the adjudication of competing sets of claims, and concerning the very intelligibility of one of those sets as an alternative to science. The educational response we shall recommend is not to avoid the situation, but to respond in a way that addresses the contradictions that have been introduced into the educational context.

Strategy 2: Presuppositions of first-order claims

In this section, we compare trespassing claims to the presuppositions of first-order statements of science. Take, as a first example, von Glasersfeld's (1995: 117) claim that science 'operates and produces its results in the experiential domain of observers'. The presuppositions of science are contrary to von Glasersfeld's claim. Compare the presuppositions of the claim that Albertosaurus is an extinct species whose members once lived and walked upon the earth, and of the claim that poliomyelitis is an infectious disease caused by the polio virus. These first-order scientific claims carry the presupposition that the results are not in the experiential domain of observers. Scientists presuppose that no human being has seen a living member of the Albertosaurus species or witnessed the extinction of the species. Yet science unabashedly and in an unqualified statement asserts both the previous life on earth of Albertosaurus and its extinction. Further, the methods of science involved in creating experimental designs presuppose that the causing of poliomyelitis by the polio virus is not part of the experiential domain of any scientist. With the possible exception of certain pushes and pulls that can be witnessed, one thing causing another is not something that can be witnessed or experienced in the sense meant by von Glasersfeld. Causation is a relationship that is inferred on the basis both of observations and design. The presuppositions of science and von Glasersfeld's claims about science are simply incompatible.

Consider Staver's (1998: 503) claim that 'objects, events, data, laws and theory do not exist independently of observers'. Compare his claim to the scientific claim that archaeopteryx is an extinct species and to the claim that fossils are the remains of organisms that once were alive. Not only is the existence of observers not presupposed by these scientific claims, it is presupposed that archaeopteryx and other prehistoric fossilized creatures existed before there were human observers and could have existed even if no observers like us ever evolved. It is only by presupposing the independence of the existence of archaeopteryx and other prehistoric creatures from those who have learned about them that a theory of evolution with human beings entering the picture at a very recent stage can be formulated. Although the scientific claims do presuppose the existence of former life, they are not built upon the presupposition that there are observers who could formulate a science. Indeed, the scientific claims cannot presuppose the existence of scientific observers in the present time, because claims about prehistoric fossils are used to help develop a theory of how human beings and other forms of life emerged on the earth. As a general theory, it must allow for the possibility that life as we know it, and certainly human life, never did appear. If it presupposed the existence of human life, it could hardly explain its emergence. Staver's statements at the metalevel simply conflict directly with science in its unqualified form.

As a final example, consider the claim by Saunders (1992: 136) that 'any so-called reality is . . . the mental construction of those who believe they have discovered and investigated it'. Not only is this claim arrogant and patronizing, when it is compared directly to scientific claims it is immediately exposed as a misrepresentation of science. Compare the claim to the scientific claim that human beings infected with the polio virus can become ill and die. It is clear that scientists must presuppose that the polio virus is not a mental construction. Mental constructions do not make people ill (at least in the sense intended), and certainly do not kill people (except for those evil constructions that subsequently are enacted by fiends). For something to kill and maim it must be an effective agent with physical power. Ideas in and of themselves do not have such power. Also, mental constructions are not candidates for attempts at eradication by freezing, scorching and drowning in acid, unless the aim is to eradicate the construction by eradicating the constructor. This method has proven not to work for mental constructions. Yet, scientists have tried to eliminate the virus by all of these means – and they know the effects of each attempt. Saunders' claim is incompatible with the presuppositions of science. As before, we imagine a science teacher in a difficult position: how does one deal with such contradictions in the science classroom?

Implications and a teaching strategy

It might be argued that we have made our case too easy by choosing examples narrowly, in the sense that they come from firmly established areas of scientific thought. Perhaps, if we had chosen different examples, we might have had more difficulty making the case against the trespassing claims. We agree that the trespassing claims might not lead to contradiction with substantive science in all cases. Examples avoiding contradiction might include the science of black holes, wave functions, conceptual structures and a long list of other possibilities. Where no contradiction results, our arguments do not apply. However, the trespassers are universal claims, with no boundary conditions specifying where they do and do not apply. If the truth and usefulness of the trespassing claims are to be assessed, then their makers need to be explicit about their applicability. In the meantime, our arguments are sufficient to demonstrate that they are not universally applicable, and to suggest that they are perhaps not applicable to many aspects of firmly established science. Given that most science education, including undergraduate science degrees, is in firmly established areas of thought, then these views on the nature of science have the potential to create widespread problems for science educators.

This chapter is about the potentially jarring type of educational experience for science students that the trespassing views can cause. We have tried to imagine a variety of situations to portray the potential for disturbance that we envisage. A situation that has created a powerful impact for us begins by imagining a class of science students and their teacher touring the Royal Tyrrell Museum in Drumheller, Alberta. This museum is perhaps the most famous public display of dinosaur fossils in the world. It truly is a remarkable place. It is not easy, in our view, to leave this museum without the belief that dinosaurs of many varieties once inhabited the earth. This is a major message of the museum, and it is not easy to believe that it is all a great hoax, which is the level of denial that is needed to continue to believe that dinosaurs never existed in the face of exhibit after exhibit offering the proof that they did. The exhibits for the most part were dug from the earth in close proximity to Drumheller. Anyone can go to Dinosaur Provincial Park and to archaeological sites within it and witness fossils in the earth and fossils being removed from it. To believe all of this is false is to hold an astonishing belief indeed.

It is when we juxtapose this image of students visiting the museum against another image that we imagine educational shock occurring. In the other image, the teacher and class return to their school and the teacher says (after Staver): 'Of course you know that those objects in the museum do not exist independently of us'; or (after Saunders): 'Of course you know that all in the museum is a mental construction of those who believe they have discovered these things in reality'. What would the students be expected to think when they heard these things? It seems to us that they would be encouraged to think of the museum and its displays as a hoax, as merely the mental construction of those who believe they have discovered these things in reality. They would be encouraged to think of scientists as delusional, as those who believe they have discovered things they have not discovered, and, like many schizophrenics, as so firm in their delusion that they try to entrap others in it.

This is the jarring educational experience we imagine. We have never met a science teacher who would expose students to this sort of experience by making those trespassing statements. Therefore, our concern is hypothetical, but genuine nevertheless. We have demonstrated the logical consequences of the views proposed by von Glasersfeld, Staver, Wheatley and Saunders. Our conclusion is that they are in conflict with science and create special problems for science teaching should they be adopted there.

Rather than exclude the trespassing claims from science classrooms, our proposal is to explore a coordinated educational response that not only includes the ideas but turns their inclusion into an opportunity for science instruction. The response is based upon simultaneously teaching the substantive content of science and respecting a plurality of ideas.

Teaching the substantive content of science

An aim of science teaching is to bring students to understand 'conventional scientific interpretations' (Driver 1989: 96) and the 'scientific view of phenomena' (Driver 1995: 385). We accept this aim on the whole, although it must be conditioned by the fact that, for some areas of scientific endeavour, conclusions are contested and there is, as yet at least, no conventional interpretation (Norris and Kvernbekk 1997). In the case of school science, such contestation rarely exists.

Thus, the physics teacher helps students understand the conventional scientific view of, for example, why distorting and releasing a weighted spring causes the system to oscillate. It is difficult in this context of uncontested physics to separate grasping the physical explanation of what causes the motion from being convinced of its power and truth. This is because the understanding brings with it insight into the fullness and elegance of the explanation. What would it mean, for instance, for a student to say: 'Oh yes, I understand precisely how the action of a variable restoring force leads to this kind of motion, and I see no gaps in the explanation, but of course I do not believe in the existence of variable restoring forces'? The physics teacher holds, as a subsidiary and irrevocably connected intention to that of bringing students to understand the scientific view on oscillations, that they also become *convinced* of the view. The views on the nature of science that have been under consideration attempt to create a rift between acquiring understanding and becoming convinced. It is a rift, we believe, that is impossible to create when dealing with the simple oscillator and with dinosaurs and poliomyelitis, without creating something like the incomprehensible statement of the imagined student quoted above, and the jarring educational experience of the imagined visitors to the Tyrrell museum. When one understands a scientific explanation and does not believe it, then one must be able to provide reasons that point to deficiencies in the explanation. Such reasons are not on the table for the students learning about oscillators or about dinosaurs or poliomyelitis. In other contexts, such as when the available explanations are contested or incomplete, then understanding without conviction is possible and reasonable. In this regard, a science teacher might help students discern the differences between situations in which it is reasonable to remain unconvinced and those in which it is not.

Respecting a plurality of ideas

A plurality of views exists on many matters of substantive science content, and the introduction of students to substantive debate in science is to be commended. It is a part of the fabric of science that not all substantive matters are settled, and even matters that are settled can be reopened.

There is also a plurality of views about science. However, it is a consequence of the arguments in this chapter that it is not enough simply to expose students to differences as they exist, or to try to identify common ground among the competing views, as appears to be the approach endorsed by Driver *et al.* (1996). We have shown that some views of the nature of science are in conflict with the substantive content of science. This situation presents a pragmatic problem for the science teacher that it does not present for the philosophy of science teacher. In teaching the philosophy of science, it is hardly ever the intent to bring students to conviction in terms of the philosophical position being addressed. However, in teaching science, conviction in substantive science content is more frequently than not an intended outcome, especially in school science teaching. The science teacher, therefore, would be torn between teaching for understanding and conviction that part of the substantive content of science that falls into conventional scientific interpretations, and exposing students in an honest and fair way to thinking about science in a manner that might conflict directly with those conventional scientific views. Respect for a plurality of ideas can be achieved by addressing reasons and providing coherence.

Addressing reasons

A very important set of educational goals deals with the inculcation in students of respect for reasons: of an inclination to seek and to provide reasons for beliefs and actions, and to interrogate the reasons offered both by others as well as by oneself (Siegel 1988). Accepting this goal, science teachers help students to grasp the role of reasons in science. In addition to this goal, science students can be shown by explanation and example that science is the same as other disciplined forms of human thought in respect of reliance upon reasons. As a consequence, it is important to treat in a fair and even-handed manner views on the nature of science that might conflict with the very substantive science content that is being taught. Fairness and even-handedness require that the reasons for accepting or rejecting views about science be given the same scrutiny as that given to the reasons for accepting or rejecting science itself. Neither should be held to a higher standard of proof.

Providing coherence

Science teachers are driven to look beyond science, because it is not responsible science teaching to ignore the vast body of thought about science, even if that thinking comes into conflict with science itself. There is no justification in hiding other views or in pretending that they do not exist. However, simple exposure is not enough. Students cannot be left in confusion, if conflicts arise that they recognize but are unable to resolve themselves. On the other hand, conflicts must be exposed, even if that exposure risks confusion. The teacher must help students set as a goal for themselves the construction of as coherent a body of belief as is possible. This help would include assisting them to recognize coherence and incoherence, helping them develop criteria for choosing among conflicting views when making a choice is important, and living with unresolved conflict when resolution is not possible immediately or not urgent.

This approach entails setting science squarely within the whole of human thought. Thus, it cannot be a satisfactory science education that teaches substantive scientific content as one goal, the nature of science as another goal, and ignores the connections and conflicts between them. Students should be encouraged to seek a coherent view of their own. As has been demonstrated in this chapter, such coherence cannot be had simply by accepting views from each realm without attention to their meaning in the other. Coherence can be had only through reasoning that takes both realms into account simultaneously, and may entail discounting segments of one or the other.

Coordinating the teaching response

The science teacher is called upon to engage simultaneously in each of the activities described above. How can such simultaneous engagement occur? It is important to begin by not granting a priori credibility either to science or to views about science. Both should be portrayed as ideas based upon disciplined inquiry. Where the ideas overlap, and in particular where they can be interpreted to conflict, the science teacher can use this opportunity to help students understand the conflict, discuss it, and seek to resolve it, all the while trying to engender in students the abilities and dispositions for engaging ideas in this way on their own. We stop short of arguing that the educational response must resolve any conflict in ideas. Ultimately, resolution is the goal; but in a situation it might be too difficult to achieve, or achieving it might conflict with other more important goals.

The central premise of these recommendations is that science is not a set of ideas isolated from other sets, such as those on the nature of science. Views from these two domains can come into direct conflict with one another, providing the science teacher with an opportunity to help students see the conflict and to explore its resolution. Although many views of the nature of science have much to recommend them even when they conflict with the substantive content of science, our view is that their existence does not alter science. Science keeps rearing its head and presenting itself to us as a body of thought demanding our belief. In many of the situations of conflict between substantive science and metalevel claims about science, science has the resources to defeat the metalevel claims. Yet, this is not a view to be urged upon science students. In the end, the students must decide for themselves whether to believe, for example, that dinosaurs existed or that they are a mental construction with no existence independent of human beings. The teacher's role is to make known to them that this task is theirs, and to help them acquire the resources to make the comparative judgements of credibility that the situation evokes.

Acknowledgements

The writing of this chapter was supported by a grant from the Social Sciences and Humanities Research Council of Canada, Grant No. 410-96-0053 and by a postdoctoral fellowship from the same council to Korpan. We thank Gregory J. Kelly for helpful comments.

References

BSCS (Biological Sciences Curriculum Study) (1987) *Biological Science: An Ecological Approach*, 6th edn. Dubuque, IA: Kendall/Hunt.

Debre, R., Duncan, D., Enders, J.F. *et al.* (1955) *Poliomyelitis*. Geneva: World Health Organization.

Driver, R. (1989) The construction of scientific knowledge in school classrooms, in R. Millar (ed.) *Doing Science: Images of Science in Science Education*, pp. 83–106. Bristol, PA: Taylor & Francis.

Driver, R. (1995) Constructivist approaches to science teaching, in L.R. Steffe and J.E. Gale (eds) *Constructivism in Education*, pp. 385–400. Hillsdale, NJ: Erlbaum.

Driver, R., Leach, J., Millar, R. and Scott, P. (1996) *Young People's Images of Science*. Buckingham: Open University Press.

Dworkin, R. (1996) Objectivity and truth: you'd better believe it. *Philosophy & Public Affairs*, 25: 87–139.

Galbraith, D., Dickinson, T., Garden, J. and Lynn, D. (1993) *Biology Directions*. Toronto: John Wiley & Sons.

Glasersfeld, E. von (1995) *Radical Constructivism*. London: Falmer.

Hacking, I. (1999) *The Social Construction of What?* Cambridge, MA: Harvard University Press.

Monger, G. (1992) *Nuffield Co-ordinated Sciences: Biology*. London: Longman.

Myers, G. (1990) Making a discovery: narratives of split genes, in C. Nash (ed.) *Narrative in Culture*, pp. 102–26. London: Routledge.

Nagel, T. (1997) *The Last Word*. Oxford: Oxford University Press.

Norris, S.P. (1995) Learning to live with scientific expertise: toward a theory of intellectual communalism for guiding science teaching. *Science Education*, 79: 201–17.

Norris, S.P. and Kvernbekk, T. (1997) The application of science education theories. *Journal of Research in Science Teaching*, 34: 977–1005.

Ritter, B., Coombs, R.F., Drysdale, R.B., Gardner, G.A. and Lunn, D.T. (1993) *Biology*. Scarborough. Ontario: Nelson.

Saunders, W.L. (1992) The constructivist perspective: implications and teaching strategies for science. *School Science and Mathematics*, 92, 136–41.

Siegel, H. (1988) *Educating Reason*. New York: Routledge.

Staver, J.R. (1998) Constructivism: sound theory for explicating the practice of science and science teaching. *Journal of Research in Science Teaching*, 35, 501–20.

Wheatley, G.H. (1991) Constructivist perspectives on science and mathematics learning. *Science Education*, 75: 9–22.

14 Renegotiating the culture of school science

Glen Aikenhead

Introduction

This chapter presents a view of school science that emphasizes the interaction between western science and the culture of students. A student's experience with school science is seen as a cultural event that strives to help students create new meanings about their world in terms of their cultural identity. I argue that only by taking a pluralistic cultural approach can the goal 'science for all' be attained.

The chapter shares with other chapters the rejection of school science that simply promotes social screening to maintain a privileged status quo (Apple 1996) – i.e. 'science for an élite'. However, the chapter moves beyond our current thinking about social constructivism, particularly the enculturation of all students into western science (Driver *et al.* 1994). Instead I offer a pluralistic multiscience approach for school science and the enculturation of students into their own life-worlds where their cultural identities form and evolve.

This innovation may seem controversial to some. My proposal to treat school science as a cultural phenomenon amounts to renegotiating what counts as scientific literacy in the school curriculum. The cultural literacy proposed in this chapter defines new territory for teaching and learning, and is firmly grounded in an emerging research programme: cultural studies in science education (see for example Aikenhead and Jegede 1999; Aikenhead 2000).

In a millennium publication, *Beyond 2000*, Millar and Osborne (1998: 2008) defined a scientifically literate person as one who is 'able to engage with the ideas and views which form such a central part of our common culture'. The phrase 'our common culture' inadvertently and tacitly casts the agenda for school science in terms of a monoculture in which material progress is linked to the success of western science – science for a privileged class that determines what that monoculture will be. Understandably, western science is therefore privileged knowledge in most schools. An alternative agenda views society as comprising many cultures and subcultures, each with an ideological agenda and each with a stake in what counts as knowledge in school science. By embracing this pluralistic cultural perspective on school science, we are open to hearing the voices of those conventionally underrepresented. This cultural perspective frames a science-for-all purpose for school science, a purpose Millar and Osborne persuasively advocated.

A cultural perspective on science education is founded on several assumptions listed but not fleshed out here:

- Western science is a cultural entity itself, one of many subcultures of Euro-American society.
- People live and coexist within many subcultures identified by, for example, language, ethnicity, gender, social class, occupation, religion and geographic location; and people move from one subculture to another, a process called 'cultural border crossing'.
- People's core cultural identities may be at odds with the culture of western science to varying degrees.
- Science classrooms are subcultures of the school culture.
- Most students experience a change in culture when moving from their life-worlds into the world of school science.
- Therefore, learning science is a cross-cultural event for these students.
- Students are more successful if they receive help negotiating their cultural border crossings.
- This help can come from a teacher (a culture broker) who identifies the cultural borders to be crossed, who guides students back and forth across those borders, who gets students to make sense out of cultural conflicts that might arise, and who motivates students by drawing upon the impact western science and technology have on their life-worlds (not upon the contribution western science and technology have made to a monoculture determined by a privileged class).

On the other hand, some students (called 'potential scientists' by Costa 1995) have identities and abilities that harmonize so closely with the culture of western science that the border crossing into school science is sufficiently smooth for such a barrier to cease to exist. The assumptions posited here are described in detail in Aikenhead (1996, 1997), Aikenhead and Jegede (1999) and Jegede and Aikenhead (1999).

A cultural perspective on school science is an unorthodox view for most science teachers, but it may turn out to be more intuitively practical than other perspectives on learning found in the research literature as, in our daily lives, we frequently move from one subculture to a quite different one (for example, from a family setting to a parent–teacher meeting at school). As we do this, we negotiate cultural differences between the two social settings. Science teachers are intuitively familiar with this type of cultural phenomenon. The challenge will be to persuade teachers to transfer this intuition to classroom instruction.

What does it mean to treat school science as a cultural phenomenon? An answer is formulated here in two parts. First, student learning is described in three different ways, giving emphasis to a cultural way that celebrates the process of 'coming to knowing'. Then the political dimensions of this innovation are explored in practical terms of the power and influence over what counts as 'science' in the school science curriculum.

Learning school science: different levels of meaning

Three levels of meaning derived from the experience of learning science in schools, described here, range from a shallow level, to an in-depth level, to an even richer level that has cultural significance to students.

Shallow learning

A superficial level of science's meaning tends to occur when a teacher's goal is simply to cover the curriculum for assessment purposes. For instance, Loughran and Derry (1997: 935) found superficiality when they investigated students' reactions to a science teacher's concerted effort to teach for 'deep understanding':

The need to develop a deep understanding of the subject may not have been viewed by them [the students] as being particularly important as progression through the schooling system could be achieved without it. In this case such a view appears to have been very well reinforced by Year 9. This is not to suggest that these students were poor learners, but rather that they had learnt how to learn sufficiently well to succeed in school without expending excessive time or effort.

Their teacher lamented, 'No matter how well I think I teach a topic, the students only seem to learn what they need to pass the test, then, after the test, they forget it all anyway' (1997: 925).

This age-old problem of superficial learning was systematically studied by Larson (1995) when conducting research into students' unintended learning. She found students in a high-school chemistry class who actually told her the rules they followed so that they could pass Mr London's chemistry class without really understanding much of the chemistry. Larson called these rules 'Fatima's rules', after the most articulate informant in the class. For example, one of the rules advises us not to read the textbook but to memorize its bold-faced words and phrases. Fatima's rules can include such coping or passive-resistance mechanisms as 'silence, accommodation, ingratiation, evasiveness and manipulation' (Atwater 1996: 823). Meaningful learning does not result, but instead, mere 'communicative competence' (Kelly and Green 1998). Gunstone and White (see Chapter 16) call this 'the game of schooling'. From a cultural perspective, Medvitz (1996: 5) recognized it as 'an accoutrement to specific rituals and practices of the science classroom'. Fatima's rules apply to most school subjects, of course, not just to science.

Students are not the only ones to play Fatima's rules, however. Classroom rituals and practices are usually staged by teachers. Tobin and McRobbie (1997: 366) documented a teacher's complicity in terms of Fatima's rules: 'There was a close fit between the goals of Mr. Jacobs and those of the students and satisfaction with the emphasis on memorisation of facts and procedures to obtain the correct answers needed for success on tests and examinations'. Costa (1997) synthesized the work of Larson (1995) and Tobin and McRobbie (1997) with her own classroom research with Mr Ellis, and concluded:

> Mr. Ellis' students, like those of Mr. London and Mr. Jacobs, are not working on chemistry; they are working to get through chemistry. The subject does not matter. As a result, students negotiate treaties regarding the kind of work they will do in class. Their work is not so much productive as it is political. They do not need to be productive – as in learning chemistry. They only need to be political – as in being credited for working in chemistry.
>
> (Costa 1997: 1020)

The three teachers (Ellis, London and Jacobs) exemplify the superficial teaching that can pass as legitimate instruction. This superficiality seems to be the status quo for many science classrooms worldwide (Cross 1997; Roth *et al.* 1999; see also Chapter 18).

Some teachers may not realize the pervasive power of Fatima's rules. For instance, Meyer (1998) documented a Grade 12 physics teacher's negative reaction to a student's 'success'. In the student's own words:

> I remember physics. We had to do a provincial exam. I had failed the first term and I got 53 on the second term but the provincial exam counted 100% in the end. So the week before I sat down with the physics book and memorised, wrote the exam ... It's all gone now. But I got 82%. I remember my physics teacher being so upset with me because he didn't know how I did it.
>
> (Meyer 1998: 464)

In summary, a superficial level of meaning for school science focuses on language and content to pass standardized assessments. This serves students, teachers and parents who subscribe to the narrow goal of simply accumulating credentials for leaving school. Students and teachers will often go through the motions to make it appear as if meaningful learning has occurred, but at best, rote memorization of key terms and processes is only achieved temporarily (see Chapter 9).

In-depth meaning-making

An in-depth level of meaning generally rejects Fatima's rules. This perspective is represented by most chapters in this book and is summarized here only for the purpose of contrasting it with a cultural perspective on school science.

The role of the curriculum is to 'help people in decision-making . . . and in feeling empowered to hold and express a view on issues which enter the arena of public debate' (Millar and Osborne 1998: 2007). Hurd (1998) has made a similar proposal for school science. This level of meaning serves a small proportion of students (i.e. 'potential scientists' – Costa 1995) who are predisposed to acquiring an in-depth understanding of natural phenomena from a western science point of view, a point of view that harmonizes with those students' worldviews. Teachers, however, are often faced with the challenge of motivating the rest of the students whose worldviews are quite different.

When in-depth meaning-making is the goal, teachers will engage students in the construction of scientific knowledge. Worldwide, Gallagher (1998: 4) concluded, 'Another common element of science teaching is persuading students to embrace abstract scientific concepts as valid representations of the natural world, replacing common sense concepts they have constructed or learned from others'.

In contrast to this simple concept-replacement model of meaning-making, a more sophisticated concept-proliferation model suggests that a new (scientific) concept is constructed within a new (scientific) context and added to a student's repertoire of specific contexts (Solomon 1983) or to a student's 'conceptual profile' (Mortimer 1995). Driver *et al.* (1994: 9) concur: 'We would not expect students necessarily to abandon their commonsense ideas as a result of science instruction'. Hewson and Lemberger (see Chapter 7) present evidence of concept proliferation occurring when students learned to use several genetic models.

Solomon (1987) advanced the view that making meaning in school science should include the *social* construction of knowledge. Driver *et al.* (1994) described the process this way:

Making meaning is . . . a dialogic process involving persons-in-conversation, and learning is seen as the process by which individuals are introduced to a culture by more skilled members. . . . The challenge lies in helping learners to appropriate these [western scientific] models for themselves, to appreciate their domains of applicability and, within such domains, to be able to use them . . . The challenge is one of how to achieve such a process of *enculturation* successfully in the round of normal classroom life.

(Driver *et al*. 1994: 7, emphasis added)

A social constructivist view of learning with its emphasis on 'enculturation' enjoys wide support from university science educators, including most authors of this book. However, as argued in the next section, the social constructivist view is limited by its preoccupation to enculturate all students into western science.

Learning as a cultural phenomenon

I have argued elsewhere (Aikenhead 1996) that enculturation into western science supports only those students (potential scientists) whose cultural identities harmonize with the culture of western science. What happens to the vast majority of students who do not fit this description? When placed in a classroom where enculturation is the intended process, these students mistake enculturation as an attempt at *assimilation* (forcing students to replace or marginalize their common-sense notions with scientific ones) even when concept replacement was not their teacher's goal (Aikenhead 1996). Concept proliferation seems to fail when teachers, even social constructivist teachers, attempt to enculturate all students. Most students react by playing Fatima's rules.

A cultural perspective attempts to avoid the enculturation/assimilation pitfall wherein 'students are socialised into a particular community of knowledge, a process described as a cultural apprenticeship' (Driver *et al*. 1994: 11). Brickhouse *et al.* (2000) argue that this community of practising scientists is too distant and irrelevant for most students, and that schools conventionally define this community of scientists too narrowly by ignoring the network of people who represent other communities of practice that interact with western science, communities more in line with students forging personal identities.

To avoid inadvertent assimilation we need to expand (not replace) social constructivism into a cultural anthropological understanding of school science. We need to join Pickering (1992) and others in recognizing western science as a subculture itself. We need to treat learning as a culture-making process that engages students with who they are and where they are going (Stairs 1993/4), not unlike other school subjects such as language arts. This cultural perspective differs from the social constructivist view of enculturation in which 'learners are supported in using scientific ways of knowing through social processes, making personal sense of scientific representations of phenomena in terms of their existing everyday knowledge' (Leach *et al.* 1997: 161). Although this view of enculturation is thoughtfully associated with everyday knowledge, it places western science at the focus of instruction without acknowledging the cultural nature of science nor the need by most students to gain access to western science through cultural border crossing. There are other learning processes besides enculturation. For instance, Aikenhead (1997) proposed autonomous acculturation and 'anthropological' learning that emphasize cross-cultural school science. These alternatives are associated with students' cultural identities.

Social constructivism and culture making have other defining differences in addition to the role played by enculturation in school science.

Culture making focuses on how various cultures and subcultures make different meanings of the natural world, including (but not limited to) the subculture of western science. The meaning of 'science' in school science has now shifted from the conventional western science found in social constructivism to a multicultural meaning – 'a rational perceiving of reality' (Ogawa 1995: 588). Ogawa delineated several sciences that can function in the life of a student, all of which may have valid contexts for their use. Contexts include, for example, a student's own cultural identity, a community's indigenous or common-sense culture (including a community's notion of western science), the domain of citizenship (citizen science) (see Chapter 12 and Layton *et al.* 1993) and the culture of western science (including its impact on the other cultures). This pluralistic, multiscience, cultural perspective encompasses and extends a social constructivist view of meaning-making. A cultural perspective shares with Driver *et al.* (1994: 11) the challenge to foster 'a critical perspective on scientific culture among students' by a teacher who acts as a 'tour guide mediating between children's everyday world and the world of science'. It also shares with Driver *et al.* the challenge to help students appropriate western science for themselves and appreciate the domains within which western science is applicable. But a cultural approach does not insist that every student proficiently uses western scientific knowledge in those domains, as enculturation does in a social constructivist approach.

Ogawa's (1995) multiscience view does not reject western science by replacing it with other sciences (i.e. concept replacement). A multiscience view adds contexts to a student's repertoire of life-world contexts, with each context having an identifiably different view of natural phenomena (i.e. concept proliferation). This is a pluralistic, not a relativistic, account of natural phenomena. (A similar conclusion from a phenomenological perspective is advanced by Erickson in Chapter 15.)

A simplified vignette will illustrate some features of this multiscience view. A child throws a ball into the air and catches it. Gunstone (1988) used this situation to illustrate constructivism. A diagram defined three points: (a) the ball rising, (b) the ball at the top of its arch, and (c) the ball falling. Students were asked 'whether the force on the ball was up, down, or zero for the three positions shown on the diagram' (1988: 74). In multiscience instruction students might be asked: 'What does our everyday common sense tell us about the force on the ball at positions a, b and c?' The students' responses (typically: up, zero and down, respectively) are recorded on a blackboard with the left-hand side entitled, for instance, 'common-sense culture'. We know from research that the most frequent common-sense concept of force is equivalent to the scientific concept of momentum (Barbetta *et al.* 1985). Thus, the right-hand side of the blackboard (entitled 'culture of western science') is introduced by the teacher who engages students in a need to communicate with a scientist, thus creating the need to know the term 'momentum' (rather than 'force') *in the context of western science discourse.* A scientist would describe the momentum at a, b and c as pointing up, zero and down, respectively. Other activities (for example, using balls with different masses, thrown at different speeds) are carried out, just as they would be in a social constructivist classroom (Driver *et al.* 1994). Border crossing between the everyday world (left-hand side) and the world of western science (right-hand side) is made smoother for students who (if forced to fend for themselves) would normally find the border crossing hazardous (Costa 1995) and would tend to react by playing Fatima's rules (Aikenhead 1996).

But the communication with a scientist does not end there. A puzzle is introduced by a teacher: 'Scientists imagine that something is tugging on the ball in the same direction (downwards) at a, b and c. What might that something be?' Of all the student responses, the one that is useful to scientists is the pull of gravity. Perhaps a foreign concept is being introduced to many students here, but it is contextualized within the culture of western science (concept proliferation). In the culture of science this pull of gravity is called a 'force'. A student's notebook page might look like Table 14.1. The Newtonian abstraction of force may be an interesting puzzle for the relatively few students who desire enculturation into western science (potential scientists). For all students, however, the obvious double definition of 'force' would be discussed, along with other situations familiar to students in which the same word has completely different meanings depending on the context (see Gough 1998 for several science examples).

Further group activities are needed for students to use the various concepts and to practise border crossings back and forth between common sense and western science subcultures. Whenever someone uses the word 'force' in the science classroom, the speaker must somehow indicate which subculture, or which science, they are speaking in. In such conversations,

Table 14.1 A notebook page in cross-cultural instruction concerning a ball thrown into the air

Common-sense culture	Culture of western science
Force direction at	*Momentum* direction at
a up	a up
b zero	b zero
c down	c down
What's always tugging downwards?	*Force* direction at
No answer, or gravity	a down
	b down
	c down

students should *not* feel like an apprentice being encultured into western science, but rather, they should feel a need to improve their personal understanding of their world, perhaps by acting like an anthropologist discovering things about a foreign culture. The example of the ball has only addressed two subcultures (common sense and western science) and not a wider range of cultures as illustrated later in an example about summer clothes.

The issue of different discourses between subcultures is just one of many issues that arise when border crossing is made explicit for students. The domains of discourse analysis and language structure (Applebee 1996; Gee 1996; see also Chapter 3) for instance, are generally encompassed by a cultural perspective, along with many other features of culture to which students must attend. For example, when consciously moving back and forth between different subcultures, in addition to switching their discourse and language structures, students often need to switch certain values, switch loyalties, switch epistemologies and switch ontologies (Tyson *et al.* 1997). All these differences are highlighted when we remember that the culture of western science is rationalistically centred, decontextualized puzzle solving, while common-sense cultures are human centred and contextualized in social situations (Aikenhead 1997).

When learning science in a multiscience curriculum, students not only study western science because it has a significant impact on their community's culture (including, in some communities, a status of prestige, power, progress and privilege), but they learn other sciences (for example, citizen science, or Aboriginal science if appropriate) for the purposes of having a better grasp of their own culture and of the multicultural global village, and engaging in practical action such as personal decision making, economic development and environmental responsibility (i.e. responsible citizenship – see Chapter 9). Some students and teachers may resist a multiscience curriculum simply because they are uncomfortable negotiating the movement (border crossing) between one science and another. Others may resist it on ideological grounds (Cross 1995, 1997).

A curriculum dedicated to teaching science as a cultural phenomenon will identify a network of communities in students' life-worlds – for example, the media, funding agencies, legal and political systems, environmental groups and industry. Each network interacts with communities of scientists. A network of communities reflects/distorts the culture of western science into what Weinstein (1998) called 'science-as-culture':

> The meaning making that we call science happens in a way that is distributed over the society spatially and temporally. It happens through science fiction, it happens through laboratory work ... it happens in hospitals, it happens in advertising, and it happens in schools. To emphasise this, I explicitly refer to *science-as-culture* rather than to just *science*. I do this as a reminder to the reader that I am concerned with science in all parts of the network and not just the laboratory, field station, and research institute.
>
>   (Weinstein 1998: 492, original emphasis)

Part of students' knowledge of their everyday world is science-as-culture, which is more than just pop culture (Solomon 1998). The cultural contributions to society by western science are partly embedded in science-as-culture. These cultural contributions need to be accessible to students in a context that affirms their cultural identities, not in a context that encultures students into western science. Although students' identities may cause them to reject an apprenticeship into western science, they are likely to openly embrace a critical perspective on both science-as-culture and western science. Examining science-as-culture can be a supportive form of enculturation into students' common-sense (life-world) cultures.

Learning science as a cultural phenomenon is experienced as 'coming to knowing', a phrase borrowed from First Nations (Canadian Indian) educators. Coming to knowing occurs within a cultural setting linked to human action (see Chapter 3). It is reflected in John Dewey's (1916: 393) participatory learning: 'If the living, experiencing being is an intimate participant in the activities of the world to which it belongs, then knowledge is a mode of participation'. The world in which most students participate is not the world of western science, but another world increasingly influenced by western science and technology.

Coming to knowing engages students in their own cultural negotiations (Stairs 1993/4). These negotiations involve students interacting with their cultural surroundings for the purpose of cultural development, such as enriching their cultural identity. A cross-cultural science class will engage students in their own cultural negotiations with several sciences found within school science. (Enculturation into only one science is not the agenda.) As students cross cultural borders into various sciences, they become more aware of their own understanding of the physical and biological world; their community's common-sense understanding (for example, citizen science); perhaps another subculture's or another culture's way of knowing (for example, technology or Aboriginal science, respectively); and the norms, beliefs, values and conventions of western science. Science-as-culture can often provide a useful starting point.

When in contact with the four different sciences stated above, students are free to take what makes sense to them. This appropriation is a meaning-making process of intercultural borrowing or adaptation which anthropologists call 'acculturation'. Acculturation occurs when people of one culture take on features of another culture that are attractive to them. (A simple example of acculturation would be Anglo-British homes habitually serving multinational dishes). Acculturation can lead to participation and empowerment in a community without altering one's cultural allegiance, and therefore, neither enculturation nor assimilation occur (Aikenhead 1997).

The example of a child throwing a ball into the air given earlier illustrated some features of cross-cultural science teaching. Another example will show other characteristics of coming to knowing. Although the illustration by itself is not intended to be an exemplar of practice, it nevertheless illustrates the selection of school science content in a multiscience curriculum.

Summer clothes are on the minds of most adolescents. What are students' understandings in relation to their choices of summer clothes (either personal or the community's common-sense ideas)? How have western science and technology contributed to those choices and ideas? These questions can lead to another: how can we account for summers being hot? Here are four different answers, each taken from a different subculture.

1 Expressing their 'personal science' (Ogawa 1995), students often explain that the earth is closer to the sun during the summer.
2 Western science textbooks (in North America, at least) offer the story that the 'direct' rays of the sun produce greater energy concentration than 'indirect' rays do (by a factor of 3.5, summer to winter, if we take time to calculate it for about 52 degrees latitude).
3 Some Aboriginal nations explain the phenomenon in terms of interrelationships between certain keepers of the earth and the law of circular interaction.
4 Common sense in the kitchen suggests that the longer the sun heats the earth each day, the hotter the earth becomes (by a factor of 2, summer to winter, at about 52 degree latitude).

Coming to knowing about hot summers may involve negotiating borders between all these subcultures, rejecting ideas that are not defensible (the earth is closer to the sun in summer), and appropriating ideas that do make sense – a process of acculturation.

In the case of hot summers, the answer found in western science textbooks (in North America, at least) leaves out the common-sense effect of time that the sun shines. But neither of these mechanistic explanations engages us in issues of values as Aboriginal explanations tend to do. For some cultural negotiators ('intimate participant', to use Dewey's 1916 term), western science's mechanistic knowledge may not be worth acculturating in the context of hot summers and cold winters, because the idea may not fit comfortably with a student's worldview or cultural identity. However, in classrooms dedicated to enculturation into western science, mechanistic knowledge is expected to be appropriated by students, and in response, students often resort to playing Fatima's rules (Aikenhead 1996).

One significant feature of cultural border crossing is the confusion that arises when one subculture uses the same word as another subculture (for example, the word 'heat') but the word has a totally different meaning. Although concept proliferation allows us to keep the word meanings of common-sense subcultures, concept proliferation does not help clarify the cultural borders that need to be crossed to gain access to the word meaning within the subculture of western science. Students' cultural negotiations need to be facilitated by making those cultural borders explicit and by helping students cross them (Jegede and Aikenhead 1999).

In summary, learning science as a cultural phenomenon (coming to knowing) is an activity that involves students in an increasingly competent participation in a community of practice, by enriching their self-identities within the context of their cultural identity (a process that engages students with who they are and where they are going). The community of practice for students engaged in culture making is not the western scientific community as proposed by Driver *et al.* (1994) or by Millar and Osborne (1998), but instead it is the network of communities within which students' self-identities most commonly take shape.

Responses from stakeholders

Social constructivists worldwide tend to experience some resistance to their innovative ideas in schools (see Chapter 18). A cultural view of school science proposed in this chapter will receive an even stronger reaction. For either of these innovations to succeed, they must take into account the reaction of stakeholders, particularly those who see themselves as being privileged by current traditional practices, such as the status quo of playing Fatima's rules. This section summarizes the political territory that school science innovators must face if they are to renegotiate the culture of school science.

The twentieth century began with nature divided into physics, chemistry, biology and geology by an emerging community of scholars calling themselves scientists, but the century ended with nature viewed as a transdisciplinary collage by communities of engineers, technologists, scientists and funding agencies (Latour 1987). The twentieth century began with the high-school science curriculum divided into the content of physics, chemistry, biology and geology, taught to an intellectual and occupational élite. The century ended with a curriculum that adhered largely to its nineteenth-century roots, in spite of many innovative attempts to change it (Fensham 1992; Hurd 1998). In short, school science resisted co-evolving with western science during the twentieth century (Aikenhead 1994; Cross 1997).

This successful resistance suggests that school science must somehow be serving the interests of dominant stakeholders who enjoy social, economic and political power in society (Apple 1996). 'The control over what counts as knowledge, and the control over the institutions where such knowledge is practised, allows for dominant interest groups to perpetuate and maintain their positions of dominance and advantage' (Jones *et al.* 1995: 194). Therefore, whoever attempts to renegotiate school science automatically threatens society's dominant stakeholders, the keepers of this status quo. Renegotiating school science is fundamentally a political event (Roberts 1988) in which power is the currency of social change (Blades 1997).

By recognizing the successful influence exerted by the keepers of the status quo, we can become vigilant to their tacit control over the school science agenda that privileges 'science for an élite' over 'science for all'. These two agendas represent two ends of an ideological spectrum. The science for an élite agenda is often couched in the discourse of raising standards and competing in international assessment tests. The science for all agenda is often expressed in the discourses of equity and of meaningful learning. These ideologies influence school practice in several contexts (Fensham 1992). These contexts are summarized here.

National context

School science trains future scientists and engineers. To be internationally competitive, the argument goes, a nation needs an élite pool of mathematicians, scientists and engineers. Corporate profits drive the engines of free enterprise in the global village. Fensham (1992) referred to this special interest in controlling school science as 'economic'. Ultimately, school science is seen as maximizing corporate profits.

By responding to national interests, school science takes on a gatekeeping role by identifying and promoting talented students, and by employing a 'survival of the fittest' type of curriculum. Changes to this gatekeeping role are often resisted in the name of national security and economic competitiveness. However, an appraisal of these reasons exposes their false claims (summarized in Aikenhead 1997; Gibbs and Fox 1999). For instance, there are ample students in first year university science courses to meet the national needs of industrial nations. School science is not a significant factor in the production of national wealth.

Academic context

University science departments are the gatekeepers to the scientific, engineering and health professions. In turn, the science departments give school science the gatekeeping role of maintaining the integrity of scientific disciplines. 'Scientists, particularly in research institutions and universities, are now a power faction in society with a major interest in *maintaining their discipline* as an elite and important field' (Fensham 1992: 793, original emphasis).

In keeping with this rather self-serving interest, some academic scientists portray their profession in terms of a platonic idealism that demands uncritical respect because their valid knowledge is superior to (has greater predictive validity than) other domains of knowledge. This extreme though common ideology is called 'scientism' (Smolicz and Nunan 1975). Science teachers often harbour a strong allegiance to scientism by viewing science as authoritarian; non-humanistic; objective; purely rational and empirical; universal; impersonal and unencumbered by the vulgarity of human imagination, dogma, judgements or cultural values (Smolicz and Nunan 1975; Brickhouse 1990; Gaskell 1992).

A wall of scientism will invariably confront science educators whenever they try to negotiate a sociological or cultural approach to school science that privileges science for all. Confrontations can surface as *ad hominem* arguments (for example, associating innovative educators with Nazis; Matthews 1997) or as a spirited defence of science's monopoly on truth (for example, 'We believe that there is only one science, not Western, not indigenous, not even Maori . . . We agree that science is value-free knowledge about the world' – Lederman 1998: 132). These are extreme examples perhaps, but they do represent the lived experiences of students and education innovators whose interests are systemically marginalized by gatekeeping science curricula (Roth and McGinn 1998). The academic community has successfully vetoed innovations that challenged the maintenance of its disciplines (Blades 1997; Fensham 1998). On the other hand, we must also recognize those scientists who have instigated science-for-all projects themselves (see Chapter 1).

One political ploy to avoid academic vetoes is to enlist members of the scientific community who subscribe to a science-for-all ideology, and to marginalize the others before they marginalize you. Co-opting the academic context is essential to successful negotiations.

Social, economic and political context

The social, economic and political (SEP) context is populated by stakeholders who subscribe to national and academic interests for purely pragmatic reasons: to become credentialed, to gain access to post-secondary institutions, and hence, to join the privileged class (Apple 1996). In Fensham's words:

> The sciences, particularly the physical sciences, in many societies are gateway subjects that filter the relatively few students who are allowed to move into certain professions of high status, societal influence, and economic security. Because of the societal power associated with these positions, we can call this a *political* interest in schooling.
>
> (Fensham 1992: 793, original emphasis)

The ideology of rugged individualism blossoms here.

When attempting to rationalize a science-for-all curriculum, science educators often cite the need for a strong democracy, an equitable access to social power and a literate citizenry (for example Millar and Osborne 1998). However, privileged stakeholders will translate these arguments into one issue only: sharing their SEP power. For most keepers of the status quo, sharing power is not negotiable. Therefore, successful negotiations over the culture of school science must somehow marginalize or co-opt those stakeholders.

School context

Most schools face the tension between, on the one hand, providing worthwhile and genuine experiences for all students, and on the other hand, serving as gatekeepers for national interests and for the integrity of a discipline. Moreover, the culture of a school is directly affected by the SEP status of the community it serves and by the middle-class aspirations held by many of the school's personnel – aspirations that rely on obedience, management techniques and narrow assessment policies (Anyon 1981; Cross 1995). We cannot renegotiate the culture of school science within a school hostile to a science-for-all curriculum. Therefore, successful negotiators must select appropriate schools.

Science classroom context

A science classroom can be as idiosyncratic as the individual teacher, and so there is always potential for renegotiating what counts as 'science' in school science for that teacher. Teachers make pedagogical decisions based on practical knowledge that holistically integrates culture-laden principles, values and worldviews (Duffee and Aikenhead 1992). However, a teacher's loyalty to a limited number of ideologies and paradigms greatly reduces the variety of science classroom subcultures found the world over (Cross 1997; Gallagher 1998). In a case study of five rather typical high-school science teachers in Canada, Aikenhead (1984: 182) discovered a strong loyalty towards socializing students for post-secondary institutions where the teachers themselves had developed self-images and cultural identities:

> From a teacher's perspective, if a teacher drastically altered the curriculum content, this would limit the student's ability to take courses for which the current course is a prerequisite; courses which would lead to good careers with social status. Even a lower ability student ought not to be severely cut off from taking courses that have potential for social status.

For these teachers to renegotiate their science curriculum, they would need to change their values about teaching, evaluate the socializing function of any new curriculum, and reformulate the 'practical holistic, decision-making system that currently supports and sustains them on a day to day basis' (Aikenhead 1984: 184).

Fensham identified interest groups who generally support teachers in favour of science for all:

> There are clearly many ways in which the *cultural* and *social life* of groups in society are now influenced by technology and by knowledge and applications from the sciences. Science education can assist these groups to have a sense of control rather than of subservience and to take advantage of what science in these various ways has to offer them.
> (Fensham 1992: 793, original emphasis)

This point was developed in detail by Millar and Osborne (1998) when they included Fensham's cultural argument within their notion of scientific literacy.

The stakeholders in science classrooms with the least power to influence the curriculum are the students themselves. Students have interests in personal growth, satisfaction and self-esteem (Fensham 1992). When their voices were heard in a national curriculum renewal project (Science Council of Canada 1984), students uniformly criticized school science as being socially sterile, intellectually boring and invalid in its assessment of what they learned in class. On the other hand, students can also be keepers of the status quo when they embrace Fatima's rules and the gatekeeping function of schools. These are often students well served by national, academic and SEP interests (Aikenhead 1996). Student expectations are part of the political landscape and hence their voices must be part of the negotiation process. Like teachers, students must sense the benefit of an innovation.

Conclusion

As has already been stressed, the point of this chapter is not to sweep aside western science and replace it with other sciences. Instead, the point is to negotiate a balance among several legitimate sciences important to a students' cultural identity (for example, science-as-culture, citizen science and western science). In doing so, we need to resolve the contradiction between a science-for-all goal for school science and the necessity that western science be the *only* science in 'science for all'. Similarly, Jenkins (see Chapter 12) argues for 'a more generous view of science in the school curriculum'. Because science content (western or otherwise) determines in large measure the culture of school science, selecting that content is a process of negotiation that uses both rational criteria (see Chapter 9) and the political power to ameliorate influences by various stakeholders (as described above).

The cross-cultural approach to school science proposed in this chapter is beginning to be implemented for Aboriginal students in Australia, Canada, New Zealand, South Africa and the USA. With experience and empirical research, cross-cultural science education will mature as it develops richer descriptions of coming to knowing. I predict that this research programme will support any science educator committed to renegotiating the culture of school science for *all* students, not just for Aboriginal students.

References

Aikenhead, G.S. (1984) Teacher decision making: the case of Prairie High. *Journal of Research in Science Teaching*, 21: 167–86.

Aikenhead, G.S. (1994) The social contract of science: implications for teaching science, in J. Solomon and G. Aikenhead (eds) *STS Education: International Perspective on Reform*. New York: Teachers College Press.

Aikenhead, G.S. (1996) Science education: border crossing into the subculture of science. *Studies in Science Education*, 27: 1–52.

Aikenhead, G.S. (1997) Toward a First Nations Cross-cultural Science and Technology Curriculum. *Science Education*, 81: 217–38.

Aikenhead, G.S. (2000) Cross-cultural science & technology units project. http://capes.usask.ca/ccstu.

Aikenhead, G.S. and Jegede, O.J. (1999) Cross-cultural science education: a cognitive explanation of a cultural phenomenon. *Journal of Research in Science Teaching*, 36: 269–87.

Anyon, J. (1981) Social class and school knowledge. *Curriculum Inquiry*, 11: 3–42.

Apple, M. (1996) *Cultural Politics and Education*. New York: Teachers College Press.

Applebee, A. (1996) *Curriculum as Conversation: Transforming Traditions of Teaching and Learning*. London: Chicago University Press.

Atwater, M.M. (1996) Social constructivism: infusion into the multicultural science education research agenda. *Journal of Research in Science Teaching*, 33: 821–37.

Barbetta, M.G., Loria, A., Mascellani, V. and Michelini, M. (1985) An investigation on students' frameworks about motion and the concepts of force and energy, in P.L. Lijnse (ed.) *The Many Faces of Teaching and Learning Mechanics*. Utrecht: GIREP/SVO/UNESCO.

Blades, D. (1997) *Procedures of Power & Curriculum Change*. New York: Peter Lang.

Brickhouse, N.W. (1990) Teachers' beliefs about the nature of science and their relationship to classroom practice. *Journal of Teacher Education*, 41: 52–62.

Brickhouse, N.W., Lowery, P. and Schultz, K. (2000) What kind of a girl does science? The construction of school science identities. *Journal of Research in Science Teaching*, 37: 441–5.

Costa, V.B. (1995) When science is 'another world': relationships between worlds of family, friends, school, and science. *Science Education*, 79: 313–33.

Costa, V.B. (1997) How teacher and students study 'all that matters' in high school chemistry. *International Journal of Science Education*, 19: 1005–23.

Cross, R. (1995) Conceptions of scientific literacy: reactionaries in ascendency in the state of Victoria. *Research in Science Education*, 25: 151–62.

Cross, R. (1997) Ideology and science teaching: teachers' discourse. *International Journal of Science Education*, 19: 607–16.

Dewey, J. (1916) *Democracy and Education: An Introduction to the Philosophy of Education*. New York: Macmillan.

Driver, R., Asoko, H., Leach, J., Mortimer, E. and Scott, P. (1994) Constructing scientific knowledge in the classroom. *Educational Researcher*, 23(7): 5–12.

Duffee, L. and Aikenhead, G.S. (1992) Curriculum change, students' evaluation, and teacher practical knowledge. *Science Education*, 76: 493–506.

Fensham, P.J. (1992) Science and technology, in P.W. Jackson (ed.) *Handbook of Research on Curriculum*. New York: Macmillan.

Fensham, P.J. (1998) The politics of legitimating and marginalizing companion meanings, in D.A. Roberts and L. Ostman (eds) *Problems of Meaning in Science Curriculum*. New York. Teachers College Press.

Gallagher, J.J. (1998) Science teaching as shared culture: an international perspective. *NARST News*, 41(3): 4.

Gaskell, P.J. (1992) Authentic science and school science. *International Journal of Science Education*, 14: 265–72.

Gee, J. (1996) *Social Linguistics and Literacies*, 2nd edn. London: Taylor & Francis.

Gibbs, W.W. and Fox, D. (1999) The false crisis in science education. *Scientific American*, 281: 86–93.

Gough, N. (1998) All around the world: science education, constructivism, and globalization. *Educational Policy*, 12: 507–24.

Gunstone, R.F. (1988) Learners in science education, in P. Fensham (ed.) *Developments and Dilemmas in Science Education*. London: Falmer.

Hurd, P.deH. (1998) *Inventing Science Education for the New Millennium*. New York: Teachers College Press.

Jegede, O.J. and Aikenhead, G.S. (1999) Transcending cultural borders: implications for science teaching. *Research in Science and Technology Education*, 17: 45–66.

Jones, A., Marshall, J., Matthews, K.M., Smith, G.H. and Smith, L.T. (1995) *Myths and Realities: Schooling in New Zealand*, 2nd edn. Palmerston, NZ: The Dunmore Press.

Kelly, G.J. and Green, J. (1998) The social nature of knowing: toward a sociocultural perspective on conceptual change and knowledge construction, in B. Guzzetti and C. Hynd (eds) *Perspectives on Conceptual Change: Multiple Ways to Understand Knowing and Learning in a Complex World*. Mahwah, NJ: Erlbaum.

Larson, J.O. (1995) Fatima's rules and other elements of an unintended chemistry curriculum. Paper presented to the American Educational Research Association Annual Meeting, San Francisco, April.

Latour, B. (1987) *Science in Action*. Cambridge, MA: Harvard University Press.

Layton, D., Jenkins, E., Macgill, S. and Davey, A. (1993) *Inarticulate Science?* Driffield: Studies in Education.

Leach, J., Driver, R., Millar, R. and Scott, P. (1997) A study of progression in learning about 'the nature of science': issues of conceptualisation and methodology. *International Journal of Science Education*, 19: 147–66.

Lederman, L. (1998) A response. *Studies in Science Education*, 31: 130–5.

Loughran, J. and Derry, N. (1997) Researching teaching for understanding: the students' perspective. *International Journal of Science Education*, 19: 925–38.

Matthews, M. (1997) James T. Robinson's account of philosophy of science and science teaching: some lessons for today from the 1960s. *Science Education*, 81: 295–315.

Medvitz, A.G. (1996) Science, schools and culture: the complexity of reform in science education. Paper presented to the 8th symposium of the International Organization for Science and Technology Education, Edmonton, Canada, August.

Meyer, K. (1998) Reflections on being female in school science: toward a praxis of teaching science. *Journal of Research in Science Teaching*, 35: 463–71.

Millar, R. and Osborne, J. (eds) (1998) *Beyond 2000: Science Education for the Future*. London: School of Education, King's College.

Mortimer, E. (1995) Conceptual change or conceptual profile change? *Science and Education*, 4: 267–85.

Ogawa, M. (1995) Science education in a multi-science perspective. *Science Education*, 79: 583–93.

Pickering, A. (ed.) (1992) *Science as Practice and Culture*. Chicago: University of Chicago Press.

Roberts, D.A. (1988) What counts as science education? In P.J. Fensham (ed.) *Development and Dilemmas in Science Education*. New York: Falmer Press.

Roth, W.-M. and McGinn, M.K. (1998) >unDELETE science education:/lives/work/ voices. *Journal of Research in Science Teaching*, 35: 399–421.

Roth, W.-M., Boutonné, S., McRobbie, C.J. and Lucas, K.B. (1999) One class, many worlds. *International Journal of Science Education*, 21: 59–75.

Science Council of Canada (1984) *Science for Every Student.* Ottawa: Science Council of Canada.

Smolicz, J.J. and Nunan, E.E. (1975) The philosophical and sociological foundations of science education: the demythologising of school science. *Studies in Science Education*, 2: 101–43.

Solomon, J. (1983) Learning about energy: how pupils think in two domains. *European Journal of Science Education*, 5: 49–59.

Solomon, J. (1987) Social influences on the construction of pupils' understanding of science. *Studies in Science Education*, 14: 63–82.

Solomon, J. (1998) The science curricula of Europe and notion of scientific culture, in D.A. Roberts and L. Ostman (eds) *Problems of Meaning in Science Curriculum.* New York: Teachers College Press.

Stairs, A. (1993/4) The cultural negotiation of indigenous education: between microethnography and model-building. *Peabody Journal of Education*, 69: 154–71.

Tobin, K. and McRobbie, C. (1997) Beliefs about the nature of science and the enacted science curriculum. *Science and Education*, 6: 355–71.

Tyson, L.M., Venville, G.J., Harrison, A.G. and Treagust, D.F. (1997) A multidimensional framework for interpreting conceptual change events in the classroom. *Science Education*, 81: 387–404.

Weinstein, M. (1998) Playing the paramecium: science education from the stance of the cultural studies of science. *Educational Policy*, 12: 484–506.

Section 3   RESEARCHING SCIENCE EDUCATION

In this final section of the book, the focus of attention is science education research itself. We asked five very experienced science educators to address some fundamental questions about the nature of research in science education, to reflect critically on its achievements, and to say what they thought its future agenda should be. We suggested that they might address some of the following more specific questions:

- What is the nature of science education research as a 'discipline'? What can it aspire to produce?
- What has science education research to date produced that offers help to classroom teachers or policymakers in making real practical decisions? Is it reasonable to expect science education research to do so? If not, is it worth continuing to do it?
- Can science education 'make progress' as a research field? If so, what sort of progress: in our understanding, in the practices of researchers, in the practices of teachers?
- What should now be the agenda for research in science education?

In Chapter 15, Gaalen Erickson reflects on the major shifts in the programme of research on student learning in science, using as a framing device Lakatos' idea of 'research programmes', with a *hard core*, a *protective belt* and *heuristic methods*. He identifies three research programmes in student learning in science, distinguished by their different hard core commitments: the Piagetian programme, the constructivist programme and the phenomenological programme. He then outlines the main ideas underpinning each programme and the issues each faces. For Erickson, the purpose of science education research is 'not only to generate new understandings and methods for inquiring into the phenomena of students learning science, but also to generate new methods for engaging in the actual practice of teaching science'. He notes that curriculum interventions based on the Piagetian programme continue to influence practice, but uses White's data on the frequency of terms used in a sample of research articles over the past three decades to show a decline in work in the Piagetian programme since the late 1980s – matched by a dramatic rise in the frequency of terms associated with the constructivist programme. Unlike some other commentators he does not see the shift of emphasis from personal to social constructivism as signifying a new research programme; both in his view share the same hard core commitments. He is less optimistic than some other recent comment-ators that a genuine theoretical synthesis is emerging within the constructiv-ist programme, but endorses Cobb's plea for a more pragmatic research approach which focuses on the improvement of classroom instruction. Erickson also sees considerable promise in the emerging phenomenological programme. Unless an overarching theoretical framework is developed, he predicts that 'the field will continue to be characterized by fragmented research methods, contested findings, and differing approaches to the develop-ment of new pedagogical perspectives'.

In Chapter 16, Richard Gunstone and Richard White focus not on how research on student learning in science has evolved, but on what it has achieved. They begin by characterizing science education research as a social science; it cannot therefore hope to produce the kind of generalizable knowledge that is characteristic of the natural sciences. Progress, they claim, is evident not in a steadily accumulating fund of agreed knowledge about science learning, but in the slow emergence of consensus about some funda-mental principles, such as that *beliefs formed from experience can impede understanding, the science concept/topic to be learned is a significant variable in teaching*, and *people construct their own meanings from what they experi-ence*. Gunstone and White identify several phases in the research effort on students' conceptions. The first was a rather eclectic set of studies of stu-dents' ideas in a range of science topics, carried out in the late 1970s and early 1980s. This was followed by a second phase in which further studies on the same science topics largely corroborated the earlier findings. In the third phase, researchers began to address the question of how to change students' conceptions. Here, Gunstone and White note, the difficulties began to mount, as the persistence of many 'alternative conceptions' became appar-ent. This may have stimulated the fourth phase, in which questions about the source and nature of alternative conceptions were raised and debated. Finally cross-age (or cohort) studies and longitudinal studies signal a fifth phase, in which the aim is to map characteristic pathways of groups and individuals as their understanding of a science topic grows.

Turning to the question of what this research effort has produced to help the science teacher (or curriculum planner), Gunstone and White identify a number of broad principles which can guide teachers and others as they reflect on their practices, citing the Programme Enhancing Effective Learn-ing (PEEL) as a prominent example. They see the future agenda taking greater account of the perspectives of learners, by exploring student perceptions on the purposes of learning (in science, and more generally), and improving our understanding of how to incorporate principles derived from research in teaching programmes, thus bridging the researcher–practitioner divide.

In Chapter 17, Piet Lijnse is rather more doubtful about the achievements of the science education research effort, asking how far it has really told us 'how to teach X better'. He takes a pragmatic view of the purposes of science education research, noting that others outside the community expect it to have something useful to say about how to teach science topics effectively. He contrasts the Anglophone tradition in science education with the continental European tradition of disciplines of 'didactics of physics' (and chemistry and biology). He sees the former as more interested in general principles, and the latter as having a stronger focus on the content that is to be taught and learned. In Lijnse's view, each science topic has to be analysed to determine what should be taught, followed by research to establish how this can be done effectively. The 'what' question he sees as largely a matter of society's preferences, which change over time; we cannot really speak of 'progress' in our answers to it. On the other hand, Lijnse argues, progress in answering the 'how' question is possible. He disagrees, however, with Fensham (see Chapter 9) that the research effort to date *has* in fact made much progress on this question, though he regards the idea of 'teaching experiments' (which Erickson discusses) as a positive development. However, he is sceptical regarding the value of intensive discussion about the philosophical basis of constructivism(s), and introduces instead the idea of 'didactical quality' as a characteristic of effective instruction. To illustrate the issues involved, he contrasts the approach taken by two teaching schemes designed to teach introductory ideas about the particulate nature of matter, one developed by the Children's Learning in Science Project (CLISP), the other by Lijnse's own group in Utrecht. He identifies a key difference between the schemes in how they interpret learners' utterances which use terms from the accepted scientific model, and argues that learners must first be led to pose problems about matter so that 'they themselves come to see the point of extending their existing conceptual knowledge, experiences and belief systems in a certain direction'. In this approach, the learners have to reflect on the nature of model-making as they consider how well their models account for observed phenomena.

Lijnse is clearly less convinced by the outcomes and directions of science education to date than Erickson or Gunstone and White. He raises questions that need, perhaps, to be taken more seriously and discussed more openly – about the real value to practitioners of the reported outcomes of science education research. In this he echoes the views of many influential voices outside the science education community. Similar questions about the impact of educational research are being increasingly asked in the UK and elsewhere. Lijnse advocates one particular kind of research programme to address this critique. Whether or not we agree with his vision of the way forward, these are questions that we need to take seriously.

The final chapter, by Paul Black, considers a different area of research in science education. Black reviews issues and research findings on testing and assessment. Drawing extensively on his own personal involvement in many of the initiatives and developments he discusses, he draws out a number of important issues concerning surveys of student performance, 'high stakes' summative assessment in the school system, and formative classroom assessment. In reviewing the work of the Assessment Performance Unit (APU) (in which Ros Driver was also involved) he highlights the contribution that assessment can make to clarifying objectives, commenting that 'when broad aims have to be operationalized in specific achievement exercises, their ambiguities are cruelly exposed'. He notes, however, that this major project made almost no impact on the public examination system in the UK. He goes on to review research which questions the reliability and validity of many of the methods used for summative testing of students. The contribution of researchers in this area he likens to 'guerrilla attacks' on outposts of an occupying army, rather than a concerted effort to take control or to secure a permanant involvement. In contrast to the research evidence which exposes the weaknesses of much summative assessment, work on formative assessment (also discussed by Bell in Chapter 3) shows consistently that this can be a major tool for improving performance.

In the course of this overview, Black notes the lack of a sense of a 'research programme' on assessment; articles on similar topics often do not cite each other. He raises some important general questions about the insulation of research domains, asking how much science education researchers know about research on the teaching and learning of other school subjects, and suggesting that researchers should budget more time for reading – and not only in their immediate area of interest. The chapter ends with an audit of the contribution of research on assessment to solving the main problems in the field. In contrast to Lijnse's evaluation of what research has added to our knowledge of pedagogy, Black clearly considers that research has added significantly to our knowledge of the effects and outcomes of assessment practices. The problem is rather that, despite a strong body of research evidence that many official policies are dysfunctional, these persist, because they satisfy other needs and requirements of powerful groups. Black ends his chapter by arguing that researchers need to try to close two 'fault lines': between researchers and teachers, and between acceptance of results in the academic community and their acceptance in the media and among those who make the policy decisions.

While communication is clearly important, the key questions raised in Section 3 are about the extent to which researchers in science education do, indeed, have 'something to say', what this 'something' might be, and how we might increase the quantity or quality of this 'something' in the future. These are questions that the science education community, of which we are all a part, ought perhaps to be putting more effort into addressing. We hope that these four chapters might help to start that discussion.

Research programmes and the student science learning literature

Gaalen Erickson

Introduction

Over 15 years ago Ros Driver and I wrote an article aimed at clarifying a number of conceptual and empirical issues in the rapidly expanding field of research on students' understanding of science (Driver and Erickson 1983). My aim in this chapter is to provide a personal perspective on the conceptual shifts that have occurred in this field over the past two decades and speculate on where it may move in the future. The aim of clarifying issues remains important, as the field still exhibits considerable 'diversity of approaches [which] has created a proliferation of terms, techniques and supporting theoretical rationales for describing students' cognitive commitments' (Driver and Erickson 1983: 39). Indeed, if anything, this diversity has increased.

Shifting perspectives on students' conceptions in science

To help identify conceptual shifts in the field, I have decided to employ one of the ideas that Ros and I used in our earlier article – that of a 'research programme', most commonly associated with Lakatos' (1970) analysis of scientific progress. We framed the earlier article around our reconstruction of 'the argument used by researchers, either implicitly or explicitly, to justify their research programme' (Driver and Erickson 1983: 39). In this chapter I will develop further some aspects of this notion of a 'research programme'.

What is a research programme?

For Lakatos (1970), a research programme consists of a cluster or series of interconnected hypotheses or theories, typically crafted over a period of time, which permit its proponents to explain existing phenomena of interest. A further function of a research programme is to point the way to new, interesting questions that need to be addressed. It is this latter heuristic, problem-solving feature of research programmes that I think has applicability to social science theories in general and to the student science learning literature in particular. I will focus on two heuristic aspects of research programmes. The first is the ability to generate new ways of understanding phenomena and hence create novel and more interesting research agendas. The second is the ability to generate new approaches for curricular organization and for teaching science concepts.

In simplified form, Lakatos argues that there are three important features that characterize a research programme: the 'hard core' commitments, the auxiliary hypotheses comprising the 'protective belt', and the 'heuristic methods'. The hard core of the programme refers to the 'irrefutable' unquestioned assumptions that are never challenged or subjected to serious inquiry. The protective belt is the active part of the programme that is frequently being put to empirical tests, getting adjusted through 'auxiliary hypotheses', and being changed in the light of persuasive empirical work. The heuristic methods are the research approaches that are used in empirical inquiries judged to be relevant to the programme. In a field of study like science education, the purpose of a research programme is not only to generate new understandings and new methods for *inquiring into the phenomena of students learning science*, but also to generate new methods *for engaging in the actual practice of teaching science*. I will use the three features to trace and examine the trajectory of the research programmes that have emerged in the science learning literature over the past 20 years.

Research programmes and the student science learning literature

So what are the research programmes in the student science learning literature and how have they changed over the past 20 years? I argue that there have been two broadly-based research programmes in this field, with a third beginning to emerge in the last few years. The first I refer to as the 'Piagetian programme', the second is the 'constructivist programme' and the third is the 'phenomenological programme'. While the first two programmes are well-known by researchers and increasingly by classroom teachers, the breadth of these categories, particularly the constructivist programme, may surprise some. Other reviewers of the field such as Eylon and Linn (1988), Farnham-Diggory (1994) and Duit and Treagust (1998) have used finer distinctions in their respective analyses. I claim that we must look for differences in the hard core components of the programmes to detect significant shifts in these perspectives, and that the categories used by these reviewers reflect differences in the protective belt of these two larger programmes.

Before discussing these three research programmes, I will clarify what I consider to be a core commitment of each. Given the focus on student learning, it is not surprising that a perspective on learning, or cognition, is a primary theoretical tenet. This perspective provides the researchers with both a language and a set of theoretical lenses through which to see and interpret the phenomena under scrutiny. In our earlier article we identified competing perspectives on learning: Piagetian views of development, information-processing views of learning, and a general perspective just beginning to coalesce, which we referred to as a 'constructivist view of learning'. Thus the perspectives on learning underlying the two dominant research programmes were already in place 20 years ago.

Unfortunately, many researchers and curriculum developers seemed to think that by embracing a particular perspective on learning they would be able to derive instructional programmes directly from it. However, as the field matured, it became apparent that a theory of learning was not in itself a sufficient foundation to develop curricular and instructional programmes. These require a much greater empirical and normative content base than is provided by any theory of learning (Millar 1989; Cobb 1994; Driver *et al.* 1994). It is important to note that this comment on the problems of overextending learning theories into the domain of instructional models is a general one which applies to all of the research programmes outlined below.

The Piagetian research programme

Virtually all reviews of research on student learning in science acknowledge the profound impact of Piaget's prodigious body of work in the field. From the early 1920s, Piaget's far-reaching research programme provided many examples of student reasoning and understanding in a large variety of science- and mathematics-related content areas. More importantly, his underlying model of cognitive development and his stage theory fitted nicely with the 'student-centred approach' to instruction and curriculum design that was being advocated at the time. Piaget's preference for a logical–mathematical description of the underlying structures of cognition also made his work attractive to mathematics and science educators.

Of all the theoretical perspectives on cognition which have informed science education research, I suspect that Piaget's research programme may have suffered the greatest misinterpretation. This is a result of many factors: the sheer volume of his writings, the opaqueness of his writing style, and his disciplinary breadth – from evolutionary biology and ethology, to philosophy, to developmental psychology. Many science education researchers during the 1960s and 1970s used Piaget's stage theory of intellectual development to generate numerous studies categorizing students into the various stages (or sub-stages) and comparing them on other measures of achievement or with success in learning particular curricular topic areas.

Hard core commitments

What are the hard core commitments that underlie Piaget's accumulated body of writings and, in turn, the work of the science educators who have drawn upon his ideas? As several researchers who have examined Piaget's work have noted (Feldman 1980; Lawson 1994; Metz 1998), he was concerned first and foremost with questions of 'genetic epistemology' (Piaget 1970). His focus was on biological factors and his central interest was the nature and growth of knowledge. The first core commitment of the Piagetian programme is to the idea of *development*. The aim is to understand how the child comes to develop complex and sophisticated ways of seeing and acting upon the world. The key word in this sentence is 'develop', which is used in contrast to 'learn'.

Feldman (1980) and others have rightly emphasized Piaget's dominant interest in the 'universal' components of cognitive development – those mental capabilities that are developed by all children who have access to a reasonable level of engagement with their physical and cultural environments. He was not, for the most part, interested in problems related to the teaching and learning of subject matter, nor was he interested in trying to accelerate the developmental process.

Two other core commitments are an *invariant stage model* of development and an *equilibration model* of conceptual growth or change. A final structural feature of Piaget's work, which emerges from all of the above commitments, is his focus on the development of *mental structures in an individual*. While there are many other facets and important theoretical contributions of Piaget's work, these seem to me to be the central ones, particularly in view of the manner in which his theory was interpreted and applied by science educators.

What are the pedagogical commitments associated with this research programme? Since Piaget's primary focus was on the development of universals, the task of generating an instructional agenda was left to those science educators who drew upon his work. Their primary strategy was to use Piaget's stage theory as an organizing principle for developing curriculum and teaching approaches intended to accelerate students' progress through the stages. Many researchers also classified students into stage categories for the purpose of comparing the effectiveness of different instructional strategies and programmes. A second important commitment was Piaget's equilibration mechanism for cognitive growth, often operationalized in terms of creating cognitive dissonance or conflict. This equilibration model was used for the development of curricular programmes as well as for designing new instructional approaches – for example, the Science Curriculum Improvement Study (SCIS 1970).

Protective belt

The protective belt of a research programme consists of those auxiliary hypotheses created to account for anomalies that arise and threaten hard core commitments. In the Piagetian programme, the most empirically exposed component was the stage theory, which was subject to considerable criticism (for example Driver 1978; Siegel and Brainerd 1978). This commitment to an invariant sequence of developmental stages, combined with Piaget's concern for identifying universal, context-independent mental structures, has created more empirical difficulties for the Piagetian programme than any other. A 'textbook example' of an auxiliary hypothesis, created to account for empirical challenges to the invariant sequence in Piaget's stage theory, was his invention of 'horizontal décalage'. According to Piaget, when a child was in the process of constructing a new operational structure, gaps (i.e. décalage) in the child's ability to apply the emergent mental structures in new settings should be expected.

A second core commitment that has been challenged is Piaget's focus on development rather than learning. Piagetian researchers in science education, with a strong interest in learning, adapted aspects of the Piagetian programme to fit their own particular research agendas (Adey and Shayer 1994; Abraham 1998).

Heuristic methods

What new approaches to research and to problems of practice were generated by the Piagetian programme? Part of the science education research agenda of the 1960s and 1970s, which focused on Piagetian stages, was the development of convenient, paper-and-pencil instruments that would enable researchers to categorize students at a given stage. While the stage categories themselves typically reflected those reported in Piaget's writings, the purpose and methods used by science educators differed dramatically from those of Piaget. Piaget's 'clinical method' involved an in-depth exploration of students' reasoning, often using counter examples and other techniques for checking the stability and degree of commitment of their response – quite unlike the favoured questionnaires.

Another genre of Piaget-inspired research emerged from the long-term work of Adey and Shayer in England. Over the past 20 years they have developed teaching materials for accelerating the growth of logical thinking in adolescents, culminating in the Cognitive Acceleration through Science Education (CASE) project (Adey and Shayer 1994). They use Piaget's schemata of formal operational thought but, unlike Piaget, argue that the teacher, the materials and the peer group play a strong mediating role. In another genre of research that draws upon Piaget's foundational studies, particularly his 'equilibration model' of cognitive growth, Lawson (1994) has included neural physiology and neural modelling in his endeavour to explain how knowledge is acquired. While acknowledging concerns expressed by others regarding the rigidity of Piaget's stage model, Lawson claims to go beyond Piaget's work on equilibration theory 'to consider neurological mechanisms involved in learning and knowing' (p. 131).

Perceived curricular and instructional applications of the Piagetian programme were reflected in a flurry of curriculum development projects, particularly in elementary science education, following the 'discovery' of Piaget in the early 1960s. In the USA, two very prominent programmes were developed using Piagetian principles – the Elementary Science Study (ESS) and the Science Curriculum Improvement Study (SCIS). In England, Nuffield Junior Science had a similar emphasis. Later a more structured programme was developed in England called 'Science 5/13', with perhaps the most explicit set of objectives tied to Piagetian stages ever produced. While many of these programmes had an implicit instructional approach built into the materials and the teacher's guides, only the SCIS programme developed a formal instructional model, which came to be known as 'the learning cycle'. This, at its most basic, consisted of three instructional phases: exploration, invention and application. This model continues to be employed in a variety of curricular contexts (Abraham 1998).

What has been the overall influence of Piaget's work on science education over the past 30 years? White (in press) presents data that examines that question. He documents the frequency of descriptive terms per 1000 entries reported in Educational Resource Information Center (ERIC) summaries over five-year periods from 1966 to 1995. The number of summaries using the word 'Piaget' or 'Piagetian' is shown in Table 15.1. The table shows a gradual increase from 1966 to 1980, followed by a tailing off over the next decade and a virtual collapse in the 1990s.

Table 15.1 Number of ERIC summaries using the word 'Piaget'

1966–70	*1971–5*	*1976–80*	*1981–5*	*1986–90*	*1991–5*
45	77	140	84	92	13

The constructivist research programme

In looking at the origins of the constructivist programme, we argued in our 1983 article that serious challenges were being mounted to the Piagetian position in the 1970s. One group of critics, led by Novak (1978), argued that Ausubel's focus on 'meaningful reception learning' (Ausubel *et al.* 1978) was a much more appropriate cognitive model for educational research and instruction than Piaget's developmental stage model. Another model, based upon the creation of content-oriented, learning hierarchies, was offered initially by Gagné (1970) and later modified by Gagné and White (1978). Yet another important development was the emergence in the 1960s of the field of cognitive science. Spurred on by the growth of computer technologies, some of the earliest information-processing models of cognition were beginning to appear. All of these perspectives on intellectual growth had one thing in common: the importance they placed on the learning of content knowledge, as opposed to Piaget's focus on the development of context independent, operational structures. While there were clearly differences between these approaches, they were all engaged in analysing how individuals learn content that is organized according to the frameworks of what might be called 'disciplinary knowledge bases'.

While the learning hierarchy work continued to attract some attention in the 1970s, its appeal faded in the 1980s and 1990s. By contrast, the field that gathered momentum was identified variously in terms of: 'alternative conceptions' (Driver and Easley 1978; Wandersee *et al.* 1994); 'misconceptions' (Helm and Novak 1983); or 'children's science' (Gilbert *et al.* 1982). Work in this research genre encompassed a diverse collection of theoretical and methodological approaches but the common element was a focus on examining students' understanding in a given conceptual domain. I am not going to review either the growth of this field or the huge literature that it has spawned, as this task has been done by many other reviewers. In addition, two comprehensive bibliographies have categorized the thousands of studies in the field (Carmichael *et al.* 1990; Pfundt and Duit 1994); and work in the genre has been presented and discussed at many conferences (notably the three international seminars held at Cornell in 1983, 1987 and 1993). There is, therefore, clear evidence of a strong field of research in a state of maturity.

Hard core commitments

Both the Piagetian and constructivist research programmes acknowledge the critical mediating role of prior knowledge in interpreting new experiences. However, constructivists focus on prior knowledge in the content domain, rather than universal, operational knowledge. A second related commitment concerns how this constructed knowledge is represented. Researchers in both groups represent this knowledge in terms of mental structures or mental models (Gentner and Stevens 1983; Gilbert and Boulter 1998) that reside in the individual's mind – although the nature of the analysis and the types of mental models proposed differ significantly. Furthermore, both groups tend to think of this knowledge as relatively well structured and fairly stable. However, in the constructivist programme, the issue of how to bring about changes in these mental structures is paramount.

Other core commitments unique to the constructivist programme relate to instructional design issues. Most researchers working in this programme are concerned with understanding how students engage with particular science content, and the nature of the relationship between the learner's prior knowledge and the learning environment. A corollary commitment, and one that might have been overly optimistic, was identified in our earlier article: 'Well-planned instruction employing teaching strategies which take account of student frameworks will result in the development of frameworks that conform more closely to school science' (Driver and Erickson 1983: 39).

Protective belt

The constructivist programme has been subjected to criticism in a number of areas, and significant 'problem shifts' (to use Lakatos' term) have occurred. Some critics, basically sympathetic to the field, were merely pointing out problems, such as the unwarranted derivation of an instructional model from a constructivist view of learning, as discussed earlier. Others rejected many of the central tenets of the programme (Matthews 1992, 1994).

Matthews' argument against constructivism was twofold. First, the strong focus on personal construction of meaning (by both students and by scientists) leads to a form of conceptual or ontological 'relativism'. Second, constructivism is really just another form of empiricism wherein students construct meaning directly from their encounters with the empirical world without any recourse to the conceptual inventions and symbols created by scientists. Both of these arguments have been addressed, primarily by Driver although she claimed (like many involved in the constructivist programme) that much of Matthews' critique came from a serious misreading of the literature (Leach 1998).

In another critique, Solomon (1994) argued that the field grew rapidly as a result of a paper by Driver and Easley (1978) which provided the necessary language and theoretical framing to initiate and sustain this growth.

But Solomon goes on to claim that constructivism is in decline because: (a) there continues to be a lack of unanimity around the best language to describe student conceptions (for example, student conceptions, alternative frameworks, children's science, misconceptions, etc.); (b) there remains a continuing debate about the nature and stability of these conceptions and whether they really are like scientists' theories; (c) efforts to design curricular packages and instructional strategies based upon the constructivist view of learning have not yet produced significant effects; and (d) the focus on individuals' construction of knowledge, as reported in many of the research studies, is incongruent with the kind of learning that occurs in most authentic settings, be it in classrooms, playgrounds or scientists' laboratories.

This latter issue of whether learning ought to be conceptualized as primarily an individual activity or as a product of more complex sociocultural processes has been debated within the constructivist research community in recent years. The appearance in the general education literature of a number of learning theorists who take a sociocultural view of learning (for example Bruner 1990; Lave and Wenger 1991; Wertsch and Toma 1995; Lave 1996) indicated that a significant shift in emphasis in theories of learning was occurring. New sub-fields of learning were also being created, such as 'situated cognition' (Brown *et al.* 1989; Hennessy, 1993).

Over the past ten years there has been a move toward 'social constructivism' (Driver *et al.* 1994; Roth 1995; Duit and Treagust 1998). These changes are, in my view, an adjustment in the protective belt of this programme – accompanied by shifts in the research methods and settings used and in the language and concepts employed to interpret the phenomena of student learning. While some might claim this change represents a new research programme, the core commitments remain unchanged and so I include this work within the constructivist research programme.

Other criticisms have centred on an over-reliance on rational models to the exclusion of important affective components of cognition (Simpson *et al.* 1994; Alsop 1999). This issue appeared most explicitly in the criticism of the conceptual change model (Posner *et al.* 1982) by Pintrich *et al.* (1993). There has also been a growing interest in exploring alternative ways of thinking about learning science which do not presuppose western norms of rationality as a starting point (see Chapter 14; Aikenhead 1996; Cobern and Aikenhead 1998).

Heuristic methods

The constructivist research programme introduced a number of important conceptual and methodological advances, the most notable being the recognition that all learners, even very young children, are capable of constructing plausible conceptions while engaging with their physical and social worlds. While Piaget's clinical interview was a common method used by a number of the early researchers in the field, many new techniques for exploring students' understanding were invented (see White and Gunstone 1992 for an excellent elaboration of these methods).

The substantive findings of the numerous studies that have probed student understanding have provided a strong foundation both for theorizing about the learning process and for developing pedagogical programmes aimed at improving student learning in science. From the outset it was clear that pedagogical issues were critical for most researchers in this tradition, with many studies involving the design of instructional sequences and curricular materials. More recently, the constructivist perspective has been one of the primary organizing frameworks for a popular science textbook series used in Canada and the USA called *SciencePlus* (McFadden *et al.* 1990) and two methods textbooks for elementary science teaching (Bloom 1997; Ebenezer and Haggerty 1999).

The shift from a focus on individual learning to more sociocultural forms of learning has resulted in new pedagogical approaches. Those who focus on the cultural aspects of learning argue that educational settings ought to foster a type of enculturation into the practice of scientific communities (for example Nespor 1994; Lave 1996), whereas those who focus more on the social aspects of learning tend to prefer the establishment of dynamic, collaborative, learning environments where the focus is on group rather than individual learning (for example Brown 1992; Bereiter and Scardamalia 1993). This difference in instructional focus between the individual and the group was at the heart of a series of three articles in *Educational Researcher* by Bereiter (1994), Cobb (1994) and Driver *et al.* (1994).

As with the Piagetian Programme, White's (in press) compilation of the frequency of terms used in ERIC summaries shows trends in the constructivist programme (see Table 15.2). Comparing these figures with those on the Piagetian programme, it seems clear that the constructivist programme has gained a dominant position in the student science learning literature.

Table 15.2 Number of ERIC summaries using terms associated with the constructivist programme

Terms used	1971–5	1976–80	1981–5	1986–90	1991–5
Constructivism	0	2	3	57	214
Conception or misconception	24	36	134	269	355
Analogies or metaphors	24	34	58	69	135

The phenomenological research programme

The emergence of the phenomenological programme can be traced in part to criticisms of the constructivist programme. These critiques were aimed at the core commitments and so represent in my view an endeavour to develop a new and unique research programme. The two core commitments which these critics reject are: that the task of the researcher is to describe the evolving mental models being constructed by the learner; and that the locus of inquiry should primarily be on the individual cognizing agent who is responding and adapting to his or her personal, social and cultural contexts.

For phenomenologists, learning is not an act of construction of mental structures, but rather consists of a set of relationships between the learner and the world. One of the tasks of phenomenological researchers, then, is to focus on illuminating the nature of these relationships. Although a number of different phenomenological approaches have emerged in the educational literature in the past 20 years, I will only discuss in detail one of these approaches, called *phenomenography* (Marton and Booth 1997), because this research community has a longer history than most others and its members have investigated a number of topics relevant to science education. I will also allude briefly to an emergent approach called *enactivism* (Varela *et al.* 1991; Davis *et al.* 1996; Davis *et al.* in press), which I think has considerable potential, but is still in the early stages of development in the educational literature. Both approaches share some important core commitments, although they also draw upon different intellectual literatures.

Hard core commitments

At the centre of phenomenological approaches is a commitment to understanding how people experience the world and learn to act in the world. This perspective on learning is different from that of the Piagetian and the constructivist programmes in that these earlier programmes posited an independent, external world and that learners progressively develop or construct more sophisticated internal models of that world. However, the phenomenological programme rejects this notion of a *person–world dualism*. As Marton and Booth (1997: 122) put it: 'being located neither in the subject nor in the world, being neither psychological nor physical, being neither mind nor matter, experiences do comprise an *internal relationship* between the subject and the world, and that is their fundamental characteristic: An experience is of its essence *nondualistic*' (original emphasis).

Rejection of this dualism goes against the grain of much western intellectual thought, which has long searched for reliable and valid ways of making claims about the external world. It is interesting to note, therefore, that

Varela *et al.* (1991) look to Buddhism as a source of ideas about non-dualist ways of thinking about experience in our world. Since they are interested in cognition, and creating a 'middle space' between contemporary work in cognitive science and phenomenology, they frame the issue of dualism from the perspective of a cognitive scientist:

> A phenomenologically inclined cognitive scientist reflecting on the origins of cognition might reason thus: Minds awaken in a world. We did not design our world. We simply found ourselves with it; we awoke both to ourselves and to the world we inhabit. We come to reflect on that world as we grow and live. We reflect on a world that is not made, but found, and yet it is also our structure that enables us to reflect upon this world. Thus in reflection we find ourselves in a circle; we are in a world that seems to be there before reflection begins, but that world is not separate from us.
>
> (Varela *et al.* 1991: 3)

Given this non-dualist position, how do phenomenologists construe learning and what implications does it have for pedagogy? Marton and Booth's response to this question is that learning is a process of coming to experience, and subsequently *to see*, the world in different ways. They distinguish their phenomenological stance from the constructivist research programme position on learning by referring to learning as a process of constituting (or often reconstituting) the world rather than constructing representations of the world. Because these ideas and the language used to express them are quite new, I will quote Marton and Booth (1997: 139) at some length on this point. For them, experience is:

> ... generally a mediated experience: We do not face the phenomenon as such, but the phenomenon as described by others. To an increasing degree we see the world in terms of patterns of a shared culture through a shared language. Our own world becomes increasingly the world of others as well, and the latter world, the world as already experienced, is a constitutive force in learning just as the individual's constitutive acts are. This is an important difference compared with individual constructivism, which sees knowledge as being an individual construction – within the individual. We also find a difference if we make a comparison with social constructivism, which sees the social, the cultural, the situational outside the individual as the fabric of knowledge ... According to the view we are presenting, learning takes place, knowledge is born, by a change in something in the world as experienced by a person. The new way of experiencing something is constituted in the person-world relationships and involves both. .... Learning is mostly a matter of reconstituting the already constituted world.

What are the pedagogical commitments that emerge from this phenomenological stance? Marton and Booth identify two principles of 'learning to experience'. They refer to these principles as:

- the relevance structure of the situation;
- the architecture of variation.

The relevance structure entails not only the learner becoming aware of the relevant features of the situation, but also learning which aspects of the situation appear to be more or less relevant to the aims or purpose of the activity. If learning constitutes a change in one's capability to experience a phenomenon, then we must have some account of what is required to bring about this change. Marton and Booth argue that this 'mechanism is variation'.[1] Further they posit that the sources of this variation may come from within the individual – for example, a type of 'reflective variation'; or it may come from without – for example, from alternative ways of experiencing a phenomenon offered by other participants in the setting. These sources for creating an effective learning environment are reminiscent of those identified earlier under the constructivist programme.

Protective belt

Since the phenomenological programme is relatively new in the field, it has not been subject to any sustained criticism in the area of student science learning. However, Marton and his colleagues at the University of Göteborg have been developing their 'phenomenographic perspective' for over 20 years, and several years ago a collection of papers (Dall' Alba and Hasselgren 1996) critically examined the accumulated body of work in this tradition. There were several common themes to these criticisms. Summarized briefly they are:

- the need to develop and clarify the ontological and epistemological assumptions underlying phenomenography;
- the need to obtain consistency between aims, ontology, epistemology and methodology;
- the need to consider the social and discursive nature of human experience as part of the research process; and
- the need to show a stronger link between phenomenography and pedagogy.

These criticisms are fairly general in nature and most could be raised with virtually any research agenda. Since this research programme is still emerging and these papers were published quite recently, there has not been sufficient opportunity to determine whether these critiques have had any impact on the phenomenographic programme. Marton (1996) did respond to a number of these issues in a concluding paper in this collection, and with Booth he has outlined a more comprehensive position on pedagogy (Marton and Booth 1997), possibly in response to the last point above.

Heuristic methods

Interestingly, the primary data collection method used by phenomenographers is similar to that of the earlier research programmes – the in-depth clinical interview. However, their methods of analysis and the way in which they interpret the interview data are very different (Johansson *et al.* 1985; Marton 1988). Rather than positing mental structures that have been constructed by the students, the phenomenographic approach identifies, qualitatively, different ways of experiencing the world. These variations in the way people experience a given phenomenon are then depicted as 'categories of description'. The researcher's task is to depict as complete a set of categories as possible, given the particularities of the phenomenon and the participants, but recognizing that this set will never be exhaustive.

A further crucial difference between the phenomenological programme and earlier research programmes is that individuals are not placed in particular categories; it is the relationship between the individual and the setting that is being mapped and this relationship can change dramatically for an individual, even within the course of the same interview (cf. Linder and Erickson 1989). Thus, phenomenography does not suffer from the problems of creating rigid descriptions of cognitive functioning, as did the earlier programmes. Linder (1993) takes this feature of phenomenography to be one of its great strengths as he argues against a view of conceptual change whereby one conception is changed in favour of another. Rather, he posits that we should aim to enhance students' capabilities to 'appreciate' the variability of conceptions (i.e. different ways of experiencing the world) and to recognize which way is most appropriate for the context and purpose at hand.

The Göteborg group has undertaken studies on a range of conceptual domains such as density, force, matter, the mole concept and motion. One of the topic areas studied most comprehensively by the group is the mole concept (Lybeck *et al.* 1988; Tullberg *et al.* 1994). This work was used to develop a very effective teaching sequence that enabled both teachers and students to explore and appreciate the different ways in which the mole concept can be interpreted and used in solving chemistry problems (Tullberg 1998).

While there are a limited number of studies which have carefully examined the pedagogical dimensions of the phenomenological programme (Davis 1996; Sumara 1996; Tullberg 1998; Kass and MacDonald 1999; Davis *et al.* in press), some important features distinguish this pedagogical programme from those arising from the earlier research programmes. Given the emphasis upon experiencing the world in ever more complex ways,

> teaching seems to be less about helping students to *know* what they don't know and more about helping them to *notice* what they haven't noticed. Teaching is about affecting perception – that is, about pointing to various aspects of the world in a deliberate attempt to foster different habits of perception/interpretation ... It also involves a study of perspectives, positionings, and points of view.
>
> (Davis *et al.* in press: 25)

The task of the teacher is therefore to establish a pedagogical environment that encourages students to compare and contrast present experiences with previously remembered ones, in order to create novel interpretations of these experiences. Further, the teacher must be prepared deliberately to disrupt 'students' everyday habits of mind and practice' (Davis *et al.* in press: 180) so as to encourage them to engage in these creative acts of invention.

Some concluding remarks

In this chapter I set out to document how the field of students' science learning has evolved over the past 20 years and to identify some of the issues that have emerged. I have done this, in part, by conjecturing that there has been a shift in research programmes over this period that has resulted in changes in preferred theoretical perspectives, methodological practices and substantive findings in this research community. Unfortunately there is very little evidence, that I am aware of, which has systematically examined concomitant changes in practice in the science teaching community. The evidence available regarding any such shifts is anecdotal at best or from secondary sources, such as curriculum or policy documents.[2]

What is clear is that there have been some significant changes in the ways in which the research on teaching has been conducted. As with the changes in research methods aimed at describing student learning, research on teaching has become much more sophisticated, more comprehensive and more complex. In contrast to the earlier designs where a two- or three-week module was aimed at teaching a particular concept, more recent classroom studies recognize the inherent complexity of classroom learning, by foregrounding the important role played by linguistic and cognitive exchanges between all of the participants in a classroom setting, and acknowledging that the kind of learning outcomes that should be assessed require a significant amount of time to nurture and to assess. These shifts in the nature of classroom studies emerge from the newer theoretical perspectives, which focus on the 'sociolinguistic environment' of science learning.

The road ahead

While the field of student science learning has undergone many changes over the past 20 years, many theoretical and methodological issues remain problematic. I have argued above that the constructivist programme has dominated much of the research literature on student learning over the past 20 years. Nevertheless there is still an uneasy tension between those advocating a focus on mapping the mental structures of individuals and those arguing for more holistic methods and descriptions of the social co-construction of knowledge, focusing on the enculturation of students into a community of practice. Cobb (1995) has endeavoured to bring these two approaches together in what he refers to as 'an emergent perspective'. He argues that researchers ought to take a more pragmatic approach to their work and focus on the improvement of classroom instruction, rather than developing a theory of cognition or learning. On the other hand diSessa (1991) makes a plea for becoming more 'theoretically attentive [in our] practice of educational research' (p. 221). He even outlines a number of heuristic strategies for attending more to the theoretical commitments in our research. Given my endeavours in this chapter, where the theoretical core commitments played a crucial role in distinguishing between research programmes, I am clearly sympathetic to diSessa's concerns. However, we must also attend to Cobb's concern for the improvement of classroom instruction. Fortunately these two initiatives are compatible, as is nicely illustrated in a forthcoming text by Davis *et al.* (in press).

It is encouraging to see an increasing trend towards much more classroom-based research over the past 20 years. However, I think that we need to become much more systematic and deliberate in our efforts. A very promising recent movement in classroom-based research is towards what have been referred to as 'design experiments' (Brown 1992; Hawkins and Collins in press) or 'teaching experiments' (Cobb 1994, 1995; Cobb and Yackel 1995). What distinguishes these experimental approaches from most of the current classroom-based studies in the field are the efforts to make explicit the design principles used, and to develop a cumulative literature around the use of this type of approach to educational research.

Another promising trend, in my view, is for practising teachers to become more active in researching their own practices and their own classrooms (Loughran and Northfield 1996; Mitchell and Mitchell 1997; Loughran 1999; Mitchell 1999). Until recently, much of the classroom-based research reported in the literature was initiated and supported by university researchers (for example much of the classroom-based work of the Children's Learning in Science Project (CLISP) and Roth's work). While this is an important first stage of working with and empowering classroom teachers, the power to make decisions about the object of inquiry and the methods of inquiry has to shift significantly in the direction of the classroom teacher. We need to develop much more equitable and sophisticated models of collaborative inquiry than the ones that are currently in use (Hoban and Erickson 1998).

Finally, I think that we are at a stage in both the research literature on students' conceptions and the emerging classroom-based literature on student learning in science where some serious consolidation of previous results needs to be undertaken. This synthesis of studies needs to move well beyond the important bibliographic work that has already been done in the field, to try and bring some conceptual and pedagogical coherence to findings that have been reported using different methods and very different educational contexts. Two important orientating frameworks need to be revealed by any reviewers undertaking such a task. The first is an explicit statement of the theoretical commitments being used by the reviewer; the second is the pedagogical perspective being used to inform this synthesis. Some synthetic efforts of this nature have occurred – for example, the earlier publication by Driver *et al.* (1985) and a later one by Fensham *et al.* (1994). The former used an implicit constructivist framework while in the latter text it was explicit. Nonetheless, I think that much more sustained activity focused on particular content domains with explicit orientating frameworks would be most worthwhile.

In concluding this chapter, I am not as optimistic as Wandersee *et al.* (1994) who claimed that 'the emerging constructivist synthesis appears to be gaining wide support and may become the first broad-based research perspective in the field. It has already begun to be "translated" for science teachers and is now affecting classroom practice' (p. 198). I think that the 'alternative conceptions' literature has become somewhat moribund (to borrow a term from Schwab) and I certainly do not see any sustained evidence of changes in classroom practice. Rather, I concur with a number of the generalizations constructed by Wandersee *et al.* (1994) from a survey of a group of 'leading researchers' regarding future research in the field. Some of these generalizations (for example, the need to *explore the cultural dimensions of student learning*, and the move to a *focus on conceptual change*) have already been acted upon (cf. Chapter 14; Cobern and Aikenhead 1998; Hewson *et al.* 1998). Others (for example, the need for a *well developed theoretical foundation*, a stronger focus on *integration of research findings*, and on *classroom processes and practices*) are still largely unfulfilled.

In a recent review of the student learning literature, Duit and Treagust (1998: 3) acknowledge the tension between the personal and social construction of knowledge viewpoints but conclude:

the rival positions emphasise different aspects of the learning process. Further research should not focus on the differences but present an inclusive view of learning and conceptualise the different positions as complementary features that allow researchers to address the complex process of learning more adequately than from a single position.

I think that this 'non-competitive' option neglects the important role that is played by the underlying theoretical commitments of the researchers, as noted in my analysis above. Unless efforts are made to develop an encompassing conceptual framework on student learning, as Cobb (1995) and Davis *et al.* (in press) are doing, then I predict the field will continue to be characterized by fragmented research methods, contested findings and differing approaches to the development of new pedagogical perspectives. In my view, the way forward is to consider carefully the more holistic position being advanced by those advocating a phenomenological research programme. These researchers argue that the distinction between the individual and their social context is a spurious one, as is the body–mind dualism. The conceptual and empirical work that has begun in this emergent research programme warrants careful attention by the science education community in the years ahead.

Notes

1 A similar mechanism is posited by Stephen Gould (1996) for the changes which occur in biological organisms over time, though he refers to it as a 'principle of diversity'.
2 For example, there has been a shift in focus from the structure of content knowledge towards student inquiry and the ability to communicate scientific ideas. This is manifested in the USA in several 'standards' documents (AAAS 1993; NRC 1996). In England it has been captured in the National Curriculum (DFEE/QCA 1999) as one 'attainment target'.

References

AAAS (American Association for the Advancement of Science (1993) *Benchmarks for Scientific Literacy*. Washington, DC: AAAS.
Abraham, M. (1998) The learning cycle approach as a strategy for instruction in science, in B.J. Fraser and K.G. Tobin (eds) *International Handbook of Science Education*, pp. 513–24. Dordrecht: Kluwer Academic Publishers.
Adey, P. and Shayer, M. (1994) *Really Raising Standards: Cognitive Intervention and Academic Achievement*. London: Routledge.
Aikenhead, G.S. (1996) Science education: border-crossing into the subculture of science. *Studies in Science Education*, 27: 1–52.
Alsop, S. (1999) Testing the temperature: exploring the affective domain in science education. Paper presented at the Annual Meeting of the Canadian Society for the Study of Education, Sherbrook, Quebec, June.
Ausubel, D., Novak, J. and Hanesian, H. (1978) *Educational Psychology: a Cognitive View*. New York: Holt, Rinehart & Winston.
Bereiter, C. (1994) Constructivism, socioculturalism and Popper's World 3. *Educational Researcher*, 23(7): 21–3.

Bereiter, C. and Scardamalia, M. (1993) *Surpassing Ourselves: An Inquiry into the Nature and Implications of Expertise*. Chicago: Open Court.

Bloom, J. (1997) *Creating a Classroom Community of Young Scientists*. Toronto: Irwin.

Brown, A. (1992) Design experiments: theoretical and methodological challenges in creating complex interventions. *Journal of the Learning Sciences*, 2(2): 141–78.

Brown, J.S., Collins, A. and Duguid, P. (1989) Situated cognition and the culture of learning. *Educational Researcher*, 18(1): 32–42.

Bruner, J. (1990) *Acts of Meaning*. Cambridge, MA: Harvard University Press.

Carmichael, P., Driver, R., Holding, B., Phillips, I., Twigger, D. and Watts, M. (1990) *Research on Students' Conceptions in Science: A Bibliography*. Leeds: Centre for Studies in Science and Mathematics Education.

Cobb, P. (1994) Where is the mind? Constructivist and sociocultural perspectives on mathematical development. *Educational Researcher*, 23(7): 13–20.

Cobb, P. (1995) Continuing the conversation: a response to Smith. *Educational Researcher*, 24(7): 25–7.

Cobb, P. and Yackel, E. (1995) Constructivist, emergent, and sociocultural perspectives in the context of developmental research. Paper presented at the annual meeting of the North American Chapter of the International Group for the Psychology of Mathematics Education, Columbus, Ohio, May.

Cobern, W.W. and Aikenhead, G.S. (1998) Cultural aspects of learning science, in B.J. Fraser and K.G. Tobin (eds) *International Handbook of Science Education*, pp. 39–52. Dordrecht: Kluwer Academic Publishers.

Dall' Alba, G. and Hasselgren, B. (eds) (1996) *Reflections on Phenomenography: Toward a Methodology?* Göteborg, Sweden: Acta Universitatis Gothoburgensis.

Davis, B. (1996) *Teaching Mathematics: Toward a Sound Alternative*. New York: Garland.

Davis, B., Sumara, D. and Kieren, T. (1996) Cognition, co-emergence, curriculum. *Journal of Curriculum Studies*, 28(2): 151–69.

Davis, B., Sumara, D. and Luce-Kapler, R. (in press) *Engaging Minds: Learning and Teaching in a Complex World*. Mahwah, NJ: Erlbaum.

DFEE/QCA (Department for Education and Employment/Qualifications and Curriculum Authority) (1999) *Science. The National Curriculum for England*. London: DFEE/QCA.

diSessa, A. (1991) If we want to get ahead, we should get some theories, in *Proceedings of the 13th Annual Meeting of the Psychology of Mathematics Education, Vol. 1*. Blacksburg, VA: Psychology of Mathematics Education Group.

Driver, R. (1978) When is a stage not a stage? A critique of Piaget's theory of cognitive development and its application to science education. *Educational Research*, 21(1): 54–61

Driver, R. and Easley, J. (1978) Pupils and paradigms: a review of literature related to concept development in adolescent science students. *Studies in Science Education*, 5: 61–84.

Driver, R. and Erickson, G. (1983) Theories-in-action: Some theoretical and empirical issues in the study of students' conceptual frameworks in science. *Studies in Science Education*, 10: 37–60.

Driver, R., Guesne, E. and Tiberghien, A. (1985) *Children's Ideas in Science*. Buckingham: Open University Press.

Driver, R., Asoko, H., Leach, J., Mortimer, E.F. and Scott, P. (1994) Constructing scientific knowledge in the classroom. *Educational Researcher*, 23(7): 5–12.

Duit, R. and Treagust, D. (1998) Learning in science – from behaviourism towards social constructivism and beyond, in B.J. Fraser and K.G. Tobin (eds) *International Handbook of Science Education*, pp. 3–25. Dordrecht: Kluwer Academic Publishers.

Ebenezer, J. and Haggerty, S. (1999) *Becoming a Secondary School Science Teacher*. Upper Saddle River, NJ: Merrill.

Eylon, B.-S. and Linn, M.C. (1988) Learning and instruction: an examination of four research perspectives in science education. *Review of Educational Research*, 58(3): 251–301.

Farnham-Diggory, S. (1994) Paradigms of knowledge and instruction. *Review of Educational Research*, 64(3): 463–77.

Feldman, D. (1980) *Beyond Universals in Cognitive Development*. Norwood, NJ: Ablex.

Fensham, P., Gunstone, R. and White, R. (eds) (1994) *The Content of Science: A Constructivist Approach to its Teaching and Learning*. London: Falmer.

Gagné, R. (1970) *Conditions of Learning*. New York: Holt, Rinehart & Winston.

Gagné, R. and White, R. (1978) Memory structures and learning outcomes. *Review of Educational Research*, 48(2): 187–222.

Gentner, D. and Stevens, A. (1983) *Mental Models*. Mahwah, NJ: Erlbaum.

Gilbert, J., Osborne, R. and Fensham, P. (1982) Children's science and its consequences for teaching. *Science Education*, 66(4): 623–33.

Gilbert, J.K. and Boulter, C.J. (1998) Learning science through models and modelling, in B.J. Fraser and K.G. Tobin (eds) *International Handbook of Science Education*, pp. 53–66. Dordrecht: Kluwer Academic Publishers.

Gould, S. (1996) *Full House: The Spread of Excellence from Plato to Darwin*. New York: Harmony Books.

Hawkins, J. and Collins, A. (eds) (in press) *Design Experiments: Using Technology to Restructure Schools*. New York: Cambridge University Press.

Helm, H. and Novak, J. (1983) *Proceedings of the First International Seminar on Student Misconceptions in Science and Mathematics*. Ithaca, NY: Cornell University, Department of Education.

Hennessy, S. (1993) Situated cognition and cognitive apprenticeship: implications for classroom learning. *Studies in Science Education*, 22: 1–41.

Hewson, P.W., Beeth, M.E. and Thorley, N.R. (1998) Teaching for conceptual change, in B.J. Fraser and K.G. Tobin (eds) *International Handbook of Science Education*, pp. 199–218. Dordrecht: Kluwer Academic Publishers.

Hoban, G. and Erickson, G. (1998) Frameworks for sustaining professional learning. Paper presented at the Australasian Science Education Research Conference, Darwin, Australia, July.

Johansson, B., Marton, F. and Svensson, L. (1985) An approach to describing learning as change between qualitatively different conceptions, in L. West and L. Pines (eds) *Cognitive Structure and Conceptual Change*, pp. 233–57. New York: Academic Press.

Kass, H. and MacDonald, L. (1999) The learning contribution of student self-directed building activity in science. *Science Education*, 83(4): 449–71.

Lakatos, I. (1970) *The Methodology of Scientific Research Programmes: Philosophical Papers, Vol. 1* (edited by J. Worrall and G. Currie). Cambridge: Cambridge University Press.

Larkin, J., McDermott, J., Simon, D. and Simon, H. (1980) Expert and novice performance in solving physics problems. *Science*, 208: 1335–42.

Lave, J. (1996) Teaching, as learning, in practice. *Mind Culture and Activity: An International Journal*, 3(3): 149–64.

Lave, J. and Wenger, E. (1991) *Situated Learning: Legitimate Peripheral Performance*. New York: Cambridge University Press.

Lawson, A.E. (1994) Research on the acquisition of science knowledge: epistemological foundations of cognition, in D. Gabel (ed.) *Handbook of Research on Science Teaching and Learning*, pp. 131–76. New York: Macmillan.

Leach, J. (1998) Rosalind Driver (1941–1997): a tribute to her contribution to research in science education, in M. Méheut and G. Rebmann (eds) *Theory, Methodology and Results of Research in Science Education: Proceedings of the Fourth European Science Education Summer School*, pp. 12–29. Paris: Université Paris 7.

Linder, C. (1993) A challenge to conceptual change. *Science Education*, 77(3): 293–300.

Linder, C. and Erickson, G. (1989) A study of tertiary physics students' conceptualizations of sound. *International Journal of Science Education*, 11(5): 491–501.

Loughran, J. (1999) Researching teaching for understanding, in J. Loughran (ed.) *Researching Teaching: Methodologies and Practices for Understanding Pedagogy*, pp. 1–9. London: Falmer.

Loughran, J. and Northfield, J. (1996) *Opening the Classroom Door: Teacher, Researcher, Learner*. London: Falmer.

Lybeck, L., Marton, F., Strömdahl, H. and Tullberg, A. (1988) The phenomenography of the 'mole concept' in chemistry, in P. Ramsden (ed.) *Improving Learning: New Perspectives*, pp. 81–108. London: Kogan Page.

McFadden, C., Armour, N., Moore, A. and Morrison, E. (1990) *SciencePlus: Technology and Society*. Toronto: Harcourt Brace Jovanovich.

Marton, F. (1988) Phenomenography: exploring different conceptions of reality, in D.M. Fetterman (ed.) *Qualitative Approaches to Evaluation in Education*, pp. 176–205. London: Praeger.

Marton, F. (1996) Cognosco ergo sum – reflections on reflections, in G. Dall' Alba and B. Hasselgren (eds) *Reflections on Phenomenography: Toward a Methodology?* pp. 163–87. Göteborg, Sweden: Acta Universitatis Gothoburgensis.

Marton, F. and Booth, S. (1997) *Learning and Awareness*. Mahwah, NJ: Erlbaum.

Matthews, M. (1992) Constructivism and empiricism: an incomplete divorce. *Research in Science Education*, 22: 299–307.

Matthews, M. (1994) Discontent with constructivism. *Studies in Science Education*, 24: 165–72.

Metz, K.E. (1998) Scientific inquiry within reach of young children, in B.J. Fraser and K.G. Tobin (eds) *International Handbook of Science Education*, pp. 81–96. Dordrecht: Kluwer Academic Publishers.

Millar, R. (1989) Constructive criticisms. *International Journal of Science Education*, 11(5): 587–96.

Mitchell, I. (1999) Bridging the gap between research and practice, in J. Loughran (ed.) *Researching Teaching: Methodologies and Practices for Understanding Pedagogy*, pp. 44–64. London: Falmer.

Mitchell, I. and Mitchell, J. (1997) *Stories of Reflective Teaching: A Book of PEEL Cases*. Melbourne: PEEL Publishing.

Nespor, J. (1994) *Knowledge in Motion: Space, Time and Curriculum in Undergraduate Physics and Management.* London: Falmer.

Novak, J. (1978) An alternative to Piagetian psychology for science and mathematics education. *Studies in Science Education,* 5: 1–30.

NRC (National Research Council) (1996) *National Science Education Standards.* Washington, DC: National Academy Press.

Pfundt, H. and Duit, R. (1994) *Bibliography: Students' Alternative Frameworks and Science Education,* 4th edn. Kiel: IPN.

Piaget, J. (1970) *Genetic Epistemology.* New York: Columbia University Press.

Pintrich, P.R., Marx, R.W. and Boyle, R.A. (1993) Beyond cold conceptual change: the role of motivational beliefs and classroom contextual factors in the process of conceptual change. *Review of Educational Research,* 63(2): 167–99.

Posner, G.J., Strike, K.A., Hewson, P.W. and Gertzog, W.A. (1982) Accommodation of a scientific conception: toward a theory of conceptual change. *Science Education,* 66(2): 211–27.

Roth, W.-M. (1995) *Authentic School Science: Knowing and Learning in Open-inquiry Laboratories.* Dordrecht: Kluwer Academic Publishers.

SCIS (1970) *Science Curriculum Improvement Study.* Chicago: Rand-McNally.

Siegel, L. and Brainerd, C. (eds) (1978) *Alternatives to Piaget: Critical Essays on the Theory.* New York: Academic Press.

Simpson, R., Koballa, T. and Oliver, S. (1994) Research on the affective dimension of science learning, in D. Gabel (ed.) *Handbook of Research on Science Teaching and Learning,* pp. 211–34. New York: Macmillan.

Solomon, J. (1994) The rise and fall of constructivism. *Studies in Science Education,* 23: 1–19.

Sumara, D. (1996) *Private Readings in Public: Schooling the Literary Imagination.* New York: Peter Lang.

Tullberg, A. (1998) 'Teaching the mole: a phenomenographic inquiry into the didactics of chemistry', doctoral dissertation. University of Göteborg.

Tullberg, A., Strömdahl, H. and Lybeck, L. (1994) Students' conceptions of 1 mol and educators' conceptions of how they teach 'the mole'. *International Journal of Science Education,* 16(2): 145–56.

Varela, F., Thompson, E. and Rosch, E. (1991) *The Embodied Mind: Cognitive Science and Human Experience.* Cambridge, MA: MIT Press.

Wandersee, J.H., Mintzes, J.J. and Novak, J.D. (1994) Research on alternative conceptions in science, in D. Gabel (ed.) *Handbook of Research on Science Teaching and Learning,* pp. 177–210. New York: Macmillan.

Wertsch, J. and Toma, C. (1995) Discourse and social dimensions of knowledge and classroom teaching, in L. Steffe and J. Gale (eds) *Constructivism in Education,* pp. 159–75. Hillsdale, NJ: Erlbaum.

White, R. (in press) The revolution in research on science teaching, in V. Richardson (ed.) *Handbook of Research on Teaching.*

White, R. and Gunstone, R. (1992) *Probing Understanding.* London: Falmer.

16 Goals, methods and achievements of research in science education

Richard Gunstone and Richard White

Introduction

The central issues we wish to address in this chapter concern the nature of science education research as a discipline, the nature of progress (if any) in this research, and the question of what the agenda for the field ought now to be. In considering the second and third of these, we will restrict our focus to student learning of science. Our aim is not to trace the conceptual shifts in this field of research (that task is undertaken by Erickson in Chapter 15), but rather to place the growth of research on students' alternative conceptions in science in the context of its antecedents, and then to derive some general principles that are evident from this work.

The discipline of science education

A cursory glance at the titles of journal articles could give the impression that science education divides into diverse categories. There are studies of curricula, teaching styles, behaviour in laboratories, motivation, students' beliefs, classroom management and many other topics. We see that one theme, however, unites all. The single purpose behind the diversity is to discover how to bring students to understand concepts and natural phenomena in the terms that scientists use. Even the most apparently esoteric study shares the goal of improving learning. Science education is about the practice of teaching and learning.

A second unifying characteristic is that science education concerns the understanding of specific content. In this it differs from general studies of the psychology of learning, in which the content is merely a vehicle and not of interest in itself. In science education, content is a vital variable. Content is the factor which has given science education an identity distinct from education in general.

Does science education merit the title of 'discipline'? Disciplines are coherent collections of principles. In some discipline areas, most obviously the natural sciences, principles, when sufficiently confirmed by investigations, become laws. Science education has not yet arrived at laws. As with other social sciences, the nature and complexity of its variables make it highly likely that laws will forever evade it. Examples of this are the variables of context and time. Not only are these complex alone, they interact – contexts change with time (among other things). Any formulation of a law in science education will initially be embedded in some particular context. Over time that context will change, and thus the law may no longer be applicable. Even the generation of understanding sufficient to result in the postulation of a law may result in the context of the law being changed by that greater understanding.

The extent to which laws are an appropriate criterion to apply to consideration of whether a field of study merits the label 'discipline' depends on the nature of the knowledge claims that that area can reasonably make. In this regard science education is distinct from science. Another closely related distinction between science education and science is in the nature of theories and the roles these play in the development of the field. While the worth of theories in all disciplines is judged by their explanatory and predictive value, the nature of this value is different in different disciplines. Much of science values theories that provide broad explanations, and that provide predictions that can be framed in precise mathematical terms. Science education at the current stage of its development cannot do this, and, again for reasons of complexity and variation in its variables, is unlikely ever to be able to do so, at least for units such as single school classes or single school populations. Many writers have pointed to the inappropriateness of seeing educational research in terms of the extent to which prediction and control result (for example Gage 1989; Darling-Hammond and Snyder 1992). A failure to consider this fundamental difference between the nature of scientific theories and the theories of science education is damaging to science education.

The notion of causality provides a good summary of these issues. Some years ago we wrote the following in comparing notions of causality in science and in science teaching. The same statement can be applied to comparisons of cause in science and science education research, and to both empirical and analytical research.

Conceptions of cause that pervade science and much school teaching and learning of science are often monistic (focus on unity) and absolutist (invariant). That is, there is a striving to discover the *one* correct explanation of a particular scientific phenomenon, the *one* most elegant procedure for testing an hypothesis, and so on. The veracity and applicability of such explanations or procedures are taken to transcend time, context, and, for some 'universal laws', content. Unlike science itself, however, cause in [science] teaching and learning is unlikely to be unitary and invariant. It is much more likely to be multiple (pluralistic) and content-, context-, and time-dependent (relativistic).

(Baird *et al.* 1991: 181)

We see science education then as a discipline, but one that is different in form from the natural sciences. If it is to be characterized in a general way, it is a *social science* discipline. Though that may seem obvious, we wish to emphasize its significance for understanding the nature, methods and outcomes of research.

We do not expect laws stated in mathematical terms to emerge in science education. Science education can, however, aspire to *principles*. One measure of its progress is the formation of principles which illuminate the learning and understanding of scientific concepts. We need to look at whether research has generated such principles.

Progress in science education

Central to research in science education are studies of how effective certain practices are in producing understanding of content. This research has given scholars an increasing appreciation of the complexity of both classrooms and science.

Earlier theories of learning (for example Gagné 1965; Ausubel 1968), and motivation (for example Maslow 1954) treat learners as individuals, with slight attention to their interactions with each other in social groups. A typical study of the 1960s (e.g. Tanner 1969) would attend to the details of teaching procedures being compared, the tests to measure outcomes, and to the statistical analysis of the test scores. It would not attend to the context in which the learning was to occur. It would ignore the feelings of the students for the topic and their prior knowledge of it, their beliefs about the purpose of schooling and about the learning of the topic, and their feelings for each other and the teacher. The study would treat them as separate, independent units, as indeed was required by the statistical analysis. The nature of process involved in any change from pre- to post-test was ignored, and thus issues of causality were not addressed. Consequently, few principles relevant to classrooms could emerge.

In the same period there was little questioning of the nature of science. In particular, theorists, researchers and teachers took the content as unproblematic. Of course they recognized that some topics were more complex and difficult to learn than others, but saw teaching as essentially a matter of clarity in explanation and logical sequencing. Students would learn propositions and algorithms in the form that was presented to them. Prior knowledge would either be a benefit to understanding, or would be seen as irrelevant. It was never seen as a possible obstacle. Again no useful principles, this time about content, emerged.

The research of the 1960s did not produce principles. For science education to progress, there had to be a change in style. Certainly in the 1970s the quantity of research increased markedly. A comparison of the review of science education research by Watson (1963) in the first edition of the *Handbook of Research on Teaching* with those in the second edition by Shulman and Tamir (1973) and the third by White and Tisher (1986), and with the numerous chapters in the *Handbook of Research on Science Teaching and Learning* (Gabel 1994), reveals a surge in the amount, richness and diversity of research. However, energy in research, though welcome, is not an end in itself. To judge whether there has been progress in science education, we should look at the *style* of research. Has it changed in ways that appear more likely to create principles which are useful guides to practice? Then, have any such principles appeared? Third, what evidence is there that the research has influenced classroom practice?

White (1997; in press) analysed the shifts between 1965 and 1995 in research style, and concluded that the change in style amounted to a revolution. There had been a marked shift from interventionist studies, in which the researcher imposed an experimental form of teaching, often in artificial circumstances, to descriptive ones, where the researcher made observations over lengthy periods of time of events in working classrooms. This shift involved much greater reliance on qualitative data, and the verbatim reporting of teachers' and students' words rather than means of scores on tests. Naturally there was an accompanying move from reporting of sophisticated inferential statistics to simple descriptive statistics or no statistics at all.

The revolution was a consequence of three perceptions. One was that mechanisms of causation had to be elicited. Where earlier researchers were content, in the main, to record that a method of teaching led to certain outcomes with only mild speculation about why that happened, later ones became much more interested in how the effect occurred. This perception led them to investigate teachers' and students' epistemologies of teaching and learning, and of science. A special issue of the *Journal of Research in Science Teaching* (1991, 28 (9)) concentrated on this.

The second perception was that research needed to produce principles relevant to the practice of teaching. Teachers had little interest or faith in the conclusions from studies in psychology laboratories. Nor did brief, artificial interventions in classrooms impress them, for they knew classrooms to be complex places where a change needed time to bed down before its outcomes could be relied upon.

Researchers' recognition of teachers' perspectives encouraged them to attend to ecological validity in their studies. They ceased to treat the 'subjects' in their research as puppets, and began to listen to what they had to say about what was going on. Teachers emerged first as partners and then as principals in research. It may be that this will occur with students at some time.

The third perception was that content mattered. In most studies from the 1960s, content is no more than a necessary vehicle. In comparisons of the effectiveness of teaching methods, students had to learn something, and one topic was as good as another. The research on alternative conceptions destroyed that comfortable assumption. Students' beliefs affect what they learn from instruction, and beliefs are content-specific. Content emerged as an important variable.

The number of studies that refer to content rose markedly between 1965 and 1995. Although it is unlikely that any single scholar or publication was solely responsible for this rise, Ros Driver's doctoral study (1973) and her subsequent articles and books (for example Driver and Easley 1978; Driver 1981, 1983; Driver and Erickson 1983; Driver *et al.* 1985; Driver and Bell 1986) certainly had significant effect. Where Gagné and White (1978) had conceived of memories for events as wholly beneficial to understanding, Driver perceived that *beliefs formed from experience could impede understanding*. This perception constitutes an important principle.

Soon after Driver's initial work, whether germinated by it or not, studies of students' conceptions, revealing differences between their beliefs and scientists' explanations, proliferated. Research on alternative conceptions soon dominated science education. The bibliography compiled by Pfundt and Duit (1985, 1988, 1991, 1994) grew edition by edition, until the fourth listed around 3500 studies. Embedded in the early studies of alternative conceptions was another significant principle: *science concepts/topics to be learned are a significant variable in teaching the concepts/topics.*

The research on alternative conceptions illustrates progress in style. The initial studies – such as Za'rour (1975), Erickson (1979), Viennot (1979), Champagne *et al.* (1980) and Osborne (as reviewed in Osborne and Freyberg 1985), – were ones of eclectic discovery. They investigated beliefs of topic after topic, usually from physics but also from chemistry (for example Wheeler and Kass 1978), biology (for example Brumby 1979, 1981), astronomy (for example Nussbaum and Novak 1976) and earth science (for example Happs 1985). At that stage there was little theory behind the studies.

The second phase of this research was replication. Results of the initial probes were confirmed, in country after country and school system after school system. Such extensive replication and confirmation is rare in educational research. There were a small number of exceptions to this pattern of replication. In content areas rich in social/cultural explanatory forms (most obviously health and sickness) variations across cultures were found.

However, these variations were consistent with the social/cultural differences associated with the concepts, and so served to reinforce rather than oppose the principle that we derive from these studies and give in the next paragraph.

The replications showed that beliefs contrary to those of scientists are not the result of isolated instances of poor teaching, but arise from common experiences and common interpretations of these experiences. From this came a fundamental principle: *people construct their own meanings from what they experience.*

Two important questions followed:

• Why do beliefs persist in the face of contrary teaching?
• Why are there relatively few alternative conceptions about a particular phenomenon?

The third phase of research began with researchers confident that they would find readily effective methods of teaching to eradicate inappropriate beliefs and replace them with scientists' conceptions. The most promising method appeared to be a combination of demonstrations or direct experience with discussion. An example is the study by Champagne *et al.* (1985), in which the investigators provided a small group of students with experiences with air tracks and other devices, in order to shift their beliefs about force and motion from an Aristotelian to a Galilean perspective. In almost all studies, the investigators were surprised to find that alternative conceptions persisted despite carefully designed, concentrated efforts. Whatever other outcomes there were, this failure generated greater respect for the work of teachers, and appreciation of the difficult task of science teaching.

Posner *et al.* (1982) provided an explanation for the durability of alternative conceptions, which was cited frequently during this third phase of research: *learners would not abandon an existing belief and accept a new one unless they were dissatisfied with the first and found the latter intelligible, plausible and fruitful.* Despite this identification of the four elements required for change, getting learners to discard a belief remained difficult. Making the scientists' version intelligible and plausible caused no problem; teaching had long been directed at those matters. The difficulties seemed to be in bringing about dissatisfaction with existing beliefs, and in obtaining acceptance that change to the scientists' view would be fruitful in wider contexts than just learning to pass examinations.

Although some attempts to promote conceptual change were promising (for example Hewson 1982), a fully satisfactory procedure continued to elude researchers. The issue now appears to be not one of abandonment and replacement, but one of *addition*, so that the earlier belief and the scientific belief co-exist. The learner's task is to learn the scientific belief, and to become clear about when it is appropriate to apply one belief or the other. For instance, for much of daily life, thinking as Aristotle did that force is required for motion causes no problem, and indeed may be a more useful way of coping with the physical world than a strict Galilean and Newtonian view.

Changing the focus of the research problem does not necessarily make it easier to solve. Effective ways of bringing learners to proper appreciations of their alternative beliefs remain a goal for researchers and teachers. In this, the third phase of research continues alongside later phases.

The fourth phase in the study of alternative conceptions is the search for explanations of how they arise in the first place. Obviously, they are derived from experience. Interaction with objects and 'common sense' interpretations lead to the Aristotelian notion of force and motion, and parallels with real fluids lead to the caloric notion of heat. Theories of the formation of conceptions naturally emphasize the role of experience.

Perhaps the main issue which divides current theories is whether they regard young children's views about natural phenomena as coherent alternatives to scientists' explanations. Carey (1985), Bliss and Ogborn (1994) and Vosniadou (1994) say that they are, diSessa (1983) that they are not. Carey refers to intuitive theories, Bliss and Ogborn to schemes, rules, and prototypes, and Vosniadou to naive framework theories.

A theory of conceptions that includes the notion of naive or intuitive theories must depict the shift from such beliefs to scientists' explanations. For Carey, this shift has parallels with Kuhn's (1962) notion of paradigm shifts with scientific theories. Just as the mass of scientists accumulate knowledge within the current paradigm despite an increasing sense of incoherence, until there is a major revision to resolve the incoherence, such as from classical physics to quantum mechanics, so children acquire knowledge until they discard one picture of the world and accept another.

Carey (1985) distinguished between weak and strong restructuring. Weak restructuring involves seeing new relations between concepts without major change in the concepts themselves. In strong restructuring the learner accepts a view that differs from his or her prior one in the range of phenomena it accounts for, the sorts of explanations that are acceptable, and in its central concepts. Carey's distinction between weak and strong restructuring is similar to Piaget's between assimilation and accommodation, Ausubel's (1968) between subsumption and integrative reconciliation, and White's (1994b) between conceptual and conceptional change.

For diSessa (1983), children do not combine their basic beliefs into coherent theories. Their knowledge remains unconnected, 'in pieces'. DiSessa terms the basic beliefs 'phenomenological primitives'. With knowledge in pieces, there can be no major change in which one view of the world replaces another, but a gradual acquisition of knowledge in which the learner eventually subsumes the phenomenological primitives under general principles. The individual might never lose completely the phenomenological primitives formed early in life.

Although this fourth phase in the study of alternative conceptions includes empirical studies, it is mainly theoretical in character. Research is now entering a fifth, more empirical phase, of longitudinal studies which monitor development of conceptions over long periods. If we knew the factors that influence development of conceptions of natural phenomena and scientific principles, we should be better able to design curricula and teaching procedures for science. Longitudinal studies appeal as the most promising means for identifying those factors, whether they are characteristics of individuals or of teaching. Longitudinal studies in science education are rare, however, because they are time-consuming and difficult.

Cohort studies are an alternative to longitudinal studies. In a longitudinal study the researcher makes a series of observations on the same individuals, while in a cohort study the observations or measures are made at more or less the same time on groups of people of differing ages. Although cohort studies are easier to do than longitudinal ones, they provide less information about the causes of students' formation of beliefs. While a longitudinal study shows the changes that *did* occur in an individual, a cohort study can only show what changes *probably* occur with age and experience. Probably, because the cohort researcher does not know for certain that an older group was initially similar to a younger one. Any observed difference might be a consequence of getting older, but the groups might have been different when they were of the same age. One potential source of difference is the contexts that the learners experienced. Any change in a relevant factor – such as the curriculum, quality of teaching or societal views of science – that occurred after the older groups had passed the base age in the study but before the youngest had reached it would make the groups non-equivalent. A longitudinal study has some chance of discovering the effect of such factors.

Longitudinal studies provide information about the consistency, or lack of it, in a learner's expression of beliefs. An effective longitudinal study should reveal how a learner builds up knowledge, and should show the source of individual differences in beliefs. A cohort study can only report individual differences, and not explain them. Longitudinal studies are likely to lead to refinement of the theories for conceptional development and change.

Change in research style is one piece of evidence needed to support the proposition that research in science education is making progress. A second, and perhaps more stringent, test of the proposition is the identification of principles which would guide practice. A set of principles from research on alternative conceptions is:

- Learning involves the construction of meanings.
- Existing knowledge and experience affects the meaning constructed.
- Different people have different knowledge, so are likely to construct different meanings from the same information.

- There are patterns in the meanings students construct due to shared experiences of the natural world.

Though not directly connected with practice, these principles lead readily to others, about teaching:

- Good teaching involves checking before instruction on students' prior meanings.
- Good teaching involves checking on students' constructions of meaning following instruction.

Of course these last two could have been formulated before research on alternative conceptions, but that research has made it clear how important they are. A principle of teaching that would have been less obvious before the research is:

- Good teaching involves clarifying the contexts in which beliefs are appropriate.

One might expect research on alternative conceptions to yield principles that concern content. White (1994a) provides examples:

- The more abstract the concept, the less it is open to direct experience, and the less likely that learners will come to the classroom with alternative conceptions for it.
- Discussion of students' beliefs will be advantageous for topics that are open to experience and concrete, and harmful for topics that are closed to experience and abstract.
- The more complex the topic, the greater the need to attend to integrating it and to showing its unity.
- The incidence of alternative conceptions will be greater for topics that employ specialized use of common words.
- Rote learning will be more prevalent in topics with a high proportion of unfamiliar words.

Although research can be an end in itself, the chief justification for research in science education is that it has led to improvements in practice. The principles that come from it should lead teachers, curriculum designers and test constructors to better ways of doing their work. The outcome of that has to be better learning.

Has the research on alternative conceptions led to better teaching and better learning? In answering this, we have to recognize that the relation between research and practice is not simple and direct, even in science. Discovery of a wonder drug, such as penicillin, is not followed immediately by widespread successful application, and even after it comes into general use complicating issues arise such as the evolution of resistant bacteria. In education it is even more complex, because contexts affect the success of methods. The fate of package solutions such as national curricula illustrates this. The way research influences practice in education is not through discovery of a detailed and specific mode of teaching, but through substantiation of principles which pervade thinking about teaching and learning.

The research in science education on alternative conceptions also illustrates this point. Another principle from that research is that *students' beliefs persist despite direct teaching of a different view*. In their search for a way to escape from this principle, researchers turned to explorations of metacognition. The reasoning ran: alternative conceptions persist because students do not reflect on what they are learning, to check its consistency with what they believe; if they can be brought to compare information with beliefs, and test their relative accuracy through experiments, they will be more likely to adopt the scientific view. That checking and comparing requires the students to control their learning – that is, to be metacognitive.

The research on alternative conceptions had much to do with two large-scale projects to improve the quality of learning through metacognition: the Project for Enhancing Effective Learning (PEEL) and the Cognitive Acceleration through Science Education (CASE) project. Each of these has somewhat different origins and approaches. Both have important implications for the curriculum as a whole, not just science.

PEEL arose in 1985 from two apparently diverse areas: studies of students' conceptions (for example Mitchell and Gunstone 1984) and studies of students' learning approaches (for example Baird and White 1984). The project had as its beginning two assertions: students are very passive learners, and most students regularly display some poor learning tendencies. The essential intention was to move students to being informed, purposeful, independent, intellectually active learners – to have students become more metacognitive in their learning.

Since then, PEEL has involved many teachers, academics and students in collaborative action research in many classrooms. From its inception it has had a clear devolved, decentralized grass-roots nature. While academics have been involved, they have been genuine collaborators, not directors of the project. The project has resulted in a number of publications, with teacher, not academic, audiences in mind (for example Baird and Northfield 1992; Mitchell and Mitchell 1997), and has spread widely. It has also fostered new research directions.

In outline, the outcomes of this extensive activity include: increased understanding of the nature of quality learning in classrooms; identification and description of good learning behaviours (behaviours more likely to lead to quality learning); classroom approaches and procedures for promoting a metacognitive awareness of learning; increased understanding of the nature of student change that is always required for classroom change to be achieved;

increased understanding of the risks for students and teachers associated with quality learning; increased understanding of the trusts that need to be developed if quality learning is to result from classrooms; and increased understanding of the role of student questions and student talk in achieving quality learning.

The intent of the CASE project (Adey and Shayer 1994) was to raise the quality of learning by junior secondary school students through direct teaching of skills of thinking. The teaching continued over two years, with one lesson a fortnight in science classes. The training focused on 32 activities, each linked with one of the aspects Piaget had identified for operational thought such as classification, compound variables or probability. As in PEEL, the students' usual teachers taught the CASE lessons. The teachers received training in this from Adey and Shayer. Unlike PEEL, CASE did not pervade the whole of the students' schooling, though Adey and Shayer report that it had a positive and lasting effect in mathematics and English as well as in science.

An agenda for science education research

Although research should never be limited to the programme set out by one or two, it is appropriate for individuals to set out their vision for it, as this may suggest creative projects which others develop. Our view is that the track on which Ros Driver first set foot a quarter of a century ago remains central to science education.

Research on alternative conceptions is vital to discovering principles and methods for improving the quality of learning, not just of science but of any content. The latest phase of that research, of longitudinal studies of the growth of alternative conceptions, should continue. These studies are likely to emphasize that learners should not be considered, or studied, as isolated individuals but as members of social groups. Research in science education will have to study the social dynamics of classrooms and the impact on these of different content and different modes of teaching and assessment.

New variables will be important. Among them will be students' perceptions of the 'game of schooling' – their notions of the purposes of learning and the scripts they have for classroom behaviour. The emotional environment of the learner is another variable. Old notions may revive, such as Havinghurst's (1948) developmental tasks.

Perceptions of teachers and systems of the 'game of schooling' are also significant. While the impact of system views on the purpose and conduct of science education is clear in the broad sense, through the growing use of system-wide testing as a form of accountability, there are fundamental issues for research in the detail of the impact of these views on the intended, implemented and learned science curriculum. The specifics of the ways modes of assessment more generally influence the intended, implemented and learned curriculum need to be better understood.

Another major curriculum issue involves understanding how to better incorporate the principles developed over the last 20 years, in particular the ways in which we now understand that 'intellectual engagement' is different from students physically manipulating apparatus in fostering the learning of science.

New forms of research are likely, which synthesize quantitative and qualitative methods. In describing above the changes in research approach we indicated the general nature of quantitative studies in the 1960s. In most cases these earlier studies took as their starting point the reductionist approach that is typical of science. One small part of a complex whole was carved off for investigation, and assumptions made about the ways in which particular methodologies would allow the other parts of the whole to be ignored. One major aspect of the failure of this approach to reveal principles is that the complexity of science classrooms is not as amenable to reduction as the complexity of aspects of nature – the variations of context and time already mentioned are one reason. Thus qualitative methodologies became accepted. To assert the appropriateness of syntheses of qualitative and quantitative methodologies is in itself obvious. The methodological advance that is needed is to generate such a synthesis while also maintaining the complexity of the issues to be investigated.

From the new research, we expect a more extensive set of principles that can guide practice. But before that potential guidance can have an effect, we need to know a lot more about students' reactions to change, and about teachers' knowledge, or ignorance, of research and theory. We need to study the ways in which teachers' professional knowledge is deficient: what obstacles prevent them from learning about the useful outcomes of research, and putting them into practice. The last decade has seen substantial growth in explorations of teacher knowledge, mostly directed by Shulman's (1986) notion of pedagogical content knowledge. Thus far, that research has not been as fruitful as was initially hoped, and there is still no clear consensus about what pedagogical content knowledge might be. What we are suggesting here is not a focus on pedagogical content knowledge *per se*. Rather we are advocating the exploration of why the results of research that researchers see as significant for classroom practice are not embraced by teachers: are the researchers not correct in their views of relevance for classrooms? Does the knowledge generated by researchers need to be reformulated through research undertaken by teachers? What kinds of knowledge do teachers draw on? And so on. In carrying out such studies, we may well find that Ros Driver, in her work in the Children's Learning in Science Project (CLISP), had again started before us.

References

Adey, P. and Shayer, M. (1994) *Really Raising Standards: Cognitive Intervention and Academic Achievement.* London: Routledge.

Ausubel, D.P. (1968) *Educational Psychology: A Cognitive View.* New York: Holt, Rinehart & Winston.

Baird, J.R. and Northfield, J.R. (eds) (1992) *Learning from the PEEL Experience.* Melbourne: Faculty of Education, Monash University.

Baird, J.R. and White, R.T. (1984) Improving learning through enhanced metacognition: a classroom study. Paper presented at the annual meeting of the American Educational Research Association, New Orleans, April.

Baird, J.R., Fensham, P.J., Gunstone, R.F. and White, R.T. (1991) The importance of reflection in improving science teaching and learning. *Journal of Research of Science Teaching,* 28(2): 163–82.

Bliss, J. and Ogborn, J. (1994) Force and motion from the beginning. *Learning and Instruction,* 4(1): 7–25.

Brumby, M. (1979) Problems in learning the concept of natural selection. *Journal of Biological Education,* 13(4): 119–22.

Brumby, M. (1981) Learning, understanding and 'thinking about' the concept of life. *Australian Science Teachers Journal,* 27(3): 21–5.

Carey, S. (1985) *Conceptual Change in Childhood.* Cambridge, MA: MIT Press.

Champagne, A.B., Klopfer, L.E. and Anderson, J.H. (1980) Factors influencing the learning of classical mechanics. *American Journal of Physics,* 48(12): 1074–9.

Champagne, A.B., Gunstone, R.F. and Klopfer, L.E. (1985) Effecting changes in cognitive structures among physics students, in L.H.T. West and A.L. Pines (eds) *Cognitive Structure and Conceptual Change,* pp. 61–90. New York: Academic Press.

Darling-Hammond, L. and Snyder, J. (1992) Curriculum studies and the traditions of inquiry: the scientific tradition, in P.W. Jackson (ed.) *Handbook of Research on Curriculum,* pp. 41–78. New York: Macmillan.

DiSessa, A.A. (1983) Phenomenology and the evolution of intuition, in D. Gentner and A.L. Stevens (eds), *Mental Models,* pp. 15–33. Hillsdale, NJ: Erlbaum.

Driver, R. (1973) 'The representation of conceptual frameworks in young adolescent science students', Unpublished PhD thesis. University of Illinois.

Driver, R. (1981) Pupils' alternative frameworks in science. *European Journal of Science Education,* 3(1): 93–101.

Driver, R. (1983) *The Pupil as Scientist?* Milton Keynes: Open University Press.

Driver, R. and Bell, B.F. (1986) Students' thinking and the learning of science: a constructivist view. *School Science Review,* 67(240): 443–56.

Driver, R. and Easley, J. (1978) Pupils and paradigms: a review of literature related to concept development in adolescent science students. *Studies in Science Education,* 5: 61–84.

Driver, R. and Erickson, G. (1983) Theories in action: some conceptual and empirical issues in the study of students' conceptual frameworks in science. *Studies in Science Education,* 10: 37–60.

Driver, R., Guesne, E. and Tiberghien, A. (eds) (1985) *Children's Ideas in Science.* Milton Keynes: Open University Press.

Erickson, G.L. (1979) Children's conceptions of heat and temperature. *Science Education*, 63(2): 221–30.

Gabel, D.L. (ed.) (1994) *Handbook of Research on Science Teaching and Learning*. New York: Macmillan.

Gage, N.L. (1989) The paradigm wars and their aftermath. *Teachers College Record*, 91(2): 135–50.

Gagné, R.M. (1965) *The Conditions of Learning*. New York: Holt, Rinehart & Winston.

Gagné, R.M. and White, R.T. (1978) Memory structures and learning outcomes. *Review of Educational Research*, 48(2): 187–222.

Happs, J.C. (1985) Regression in learning outcomes: some examples from the earth sciences. *European Journal of Science Education*, 7(4): 431–43.

Havinghurst, R.J. (1948) *Developmental Tasks and Education*. New York: Longmans, Green.

Hewson, M.G.A'B. (1982) 'Students' existing knowledge as a factor influencing the acquisition of scientific knowledge', unpublished PhD thesis. University of Witwatersrand.

Kuhn, T.S. (1962) *The Structure of Scientific Revolutions*. Chicago: University of Chicago Press.

Maslow, A.H. (1954) *Motivation and Personality*. New York: Harper & Row.

Mitchell, I. and Gunstone, R. (1984) Some student conceptions brought to the study of stoichiometry. *Research in Science Education*, 14(1): 78–88.

Mitchell, I. and Mitchell, J. (eds) (1997) *Stories of Reflective Teaching: A Book of PEEL Cases*. Melbourne: PEEL Publishing.

Nussbaum, J. and Novak, J.D. (1976) An assessment of children's concepts of the earth utilizing structured interviews. *Science Education*, 60(4): 535–50.

Osborne, R. and Freyberg, P. (1985) *Children's Learning in Science*. London: Heinemann.

Pfundt, H. and Duit, R. (1985, 1988, 1991, 1994) *Bibliography: Students' Alternative Frameworks and Science Education* (1st, 2nd, 3rd, 4th edns). Kiel: Institute for Science Education (IPN).

Posner, G.J., Strike, K.A., Hewson, P.W. and Gertzog, W.A. (1982) Accommodation of a scientific conception: towards a theory of conceptual change. *Science Education*, 66(2): 211–27.

Shulman, L.S. (1986) Those who understand: knowledge growth in teaching. *Educational Researcher*, 15(2): 4–14.

Shulman, L.S. and Tamir, P. (1973) Research on teaching in the natural sciences, in R.M.W. Travers (ed.) *Second Handbook of Research on Teaching*, pp. 1098–148. Chicago: Rand McNally.

Tanner, R.T. (1969) Expository-deductive versus discovery-inductive programming of physical science principles. *Journal of Research in Science Teaching*, 6(2): 136–42.

Viennot, L. (1979) Spontaneous reasoning in elementary dynamics. *European Journal of Science Education*, 1(2): 205–21.

Vosniadou, S. (1994) Capturing and modelling the process of conceptual change. *Learning and Instruction*, 4(1): 45–69.

Watson, F.G. (1963) Research on teaching science, in N.L. Gage (ed.) *Handbook of Research on Teaching*, pp. 1031–59. Chicago: Rand McNally.

Wheeler, A.E. and Kass, H. (1978) Student misconceptions in chemical equilibrium. *Science Education*, 62(2): 223–32.

White, R.T. (1994a) Dimensions of content, in P.J. Fensham, R.F. Gunstone and R.T. White (eds), *The Content of Science: A Constructivist Approach to its Teaching and Learning*, pp. 255–62. London: Falmer.

White, R.T. (1994b) Conceptual and conceptional change. *Learning and Instruction*, 4(1): 117–21.

White, R.T. (1997) Trends in research in science education. *Research in Science Education*, 27(2): 215–21.

White, R.T. (in press) The revolution in research on science teaching, in V. Richardson (ed.) *Handbook of Research on Teaching* (4th edn). New York: Macmillan.

White, R.T. and Tisher, R.P. (1986) Research on natural sciences, in M.C. Wittrock (ed.) *Handbook of Research on Teaching* (3rd edn), pp. 874–905. New York: Macmillan.

Za'rour, G.I. (1975) Science misconceptions among certain groups of students in Lebanon. *Journal of Research in Science Teaching*, 12(4): 385–91.

Didactics of science: the forgotten dimension in science education research?

Piet Lijnse

In loving memory of my dearest wife, Yvonne, and my dear friend, Rosalind, two strong women who died of the same disease.

Introduction

> I would be quite happy if more research dealt with how to teach Xs.
>   (Driver 1994 private communication)

In this chapter I want to deal with some questions that Ros Driver and I often discussed – questions like 'What is actually the value of the research we're doing?' and 'How, and in what direction, should we go on?' Of course, to answer such questions is not easy and my attempts cannot be anything other than personal constructions. The perspective from which I approach these questions will be that of 'a didactician of physics' (in translated Dutch) – that is, someone who deals with the improvement of physics education in all its aspects: through research, curriculum development and teacher training. So, my interest in the field of physics education research is of a rather practical and pragmatic nature. I am not interested in research on understanding teaching and learning as an aim in itself, even if the teaching and learning concerns physics. What I am interested in is research that can, and does, improve the practice of teaching and learning physics.

It is often said that science education research suffers from a theory–practice gap (for example de Jong *et al.* 1998). Concerns are expressed about the fact that teachers are too unaware of research outcomes, or about their being unable or unwilling to put those outcomes adequately into practice. This may be true to a large extent, but here I would like to argue that, above all, the theory–practice gap is largely due to the nature of the research that is being done.

I also cannot help looking at science education research from the perspective of a (former) physicist. In spite of all the conceptual relativism that is so fashionable nowadays, I still look at physics as a body of largely reliable knowledge with which one can successfully explain and predict, as well as develop new technology. Above all it is a field in which we now know considerably more than, say, 30 years ago – that is, in which real progress seems to be possible. Is this also the case for research in (physics) education?[1] I still remember my disappointment when, as a newly appointed didactician, I had to develop an innovative series of lessons to introduce quantum mechanics at secondary school. I turned to theories of education and educational psychology for help. However, hardly any such help appeared to be available, a frustrating result which unfortunately was (and is) in line with the 'traditional' scepticism of physicists concerning the 'soft' sciences. That this was not just a personal experience of mine may be illustrated by the following report by one of the participants at the 1982 conference of the American Educational Research Association. Seven prominent educationalists were given the task of designing a lesson on elementary optics. It turned out, to their increasing amazement, that in spite of their totally different theoretical starting points, their designs were remarkably similar (de Klerk 1982). At that time, apparently, educational theories had little specific guidance to offer for the design of educational practice. Has any progress been made since then, at least for science education? My own answer, for reasons to be explained below, would be rather sceptical, even though the past 25 years of curriculum development and research, particularly in the field of 'alternative frameworks' as co-initiated by Ros Driver, have convinced me that, for progress to be made, appropriate science education research is badly needed. The question then is, what is 'appropriate'?

Didactics of science and science education research

I have used the term 'didactics of science' above, as well as the term 'research in science education'. It may be appropriate to go into some more detail as to what the differences between the two might be. Let me first say a little more about contemporary research in science education. To define it operationally, we have available, in addition to many volumes like this one, two major recent publications, the *Handbook of Research on Science Teaching and Learning* (Gabel 1994) and the *International Handbook of Science Education* (Fraser and Tobin 1998). On the whole, these handbooks make interesting reading (for a researcher, though not perhaps for a teacher), and give a good impression of, and valuable insights into, many aspects of science education and of developments in the field. Having said this, however,

I also felt rather disappointed after having read them, because of the one-sidedness and the lack of didactical relevance of most of the reported studies.[2]

A first feature that is very striking is the almost complete lack of attention to 'science content' (see Chapter 9). As far as theorizing is concerned, science education research seems to aim primarily for a content-independent meta-position that links closely with general research in education. A second feature is the almost complete lack of studies that deal with what I would like to call the 'hard core' of didactics: the interrelation of teaching and learning activities.[3] Little attention is paid to a thorough didactical conceptual analysis of the content to be taught – a conceptual analysis, that is, from the perspective of learnability and teachability. What is also almost always lacking is a description and discussion of the didactical quality of the teaching/learning situations that were studied.[4]

What seems to be apparent from the literature is that science education research does not aim to develop content-specific didactical knowledge (possibly to be described as 'small-scale theories') but to contribute to (if only by simply applying) general educational and/or psychological theories. I consider this 'flight away from content' detrimental, because thereby a level is skipped that I consider necessary for making a real impact on science education and for making didactical progress. The missing level is that of describing and understanding what is, or should be, going on in science classrooms in terms of content-specific teaching–learning processes, and of trying to interpret them in terms of didactical theory.

This criticism also applies to studies that seek to 'understand' learning processes in great detail. For instance, I fail to see the didactical relevance of describing learning processes in terms of detailed cognitive processes (Welzel 1997; Roth 1998), or as individual conceptual learning pathways (Scott 1992). From a didactical perspective, research of the first kind often amounts to little more than describing didactical common sense in complicated cognitive terms, while research of the latter kind often is not interpreted in direct relation to the teaching process (and is therefore of little didactical interest).

I also have my doubts concerning the didactical value of conceptual change theory, and theories concerning 'general' problem-solving strategies (see Chapter 7) and/or other 'general' metacognitive skills. Quite often such 'detours into the brain' appear to be didactically unnecessary or non-productive. If one attempts to interpret what is going on in science classrooms directly in terms of such general (learning) theories, one immediately faces the problem that on application such theories only result at best in heuristic rules. Such rules simply cannot guarantee that the teaching situations that are supposed to be governed by them will have the necessary didactical quality.

How does this relate to 'didactics of science'? In line with my pragmatic and practical perspective, the aims of 'didactics of science' can be simply formulated as dealing with the basic questions of why, what and how to teach science to whom, in all its aspects. The hard core of this activity, therefore, is not the understanding of (science) learning as a psychological process (though appropriate knowledge about this may, of course, be useful), but the improvement of science teaching and learning. And for this purpose it cannot but focus on the teaching and learning of the contents and other particularities of science as a (school) subject.

Now, of course, every experienced science teacher has much practice-built and/or theory-inspired knowledge about his or her subject, and about why and how and what to teach (of it) and learn (from it).[5] In fact, because of this, in many policy documents and in most educational research that deals with science education, teachers are considered to be *the* didactical experts, who have to transform new curriculum ideas or learning theories into manageable practice. However, past research on 'alternative frameworks' (as well as the disappointing effects of the major curriculum development projects of the past) have shown that this didactical expertise, even in the case of experienced teachers, is insufficient. This is not at all meant to devalue the didactical knowledge of experienced teachers, but only to argue that an extension of such knowledge is badly needed. This cannot be left as a task only for practitioners themselves, but should be considered an area in need of proper research: didactics of science.

In didactical research two interrelated aspects may be distinguished: namely, the problem of curriculum choice and justification (the 'why' and 'what' and to 'whom'; Millar and Osborne 1998; see also Chapter 9), in recursive relation to the problem of teaching and learning the chosen curriculum (the 'how'). Research in science didactics thus basically comes down to analysing, describing and improving the teachability and learnability of science. It does not take the science content for granted, but studies it from this particular point of view. Its relation to science itself, therefore, can best be compared with that of the history or philosophy of science.

As far as the content and justification of science curricula are concerned, one cannot, I think, properly speak of 'progress'. As the mathematics educator Freudenthal (1991: 156) once remarked: 'Pictures of education taken at different moments in history are incomparable. Each society at a given period got the education it wanted, it needed, it could afford, it deserved and it was able to provide. Innovation cannot effect any more than adapting education to a changing society or at best can try to anticipate the change. This alone is difficult enough'.

In my opinion, however, things stand differently as regards the 'how'. Although I completely disagree with Fensham (see Chapter 9) that 'there is now no shortage of pedagogical knowledge in science education', I do think that progress in didactics of science as regards such knowledge is possible, provided we intensify our search for it. Such a search demands, I think, a special methodology – namely, 'developmental research' (Gravemeijer 1994; Lijnse 1995), which is rather similar to what others have called 'design experiments' or 'teaching experiments' (see Chapter 15). Though such research should take the didactical knowledge of experienced teachers quite seriously, its task is to seek for essential improvement and scientific extension of that knowledge. This can probably best be done by developing exemplary practices for the teaching of specific topics. Starting from explicit views of science, and science teaching and learning, such developmental research involves a cyclical process of conceptual analysis, small-scale curriculum development with teacher cooperation and training, and classroom research on teaching–learning processes. In this process, one should of course apply anything that is useful (one's scientific knowledge, educational theories, views from the history and philosophy of science, and so on).

Through reflection on such practices, one might come to formulate content-specific theories regarding the teaching/learning of particular topics, which can perhaps be generalized to a certain extent to similar topics. And one may even come to formulate more general 'theoretical' principles for 'good' science teaching and learning. Thus one could give content to didactics of science as a scientific activity.

In the discussion above, I hope to have made clear that didactics of science differs considerably from mainstream science education research. The main distinction (as I see it) is this:

- The primary aim of (research in) didactics of science is content-specific didactical knowledge, based on developing and justifying exemplary science teaching practices.
- Mainstream (Anglo-American) science education research seems to be primarily aimed at a description and theoretical understanding of (existing) science teaching practices, mainly in terms of content-independent factors.[6]

Didactics, taken as a scientific activity, can, I think, best be characterized as a kind of 'educational engineering', whereas much of science education research seems to aim for understanding of teaching and learning (science) as a *theoretical science*. Although there may be overlap between the two, I think this difference in focus is a major reason for the problematic practical relevance of science education research.

Perhaps I should add that I am not at all against trying to develop or apply general theories. On the contrary, I think that in scientific work we always have to go back and forth between the specific and the general to make progress in our theories. My problem is, however, that in the dominant form of science education research, the general focus is taken from the start to be the psychology of the brain, or the sociology of the classroom, or the philosophy of science, etc. Consequently this neglects a necessary didactical level, with its content-specific aspects.

Take, for example, the intensive discussion about constructivism(s) in large numbers of philosophically orientated papers. As summarized and interpreted (rather charitably) by Ogborn (1997: 131), the possible didactical relevance of this whole discussion boils down to four simple ideas:

- The importance of the pupils' active involvement in thinking if anything like understanding is to be reached.
- The importance of respect for the child and for the child's own ideas.
- That science consists of ideas created by human beings.
- That the design of teaching should give high priority to making sense to pupils, capitalizing on and using what they know and addressing difficulties that may arise from how they imagine things to be.

It is hard to think of anyone who would not agree with these ideas.[7] So the real issue does not concern the theoretical or philosophical validity of those four starting points of what I would like to call 'educational constructivism', but rather the didactical quality with which they are applied in practice. Heuristic guidelines do not suffice for that. However, this problem has, as yet, scarcely been taken up as a task for researchers in science education. Its solution is largely left (as an impossible task) to teachers.

Apart from this discussion about constructivism, the stage of science education research has been dominated by topics like mental models and modelling; problem solving and other general cognitive and metacognitive processes and strategies; cooperative learning and co-construction of knowledge in communities of learners; apprenticeship and scaffolding; metaphors and analogies; and language and semiotics. Partly inspired by all of this and partly for other reasons, there has also been a spectacular rise in attention paid to the history and philosophy of science – in short, to the 'nature of science'. Noticing all these developments, Duschl and Hamilton (1992: 7) wrote: 'We find ourselves, then, at a critical and exciting time in science education'.

It may be clear from the above that I am less excited. All the developments mentioned seem to take place predominantly within a circuit of theorizing (science) educators, staying well away from the didactical practice of the science classroom (see for example the journal *Science & Education*). Therefore, at best, this work results only in 'implications' for (science) teaching, and so scarcely leads to didactical progress.

A case study: teaching about the particulate nature of matter

In order to clarify the issues discussed above, I will compare two approaches to teaching an introductory particle model. The first approach is taken from the Children's Learning in Science Project (CLISP) (1987), which developed a number of influential teaching materials that (though probably unintended by its authors) are often referred to as paradigms of constructivist teaching strategies. The second approach has been developed as part of a PhD project (Vollebregt 1998).

In view of some of my criticisms above, my choice of the CLISP work may seem strange at first sight. For the CLISP did not stop short with just formulating some general implications, but also made quite an effort to put them into practice. Nevertheless, I consider it an example of mainstream science education research in that its focus was on applying 'the constructivist view of learning'. As a result the CLISP approach suffers from severe didactical shortcomings. Or at least so I will argue, by contrasting it with our own approach.[8]

The CLISP approach

The CLISP's view on learning involves the idea that 'pupils come to science lessons already holding their *own* ideas about natural phenomena which they have developed through everyday experiences: pupils are not empty-headed' (CLISP 1987: 6). In line with this, a number of pupils' ideas about matter prior to formal teaching, as found in previous research, are described. While taking account of those ideas, a teaching scheme is then worked out that has the following aims: to introduce pupils to the particulate theory of matter as a theory that is useful in explaining a large number of seemingly unconnected phenomena relating to the nature and behaviour of matter; and to introduce pupils to scientific theory-making as an activity in which they can validly engage.

The teaching scheme itself is based on a generalized teaching sequence proposed by Driver and Oldham (1986), which consists of the following phases (Johnston 1990: 248):

- *An elicitation phase*: where students are provided with opportunities to put forward their own ideas and to consider the ideas of their peers.
- *A restructuring phase*: where the teacher introduces activities which interact with students' prior ideas and which encourage students to move their thinking towards the school view.
- *A review phase*: where students are asked to reflect on the ways in which their ideas have changed.

The application of this general scheme to the topic of particle models is described in some detail by Johnston (1990). The approach begins with asking pupils for their own ideas about a number of simple phenomena related to the behaviour of matter (for example, how smell reaches you). By means of a number of theory-making games set in non-scientific contexts (for example, solving a murder mystery), pupils are encouraged to reflect on their understanding of theories and how these are developed. Next, pupils are asked to put forward their own ideas about the properties of solids, liquids and gases and are stimulated to reach consensus on a pattern of properties. Subsequently pupils are required to generate a theory as to what solids, liquids and gases are like inside, while being reminded of the general nature of theory-making and encouraged to base their theory-making in the case at hand upon the agreed pattern of properties of solids, liquids and gases. Although up to this point pupils are left free in terms of what they bring forward, it turns out, as was expected and/or intended by the devisers:

- that in a wide range of classes pupils reach consensus on a similar sort of pattern of properties (for example, solids have a definite and fixed shape, liquids take the shape of the container, gases have no shape but rather completely fill the container);
- that pupils generate particle models in order to account for this pattern of properties of solids, liquids and gases (for example, a solid cannot be compressed because its particles are so close together that they cannot be pushed any closer);
- that some of the particle ideas pupils hold are alternative (for example, they attribute macroscopic properties such as expanding to particles or hold that there is air between particles);
- that some elements of the school science view are lacking in pupils' particle models (for example, particles have intrinsic motion).

The heart of the CLISP approach, then, consists in making pupils evaluate, develop and change their alternative ideas and adopt the appropriate scientific ones – for example, by thought experiments to encourage them to consider the possibility that there might be nothing between particles; by diffusion demonstrations to make them recognize that particles have intrinsic motion; or by direct explanations of what scientists think.

Evaluation studies showed that 'most students appeared to enjoy the scheme and appreciated the opportunity to become actively involved in their own learning' (Johnston 1990: 262). In particular, 'the most able students appreciated being given the opportunity to think in depth about an area of science' (Johnston 1990: 263). However, a comparison study between two parallel groups, of which one used the CLISP approach and the other the school's traditional approach, showed that 'there was little difference . . . overall in the conceptual change produced' (Driver 1988: 102).

Some comments on the CLISP approach

The first thing to note about the CLISP approach is that 'particle ideas' or 'particle models' are attributed to pupils because they use words like 'atom', 'molecule' or 'particle', and/or draw discrete entities in their pictures of what matter is like inside. Furthermore, some of their particle ideas are counted as 'alternative' because they attribute macroscopic properties, such as melting or expanding, to particles. This is in line with numerous studies that have been conducted on 'the way pupils relate microscopic particles to macroscopic phenomena' (Lijnse *et al.* 1990).

Now, one is of course free to call what pupils bring forward 'particle ideas' or 'particle models'. But one should then also clearly bear in mind that their ideas are not about the particles that figure in scientific particle models and that their models are of a different nature from scientific particle models. For we think it is clear from the way pupils use words like 'particle of . . .' or 'atom of . . .', that, in order to make their words make sense, one cannot do better than interpret these as 'tiny bit of . . .'.[9] So the statement that pupils come up with ideas about 'particles/atoms', some of which are alternative, simply amounts to the statement that pupils believe that a substance can be divided into little bits that, apart from their size, are just like larger amounts of the substance (have the same macroscopic properties, are subject to the same macroscopic regularities, and so on). Their particles simply *are* small-scale macroscopic objects, and their particle models essentially *are* macroscopic accounts. So one should be very careful with the conclusion that it is 'common for students to attribute macroscopic properties (such as melting or expanding) to particles' (Johnston 1990: 247).[10] If we read it as 'pupils attribute macroscopic properties to *our* molecules', we will be misinterpreting them: they are *not* talking about *our* molecules. As far as our molecules are concerned, we think it is best to say that they do not have any ideas at all.

However, because of its emphasis on the supposedly alternative particle ideas that pupils are to change to more appropriate scientific ones, which after all is the heart of the constructivist teaching sequence, the CLISP approach does in effect equate pupils' particles to the particles that figure in scientific particle models. Or, to put it from the pupils' point of view, in the CLISP approach they are to replace some of their existing ideas about *their* particles with other (and quite strange) ideas about *their* particles, which are then called 'scientific'.

So in our opinion the CLISP's approach misfires. If appropriately interpreted, there are no alternative beliefs to overcome (for example, there is no need to make pupils abandon the idea that *their* particles expand when heated) and be replaced by 'scientific' ones (for example, there is no need to make pupils learn that *their* particles have intrinsic motion or that there is nothing between *their* particles). Moreover, by inappropriately equating pupils' particles to the particles that figure in scientific particle models and by treating their particle models on a par with scientific particle models, the CLISP approach also cannot lead to a proper understanding of scientific particle models. At best, pupils will arrive at a hybrid between their particle models (in essence, macroscopic accounts) and scientific particle models. And thus the negative result of the comparative study cited above comes as no surprise.

A 'problem-posing approach'

Starting points

I will now describe our approach to the introduction of an initial particle model, in order to be able to point concretely to the sorts of didactical considerations we think are lacking in the CLISP approach. In developing our approach, we have taken as a first starting point what above has been called 'educational constructivism'. We do not adhere to the 'alternative framework' movement, however, and therefore did not try to develop 'constructivist teaching strategies' nor try to apply 'conceptual change theory'. The reason is, as will have become clear from the above, that we do not think pupils have 'alternative' ideas about particles that need to be changed. As far as cognitive learning is concerned, we think it is best to think of science learning as a process in which pupils, by drawing on their existing conceptual resources, experiential base and belief system, come to add to those (with accompanying changes of meaning). What we think needs to be added to this picture, as a second starting point, is that if this process is to make sense to them, pupils must also be made to *want* to add to those conceptual resources. Or, in other words, pupils should, at any time during the process of teaching and learning, see the *point* of what they are doing. If that is the case, the process of teaching and learning will make sense to pupils, and it can be expected that they will then accept new knowledge on grounds that they themselves understand. An approach to science education that explicitly aims at this we call *problem posing*.[11] The emphasis of a problem-posing approach is thus on bringing pupils to such a position that they themselves come to see the *point* of extending their existing conceptual knowledge, experiences and belief systems in a certain direction.

Thus formulated, the second starting point seems rather trivial, and indeed it is. Since in themselves both starting points give hardly any didactical guidance, the real non-trivial challenge lies in the didactical quality with which they can be put into practice.

A scientific particle model

Let us first give an indication of what the didactical task of making pupils see the point and direction of a process that eventually does lead to a proper understanding of scientific particle models might amount to. In order to achieve this, we think that it should not only become clear to pupils that devising a scientific particle model is a form of theory-making that, just like (for example) solving a murder mystery, involves framing tentative hypotheses on the basis of available clues, but foremost also that it is the making of a theory of a *characteristic* kind. Moreover, making it of this characteristic kind imposes constraints on the framing of hypotheses.

What is characteristic about a (classical) scientific particle model is that it aims to understand the behaviour of matter by assuming that matter consists of invariant ultimate components (the particles) whose positions and velocities change due to their mutual interactions. The two basic aspects of any such model are, therefore, 'invariance' and 'motion', which are related in the sense that if all change ultimately has to be understood in terms of basic components that themselves are invariant, this can only be in terms of the basic components being in motion.[12] All change, that is, then ultimately is motion. In order to arrive at a specific particle model, one will obviously have to supplement those basic aspects with hypotheses that allow one to derive, given the initial positions and velocities of the particles, their positions and velocities at a later time – for example, hypotheses concerning the way the particles collide, or concerning the interactions between the particles.

The only way we can test the model is, in essence, by macroscopic phenomena. So what will have to be added, in order to give the model empirical content, are hypotheses of another kind – namely, those which specify the connections between the macroscopic variables of an object and certain functions of configurations of particles: for example, the connection between the temperature of an object and the mean kinetic energy of its particles.

This brief characterization can be said to indicate a general framework within which further specific hypotheses are to be made in order to arrive at a specific scientific particle model. We therefore think that the didactical task identified above, of making pupils see the point and direction of a process that eventually leads to a proper understanding of scientific particle models, consists in making pupils achieve sufficient insight into this general framework and why it is as it is. This way of putting the didactical task not only shows that the CLISP underestimated the necessity of a thorough conceptual analysis of the content to be taught, but also that general accounts of models and modelling (for example Gilbert and Boulter 1998), are of little didactical relevance in this respect.

It is of course far from simple to solve the didactical problem of how to make pupils partners, in a meaningful way, in an enterprise that aims to explain the behaviour of objects and materials, using just the assumptions that an object is a collection of particles and that all changes of that object can be explained solely in terms of changes in position and velocity of those particles due to their mutual interactions. Among other things, the following should become clear to pupils:

- why, in the first place, one would want to improve on one's macroscopic understanding of the behaviour of matter;
- why, if there is a need for improvement, it is plausible, in order to attain the desired improvement, to assume that an object is a collection of particles;
- the sense in which those particles differ from small-scale macroscopic objects (tiny bits);
- why one wants to give explanations solely in terms of changes of position and velocity of the particles, and why it is plausible to expect that all (or at least a great number of) macroscopic changes can be explained in those terms;
- why, in order to give such an explanation, one needs the two kinds of hypothesis mentioned above, and what the explanation then consists of;
- how further specific hypotheses can be arrived at, and the sense in which one particle model can be called 'better' than another.

A particular problem has to do with inducing an appropriate initial 'theoretical orientation' – i.e. with making pupils see the point of looking for a deeper understanding of macroscopic knowledge and making them prepared to start learning about *scientific* particles. This standard problem of a first introduction of particle models cannot be solved by simply asking questions about the macroscopic behaviour of matter, as these can always be answered with still more macroscopic knowledge. Nor can it be solved by simply asking pupils for *their* ideas about the structure of matter. We think it is quite obvious that when pupils without any real experience of particle models are asked to account for the behaviour of matter in terms of what it is like inside, the result will not be 'alternative theories of molecules' but 'largely correct theories of tiny bits'. And what is even more important in this context, because the theories thus triggered are essentially accounts where smaller parts behave just like larger wholes, they are the wrong theories to trigger if one wants to introduce pupils to an account where smaller parts do *not* behave just like larger wholes (as in particle models). The problem, therefore, becomes how to trigger such accounts in the context of the behaviour of matter.[13] We do not claim to have solved this problem. But since analogies are natural tools for introducing something new, for the purpose at hand we may attempt to devise an appropriate analogy with functional or mechanistic explanations – for example, of the capacities of an organism in terms of its components, or the working of a clock in terms of springs, cogs and so on.

I hope this suffices to make clear not only that the real didactical problems are non-trivial, but also that the CLISP approach, because of its focus on general strategies, did not meet them. What we would like to retain from the CLISP approach is giving pupils an active role in the process. They enjoy such a role and will thus be more involved.[14] But now we would like this involvement to consist in their seeing the point and direction of, and their having control over, constructions and reconstructions of specific *scientific* particle models. In order to achieve this, we have pointed to the necessity of a thorough conceptual analysis from a didactical point of view – an analysis, that is, that aims to uncover the conceptual steps that pupils have to make *from their point of view* in order to be able to come to understand the content matter in the intended way. In attempting to design a teaching sequence that succeeds in making such steps acceptable for pupils, we believe we are at least on the right route to real didactical progress.

A didactical structure

Because of lack of space I cannot here describe in any detail the actual teaching sequence that was designed, tried and revised several times. Here a description and brief discussion of one of the products of the research will have to suffice: a schematic description of a didactical structure for the teaching of an initial particle model, such that pupils are actively involved in the process of modelling (see Figure 17.1). The structure relates to a sequence of approximately ten lessons for pupils aged 16 in Dutch upper-level secondary education. This should act as a reminder that outcomes of didactical research are not only content-specific but also to some extent system-specific, as they apply in the first place to a particular niche in a particular educational system.

Some remarks may shed more light on this structure and its wider applicability. The left-hand column consists of knowledge of physics and the right-hand one of knowledge of the nature of physics. The arrows show how the process of teaching and learning switches between columns and how these switches arise naturally from motives that are developed. These motives constitute the middle column. The structure shows that our two main content-specific aims (learning to use a particle model insightfully to explain macroscopic behaviour of matter and obtaining insight into the nature of particle models and scientific modelling) are not only elaborated in relation to each other, but, more strongly, as dependent on each other. Thus, learning at the one 'level' naturally *drives* the learning at the other, and vice versa. In the description of our structure, we have used 'status terms' from conceptual change theory (intelligible, plausible, fruitful) (Posner *et al.* 1982). This is not because we *applied* this theory in our didactical design, but simply because such terms happened naturally to fit.[15]

Given the chosen aims, the didactical structure above describes the essential steps of a conceptual and content-related motivational pathway through the topic, that has been shown to be possible for pupils. In our research, it is abstracted from an empirically tested scenario, in which the didactical choices are motivated and the probable teaching–learning process is described

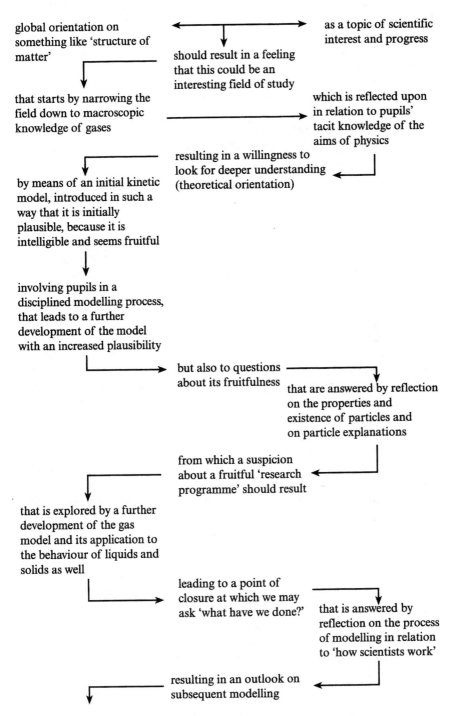

global orientation on something like 'structure of matter'

that starts by narrowing the field down to macroscopic knowledge of gases

by means of an initial kinetic model, introduced in such a way that it is initially plausible, because it is intelligible and seems fruitful

involving pupils in a disciplined modelling process, that leads to a further development of the model with an increased plausibility

should result in a feeling that this could be an interesting field of study

as a topic of scientific interest and progress

which is reflected upon in relation to pupils' tacit knowledge of the aims of physics

resulting in a willingness to look for deeper understanding (theoretical orientation)

but also to questions about its fruitfulness

that are answered by reflection on the properties and existence of particles and on particle explanations

from which a suspicion about a fruitful 'research programme' should result

that is explored by a further development of the gas model and its application to the behaviour of liquids and solids as well

leading to a point of closure at which we may ask 'what have we done?'

that is answered by reflection on the process of modelling in relation to 'how scientists work'

resulting in an outlook on subsequent modelling

Figure 17.1 The structure of our problem-posing approach

in great detail, from the perspective of both teacher and pupils, and therefore, as formulated above, from the perspectives of both learnability and teachability.

From this content-specific didactical structure a more general structure may be abstracted, consisting of phases switching between a content level and a reflective level. We feel that this more general structure may provide a possibility of generalization to teaching other topics and skills, thus providing a step to a more general didactical theory.

Discussion

Let me now go back to where I began. I have argued that (Anglo-American) science education research is very much focused on explaining science education within a psychological, sociological, linguistic and philosophical context. This has led to important insights into what is going on in science classrooms. At the same time, however, it is hard to apply such research to science education practice, because it does not pay much attention to a didactical analysis of the content to be taught and to the design of teaching/ learning situations of sufficient didactical quality. To illustrate this problem I have described two approaches for introducing an initial particle model. In my opinion, this example not only illustrates the necessity of treating didactics of science as a research field in its own right, but also explains why results of mainstream science education research have little to add. A possible and necessary (long term) outcome of such research in didactics could be, for example, (a) didactical structure(s) for all of science (or for that part that may be chosen to be in the school curriculum), (a) structure(s) that could play an essential role in decreasing the present negative image of science as incomprehensible and irrelevant. Starting from a thorough analysis of science and scientific knowledge in terms of underlying basic common-sense intuitions, one should develop, and test empirically, conceptual and motivational pathways that describe the essential conceptual steps which have to be taken, how they build on and prepare for each other, and how pupils and teachers may take those steps together.

Now, it is often questioned whether, or to what extent, research can deal with how to teach a topic most effectively. As Tiberghien (see Chapter 2) remarks, 'designing teaching situations for each domain of physics and for each level' is an endless task. Therefore in her research she focuses, within the French didactical tradition,[16] on the design of teaching situations that are representative of a *set of situations* by making use of more general *characteristics* of physics knowledge. Though I agree that the outcome of didactical research cannot only be at the level of teaching situations themselves,[17] we have taken a different route, and have ended up with the idea of an empirically supported 'didactical structure of a certain topic'. Such structures describe well-motivated possible routes to solutions of didactical problems, which are either brought forward by teachers or result from previous research. Of course, such structures, together with their worked-out teaching scenarios, cannot succeed without the experience and craftsmanship of good teachers. As such, they are not 'teacher proof' and nor can they guarantee that the learning process of each individual pupil will be successful. However, they do provide even experienced teachers with new didactical insights which can improve their teaching considerably at key points. And they do describe a stepwise learning process whose steps have been shown to be feasible for pupils and teachers, so that even though in classroom practice both the actual teaching process and the learning processes of individual pupils will always differ to some extent from those described in the struc-. ture, on the whole, the structure provides sufficient guidance to teachers to keep these differences quite small and to keep the teaching/learning processes on the right track. That is why they can improve the learning and teaching of a certain topic, in the sense that more pupils will understand and value, in the intended way, what they have been taught.

If more research is aimed at such didactical structures (or whatever one wishes to call them), then from mutual comparisons and discussions further didactical progress may be possible. And even though 'the best way of teaching a topic' may always remain an illusion, improved ways of teaching might result which could be considered (more) satisfactory. And that would be a significant result indeed!

Research in science didactics fills an essential gap between science teaching practice and Anglo-American research in science education. The adjective 'Anglo-American' is meant to indicate a restriction in this context, because in many continental European countries (research in) science didactics seems to have a more established status. This probably has to do with the fact that in many European countries didactics has a long tradition, even though this tradition may differ from country to country. In a recent review of European PhD studies in science education, I concluded that much research is being done on the teaching and learning of Xs, where X stands for a particular science topic (Lijnse 1994). Ros Driver certainly approved of this conclusion. In 1988 she wrote: 'An important point to make here is that the curriculum is not something that can be planned in an "a priori" way but is necessarily the subject of empirical enquiry' (p. 168).

So in concluding, it is worth mentioning the key role that Ros Driver played in establishing a European Science Education Research Association (ESERA). It would be an important achievement for science education if ESERA could succeed in crossing the language and cultural borders within Europe (and elsewhere), and give research in didactics of science a more prominent role on the science education research agenda.

Notes

1 Although my experience is limited to physics and physics education, from now on I will use the terms 'science' and 'science education'. It is up to the reader to decide whether this generalization is always justified.

2 This one-sidedness may well have to do with the fact that both handbooks are primarily North American and/or Anglo-Saxon in nature. In this respect it is worth noting that the term 'didactics of a subject' is quite common in most European languages, but that it is not used in this sense in the English language.

3 In fact, in both handbooks, teaching and learning are dealt with in separate chapters.

4 The following example may illustrate what I mean by this. Recently I had to review a thesis that described the development and evaluation of courseware for an inquiry-based science curriculum. The courseware was said to have 'theoretical quality' as it used a constructivist and inquiry-based view on learning; it was said to have 'empirical quality' as it appeared to have a significant learning effect; and it was said to have 'practical quality' as the teachers appeared to be able to use it in the intended way. However, in my opinion, it lacked 'didactical quality' – i.e. the quality of the designed teaching/learning activities was rather poor.

5 This often non-reflective level of knowledge of didactics of science probably comes close to what is nowadays called 'pedagogical content knowledge' in the English literature.

6 For example, in an editorial of a recent issue of the *International Journal of Science Education* Roth (1998) writes: 'An increasing number of studies in recent years were designed to generate better understandings of learning processes . . . The learning process studies [in this issue] describe in detail interrelations between various aspects of the instructional setting (social configuration, artefacts, materials, discursive resources) and cognitive processes during teaching–learning situations' (p. 1019).

7 Some people might argue that a fifth point should be added, namely that pupils' ideas have been shown to be strongly resistant to change. However, as yet, it has only been shown that such ideas are strongly resistant to our teaching, underlining the necessity of didactical progress.

8 In this section I use the plural for two reasons. First, the PhD research in which the approach was developed was partially a group effort, to which not only Marjolein Vollebregt and myself contributed, but also Kees Klaassen and Rupert Genseberger. Second, this section is my adaptation of a draft paper by Kees Klaassen.

9 For a further discussion of the general 'problem of interpretation', and of the interpretation of pupils' utterances in science education in particular, see Klaassen (1995) and Klaassen and Lijnse (1996).

10 A similar conclusion applies to a greater or lesser degree to many more reported research findings on pupils' alternative frameworks.

11 To achieve this, we often try to bring pupils to such a position that they themselves come to pose the main problems that they intend (and have) to work on. This is why we have termed our approach 'problem posing'.

12 Note that this clearly distinguishes the basic components from pupils' particles – i.e. from essentially macroscopic 'tiny bits'.

13 The historical motive of Democritus, which had to do with how to explain (the relation between) the notions 'being' and 'becoming', presupposes such a deep level of philosophical interest that we cannot assume it to function as an initial motive for our pupils.

14 In this sense we have built on the CLISP's work. We also used as much as possible from a number of French studies on the teaching of particle models (for example Meheut and Chomat 1990). This shows that, in order to make progress at the detailed level of content specific didactics it is necessary to build on previous research.

15 We did not, however, use the status term 'dissatisfaction', because we did not consider ourselves to be starting from alternative ideas. Instead of dissatisfaction, we could say that we used the motive of curiosity.

16 The French research in *didactique* tries to describe essential didactical aspects of teaching/learning situations. So terms like 'didactical transposition', 'didactical contract', 'devolution', etc. have been framed.

17 It is, however, essential that the research is based on the development of exemplary situations. These serve to test didactical hypotheses empirically, thus forming the basis for theoretical reflection, while also serving as concrete and tested operationalizations of these reflections, thus preventing a theory–practice gap.

References

CLISP (Children's Learning in Science Project) (1987) *Approaches to Teaching the Particulate Nature of Matter*. Leeds: Centre for Studies in Science and Mathematics Education.

de Jong, O., Kortland, J., Waarlo, A.J. and Buddingh, J. (eds) (1998) *Bridging the Gap Between Theory and Practice*. Hatfield: ICASE.

de Klerk, L.F.W. (1982) Verslag van het AERA-Congress 1982 te New York. *Pedagogische Studiën*, 59: 519–21.

Driver, R. (1988) Changing conceptions. *Tijdschrift voor Didactiek der β-wetenschappen*, 6: 161–98.

Driver, R. and Oldham, V. (1986) A constructivist approach to curriculum development in science. *Studies in Science Education*, 13: 5–12.

Duschl, R.A. and Hamilton, R.J. (1992) Introduction: viewing the domain of science education, in R.A. Duschl and R.J. Hamilton (eds) *Philosophy of Science: Cognitive Psychology and Educational Theory and Practice*, pp. 1–18. New York: SUNY Press.

Fraser, B.J. and Tobin, K.G. (eds) (1998) *International Handbook of Science Education*. Dordrecht: Kluwer Academic Publishers.

Freudenthal, H. (1991) *Revisiting Mathematics Education*. Dordrecht: Kluwer Academic Publishers.

Gabel, D.L. (ed.) (1994) *Handbook of Research on Science Teaching and Learning*. New York: Macmillan.

Gilbert, J.K. and Boulter, C.J. (1998) Learning science through models and modelling, in B.J. Fraser and K.G. Tobin (eds) *International Handbook of Science Education*, pp. 53–66. Dordrecht: Kluwer Academic Publishers.

Gravemeijer, K.P.E. (1994) *Developing Realistic Mathematics Education*. Utrecht: CD-β Press.

Johnston, K. (1990) Students' responses to an active learning approach to teaching the particulate theory of matter, in P.L. Lijnse *et al.* (eds) *Relating Macroscopic Phenomena to Microscopic Particles*, pp. 247–65. Utrecht: CD-β Press.

Klaassen, C.W.J.M. (1995) *A Problem-posing Approach to Teaching the Topic of Radioactivity*. Utrecht: CD-β Press (http://pablo.ubu.ruu.nl/~proefsch/01873016/inhoud.htm).

Klaassen, C.W.J.M. and Lijnse, P.L. (1996) Interpreting students' and teachers' discourse in science classes: an underestimated problem? *Journal of Research in Science Teaching*, 33(2): 115–34.

Lijnse, P.L. (1994) Trends in European research in science education? in D. Psillos (ed.) *European Research in Science Education II*, pp. 21–32. Thessaloniki: Art of Text S.A.

Lijnse, P.L. (1995) 'Developmental research' as a way to an empirically based 'didactical structure' of science. *Science Education*, 79(2): 189–99.

Lijnse, P.L., Licht, P., de Vos, W. and Waarlo, A.J. (eds) (1990) *Relating Macroscopic Phenomena to Microscopic Particles*. Utrecht: CD-β Press.

Meheut, M. and Chomat, A. (1990) The bounds of children's atomism: an attempt to make children build up a particulate model of matter, in P.L. Lijnse *et al.* (eds) *Relating Macroscopic Phenomena to Microscopic Particles*, pp. 266–82. Utrecht CD-β Press.

Millar, R. and Osborne, J. (1998) *Beyond 2000: Science Education for the Future*. London: School of Education, King's College.

Ogborn, J. (1997) Constructivist metaphors of learning science. *Science & Education*, 6(1–2): 121–33.

Posner, G.J., Strike, K.A., Hewson, P.W. and Gertzog, W.A. (1982) Accommodation of a scientific conception: toward a theory of conceptual change. *Science Education*, 66(2): 211–27.

Roth, W.M. (1998) Learning process studies: examples from physics. *International Journal of Science Education*, 20(9): 1019–24.

Scott, P. (1992) Pathways in learning science: a case study of the development of one student's ideas relating to the structure of matter, in R. Duit, F. Goldberg and H. Niedderer (eds) *Research in Physics Learning: Theoretical Issues and Empirical Studies*, pp. 203–24. Kiel: IPN.

Vollebregt, M.J. (1998) *A Problem-posing Approach to Teaching an Initial Particle Model*. Utrecht: CD-β Press.

Welzel, M. (1997) Investigations of individual learning processes – a research program with its theoretical framework and research design, in R.Pinto (ed.) *Theory and Methodology of Research in Science Education*, pp. 76–84. Barcelona: UAB.

18 Policy, practice and research: the case of testing and assessment

Paul Black

Introduction

The interaction of research with policy and practice is complex and varied. If there are any general lessons to be drawn, they can only emerge from detailed inquiry, so I have chosen to look only at testing and assessment, mainly because I have worked on these in several different roles. A further justification is that this area is of outstanding importance. It is through testing that politicians seek to control education. The demands of these tests become the 'touchstone' not only for the things that are learned by students but also for the ways in which they learn and for what they value from that learning. They also become a model for teachers' classroom assessments, and these assessments are a powerful determinant of the quality of a teacher's pedagogy.

Given such arguments, one might expect that this would be an area of great interest for researchers. This is hardly the case in the field of science education. Following the example of White (in press) I have looked over the papers in four main journals of science education research – the *International Journal of Science Education*, the *Journal of Research in Science Teaching*, *Research in Science Education*, and *Science Education* – over the 11 years from 1988 to 1998. Overall, there are about eight papers per year in this field, equivalent to about two per journal per year, but with about 11 per year in the first six years and about five per year in the last five. However, such reckoning can only be made using very arbitrary judgements about the boundaries of the field.

About a quarter of the papers are concerned with summative achievement tests, whether externally applied or set in schools. Another quarter are reports of development of test instruments, while a further third focus on classroom assessment more directly linked to learning needs. The remaining sixth comprises papers which focus on various aspects of the learner's perspective in relation to tests and assessments.

Looking from a different perspective, the 1999 issue (vol. 24) of the *Review of Research in Education* includes review articles on methodological questions in testing, on sociocultural aspects of assessment, and on the interaction between theories of cognition and learning and assessment practices. In total these three have about 580 items in their bibliographies, but not one is from any science education journal. Thus, it seems clear that there is a gulf between the scholarly worlds of measurement and assessment and of science education research, with the latter, for whatever reason, making very little general impact on the former.

Whether or not such data should cause concern is an issue to which I turn at the end of this chapter. The intervening discussion will be set out in three main sections reflecting the three main purposes of testing and assessment. The first is on survey studies of performance, the second on 'high stakes' summative tests, and the third on classroom formative assessment.

Survey studies of performance

I first came to work closely with Ros Driver in 1978, when Chelsea College and Leeds were awarded a joint government contract to conduct national science surveys for the UK Assessment of Performance Unit (APU) (Black 1990). The aim was to use samples of about 10,000 pupils at each of the ages 11, 13 and 15 to produce an annual 'portrait' of science achievements in UK schools. The stated purposes included identifying causes of underachievement and measuring changes over time. There were formidable difficulties – conceptual in relation to the purposes of science education which surveys should reflect, technical in relation to measurement theory, professional in relation to the work of teachers, and political in relation to the aims of the government ministry.

At the outset the teams were faced with a brief that was almost wholly focused on the process view of science. They struggled to clarify this brief and determine the extent to which an aim (of producing items which reflected process aims of science education free from any requirement of conceptual knowledge or understanding) could in fact be achieved. Then we had to convince the ministry's steering group to accept our argument that there had to be a concept-based component. This was unpopular, since one political reason for embracing the 'process only' ideology was a wish to avoid formulating a concept list which could look like a Trojan Horse for a national curriculum. The salient lesson overall was that when broad aims have to be operationalized in specific achievement exercises, their ambiguities are cruelly exposed. This critique of reality operates at one level when questions are proposed, at a further level when a marking scheme has to be specified, and at yet another level when trials with students reveal that the questions are evoking responses that were not envisaged, often in ways that call for reformulation of the initial conceptualization. In this respect, the practical drive was also an unfolding research exercise. A whole apparatus of categories, sub-categories and question descriptors was invented, an enterprise to which Ros Driver made particularly cogent contributions, and no comparable framework for assessments of science achievement by external survey instruments has since appeared. The most difficult category was that of testing observation, where many novel and interesting exercises were developed, yet for which the epitaph on 'content-free' was pronounced in a closing summary report:

> Thus while making and interpreting observations is included for testing in the APU science framework of scientific activity categories, it may well be that the appropriate place for its specific inclusion in taught science is a practical test closely related to the pupils' conceptual knowledge base.
>
> (Archenhold *et al.* 1988: 63)

In relation to the technical requirements, the work drew upon the use of generalizability theory to design the tests of the domains specified by the assessment aims so that optimum reliability could be secured across them. Domains that turned out to produce heterogeneous responses had either to be narrowed by restriction of the range of question demands or given a larger share of testing time. Thus issues of validity in relation to the aims were interplayed with psychometric issues. The outcome was that the items used in a full survey at any one age required about 30 hours of testing to achieve adequate reliability for each category of achievement (Johnson 1988). Those of us who had previous experience in our public certification examinations began to worry about the absence of any such approach to ensure *their* technical quality.

The responses of teachers went through a complex evolution. The government did not feel able to make the tests compulsory and the teacher unions were determined to limit what they suspected to be a move in the direction of national control. Thus, the aim of identifying causes of underachievement was never achieved because the unions refused to allow the collection of any data on the home background of the student samples taking the test. It is however doubtful whether the dream of multivariate analysis of achievement against a myriad of possible independent variables could have revealed anything – particularly when measures of teaching styles and school ethos were also ruled out.

Among science teachers our first presentations, when we could only offer abstract plans, met with hostility. However, the suspicion that we were government agents in an escalating strategy to establish control of the curriculum was forgotten when we were able to present good quality items together with samples of students' responses. Related research had already established that a sample of various education professionals was quite unable to agree in predicting students' responses to process-rich test items (Black *et al.* 1984), and attempts to collect quality items from schools had failed to produce much that was usable. The questions that a full-time team of about 12 could produce were seized upon by teachers who wanted to use them. This experience reflected the comment of Bob Linn (1989: 5) that:

> ... the design of tests useful for the instructional decisions made in the classroom requires an integration of testing and instruction. It also requires a clear conception of the curriculum, the goals, and the process of instruction. And it requires a theory of instruction and learning and a much better understanding of the cognitive processes of learners ...

This positive response led to investment by the ministry in a series of publications of samples of questions which were widely distributed, and which were attractive because they put into concrete terms previously abstract talk about the process aims of science education and their interaction with concept learning. Here we could offer resources which had been thoroughly researched and refined, both through validation by expert judgement and by qualitative and quantitative analyses of students' responses.

In this process, the bureaucrats had to struggle with seemingly awkward academics who were calling into question their carefully laid plans and perhaps forcing them, if they did not resist, to bear bad tidings to their ministers. On the other side, the team members had to make difficult distinctions between their own technical advice and their own desire to shift policies to make them more widely acceptable. They often had to accept that things could not go the way they wanted, sometimes because of conflicting principles and sometimes because of political issues to do with acceptability and the honouring of bargains.

Overall, it could be asked whether the time devoted by the teams of university researchers to a conceptually and logistically complex exercise was well spent. In defence of the efforts, the first of several justifications is the contribution, already mentioned, to teachers' own resources and perspectives. The work also helped to clarify the process approach in school science through setting out clearly defined categories, illustrated by sample questions which provided an empirically based framework of reference.

A further outcome was that the work was a starting point for other developments in science education. Here, the most significant new ventures were a project at King's College London on 'Open Ended Work in Science' (Jones *et al.* 1992) and, outstandingly, the Children's Learning in Science Project (CLISP) at Leeds (Driver *et al.* 1994). Ros Driver took a particular interest in the APU category that assessed understanding of concepts. Indeed, in my very first encounter with her, at a physics teachers' centre founded at the University of Birmingham, she came across as a very unusual school-teacher as she explained to me over coffee her PhD work and her commitment to research further into pupils' understanding of science concepts. Among the APU questions she embedded many that served her targets (and the tests were all the better for having her conceptual underpinning) so that they gave a significant empirical start to the work of CLISP.

Looking back at the whole exercise, it can be seen that the pressures of the yearly testing meant that the data were not as fully exploited as a basis for research studies as they might have been. On the other hand, some commentators have kindly said that a consequence of having academic researchers implement this particular policy enterprise was that it was turned into the research and professional exercise that it was never meant to be. The sequence here was that a policy need provoked more thorough conceptualization of curriculum, through the discipline of producing well researched assessment instruments, and so led to enhanced resources to enrich practice. Research was an enrichment and neither the starting point nor the main purpose, but one consequence of its in-depth examination of the issues was to make clear that assessment policy and curriculum policy are bound to be closely interrelated.

High-stakes summative tests

The APU work made almost no impact on the work of the UK public examination agencies. Attempts to disseminate the findings to examination board officers met with genuine interest, but they seemed unable to work with the findings. Their own research efforts were modest and narrowly focused, and the APU approach was so different that it would have taken a sustained effort, supported by development work, to translate the findings into ideas and procedures which could be incorporated within their constraints. There may also have been more fundamental obstacles; historical and comparative studies of assessment show that the methods seen as natural in any one country have cultural and historical roots that run deep (see for example Black 1998, Chs 2 and 9), so that attempts at fundamental change offer threats to a culture, rather than merely technical improvements.

Studies of the histories and sociology of assessment are important in this respect (see for example Broadfoot 1996). For example, very few countries have relied as heavily as the USA on standardized forms of multiple-choice tests both for accountability and personal testing. The variety of test instruments used in science in the UK was enhanced in the 1960s and 1970s, partly through the influence of multiple-choice tests from the USA and partly because several curriculum projects in the sciences were able to generate new modes of questioning and assessment in order that their examinations would reflect their aims as authentically as possible (see for example Black *et al.* 1970; Black and Ogborn 1977). Research contributed little here, although some evaluation studies and some statistical analyses of the outcomes tended to lend support to the new departures, in that they showed that novel components of the examinations were both internally consistent yet did not measure the same qualities as the conventional components.[1]

There is a very extensive literature in the USA on psychometrics, much of it originating in the refinement of IQ and other multiple-choice tests, but developed to apply to other forms of testing, sometimes setting standards of reliability which newer forms of assessment find hard to meet. The assessments used in many other countries, including the UK, have never been the subject of such close scrutiny. The downside of this is that it is not possible to obtain a figure for the reliability of UK public examinations – little serious work has been done to research the issue. One estimate, made in respect of national assessment tests at age 14, produced an estimate that between 30 and 50 per cent of students are probably misplaced by at least one level – this estimate has been published, not challenged, and largely ignored (Wiliam 1995). One can wonder why both the public and the research community show little concern here, particularly when contributions of alternatives to external testing, involving the use of coursework assessments by teachers to contribute to public examination results, have been cut back on the grounds that such assessments are bound to be unreliable.

Here the scale and scope of the problems facing improvement of practice expands. Teachers will commonly report on the harmful effects on their teaching of the pressure to train their students for success in external examinations. In school science, one example is the study by Wood (1988) who used a qualitative inquiry among four teachers and 165 seventh-grade students about the state mandated tests, which led him to the general conclusion that: 'These unintended consequences of the implemented state policy, instead of improving science teaching and learning, continue to reduce science instruction to the literal comprehension of isolated facts and skills' (p. 631).

A study of advanced placement examinations set for high-school physics students in the USA has also revealed the narrowing effect (Herr 1992), while a review of the literature by Smith *et al.* (1992) concluded that test pressure inhibits teachers' innovation and diversity, reduces their autonomy, and leads them to engage in 'orchestrated cheating' – students being taught how to do tests at the expense of time devoted to teaching the subject. Such reports are both commonplace and amply confirmed by many research studies, yet the public and politicians continue to believe in the use of testing to raise standards. Ironically, any new high-stakes test will show improvement in scores over time as teachers learn how to drill students to meet its demands, so there can be apparent improvement with no real basis (Linn *et al.* 1990; Linn 1994).

Another way in which research studies challenge practice is through studies which examine students' beliefs, understandings and practices in respect of testing. When students were interviewed on their responses to APU questions, most of which were short open-response questions, it emerged that many whose answers were apparently incorrect had underperformed because of misunderstandings of the demand (Gauld 1980). Tamir (1990) showed that when students were asked to give reasons for their responses to a multiple-choice test, a typical outcome for a question might be that, while 70 per cent made a correct choice, only 50 per cent did so for the correct reason, while a further 8 per cent offered correct reasoning but made an incorrect choice; thus a total of 28 per cent had been incorrectly assessed. In a similar study, Yarroch (1991) arrived at a figure of 35 per cent of test-takers being wrongly assessed. He also found that for essay questions there were far fewer wrong classifications. Multiple-choice questions may be invalid because they can be tackled by 'test-wise' students who use strategies that are quite independent of the subject area (Towns and Robinson 1993). In a study of students' abilities to construct and interpret graphs, Berg and Smith (1994) compared results of multiple-choice with free-response methods and found a 19 per cent difference in success rates, so that they concluded that results of research studies using multiple-choice questions may be invalid. Similarly, an interview study by Fensham (1998) of responses to the Third International Mathematics and Science Study (TIMSS) tests for population 3 raised 'some doubts about how well their scores for TIMSS do reflect their actual learning of science' (p. 10). Further problems about common approaches to summative assessment in science are raised by a study of performance across heterogeneous contexts, which showed that students' responses varied in kind and in extent across assessment contexts and formats (McGinn and Roth 1998).

The collection of seven papers discussed above all serve to undermine confidence in standard test methods, yet they cannot be said to form a programme of research: none of the later six refer to Gauld (1980), and of the two 1998 papers one refers to none of the others and the second refers to only one.

The difficulties that students may have in doing themselves justice in test environments may spring in part from misperceptions of the processes and purposes of assessment as a whole. For example, it has been shown that students' understanding of their teachers' evaluation criteria influences their science achievement, especially in complex competencies, and that students of higher social class grasp more readily the rules and procedures of their teachers (Morais and Miranda 1996). The general difficulty that students have in achieving any metacognitive overviews of their work has been well documented, and applies to any attempt to develop their understanding of assessment practices (Baird and Northfield 1992; Fairbrother *et al.* 1994).

The research base has been deployed to good effect in other areas of policy. Thus, an expert review of the work of the National Assessment of Educational Progress (NAEP) in the USA revealed grave shortcomings in the procedures used for setting the cut scores which determine the assignment of each numerical result to one of the four basic bands for reporting (Pellegrino *et al.* 1998: 162–84). Similarly, enquiries ordered by the US Congress trying to block a presidential proposal to establish a voluntary national test led to an expert report demonstrating that it was not possible to achieve the goal of a common national scale of reporting by any statistical manipulation to equate the results of the many different tests set between the different states (Feuer *et al.* 1998). These examples of effective deployment of research expertise are noteworthy because they both arose through the referral of issues, for expert opinion, to the Board of Testing and Assessment of the US National Academy of Sciences.

There is less comfort in other areas. The varied interpretations (or often misinterpretations) of the results of the narrowly focused tests in the TIMSS exercises are a typical case. What seems to be emerging slowly, from fine-grained studies which seek to align results question by question to each country's curricula and textbooks, is that the main determinant of success is whether or not the material in question has been taught at all (Schmidt *et al.* 1999), a lesson which might redirect some of the debates in countries worrying about their ranking. Even more open to misinterpretation is the issue of the variations of test scores over time, where it is hard for the public to accept that if both the curriculum aims and the methods of assessment have changed over the years, any question about whether standards of performance have risen calls for a value judgement and cannot be answered by simple comparison of any pair of test scores.

What is presented in this section has been a diverse set of issues bearing on 'high-stakes' and accountability testing. The overall picture is that researchers seem to function rather like a guerrilla force, engaged in more or less successful attacks on the outposts of the occupying army of public test practice, but rarely able either to take control of any important area or to secure a significant share in the region's administration. Such a role can provide that form of satisfaction that comes from showing that 'authority' is less competent than oneself, or, to be more generous, it may be the only role available, for the task of changing policy requires that effort be directed to lobbying or to influencing public opinion, both of which require time and effort for which researchers receive little reward in their own communities and institutions.

Classroom formative assessment

In 1987 a group convened by the then minister of education in the UK produced advice on a framework for a new national assessment scheme to be introduced with the new National Curriculum. The group's report set out four main criteria that the assessments in the system should meet: they should be criterion-referenced, formative to serve learning needs, moderated to ensure comparability within and between schools, and related to the learning progression of students (DES 1987). The report's strong emphasis on formative assessment was accepted as a part of policy, but completely ignored in subsequent developments (Black 1997). With hindsight it can be seen that the group did not know enough about the empirical or conceptual basis for what they were recommending and did not make an adequately strong argument about both the benefits and the radical changes entailed.

Ten years later, Dylan Wiliam and I produced a 70-page review citing about 250 references, drawn mainly from the literature of the 1990s (Black and Wiliam 1998a). The review set out first to seek evidence on whether development of formative assessment raises standards of learning. Our definition of formative assessment was as follows: 'In this review, it is to be interpreted as encompassing all those activities undertaken by teachers, and/ or by their students, which provide information to be used as feedback to modify the teaching and learning activities in which they are engaged' (p. 7). In preparing this review, we looked for studies with matched experimental and control groups, using pre- and post-tests, incorporating frequent assessment used as feedback to guide learning, and reporting quantitative analysis to compare learning gains between the experiment and the control groups. We found between 20 and 30 studies all of which showed significant learning advantage for their formative assessment experiments, with effect sizes ranging from 0.4 to 0.7 – remarkably large for any educational experiment.[2] Several also reported that 'low attainers', or 'slow learners' showed the largest gains, and many involved emphasis on self- and peer-assessment by pupils. The strongest example in science is a study by White and Frederiksen of the incorporation of formative self-assessment work into a new inquiry-based practical course on forces and motion (White and Frederiksen 1998). These studies were not part of a coherent programme, and there is very little cross-referencing between them. Such features show that this is not a well-established field of research, but given that the studies each had their own distinctive ways of enhancing learning through formative assessment, the diversity also supports the conclusion that the learning advantage of enhanced formative assessment is a robust effect, not dependent on particular details of implementation.

The literature also confirmed that classroom assessment practices are weak. In science, a comprehensive evaluation of the implementation of the UK

National Curriculum concluded that formative assessment was 'seriously in need of development' (Russell *et al.* 1995: 489), while a more recent survey of science classrooms in the UK summarized its findings with the question, 'Why is the extent and nature of formative assessment in science so impoverished?' (Daws and Singh 1996). Common features of these findings were that assessments encourage rote and superficial learning, that in the questions that teachers used they were not critical about what was being assessed, and that in the use of assessments the grading function was over-emphasized and the learning function underemphasized.

The review was followed up by a 20-page pamphlet which summarized the findings, and recommended a series of changes in both policy and practice needed to realize the potential gains of improved formative assessment (Black and Wiliam 1998b). Such recommendations went beyond the research evidence, and it was emphasized that the evidence could only suggest a set of possible ideas that needed to be tried (and thereby reformulated and rearticulated) through the involvement of teachers in action research. In saying this we were reflecting a general belief about the gap between research results and classroom practices (see for example Hargreaves 1998). In order to carry this idea through, we are currently working with and through 24 science and mathematics teachers in six schools in a search for implementation strategies.

The publication of the pamphlet was made the occasion for a press release which led to intensive media exposure for about 48 hours. Subsequently, through requests to King's College for copies, and offers of copies for sale at the many lectures and workshops which Dylan Wiliam and I have been invited to give (around 40 in the last 18 months and still coming), we have sold over 12000 copies. A version of the pamphlet has also been published in the USA (Black and Wiliam 1998c).

I have indulged in this personal story because I believe that it raises several issues relevant to the main argument here. The first relates to the research literature. Our review took as its starting point reviews published in 1987, listing 91 references (Natriello 1987), and in 1988, listing 241 references (Crooks 1988). Only 9 references appeared in both lists. We subsequently found a review reporting a thorough meta-analysis of 21 selected formative assessment experiments, published in 1986 (Fuchs and Fuchs 1986), which was not referred to in either of the other two reviews. As we searched the literature, we found that both citation analyses based on the two reviews and the use of key words were inadequate. The only effective search procedure was to turn the pages of 76 of the most likely journals, covering the last ten years, and make rapid judgements (first from titles and then from abstracts) about likely relevance.

The general conclusion is that most researchers, in most countries, do not know of much of the literature, national or international, that could inform their work. Given the effort involved to scan the literature thoroughly, this is understandable, but raises the question as to whether this field can form productive programmes of research when the pressures to publish leave too little time for wider reading of, and reflection on, the work of others.

The second issue is raised by the surprisingly strong response of teachers to this work. A typical explanation is given by teachers who say, 'We always believed that this approach was important, but to know that this is backed by your research gives us confidence to give it fresh attention' (we had not done any research, simply reviewed the work of others). However, one set of results is so surprising to teachers that a few simply reject it. This came from research that explores the effect, on learning gains, of giving feedback on written work in different ways. The research has shown that feedback through comments alone on such work leads to learning gains, while giving marks alone, or comments accompanied by marks, or giving praise, do not (Butler, 1988). This calls into question the whole classroom culture of marks, grades, gold stars, merit awards and so on, a culture which emphasizes competition rather than personal improvement, so that feedback teaches weak pupils that they lack 'ability', and hence demotivates them.

The problems about grades and praise raise more fundamental questions about students' motivation, self-concept, ego-involvement and so on, and about the classroom as a learning community. Thus the third issue is the need for an adequate theoretical basis for further reflection and action in formative assessment. Various authors have made contributions here (Sadler 1989; Perrenoud 1991; Tittle *et al.* 1993; Deci and Ryan 1994; Butler and Winne 1995; Aikenhead 1997) and a further contribution is made in Chapter 3 by Beverley Bell. This is not the place to attempt a synthesis. However, it becomes clear that effective formative feedback can be all-pervasive, as the host of issues raised in the quotation by Linn earlier in this chapter makes clear. It takes place through written and oral questions, through the quality of classroom dialogue and through the formulation of classroom tasks so that pupils are sufficiently active to produce feedback evidence. Furthermore, it must involve pupils in self- and peer-assessment. Given this broad agenda, it becomes questionable whether any theory can be cogent without being integrated within, and influencing strongly, a theory of pedagogy as a whole. Given that, as already pointed out above, curriculum and assessment policies interact strongly, it is clear that assessment policies have to be informed by an understanding of the curriculum–pedagogy–assessment triangle; in the absence of such a perspective, policies are sure to have effects which are not anticipated, and which may not be desired even by those formulating those policies.

The fourth and final issue concerns the implications for public policy. What, policymakers might ask if they accepted the evidence, should they do about formative assessment? The answer is definitely *not* to start a national programme to require all teachers to improve their practice, but rather to build up practice slowly through programmes of development and dissemination which are matched to the capacity of teachers to take ownership of change, and to reduce some of the obstacles, such as overcrowded curricula and oppressive external tests, all on a promise that things will get better slowly, and certainly not before the next election. Could such an answer ever be acceptable as a basis for policy investment?

Reflections

This account is not a balanced and comprehensive overview of research in testing and assessment. On the contrary, it is idiosyncratic, being focused mainly on areas where I have been directly involved, following my opening justification that issues of interplay between research, practice and policy are best illustrated by a close look at a few cases. Some of these issues will be explored in this closing section.

Crossing boundaries

One issue concerns the interplay between educational research in general and research in the field of one particular subject discipline, in our case science. Research into learning became far more interesting when it broke away from the narrow range of purely logical problems and confronted the epistemologies of particular knowledge disciplines. Yet much of the literature in education is still focused on language and mathematics. Science education may achieve third place, but my experience is that its literature is not read by others, and that some of its practitioners do not pay enough attention to work in other fields of education (what do researchers in science education know about research into education in mathematics or in history?). Yet the practice of science education in the classroom requires attention to other curriculum disciplines, notably to language skills and to numeracy, and if researchers do not develop an interdisciplinary approach, they are leaving it to schools to make interdisciplinary connections when they try to implement proposals arising from research.

Are our institutions adequate?

This second issue is suggested by the example of the National Academy of Sciences in the USA, which was founded by Thomas Jefferson to give independent and public advice to government. Its Board of Testing and

Assessment, for example, is composed of leading professionals in several arenas of research and of practice. Its work is both reactive, to issues coming from government, and proactive on its own agenda. Its publications are rigorously refereed and then made public. I have referred above to two examples – the critique of the NAEP and the work on the possible link between state test results, both of which have influenced policy. The issue is: do we need new institutional structures to serve as an interface between academic and professional experts and those responsible for public policies?

Audit and agenda for research

The big issue however is whether research has helped, or could help, to enhance policies and practices in testing and assessment. One way to consider this question is to audit these contributions against a view of the main problems in the field of professional, political and public action, and to suggest how research may make further contributions. My personal audit would be as follows:

- *Teachers' formative assessment is very weak and ought to be developed.* The body of research does serve to support both parts of this assertion, but can only give clues about how to take the action that ought to follow. Thus it is necessary now to have research which looks to the problems of formulating and implementing new classroom work starting from the results of existing research 'experiments' rather than to add more results about more 'experiments'.
- *That current practices in summative assessment are more deeply flawed than is generally realized, both in regard to reliability and validity.* Here research has provided numerous pieces of relevant evidence, but has not been articulated into programmes or syntheses that can make the case clear enough to have public impact. There is therefore a need for programmes that can forge this synthesis as a basis for achieving such impact.
- *Short, affordable, externally set and marked tests cannot produce a reliable and valid assessment of a student's capability except in particular and limited areas of achievement.* It follows that, while such tests have a part to play in any system, a substantial component of assessment for personal certification must be based on extensive records of coursework. Teachers should have significant responsibility in such assessment. The research that would be helpful here would be work which explored ways to evaluate the reliability of, and public confidence in, teachers' summative assessments, whether these be based on specific pieces of coursework or based broadly on a long-term overview of a pupil's work.

- *That teachers have to bear the dual role of being guides and assessors of their students' work.* Here the research contribution has been clouded. Some have argued on technical grounds that the formative and summative purposes are different, so they cannot be served by the same instruments, hence the two roles should be kept apart (for example Harlen *et al.* 1992). The links in this chain of logic are open to challenge (see Black 1993; Wiliam and Black 1996) and more recently some of its former proponents now accept that the roles should not, in practice, be separated. However, there are hardly any studies of the practice of this duality of role by teachers: thus research into possible 'formative-summative' tensions, and into whether or not these could be replaced by a formative-summative synergy, is needed. Although in most areas of the higher education sector the dual role is accepted as a necessary part of practice, at least some teachers in schools will resist, partly because of the extra work involved, and partly because they foresee personal conflict for them between the two roles.
- *Current systems for assessment and testing command far more confidence than they should, and are adopted in the belief that tests will raise standards when in fact they impoverish learning: a radical reconstruction of policies about assessment is called for.* It is questionable whether the research community could or should contribute here. One way would be comparative studies looking in detail at those school systems where teachers' roles in public assessment are strong – for example, in Queensland (Butler 1995) or in Sweden (Eckstein and Noah 1993: 36–40). Another way would be to devote more energy to promoting the public understanding of education, perhaps following the example of the community of scientists in promoting the public understanding of science.

Changing public policy

The considerations above do set out a research agenda, but they imply much more by suggesting an agenda for researchers that is broader than that of the typical academic research programme. Here the argument homes in on the main message of this chapter, which has two components. One is to draw attention to a contradiction between public policies in testing and assessment, and their attendant implications for school practices. To summarize, the conclusions arising from research are first that summative assessments by current external tests do not give the evidence about attainment and potential that individuals and society need, and that society is mistaken in its belief that they provide trustworthy evidence. The second is that these tests mislead and oppress teachers: the paradox here is that formative assessment practices could have a powerful effect in raising standards of attainment, but wither for lack of support and are actually inhibited by the pressures of summative testing which politicians have intensified because they believe, in the face of evidence to the contrary, that such tests can raise standards.

Given such conclusions, backed by a strong body of research evidence, it seems remarkable that such dysfunctional policies are so strongly sustained. One reason may be that they serve social purposes in ways that are generally accepted as satisfactory, at relatively modest cost. Teachers are accustomed to the system, and changes of the type implied by the critique presented in this chapter are seen by them to call for extra work, for risky changes in their classroom practices, and for them to adopt a new level of responsibility for their pupils which could expose them to new types of parental and even legal challenge. For the general public there are other reasons for unease about any proposed changes in the system. One is the belief that external tests are fair and reliable, coupled with a belief that teachers' own judgements of their pupils can never command the degree of trust needed if they are to determine those pupils' life chances. As for any other public service, people want to see in place independent checks so that they can have confidence, notably in the results of high-stakes assessments: if such confidence is lost by the present assessment system, the various users, notably higher education and employers, will set up their own tests to do the job. Thus politicians and others may fear that any changes which are perceived as a threat to confidence might simply undermine the system that they are meant to improve. Furthermore, the view that the present system is not seen as problematic may stem in part from the view that the relationships between curriculum, pedagogy and assessment are relatively straightforward, so that the ways in which negative, albeit unintended, consequences of common assessment practice can undermine the aims of a curriculum are not understood.

The contribution of the research community

Given that it would be very difficult at present to change the system in the face of these entrenched positions, it seems important to ask why the contributions of research have not made the strong impact that is needed to change present beliefs and practices, and how that impact may be enhanced in future.

One way to respond to this question is to examine the nature and status of research evidence. Here there are two fault lines. The first line lies between evidence that can be published in a research journal and ideas that teachers can apply in classroom practice. To tackle this, researchers need to reconceptualize their vision of a research programme. If the vision is limited to producing scholarly articles, then it is hardly possible to envisage any practical application in schools. If the vision is broadened to include publication in professional journals and through talks to teachers, the prospects of practical impact are enhanced, but are still very slim. More ambitious still will be to make the results the basis for in-service education and training (INSET) programmes, but it is notorious that, while such programmes may often produce satisfaction or even enthusiasm among their customers, they often have very little impact in daily practice.

The vision has to be broader still. What is needed are programmes in which researchers work with teachers and others to provoke and support them in turning ideas from research into classroom actions which are fashioned by teachers themselves. In the course of doing this teachers will be transforming 'research knowledge' into 'classroom knowledge'. It is only this second type of knowledge which is useful to teachers, and it is only the practitioners themselves who can create it. Thus implementation through dissemination may require that researchers pursue such work with the limited number of teachers whom they can properly support, and that this work lays the basis for further work in which these teachers become partners with the researchers in disseminating among their profession. The necessity for such extended effort implies that when a research programme has produced evidence and insights which answer the original research questions and which can be acceptable for academic publications it is very far from being finished. The programme has to move to a second stage, promoting, via teachers, transformation of the new knowledge into classroom form and then working with teachers as partners in subsequent efforts for wide-scale dissemination. This second stage may well take at least as long as the first, and will require methods and skills rather different from those needed for the pure research stage.

The second fault line lies between acceptance of results, and of their implications in the academic community, and acceptance among the teaching profession, among the public and the media, and among politicians with legislative power. It is more difficult to make recommendations about tackling this fault line. Some pressure groups have achieved political influence by a tireless campaign of meetings and publications which have impressed politicians and the media, often with arguments that are at least open to challenge and which are often supported by inadequate or illegitimate evidence, or even by none at all.

Here there is one specific point that may serve to illustrate a more general argument: that professional and public audiences are far more easily impressed by evidence based on quantitative results of learning gains than by results of qualitative research. It may be valid to argue that quantitative pre-post score gains tell us too little, so that research effort is best spent on formulating a deeper understanding of the process of an innovation, but such arguments have been taken too far in the research community. The public is bound to reply, 'Yes, but did they *learn* anything?' It is legitimate to want explicit evidence that any innovation, which will be costly and which will disturb existing practice, will actually result in pupils being better informed, more capable in using their learning, and better motivated. It is as important to work to produce evidence that an innovation is effective as it is to work to understand how and why it is effective – it is pointless to play priorities and choose one of these tasks while neglecting the other.

The more general point that this example illustrates is that it may not be enough to decide to do something about 'public impact' as an afterthought at the end of a research study. We may need instead to give some priority to considerations of public and policy impact from the outset, so that these considerations affect the selection and design of the research.

More generally, researchers with something to say may have to commit some of their time and effort to campaigns to inform and convince the public. In doing so, they must look to allies, among the teaching profession and among other education professionals, and they must also look to the types of argument and to the language that make sense to those not engaged in the researchers' peculiar discourse.

Notes

1 Unfortunately, this work was documented only in an internal report of the Oxford and Cambridge Schools Examination Board (Shoesmith 1975) and was never published.
2 An effect size is the ratio of the difference in the mean scores between the experimental and control groups, divided by the standard deviation of either of these two scores' distributions. The reliability of such estimates depends upon the reliability of the group mean scores, and not upon the (necessarily lower) reliability of the test scores of individual pupils.

References

Aikenhead, G.S. (1997) A framework for reflecting on assessment and evaluation, in B.-Y. Yi *et al.* (eds) *Globalisation of Science Education – Moving Towards Worldwide Science Education Standards*, pp. 177–80. Seoul: Korean Educational Development Institute.

Archenhold, W.F., Bell, J.F., Donnelly, J., Johnson, S. and Welford, G. (1988) *Science at Age 15: A Review of APU Findings 1980–1984*. London: HMSO.

Baird, J.R. and Northfield, J.R. (eds) (1992) *Learning from the PEEL Experience*. Melbourne: Monash University.

Berg, C.A. and Smith, P. (1994) Assessing students' abilities to construct and inter-pret line graphs: disparities between multiple-choice and free-response instruments. *Science Education*, 78(6): 527–54.

Black, P.J. (1990) APU Science: the past and the future. *School Science Review*, 72(258): 13–28.

Black, P.J. (1993) Assessment policy and public confidence: comments on the BERA Policy Task Group's article 'Assessment and the Improvement of Education'. *The Curriculum Journal*, 4(3): 412–27.

Black, P.J. (1997) Whatever happened to TGAT? in C. Cullingford (ed.) *Assessment vs. Evaluation*, pp. 24–50. London: Cassell.

Black, P.J. (1998) *Testing: Friend or Foe*. London: Falmer.

Black, P.J. and Ogborn, J.M. (1977) The Nuffield A-level physics examination. *Physics Education*, 12: 12–16.

Black, P. and Wiliam, D. (1998a) Assessment and classroom learning. *Assessment in Education*, 5(1): 7–74.

Black, P.J. and Wiliam, D. (1998b) *Inside the Black Box: Raising Standards through Classroom Assessment*. London: School of Education, King's College.

Black, P.J. and Wiliam, D. (1998c) Inside the black box: raising standards through classroom assessment. *Phi Delta Kappan*, 80(2): 139–48.

Black, P.J., Eggleston, J.F. and Matthews, J.C. (1970) *Examining in the Advanced-level Science Subjects of the G.C.E.* (JMB Occasional Publications No. 30). Manchester: Joint Matriculation Board.

Black, P.J., Harlen, W. and Orgee, A. (1984) *Standards of Performance: Expectation and Reality* (APU Occasional Paper No. 3). London: Department of Education and Science.

Broadfoot, P.M. (1996) *Education, Assessment and Society: A Sociological Analysis*. Buckingham: Open University Press.

Butler, D.L. and Winne, P.H. (1995) Feedback and self-regulated learning: a the-oretical synthesis. *Review of Educational Research*, 65(3): 245–81.

Butler, J. (1995) Teachers judging standards in senior science subjects: fifteen years of the Queensland experiment. *Studies in Science Education*, 26: 135–57.

Butler, R. (1988) Enhancing and undermining intrinsic motivation: the effects of task-involving and ego-involving evaluation on interest and performance. *British Journal of Educational Psychology*, 58(1): 1–14.

Crooks, T.J. (1988) The impact of classroom evaluation practices on students. *Review of Educational Research*, 58(4): 438–81.

Daws, N. and Singh, B. (1996) Formative assessment: to what extent is its poten-tial to enhance pupils' science being realized? *School Science Review*, 77(281): 93–100.

Deci, E.L. and Ryan, R.M. (1994) Promoting self-determined education. *Scandinavian Journal of Educational Research*, 38(1): 3–14.

DES (Department of Education and Science) (1987) *National Curriculum: Task Group on Assessment and Testing: A Report*. London: DES/Welsh Office.

Driver, R., Squires, A., Rushworth, P. and Wood-Robinson, V. (1994) *Making Sense of Secondary Science: Research into Children's Ideas*. London: Routledge.

Eckstein, M.A. and Noah, H.J. (1993) *Secondary School Examinations: International Perspectives on Policies and Practice*. New Haven, CT: Yale University.

Fairbrother, R., Black, P.J. and Gill, P. (eds) (1994) *Teachers Assessing Pupils: Lessons from Science Classrooms.* Hatfield: Association for Science Education.

Fensham, P. (1998) Student response to the TIMSS test. *Research in Science Education,* 28(4): 481–9.

Feuer, M.J., Holland, P.W., Bertenthal, M.W., Hemphill, F.C. and Green, B.E. (1998) *Uncommon Measures: Equivalence and Linkage of Educational Tests.* Washington, DC: National Academy Press.

Fuchs, L.S. and Fuchs, D. (1986) Effects of systematic formative evaluation – a meta-analysis. *Exceptional Children,* 53(3): 199–208.

Gauld, C.F. (1980) Subject oriented test construction. *Research in Science Education,* 10(1): 77–82.

Hargreaves, D.H. (1998) The knowledge creating school. Lecture given to the Symposium on Educational Research at the Annual Meeting of the British Educational Research Association, Belfast, August.

Harlen, W., Gipps, C., Broadfoot, P. and Nuttall, D. (1992) Assessment and the improvement of education. *The Curriculum Journal,* 3(3): 215–30.

Herr, N.E. (1992) A comparative analysis of the perceived influence of advanced placement and honors programs upon science instruction. *Journal of Research in Science Teaching,* 29(5): 521–32.

Johnson, S. (1988) *National Assessment: The APU Science Approach.* London: HMSO.

Jones, A., Simon, S.A, Black, P.J., Fairbrother, R.W. and Watson, J.R. (1992) *Open Work in School Science: Development of Investigations in Schools.* Hatfield: Association for Science Education.

Linn, R.L. (ed.) (1989). *Educational Measurement,* 3rd edn. London: Collier Macmillan.

Linn, R.L. (1994) *Assessment Based Reform: Challenges to Educational Measurement.* Princeton, NJ: Educational Testing Service.

Linn, R.L., Graue, E. and Sanders, N.M. (1990) Comparing state and district test results to national norms: the validity of claims 'that everyone is above average'. *Educational Measurement: Issues and Practice,* 9(3): 9–14.

McGinn, M.K. and Roth, W.-M. (1998) Assessing students' understanding about levers: better test instruments are not enough. *International Journal of Science Education,* 20(7): 813–32.

Morais, A.M. and Miranda, C. (1996) Understanding teachers' evaluation criteria: a condition for success in science classes. *Journal of Research in Science Teaching,* 33(6): 601–24.

Natriello, G. (1987) The impact of evaluation processes on students. *Educational Psychologist,* 22(2): 155–75.

Pellegrino, J.W., Jones, L.R. and Mitchell, K. (1998) *Grading the Nation's Report Card.* Washington, DC: National Academy Press.

Perrenoud, P. (1991) Towards a pragmatic approach to formative evaluation, in P. Weston (ed.) *Assessment of Pupils' Achievement: Motivation and School Success,* pp. 79–101. Amsterdam: Swets and Zeitlinger.

Russell, T., Qualter, A. and McGuigan, L. (1995) Reflections on the implementation of National Curriculum science policy for the 5–14 age range: findings and interpretations from a national evaluation study in England. *International Journal of Science Education,* 17(4): 481–92.

Sadler, R. (1989) Formative assessment and the design of instructional systems. *Instructional Science*, 18: 119–44.

Schmidt, W.H., McKnight, C.C., Cogan, L.S., Jakwerth, P.M. and Houang, R.T. (1999) *Facing the Consequences: Using TIMSS for a Closer Look at U.S. Mathematics and Science Education*. Dordrecht: Kluwer Academic Publishers.

Shoesmith, D. (1975) Private communication.

Smith, P.S., Hounshell, P.B., Copolo, C. and Wilkerson, S. (1992) The impact of end-of-course testing in chemistry on curriculum and instruction. *Science Education*, 76(5): 523–30.

Tamir, P. (1990) Justifying the selection of answers in multiple-choice items. *International Journal of Science Education*, 12(5): 563–73.

Tittle, C.K., Hecht, D. and Moore, P. (1993) Assessment theory and research for classrooms: from taxonomies to constructing meaning in context. *Educational Measurement: Issues and Practice*, 12(4): 13–19.

Towns, M.H. and Robinson, W.R. (1993) Student use of test-wiseness strategies in solving multiple-choice chemistry examinations. *Journal of Research in Science Teaching*, 30(7): 709–22.

White, B.Y. and Frederiksen, J.R. (1998) Inquiry, modelling, and metacognition: making science accessible to all students. *Cognition and Instruction*, 16(1): 3–118.

White, R.T. (in press) The revolution in research on science teaching, in V. Richardson (ed.) *Handbook of Research on Teaching* (4th edn). New York: Macmillan.

Wiliam, D. (1995) It'll all end in tiers. *British Journal of Curriculum and Assessment*, 5(3): 21–4.

Wiliam, D. and Black, P.J. (1996) Meanings and consequences: a basis for distinguishing formative and summative functions of assessment? *British Educational Research Journal*, 22(5): 537–48.

Wood, T. (1988) State-mandated acountability as a constraint on teaching and learning science. *Journal of Research in Science Teaching*, 25(8): 631–41.

Yarroch, W.L. (1991) The implications of content versus item validity on science tests. *Journal of Research in Science Teaching*, 28(7): 619–29.

Notes on contributors

Glen Aikenhead, University of Saskatchewan, Canada
I have always embraced a humanistic perspective on science, even as a young research chemist in Canada and as a science teacher at international schools in Germany and Switzerland. This humanistic perspective was enhanced during my graduate studies at Harvard University in the 1960s and has since then (at the University of Saskatchewan) guided my research into curriculum policy, student assessment, classroom materials, classroom instruction and cross-cultural science education. This research and development has resulted in such publications as: *Science in Social Issues: Implications for Teaching* (1980); *Views on Science Technology and Society* (VOSTS 1989); *Logical Reasoning in Science & Technology* (LoRST 1991); *STS Education: International Perspectives on Reform* (co-edited 1994); and *Cross-Cultural Science & Technology Units* (2000).

I first met Ros Driver in the early 1980s and I have benefited immeasurably through the years from her mentoring encouragement and critical reflections on both our research programmes. Though these programmes differed in their focus, they shared a strong concern for a humanistic perspective on science education research.

Björn Andersson, University of Göteborg, Sweden
After about ten years as a teacher and teacher trainer in physics, I completed my PhD in science education in 1977. Since then I have mainly directed projects for the National Agency of Education, including national evaluation of students' knowledge and understanding of science. I have been working in Göteborg since 1967 and became Professor in 'subject matter *didaktik*' at the university in 1997 (the first chair in the field in Sweden). My academic interests are in students' thinking and learning in

science with some focus on the upper part of comprehensive schools (age 12–16). Another area of interest is in the integration of knowledge and curriculum organization.

I first met Ros Driver in 1979 at a Leeds conference on cognitive development research in science and mathematics education. This led to several visits to Leeds University, generously hosted and organized by Ros and significantly stimulating our science education research at Göteborg University. Ros and her colleagues also visited us several times, and during the academic year 1994/5 Ros was Visiting Professor at Göteborg. This was beneficial not only to scholars from Göteborg but from other parts of Sweden as well, who took the opportunity to join her seminars. She also made contributions to a national science education conference, held in June 1995. We are grateful that Ros devoted so much time to Swedish science education and note that Leeds–Göteborg exchanges still go on, very much in her spirit of friendliness and straightforward academic exchange of criticism and ideas.

Hilary Asoko, University of Leeds, UK

I studied biochemistry at university and spent 2 years in neurochemistry research before deciding to teach. After 11 years working in schools in England, I briefly taught English in Finland and then spent 2 years in Nigeria developing a science course for student nurses. These experiences stimulated a desire to explore ideas about teaching and learning and, in 1988, I enrolled on a masters degree at the University of Leeds. Here I encountered an inspiring and thought-provoking lecturer, Ros Driver, and from 1989 had the opportunity to work with her in the Children's Learning in Science Project (CLISP). It was Ros who first stimulated my interest in primary science, the focus of my work ever since. Currently, I am involved in the initial and in-service training of primary teachers and am particularly interested in the teacher's role in the development of children's conceptual understanding of science.

Ros had a significant influence on my thinking, my teaching and my career and I feel privileged to have known her as a teacher, a colleague and a friend.

Beverley Bell, University of Waikato, New Zealand

I taught science and senior biology in New Zealand secondary schools before coming to the University of Waikato in 1979 to study for a masters and doctoral degree in science education. As a graduate student, I worked on the first Waikato Learning in Science Project team. On my return from the UK in 1985, I joined the Curriculum Development Division for the government, before moving in 1989 to the Centre for Science, Technology and Mathematics Education Research at the University of Waikato, where I was Director from 1995–8. I am now an Associate Professor in the School of Education and my research interests include teaching, learning and assessment; science education; curriculum development; and teacher development.

My colleagueship with Ros Driver began when I joined her in Leeds as a researcher and coordinator of the Children's Learning in Science Project (CLISP) from 1983–5. I much admired and respected her scholarship, energy and determination. Her stride, both physically and academically, at times left me running to catch up!

Paul Black, Emeritus Professor, King's College London, UK

I started research in physics with 6 years in the Cavendish, then with 20 more in Birmingham. Service on the Joint Matriculation Board developed my interest in testing, while leadership with Jon Ogborn of the Nuffield Advanced Physics Project immersed me in curriculum thinking. In 1976 I moved to the Chelsea Centre for Science Education, later becoming Head of Education at King's after our merger. I worked on several Nuffield curriculum projects, co-directed the Assessment of Performance Unit (APU) science team and, in 1987/8, chaired the TGAT group. Since retirement in 1995 I have been involved in work on formative assessment.

I knew Ros Driver first when, as a teacher in Birmingham, she came to our university teachers' centre, later through the sharing of the APU work between Chelsea and Leeds, and later again through her help with the primary SPACE (Science Process and Concept Exploration) project. I was always stimulated by her passion for deeper understanding, so it was a joy to me to see her, when she succeeded me in the King's chair, leading her colleagues there with enthusiasm and courage which have left their mark.

Nancy W. Brickhouse, University of Delaware, USA

After graduating with an undergraduate chemistry degree, I taught physical science, chemistry and physics in rural East Texas, USA. I then completed graduate work in chemistry and science education at Purdue University. I have been at the University of Delaware since 1988. I have an ongoing concern for understanding how to move students away from naïve, positivist views of science so that they are in a better position to understand how science functions in a society that has not always been adequately inclusive.

Ros Driver has been an inspirational figure for me since I first became familiar with her work as a graduate student. In 1992 I spent a sabbatical in Leeds and was privileged to be part of the early conversations that guided the research on what became *Young People's Images of Science*. I admired Ros's ability to be simultaneously supportive and critical of the work of her students and colleagues.

Zoubeida Dagher, University of Delaware, USA

I am Associate Professor of science education at the University of Delaware. My research interests include the social construction of explanations in science in the classroom, and student understanding of the nature of science and scientific theories.

Justin Dillon, King's College London, UK

My father was a science teacher and a middle manager. I studied chemistry at university and trained to be a science teacher at Chelsea College. I taught and managed in London schools during the 1980s and then joined King's College London. My partner is a middle manager in further education – we met while doing our masters degrees in science education at King's. I am responsible for King's overseas and professional development work. My research into teacher development in the UK and overseas feeds into our MA in education management.

Before Ros Driver arrived at King's my colleagues and our students had set high standards of scholarly activity. To have maintained such standards, in London, at the end of the twentieth century, would have been creditable. But Ros was able to raise our standards – to lead and inspire with grace, charm, insight and wisdom. We miss her physical presence but we do not miss her ideals or her vision, because they have never gone away.

Richard Duschl, King's College London, UK

I earned my BS and PhD in earth science education and science education, respectively, from the University of Maryland, College Park, and an MAT degree in geology from Michigan State University. Prior to joining the King's College London faculty as Professor of Science Education, I held academic posts at Vanderbilt University, the University of Pittsburgh, Hunter College-CUNY and the University of Houston. My present research focuses on establishing formative assessment learning environments in middle school or Key Stage 3 science classrooms. Project SEPIA (Science Education through Portfolio Instruction and Assessment) is a programme of research investigating the dynamic structures of implementing full inquiry units that facilitate feedback in three domains: epistemic rules, notational conventions and conceptual systems. *Young People's Images of Science* has been very influential on my research.

I first met Ros through the AERA SIG-Subject Matter Knowledge and Conceptual Change. She was the SIG president and I served her in the role of programme chair for two conferences. At the time of her move to King's College London, we began conversations about a joint research programme on the role of argumentation in science education classrooms and small groups. I consider myself very privileged to be given the opportunity to follow her in the Chair of Science Education at King's College London and continue the work she started there with colleagues on argumentation. Sitting at her desk is a daily inspiration.

Gaalen Erickson, University of British Columbia, Canada

After obtaining a BEd and an MSc (in chemistry) I taught high school for several years in Canada and England. I completed my EdD in science education and have been teaching at the University of British Columbia since 1975. My research interests are primarily in the areas of student and teacher learning in a variety of science education contexts. I am a Professor in Curriculum Studies and the Director of the Centre for the Study of Teacher Education at UBC.

After Jack Easley gave me Ros Driver's dissertation to read I immediately contacted her about coming to Leeds for a sabbatical leave in 1981, where I spent a stimulating six months with Ros and her colleagues. During this time we collaborated on an article and I wrote a chapter in a book that she was editing on children's ideas in science. This was a very formative time in my career and our many discussions ranging from philosophy of science to cognitive psychology to classroom practice had a profound and lasting influence on my work. We remained very close friends over the years and I always looked forward to our extended discussions at professional meetings and conferences. Ros was an exceptional academic and human being and her work will continue to influence future generations of researchers and teachers.

Peter Fensham, Emeritus Professor, Monash University, Australia

After studies in physical chemistry at the universities of Melbourne, Bristol and Princeton, I spent three years at Cambridge University as a Nuffield sociological scholar, studying human aspects of automation in the weaving industry. Ten years lecturing and research in solid state chemistry followed at the University of Melbourne. In 1967 I was invited by Monash University to a Chair in Science Education, the first in Australia. A strong research group followed with expanding international associations. One with Leeds University led to fruitful exchanges involving David Layton, Ros Driver and Douglas Barnes. My research interests are the learning of science, the politics of curriculum change and social inequalities in education. My interest in 'science for all' has provided a coherent thread across these fields.

Before I met Ros Driver we shared the influence of Jack Easley at the University of Illinois and the importance of the learner in science education. As Christine and I got to know Ros and Geoff, we found that we shared the formative influence of the Student Christian Movement, with its traditions of taking seriously the relationships between faith and scholarship, and between faith and politics.

Richard Gunstone, Monash University, Australia

After 12 years as a high-school science teacher, and substantial involvement with the Science Teachers Association of Victoria, I joined Monash University in 1974. At this time I had strong and very ill-formed concerns with the fostering of higher quality learning in science classrooms, and with the nature of professional development among science teachers. These two concerns have been at the heart of all the work I have done as an academic at Monash, where I am now Professor of Science and Technology Education.

The concerns have been constant, but are now framed in much more informed ways. My first contact with Ros Driver was through her writings, and the powerful ideas that she laid out. Then she spent time at Monash in 1982 and I saw for the first time how genuine was her commitment to better science education. That time, and many subsequent occasions at Leeds, Monash and conferences, have been of central importance to the ways I have been able to develop.

Peter Hewson, University of Wisconsin-Madison, USA

I am a Professor of Science Education at the University of Wisconsin-Madison, and interested in several commonplaces of the field: students learning science, teachers teaching science, and people becoming teachers of science. I came to these interests slowly. A doctorate in theoretical physics led to the philosophies of science and education and, in time, a deep interest in coherency across these commonplaces. Conceptual change has been a common theme in understanding them as they occur in the complexity of practice in classrooms with diverse human beings.

Ros Driver has been a major influence on my professional development. I knew her through a series of events that started with a visit to Leeds in 1980, continuing through summer schools in La Londe and Vancouver, AERA and NARST meetings, a workshop in Madrid, and culminating in Chicago when NARST honoured her with the Distinguished Contributions

Award. These moments in time were the pillars supporting a continuous bridge of nearly two decades of collegiality and friendship. My life is richer because of Ros.

Edgar Jenkins, University of Leeds, UK

Before joining the University of Leeds, I taught chemistry in secondary schools and took part in the trials of some of the materials produced by the Nuffield science teaching projects. My research interest, the social history and politics of school science education, was very different from that of Ros Driver who joined me as a colleague at Leeds in the mid-1970s. Eventually and unexpectedly, our interests came closer together as my own work on the public understanding of science showed how ordinary people develop their own understandings of the world in which they live.

It was my privilege to be a colleague of Ros for some 20 years, 8 of them as her head of department. During that time her reputation grew steadily, both as a researcher and as someone who nurtured close contact between the communities of research and practice in science education. She attracted a stream of students and visiting scholars to Leeds and established herself as a leading international figure in her field. Immensely hard-working and always intellectually stimulating, Ros was a fine colleague who served her students, her department, the university and the wider academic community with distinction. Her research was matched by the excellence of her teaching which, given her research output, it is perhaps all too easy to overlook. No colleague could have given more and she is much missed.

Connie A. Korpan, University of Alberta, Canada

I graduated from the University of Alberta with a PhD in developmental cognitive psychology. In my graduate training, I investigated many aspects of science learning, including children's and adults' understanding of biological concepts, the kinds of questions individuals ask when they read and evaluate media briefs of scientific research, and the types of informal learning activities in science that children are exposed to in their home and community. I am currently a postdoctoral fellow in educational policy studies at the University of Alberta, where I will extend my study of science learning to include issues related to curricular design.

John Leach, University of Leeds, UK

I taught chemistry in British high schools for five years before starting work as a researcher in the Children's Learning in Science Research Group at the University of Leeds. I am now Professor of Science Education, and coordinator of the Learning in Science Research Group. My academic interests in science education focus upon teaching and learning science in secondary-school classrooms, and especially teaching and learning about the nature of science. I am also interested in links between research findings on teaching and learning, teachers' practice and science curricula.

Ros Driver exerted a profound influence on my professional life. I encountered Ros' work as a young teacher, and became interested in why my students did not learn as I expected them to. Ros put her work across with characteristic integrity and enthusiasm, qualities that inspired so many teachers and researchers who came through Leeds over the years.

Ros was an exemplary colleague, friend and mentor. I feel profoundly honoured to have worked with her.

John Lemberger, University of Wisconsin-Oshkosh, USA

John Lemberger is an Assistant Professor of Science Education at the University of Wisconsin-Oshkosh. He completed his doctorate entitled 'The relationship between a model-building problem-solving classroom and conceptual change learning' at the University of Wisconsin-Madison in 1995. He is also interested in the education of science teachers.

William J. Letts IV, Charles Stuart University, Bathurst, Australia

I am a Lecturer in Science Education in the Faculty of Education at Charles Stuart University in Bathurst, Australia. I am completing my dissertation at the University of Delaware. It examines the understandings that primary-school teachers have about how issues of cultural diversity relate to school science. My research interests include examining the sociocultural contexts of science education, particularly in reference to issues of sexuality, indigenous peoples and gender.

Piet Lijnse, Utrecht Centre for Science and Mathematics Education

I was educated as a physicist at Utrecht University, and took a PhD in molecular physics in 1973. Since then, I have been a member of the physics education group, which is now part of the Utrecht Centre for Science and Mathematics Education. I have been involved in curriculum development (the PLON project) and in research on physics education. My main interest lies in improving physics education, in particular by trying to develop innovative, research-based ways of teaching.

I have worked with Ros Driver on several occasions since 1979. In particular, we worked together in setting up the first European summer school for PhD students in science education, an initiative that has been further developed by the European Science Education Research Association.

Robin Millar, University of York, UK

I graduated in theoretical physics and did a PhD in medical physics before deciding to train as a teacher. I taught in secondary schools in Edinburgh for 8 years, before moving to the University of York in 1982 as a Lecturer in Education. Since 1996 I have been Professor of Science Education. My academic interests are in students' learning in and about science, and in curriculum design issues associated with the notion of scientific literacy and public understanding of science. My research and writing is in these areas; I have also been heavily involved in several of the Salters' curriculum development projects, which have provided vehicles for trying to put some of these ideas into practice.

I first met Ros Driver shortly after moving to York. I cannot remember exactly what led us to decide that we wanted to collaborate on projects, but in 1985 we jointly organized a conference on energy teaching which resulted in the book *Energy Matters*. We subsequently wrote 'Beyond processes', and worked together on the research that led to *Young People's Images of Science*. There was always enough common ground in our views to make collaboration easy, and enough difference of emphasis to make it stimulating. I miss Ros' thoughtful commentary on events and ideas in science education (including my own) and am grateful for having had the opportunity to know her as a colleague and a friend for over 15 years.

Eduardo Mortimer, Universidade Federal de Minas Gerais, Brazil

I am an Associate Professor at the School of Education of the Universidade Federal de Minas Gerais, Belo Horizonte, Brazil. I worked in the chemical industry for three years and taught chemistry in high schools for five years before moving to the university in 1983. Since then I have been teaching and researching in the areas of conceptualization and discursive practices in science and chemistry classrooms, the professional development of science and chemistry teachers, the history and philosophy of chemistry, and curriculum development for high-school chemistry.

The writings and ideas of Ros Driver had already had a substantial influence on my teaching and research before I had the opportunity to share the friendly atmosphere of enthusiasm and thoughtful inquiry that she created in the Children's Learning in Science (CLIS) Research Group. To work with Ros and her group for a year, in 1992/3, was a great experience and had a profound impact on my professional life. I am grateful for having had the honour to collaborate with her and glad to have memories of her vigour, her thoughtful comments and her friendly smile.

Steve Norris, University of Alberta, Canada

My early educational career was as a high-school science teacher and science curriculum consultant for the Newfoundland and Labrador Department of Education. After completing my PhD, I spent nearly two decades as a Professor of Philosophy of Education at Memorial University of Newfoundland, before moving to the University of Alberta as Professor and Chair of the Department of Educational Policy Studies. My research has dealt with the philosophy of science education, the philosophy of educational research, the methodology of critical thinking testing, and the philosophy of reading.

I came to know Ros Driver most closely during a leave at the Centre for the Philosophy of the Natural and Social Sciences of the London School of Economics. Among many reasons for our discussions, one was a paper in which a colleague and I examined the structure of Ros' constructivist theory. I spent the last evening of my leave having dinner with Ros, going over the details of a response to the paper that she had been invited to write by the *Journal of Research in Science Teaching*. I shall never forget the commitment to science education, the determination not to let her illness interfere with living and working, and the sheer strength of character that she displayed that evening. It would be the last time we would meet.

Jonathan Osborne, King's College London, UK

I first encountered Ros Driver through her writings, by reading *The Pupil as Scientist?* Working as an advisory teacher at the time, after nine years of teaching science in secondary schools, the insights that this book offered had a significant effect on my understanding of my own and others' practice. I did not meet Ros personally until some years later when working on a primary science research project SPACE (Science Process and Concept Exploration) which was following very similar lines to the Children's Learning in Science Project (CLISP) in secondary schools.

Ros' major influence on my thinking, though, was to come when she joined King's College London as Professor of Science Education. Her enjoyment and interest in science and science education, and in engaging in constructive argument, was simply infectious. Even though she was with us briefly, we managed to collaborate on a proposal to Nuffield which led to the production of the report *Beyond 2000: Science Education for the Future*. We also developed funded proposals to investigate pupils' and parents' views of the school science curriculum, and to research how argument could be introduced into school science. Ros' legacy is still enduring and working with her was one of the privileges of my professional life and experience to be measured by its quality rather than its quantity.

Phil Scott, University of Leeds, UK

I taught physics in high schools for 14 years before leaving my Head of Science post to work with the Children's Learning in Science Project at the University of Leeds. My first job with the group involved running professional development programmes for science teachers, advisers and inspectors in all parts of the UK. I then became coordinator of the group, taking on responsibility for all aspects of its day-to-day running. At present I am a Senior Lecturer in Physics Education at Leeds. My research interests focus on teaching and learning science concepts in classroom settings and draw on sociocultural perspectives in exploring the role of language and the nature of teacher and pupil talk in meaning-making.

I knew Ros Driver for all of my professional life. She was my tutor during initial teacher training and supervised both my masters and doctoral theses. I count myself doubly blessed in having both gained so much from her scholarship and in having known her as an inspirational friend and colleague for all of those years.

Harry Shipman, University of Delaware, USA

I am in the Physics and Astronomy Department at the University of Delaware, where I teach science and do research in science education and astronomy. My degrees, in astronomy, are from Harvard University and the California Institute of Technology. I have been the Education Officer of the American Astronomical Society and am the author of four popular science books.

Svein Sjøberg, University of Oslo, Norway

I was trained as a nuclear physicist, but shifted to science education in the early 1970s. After some years, I also got the chance to study science education in Leeds, with David Layton as my tutor. During my stay in Leeds, Ros Driver came back from her studies in the USA with new ideas and perspectives. From that time, I had close contacts with her over more than 20 years. She was often our guest in Norway, helping us to build a group for studies and research in science education. I also had the chance to work with Ros in Africa, the continent where she started her career in science teaching. Among other things, she played an important role in the building of the African Forum for Children's Literacy in Science and Technology, a pan-African initiative that promotes innovative ideas in science education.

At present, my main interests are in the social, political, ideological and cultural aspects of science, and how science education can contribute to preparation for citizenship and participation in modern democratic society. Gender equity is an essential concern here.

Andrée Tiberghien, Université Lumière Lyon 2, France

I did a *thèse d'état* (thesis) in solid state physics before deciding to do research in the field of *didactique de la physique* (physics education). At the time (1992) a reform of science teaching at the lower secondary-school level in France was being debated. Since the beginning of my *thèse d'état*, I have been a researcher in the National Centre of Scientific Research (CNRS). I am currently responsible for the COAST (*Communication et Apprentissage des Savoirs Scientifiques et Techniques*) research group of the *Groupe de Recherche sur les Interactions Communicatives* in Lyon. My research is focused on the relations between students' evolution of knowledge during learning in the physics domain, and the conditions of learning.

I first met Ros Driver in Paris when, just after her PhD, she presented a seminar to my research team. Her type of research was very important for me at this period. In 1983 she participated in the La Londe summer school I organized with Goery Delacôte, through the International Commission of Physics Education. After that, we worked together with Edith Guesne to edit the book *Children's Ideas in Science*. This work was an opportunity for me to get to know Ros better, and to appreciate her many qualities as a researcher through shared daily work. After a long period, I had the great pleasure to meet Ros again at the beginning of the European project, Labwork in Science Education.

Richard White, Monash University, Australia

Following ten years of teaching science in high schools, I have had a long association with Monash University: research student, lecturer, Professor of Psychology in Education, Dean of Education, Pro Vice-chancellor and Director of Monash's Centre in London. Throughout my professional life my main interest has been in the quality of learning, especially of science.

In 1978 Robert Gagné and I published an article in which we defined various types of knowledge, among them episodes or memories of experiences. My first meeting with Ros Driver occurred later that year when I spoke at Leeds about episodes, and how I saw them as essential, and beneficial, to the understanding of science. Ros said that she found this theory interesting, but that her research showed that experience often led to unscientific beliefs. That was my introduction to alternative conceptions. I have been thinking about that brief conversation ever since.

Index

AAAS, 18, 149, 159
Abd-El-Khalick, F., 12
Aboriginal science, *see* culture, in science education
Abraham, M., 275, 276
ACARD, 221
Ackerman, R.J., 192, 196, 200, 201
Adey, P., 105, 106, 275, 276
Aikenhead, G., 154, 245, 246, 250, 251, 252, 255, 256, 258, 260, 261, 279, 337
Albone, E., 219
Alexander, R., 79
Alsop, S., 279
alternative conceptions, 147, 298
American Association for the Advancement of Science, *see* AAAS
Andersson, B., 63, 68, 76
Anyon, J., 259
Apple, M., 245, 257, 259
Applebee, A., 253
appraisal, *see* management, school
apprenticeship, in learning, 53
APU, 66, 328, 331
Archenhold, W.F., 329
argumentation, 190, 200, 203
Artigue, M., 32
Asimov, I., 211
Asoko, H., 91
assessment, 148, 327
  conversation, 195, 199
  development of instruments, 327

see also developmental validity, of assessment; formative assessment; national evaluation; summative assessment
Assessment of Performance Unit, *see* APU
Atkin, M., 151, 222
attitudes, 210
Atwater, M.M., 248
Augustinos, M., 53, 55, 56, 58
Ausubel, D.P., 277, 295, 299

Bachelard, S., 29
Baird, J.R., 98, 103, 295, 302, 303, 334
Bakhtin, M., 57, 58, 126, 127, 128
Balacheff, N., 31
Ball, S.F., 94, 95, 96, 100, 101
Barde, J., 35, 36
Barnes, D., 129
Bécu-Robinault, K., 27, 41, 42
Bell, B., 48, 49, 51, 52, 53, 80, 99, 101, 124, 337
Bennett, N., 81
Bereiter, C., 280
Bildung, 159
Black, P.J., 48, 49, 66, 124, 207, 328, 331, 332, 335, 336, 340
Blades, D.W., 162, 257, 258
Bloom, J., 280
Board of Testing and Assessment, *see* NAS
border crossing, 192, 195, 252, 254, 338
Boulter, C., 90

YOUNG PEOPLE'S IMAGES OF SCIENCE

Rosalind Driver, John Leach, Robin Millar and Phil Scott

- What ideas about science do school students form as a result of their experiences in and out of school?
- How might science teaching in schools develop a more scientifically-literate society?
- How do school students understand disputes about scientific issues including those which have social significance, such as the irradiation of food?

There have been calls in the UK and elsewhere for a greater public understanding of science underpinned by, amongst other things, school science education. However, the relationship between school science, scientific literacy and the public understanding of science remains controversial.

In this book, the authors argue that an understanding of science goes beyond learning the facts, laws and theories of science and that it involves understanding the nature of scientific knowledge itself and the relationships between science and society. Results of a major study into the understanding of these issues by school students aged 9 to 16 are described. These results suggest that the success of the school science curriculum in promoting this kind of understanding is at best limited.

The book concludes by discussing ways in which the school science curriculum could be adapted to better equip students as future citizens in our modern scientific and technological society. It will be particularly relevant to science teachers, advisers and inspectors, teacher educators and curriculum planners.

Contents

192pp   0 335 19381 1 (Paperback)   0 335 19382 X (Hardback)

GOOD PRACTICE IN SCIENCE TEACHING
WHAT RESEARCH HAS TO SAY

Martin Monk and Jonathan Osborne (eds)

This book offers a summary of major educational research and scholarship important to the field of science education. Written in a clear, concise and readable style, the authors have identified the principal messages and their implications for the practice of science teaching. Aimed at science teachers of children of all ages, and others who work in teaching and related fields, the book provides an invaluable first guide for science teachers. All of the chapters are written by authors from King's College London and the University of Leeds, both of which are institutions with an international reputation for their work in the field with top research ratings. Each chapter summarizes the research work and evidence in the field, discussing its significance, reliability and implications. Valuable lists of further reading and full references are provided at the end of each chapter.

Contents
Introduction – Part I: The science classroom – Strategies for learning – Formative assessment – Children's thinking, learning, teaching and constructivism – The role of practical work – The nature of scientific knowledge – The role of language in the learning and teaching of science – Student's attitudes towards science – Part II: The science department – Managing the science department – Summative assessment – Science teaching and the development of intelligence – Progression and differentiation – Information and communications technologies: their role and value for science education – Part III: The science world – GNVQ science at advanced level: a new kind of course – Science for citizenship – Index.

256pp   0 335 20391 4 (Paperback)   0 335 20392 2 (Hardback)

UNDERSTANDING SCIENCE LESSONS

Michael Reiss

In education argumentative theoretical books are two a penny so it is very good to read Michael Reiss' longitudinal account of 21 children's progress through an 11–16 secondary school learning science, year by year, up to the end of their compulsory schooling. Reiss includes the views of their teachers, the aspirations of their parents and their own hopes for the future. It adds up to a book that beginning and experienced teachers and concerned parents will find rewarding.

Professor Joan Solomon, The Open University

- What is it like to be a pupil studying science in a school in England?
- How important are home background and school teaching for pupils to succeed?
- Why do some children maintain an interest in science while others don't?

Understanding Science Lessons reports the findings of a major five-year longitudinal study into pupils' learning of science. One group of mixed-ability pupils were followed throughout their 11 to 16 science education. A combination of extensive classroom observations and in-depth interviews with pupils, parents and teachers provides a rich mass of data. These findings are interpreted with respect to such factors as the behaviours of girls and boys in lessons, the importance of the teacher, the purpose of investigations in science education and the effects of the English National Curriculum on classroom teaching and pupil motivation.

Throughout, the emphasis is on the individual pupils and their experiences. All pupil and parent interviews were carried out in their homes and the ethnographic approach allows the reader to gain a convincing insight into what it is like to be a pupil studying science at secondary school.

Contents

176pp   0 335 19769 8 (Paperback)   0 335 19770 1 (Hardback)